*AIDS and Masculinity
in the African City*

AIDS and Masculinity in the African City

PRIVILEGE, INEQUALITY, AND MODERN MANHOOD

Robert Wyrod

UNIVERSITY OF CALIFORNIA PRESS

University of California Press, one of the most distinguished university presses in the United States, enriches lives around the world by advancing scholarship in the humanities, social sciences, and natural sciences. Its activities are supported by the UC Press Foundation and by philanthropic contributions from individuals and institutions. For more information, visit www.ucpress.edu.

University of California Press
Oakland, California

Library of Congress Cataloging-in-Publication Data

Names: Wyrod, Robert, author.
   Title: AIDS and masculinity in the African city : privilege, inequality, and modern manhood / Robert Wyrod.
   Description: Oakland, California : University of California Press, [2016] | Includes bibliographical references and index.
   Identifrs: LCCN 2015047468 (print) | LCCN 2015047889 (ebook) | ISBN 9780520286689 (cloth) | ISBN 9780520286696
(pbk. : alk. paper) | ISBN 9780520961784 (ebook)
   Subjects: LCSH: AIDS (Disease)—Social aspects—Uganda. | Masculinity—Uganda.
   Classification: LCC RA643.86.U33 .W97 2016 (print) | LCC RA643.86.U33 (ebook) | DDC 362.19697/920096761—dc23
   LC record available at http://lccn.loc.gov/2015047468

25   24   23   22   21   20   19   18   17   16
10   9   8   7   6   5   4   3   2   1

Contents

List of Figures and Tables   *vii*

1.   Remaking Masculinity in Bwaise   1

2.   The Making of Masculinity in Urban Uganda   43

3.   Providing in Poverty   80

4.   Women's Rights in the Remaking of Masculinity   123

5.   The Intersection of Masculinity, Sexuality, and AIDS   160

6.   Beyond Bwaise   205

Epilogue   233

Acknowledgments   241

Appendix   245

Notes   249

References   259

Index   283

Figures and Tables

FIGURES

1.1. Kampala's central business district.   7

1.2. Bwaise's main commercial strip.   9

1.3. HIV prevalence in Uganda by year, gender, age, and region of country.   14

1.4. Masculinity as a social process.   29

1.5. Kampala, Kawempe Division, and Bwaise.   32

1.6. Housing in Bwaise.   33

1.7. Business in Bwaise.   34

2.1. Main ethnic groups in Uganda.   45

3.1. Kimombasa section of Bwaise during the day.   96

3.2. Exterior of a lodge in Bwaise.   100

3.3. A typical carpentry workshop in Bwaise.   104

3.4. Author during carpentry apprenticeship.   106

4.1. A young couple in Bwaise.   129

4.2. A family outside their home in Bwaise.   133

5.1. Bwaise's main intersection.   171

5.2. Bwaise during the rainy season.   175

5.3. A group of women in Bwaise.   187

E.1. Bwaise's main intersection in 2015.   235

TABLES

A.1. Demographic Characteristics of Interviewees, 2004   246

A.2. Demographic Characteristics of Participants in Couples
      Research, 2009   247

1 Remaking Masculinity in Bwaise

Crammed into the back of a stuffy *matatu,* one of Kampala's ubiquitous white minivan buses, I strained to see my stop. I was making my first visit to Bwaise, a densely populated slum community that became the focus of my fieldwork in Uganda. Our matatu had begun its journey in Kampala's city center, near the office towers, government buildings, and large hotels that were the pulsing core of this vibrant capital city. In twenty minutes, after many jarring stops to disgorge and ingest passengers, we had passed the main university campus, a nearby slum with mushrooming student hostels, a long stretch of carpentry workshops displaying overstuffed couches, and a Pentecostal megachurch that resembled an airplane hangar. I knew I was now close to my destination, and when I spotted Bwaise's main landmark, a three-story furniture showroom, I shouted, "*Siteegi!*" (Bus stop!), and clambered out of the matatu.

I had come to Bwaise to visit the home of Christine, a forty-four-year-old widow who had lived in Bwaise for over two decades. Christine and I met a week earlier at a nearby health clinic when I attended a support group for HIV-positive people. Christine was the treasurer of the Post-Test Club, and she had passionately channeled her own experience living with HIV into educating and counseling residents of Bwaise about AIDS.

When she learned I was interested in how AIDS had affected life in Kampala, she extended an invitation to visit her neighborhood.

As the matatu sped away, I felt conspicuous—a white American man standing alone in a neighborhood few Western foreigners ever visited. Even without the many stares, I found the congested strip of storefronts overwhelming as a thick stream of pedestrians, cars, trucks, and motorcycles clogged the sidewalk and road. To my relief, a young man approached me and politely introduced himself as Christine's youngest son, Paul. Stocky and with something of an urban swagger, Paul seemed an ideal escort in a place like Bwaise. He led me through a narrow alley beside the furniture showroom, and in moments we were in the crowded residential interior of Bwaise. The traffic noise and exhaust fumes of the main road were replaced by sounds of children playing and the stench from the shallow streams of raw sewage snaking between the homes.

Although I had visited other Kampala slums, I was surprised by the dirt and trash, and the density of dilapidated housing. Yet on this first visit I also caught glimpses of Bwaise's energy and vitality. Women sat outside their homes laughing with each other, watching their children while preparing snack food to sell. A group of men bantered loudly as they grilled the *chapatti* bread sold in the night market, teasingly calling out, "*muzungu*," white person, as I passed. Ugandan hip-hop blared from a tiny yellow stand selling cassette tapes as a man with a wheelbarrow full of bright green *matooke* (plantains) maneuvered past us on the narrow dirt path. It was this contrast between the undeniable squalor of Bwaise and the vigor, resourcefulness, and resilience of so many of its residents that became a leitmotif of my time in the community.

Paul and I wound through the mazelike housing, passing one- and two-room homes packed cheek by jowl. Some were constructed of only mud and wattle and topped with rusting metal roofs; others were older, more substantial homes long past their prime. Eventually we reached a cluster of three small homes that shared a tiny courtyard. On the right side was Christine's house, a two-hundred-square-foot, two-room rectangle made from brown bricks and covered with an aging corrugated metal roof. It sat on a two-foot concrete foundation that provided some protection from the makeshift sewage canal that encircled the compound.

Christine, a slightly stout woman with a broad nose, almond eyes, and high cheekbones, greeted me warmly and invited me into her home. She was in the middle of her morning ritual, preparing *maandazi* (sweet fried bread). Rising around six, she spent several hours over a small pot of boiling oil, frying balls of batter to sell. This was her main source of income, and her goal was a dozen batches, each with ten pieces of maandazi. Around ten, she would deliver her product to women at the market and collect the money from the previous day's sales—an effort that yielded about one dollar in profit.

As Christine plopped the batter into the oil, she began telling me about her life, including how she was infected with HIV. At twenty, she married a man with a good job as a medical assistant. They were able to afford both an official Catholic wedding and a traditional ceremony in keeping with their heritage as Baganda, the largest ethnic group in Uganda. Over the next decade they had five children together. But then her husband fell sick and died from AIDS. From that point forward, Christine said she knew she too was infected, and because she was monogamous while her husband had two other long-term relationships during their marriage she felt he was to blame. But Christine was not embittered, saying, "At that time people were not fearing AIDS so much. They were not well informed." She referred to the other women as her cowives, and she was grateful for the financial support they provided after her husband's death. Over the course of the next decade, both of these women also died from AIDS.

As I listened to Christine's story, I came to appreciate the devastating toll AIDS had taken on her family. In addition to her husband and cowives, she had lost a brother to the disease, and she was now sharing her house with her younger sister, Mary, who was in the advanced stages of AIDS. Like Christine, Mary believed her husband had infected her with HIV. Over the next six months I watched as Mary slowly succumbed to the disease, even after gaining access to antiretroviral drugs. Christine was devastated by her death. The disturbing images of Mary's frail body on their couch remain with me still, tempered only by memories of her courage and dry wit in the face of her suffering.

While other women might have remarried, Christine was not interested in a new relationship and had remained alone since her husband's death. "I had a little money, but I had to work for my children," she told me, "so I had no time for those men." Concerned a new relationship would bring more problems than benefits, Christine was resigned to survive on her own. Her income, however, was much too low to cover her family's needs, and she was now burdened by thousands of dollars of debt from microfinance loans. Caring for her sister Mary and Mary's children added to her responsibilities, which were becoming overwhelming. Christine faced the bleak prospect of never getting out of debt. If her health ever started to fail, she said, she would not even be able to continue her modest income-generating activity. She was determined that her children receive an education, hoping that they would eventually find decent employment and, in turn, support her.

Having finished her maandazi, Christine said it was time to make her weekly rounds as an AIDS counselor. Her responsibility was to check on members of her Post-Test Club who lived in Bwaise, to monitor their condition and provide encouragement. She had been doing this volunteer work for three years, compensated by only a trifling stipend from an international nongovernmental organization (NGO). As we headed deeper into residential Bwaise, crossing increasingly large sewage canals, we eventually reached a narrow alley where a woman was scaling fish. She enthusiastically greeted us, and Christine asked her about her health, taking careful notes. In the next two hours, we would make four more similar visits, all with HIV-positive widows like Christine. If there had been more time, Christine told me, there were many more HIV-positive people we could have visited in Bwaise, something I would see firsthand in my many months of fieldwork that followed.

Given her experience with her husband, I was not surprised to learn that Christine was preoccupied with how her two sons were negotiating AIDS and sexual intimacy. She was less concerned about her older son, Peter, who at twenty-two was extremely leery of relationships because of his family's experience with AIDS. In contrast to most of his male peers, Peter decided to forgo girlfriends altogether, never having had sex, and was instead focused on his studies, a strategy that eventually resulted in a government university scholarship. Christine was very worried about her youngest son, Paul, however, who she felt was heading down a risky path. At eighteen, and ostensibly still in secondary school, Paul spent most of his days hanging out with friends and many of his evenings at the local clubs. Paul's style of dress took cues from the American hip-hop culture so influential among Kampala youth: baggy jeans, unlaced Timberland-style boots, white tank tops, and loose short-sleeved shirts. He was fond of thick silver jewelry, and his most cherished accessories were his tattoos—gothic Old English designs in black ink that covered his muscular upper arms and back.

Christine viewed Paul's tattoos, jewelry, and attitude as part of a danger-ous teenage rebellion that revolved around Bwaise's rather notorious club scene. As I would see myself, Paul was a frequent club patron, and he had befriended the staff, as well as most of the edgy young men in Bwaise. In contrast to Peter, Paul boasted to me about his girlfriends but also insisted, "I can't have sex with a girl when I don't have a condom. That only hap-pened once, the first time I had sex. And ever since I've never done it with-out one." Nonetheless, Paul's club crowd worried Christine, and she often complained he was spending too much time with Bwaise's *abayaye* (thugs). As a mother raising her sons alone, Christine said it was difficult to coun-teract the influence of his peers. "These surroundings," Christine com-plained, "when you are a woman only, you get problems with children, because they mostly fear men. They fear their fathers." Without such a man in Paul's life, Christine remained concerned that she could not stop him from getting pulled deeper into the world of Bwaise's abayaye.

·　　·　　·　　·　　·

This glimpse into Christine's life encapsulates what motivates me to write about how AIDS has shaped gender and sexuality in Uganda. Christine's story reveals the ubiquity of AIDS in a place like Bwaise and shows how the disease has become a pervasive aspect of everyday life. From my visits with Christine, it was obvious that AIDS had not only ravaged her family but her community as well. Christine's story is also emblematic of the many Ugandans who take action to address the disease, whether by being part of an AIDS support group, or helping those afflicted with the disease, or simply by discussing AIDS in a frank and open manner.

Most centrally for this book, Christine's life also illustrates the role that gender relations have played in the epidemic. Both she and Mary claimed to be monogamous wives and believed they were infected with HIV by their husbands. While not resentful of her deceased husband, Christine's experiences made her concerned about her sons and how they would negotiate their intimate relationships now that the dangers of AIDS were well known. Paul and Peter were exploring very different strategies for navigating masculinity, sexuality, and AIDS, each with consequences not only for their sexual health but for their transitions into male adulthood as well.

Finally, Christine's life underscores how the challenges of AIDS were further complicated by Bwaise's grinding poverty. For Christine and her son Peter, poverty made intimate relationships too fraught with conflict and suspicion, something to be avoided altogether. This same poverty, in Christine's eyes, provided her son Paul with easy access to perilous forms of escapism and exposure to far too many male peers who reveled in the more decadent side of life. Most obviously and sadly, poverty also impeded Christine's sister, Mary, from receiving the health care she needed, hastening her death from AIDS.

The ways that Christine and her family grappled with AIDS are not unique to life in Bwaise. Their struggles are repeated in similar communities across Kampala and illustrate how AIDS shapes everyday life in many urban African settings (figure 1.1). I chose to locate this study in Uganda because the country holds a special place in the history of the global AIDS pandemic. During the late 1980s and early 1990s, HIV infection rates dropped rapidly in Uganda, in sharp contrast to skyrocketing rates in much of southern Africa. Uganda was, in fact, the first country on the continent to document a drop in HIV prevalence.[1] Given that the country had just emerged from over a decade of civil war, this was a remarkable achievement—one that earned Uganda the label of Africa's great AIDS success story.

This success has been attributed in part to political leadership but also to the attitudes and perceptions of Ugandans from all walks of life. There was an openness in talking about AIDS in the country and a flowering of grassroots responses to the crisis. A forthrightness about how sexual behavior was tied to AIDS also emerged, including emphasis on men reducing the number of their sexual partners to mitigate the spread of HIV. This in turn helped disrupt dense networks of sexual relationships, a

Figure 1.1. Kampala's central business district.

factor now seen as important to Uganda's success (Thornton 2008). By the early 1990s, Uganda was also emerging as an African leader in women's rights, propelled by both the government's promotion of a rights agenda and the more far-reaching work of a vibrant women's movement. It has been suggested that this institutionalization of women's rights also played a role in how Ugandans, especially Ugandan women, were able to respond to the epidemic (Epstein 2007; Epstein and Kim 2007).

It was this success story that drew me to Uganda. I wanted to understand how the AIDS epidemic—a tragic event of historic proportions—had shaped gender and sexuality in Africa, especially conceptions of masculinity. Modifying sexual behavior—including promoting abstinence, condom use, and limiting sexual partnerships—has figured prominently in the public health response to AIDS in Africa. There is, therefore, good reason to suspect that the AIDS crisis may have altered normative discourses of sexuality, especially in those countries where the epidemic has been intense. In addition, because sexuality and gender are deeply intertwined, it is reasonable to presume that pressure on normative notions of sexuality would have reverberations for gender relations, especially in contexts where other forces are destabilizing the gender status quo.

If AIDS had shaped these social relations anywhere in Africa, Uganda seemed the best place to find evidence for it. Prior research on AIDS in Uganda, and sub-Saharan Africa more generally, however, has largely focused on the factors that fueled the spread of HIV on the continent, including economic and gender inequalities (Kalipeni et al. 2004; Kim et al. 2007; Pronyk et al. 2006). Far less attention has been paid to how the prolonged AIDS epidemic may have altered gender relations and intimate relationships—an issue at the heart of this book. While I could have explored these issues by examining the impact of a particular government AIDS program or a specific public health AIDS intervention, I instead focused on everyday life in Bwaise (figure 1.2). As one poor community among very many in Kampala, Bwaise gave me a view into the lives of typical Kampalans and a way of tracing the deeper cultural implications of the AIDS epidemic in urban Uganda.

My fieldwork in Bwaise paid particular, but not exclusive, attention to men and masculinity. Over the past two decades, a great deal of research has shown how normative notions of masculinity have contributed to the spread of HIV across Africa (Barker and Ricardo 2005; Bujra 2000; Dworkin 2015; Foreman 1999; Gibson and Hardon 2005; Hunter 2010; Lindegger and Quayle 2009; Parikh 2009; Rivers and Aggleton 1999; Setel 1999; Smith 2009a, 2014). In this book I examine the reciprocal nature of this dynamic—how AIDS has shaped masculinity, especially male sexuality. Throughout I develop a core theme that emerged from my fieldwork: the central role of what I refer to as masculine sexual privilege, both in everyday responses to AIDS and in the reproduction of gender inequality. In the urban Ugandan context, I use masculine sexual privilege to refer to both men's authority to dictate the terms of sex and a man's

Figure 1.2. Bwaise's main commercial strip.

right to multiple sexual partners if he so chooses, whether they are wives, girlfriends, or shorter-term partners.

Importantly, my phrase "masculine sexual privilege" should not be read to suggest that male sexual behavior and power in urban Uganda is mono-lithic, with all men striving, and always able, to maximize their control of sex and the number of their sexual partners. As I discuss in historical depth in the next chapter, there is a wide spectrum of normative male sexual behavior in urban Uganda, including not only polygamous and other forms of overlapping relationships but also monogamy. What is common across this spectrum, however, is the sexual control and agency all men can claim as members of the privileged gender group. This sexual privilege remains available to all men, even monogamous and celibate men, but not to women. And as my fieldwork reveals, it can be a potent resource for all men as they navigate the complexities of intimate relation-ships in the context of AIDS.

Uganda's reputed success in addressing AIDS suggested that masculine sexual privilege may have been significantly undermined. My fieldwork with men and women in Bwaise, therefore, focused on how AIDS has prompted challenges to masculine sexual privilege and whether these challenges have significantly reworked such privilege. To what extent can Ugandan men still draw on masculine sexual privilege in their strategies for managing intimate relationships? What new paradoxes has AIDS presented for men as they grapple with embodying normative notions of masculinity and male sexuality? And how have interactions between men and women, especially in intimate relationships, reinforced, contested, and remade masculine sexual privilege in the context of AIDS?

The story of Uganda's AIDS success was what initially inspired me to explore these questions. Yet a troubling emerging trend in Uganda has made these questions particularly timely: the steady increase in new HIV infections in recent years.[2] This trend has provoked much concern that Uganda's success has unraveled, and in this book I strive to provide a complex sociological account of masculinity in Bwaise that contextualizes this unsettling development. While many conventional approaches to HIV prevention in Uganda continue to focus on promoting monogamy and "being faithful," in my view the number of sexual partners a man or woman has is not the key issue. I make the case, instead, that a serious engagement with the persistence of men's privileges to dictate the terms of sex and the freedom to choose, on their own, to establish multiple sexual partnerships is crucial to efforts to address AIDS in Uganda, as well as the many other African countries affected by HIV.

While the long-standing AIDS crisis motivated this ethnography, my fieldwork made clear that AIDS was only one aspect of the story of changing masculinities in a place like Bwaise. As I discuss in detail in the next chapter, Uganda has been experiencing heightened tensions over gender relations for nearly two decades. The first decade of current president Yoweri Museveni's rule brought improvements in women's status in the late 1980s and early 1990s. More recently, there have also been important advances, in particular the 2010 passage of the Domestic Violence Act that significantly expands penalties for gender-based violence, including the sexual abuse of women. However, there has also been an increasing backlash against some of these gains (Kyomuhendo and McIntosh 2006). A long-sought, ambitious set of legal reforms focused on improving women's marriage and property rights, known as the Marriage and Divorce Bill, was resoundingly rejected, yet again, by parliament and the president in 2013. The Anti-Pornography Act, passed in 2014, not only contains new restrictions on sexualized media but also has prompted harassment of women wearing miniskirts or any revealing clothing. In 2014 the HIV Prevention and Control Act was also unanimously adopted by parliament and signed into law by Museveni. This new law makes it easier for a woman's HIV status to be revealed to her partner against her will.[3]

The most notorious aspect of this backlash, however, is the Anti-Homosexuality Act, which was passed by parliament and signed into law by the president in early 2014. The bill broadened the criminalization of same-sex relations and mandated some of the harshest punishments for homosexuality in Africa. Much has been made of the role that evangelicals from the United States have played in spurring this bill (Sharlet 2010). The bill has also been seen as the result of rivalries within the ruling political party, with younger party members introducing the bill to create controversy for President Museveni in the lead-up to the 2016 presidential elections. Museveni's willingness to sign the bill has, in turn, been viewed as an attempt to regain his populist support by appearing as a leader able to stand up to a Western gay rights agenda. Although the Anti-Homosexuality Act was struck down by Uganda's Constitutional Court on a technicality in 2014, it is far from dead and is expected to be reintroduced in modified form.

While American evangelicals and domestic political machinations are indeed important factors in the rise of the Anti-Homosexuality Act, such explanations tend to view the anti-gay legislation in isolation. They neglect the fact that the act is part and parcel of a spate of recent legislation that attempts to capitalize on a broader unease and uncertainty in gender and sexual relations in Uganda. The anti-homosexuality legislation is, therefore, best understood as one facet of a backlash against shifts in the gender status quo, especially those shifts that are perceived as threatening men's power and privilege on several fronts. As the Ugandan feminist Sylvia Tamale (2003b) has argued about an earlier wave of homophobia in Uganda in 2003, public debate surrounding homosexuality has made homophobia a "gendered concern." "By maintaining a regime of compulsory heterosexuality," Tamale (2003b, 6) argues, "the state seeks to enforce conventional gender relationships and identities and keep a stranglehold on public discourse on these topics."

While the Anti-Homosexuality Act has drawn global attention to Uganda's sexual politics, the tensions in gender and sexual relations that underlie the bill are hardly unique to Uganda. Across the continent, similar social processes are at work challenging male privilege: precarious and uncertain work, growing economic inequality, women's expanding access to education and employment, women in politics, and the institutionalization of women's rights (Aboim 2009; Cornwall 2002, 2003; Goetz and Hassim 2003; Morrell 2001a; Smith 2014). As in Uganda, these dynamics are intertwined with the omnipresence of AIDS, which has created new problems and paradoxes for men, and women, as they try to navigate a shifting social and moral terrain (Decoteau 2013a; Hunter 2010; Setel 1999; Simpson 2009). As Daniel Jordan Smith (2014, 5) aptly notes based on his research in Nigeria, AIDS has produced a gamut of moralizing discourses that "have been so powerful because they express and stand for people's experience of and ambivalence about certain consequences of ongoing social changes and in particular, their discontent about rising levels of social inequality."

I share Smith's interest in understanding AIDS not in narrow public health terms but as a powerful lens on broader anxieties about social change and inequality. Throughout this book, I focus on three different aspects of the entanglement of masculinity, AIDS, and social change: the ways societal problems, including gender inequalities, have contributed to the spread of AIDS; how AIDS often symbolizes tensions about such wider social problems; and, importantly and distinctively, the ways AIDS itself is the engine for social change, especially through a remaking of masculinity.

AIDS AND MASCULINITY IN AFRICA

Throughout my fieldwork in Bwaise, I encountered residents committed to raising AIDS awareness in the community, and among their ranks I occasionally encountered young men. One of these men was twenty-two-year-old Patrick, born and raised in Bwaise. He lived with his wife and newborn daughter in a quiet corner of the neighborhood, in a rented, one-room home set on a high concrete foundation that kept the nearby sewage canal at bay. Like many of his male peers, Patrick had been unable to find steady work, and he had channeled his frustration into volunteering for a Ugandan NGO focused on HIV prevention. He was particularly interested in talking with his underemployed male peers, and I often came across Patrick chatting animatedly with other young men during his rounds as a peer educator in Bwaise.

When I asked Patrick why he spent his days this way, he admitted he hoped the volunteering might lead to paid employment with the NGO. But he also stressed that his family's experience with AIDS had motivated him: "We've lost one sister to AIDS so far. And I've lost several uncles and aunties because of HIV/AIDS. People who I thought would assist me have died. Very good friends, supportive ones have died. So HIV/AIDS has really affected me. . . . All the people who were supposed to help me have died."

The plague of AIDS has not only devastated Uganda. The same is true for much of sub-Saharan Africa, which has borne the brunt of the global burden of AIDS since the beginning of the pandemic. In 2011, 24 million people were living with HIV in sub-Saharan Africa, representing nearly 70 percent of all infections globally (UNAIDS 2012). Over a million sub-Saharan Africans died from AIDS in 2011 alone, and almost 2 million people were newly infected with HIV. East and southern Africa have been, and continue to be, the regions of the world most severely affected by AIDS, with one quarter of all adults in countries such as Botswana, Lesotho, and Swaziland living with HIV in 2011.

Sub-Saharan Africa is also the only global region where women are more likely than men to be infected with HIV. This is a long-standing trend; in 2011, for example, 58 percent of people living with HIV in sub-Saharan Africa were women. This trend holds true for Uganda as well. During my fieldwork HIV prevalence was higher among women than men, especially younger and urban women (see figure 1.3).[4]

These bleak statistics are tempered by some encouraging recent trends in the region. Between 2001 and 2011, the number of new HIV infections in sub-Saharan Africa dropped by 25 percent, leading to some speculation that the African AIDS crisis has crested (UNAIDS 2012). Nonetheless, the magnitude of the AIDS pandemic remains immense, and there are now

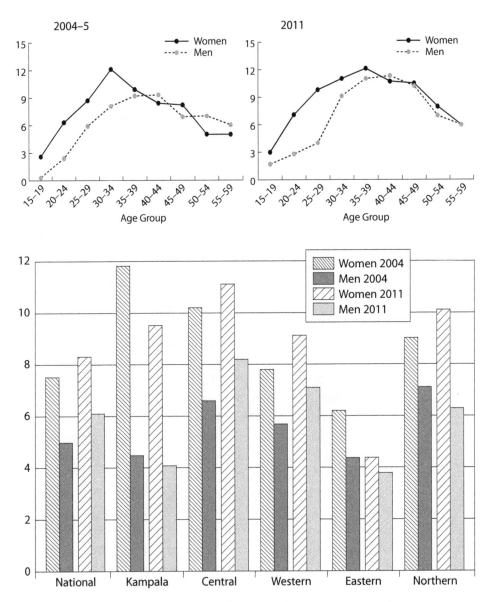

Figure 1.3. HIV prevalence in Uganda by year, gender, age, and region of country.

SOURCE: Uganda AIDS Indicator Survey 2011.

more people living with HIV in Africa than at any time in the history of the epidemic—a trend that will continue if the number of new infections remains high and increasing numbers of people receive life-prolonging AIDS drugs.

As the severity of the African AIDS crisis became evident in the 1990s, it produced an unprecedented global response. While some African countries (most notably Uganda) pioneered their own solutions to this new threat in the late 1980s, by the 1990s the response was largely being funded and overseen by the developed world, especially the United States and Western Europe. The turn of the millennium marked a massive scaling up of resources to address AIDS in Africa, including the establishment in the United States of the President's Emergency Plan for AIDS Relief (PEPFAR). At the same time, the Global Fund to Fight AIDS, Tuberculosis, and Malaria was created as an independent, international funding agency, and together PEPFAR and the Global Fund provide the vast majority of global AIDS funding.

Such institutions have provided crucial resources and have played essential roles in many successful efforts to prevent HIV infections and treat AIDS in Africa. However, this global response to AIDS has also rekindled an intense interest in African sexuality, a subject that has long fascinated Westerners. In response to AIDS, there has been an unparalleled effort to survey, quantify, and modify the sexual behavior of African men and women, such that it can now be difficult to discuss sexuality in Africa beyond the frame of HIV/AIDS. The AIDS epidemic has intensified a persistent tendency to reduce African intimate relationships to sex, which, as Lynn Thomas and Jennifer Cole (2009, 4) argue, is especially problematic given "the long history of Westerners deploying arguments of hypersexuality to dehumanize Africans and justify degrading policies."

Thomas and Cole are alluding to the nexus of AIDS and African sexuality that is part of a much longer history linking health, medicine, and sexuality to colonialism. This was especially evident in colonial South Africa, where allegedly unhealthy and unruly black bodies were disciplined by a new British public health regime (Comaroff 1993). This colonial regime emerged from nineteenth-century racial science, which gave new scientific authority to racist claims about Africans' inferiority—a legacy that remains as Westerners are often all too ready to "seek the origins of virulent disease in the uncontained nature of 'others'—in the undisciplined sexuality of Africa" (Comaroff 1993, 324).[5]

Ellen Stillwaggon (2003, 2006) has dramatically charted this legacy, arguing that metaphors rooted in nineteenth-century racial science still suffuse much AIDS analysis in Africa (see also Bibeau and Pedersen 2002; Patton 1990; Treichler 1999). Social scientists and policy makers "constructed a hypersexualized pan-African culture as the main reason for the high prevalence of HIV in sub-Saharan Africa. Africans were portrayed as the social 'Other' in works marked by sweeping generalizations and innuendo" (Stillwaggon 2003, 809).[6] For Stillwaggon, this myopic attention to a purported African sexual exceptionalism has led to a fixation on strategies for modifying Africans' sexual behavior and diverted attention from key co-factors in the spread of AIDS of Africa, including malnutrition, other diseases, and inadequate healthcare. Unlike extraordinary sexual behavior, these factors are rooted in poverty, and it is this poverty that actually distinguishes life in Africa from the West (Stillwaggon 2006, 156).

Much recent social science research on AIDS in Africa strives to avoid this problematic legacy by focusing on how political-economic and social contexts shape sexual intimacy and HIV transmission in different African settings. Analyses of how economic conditions affected the spread of HIV in Africa include the role of the *magendo* smuggling economy that emerged during Uganda's civil war in the 1970s and 1980s, the decline of rural livelihoods and resulting urban migration in northern Tanzania, and the effect of high rates of urban unemployment in South Africa (Barnett and Whiteside 2002; Hunter 2010; Setel 1996). In all these examples, AIDS and sexuality are examined in relation to how economic change and uncertainty affect social relations and social reproduction. In this sense, such work shares much with Paul Farmer's (2005) insistence on understanding the AIDS pandemic in relation to forms of "structural violence" that perpetuate poverty and illness.

A rich facet of research in this vein—and the one most relevant to this book—examines the ways gender relations are intertwined with the political economy of sexuality and AIDS in Africa. There is now a well-developed body of research linking gender inequality to women's vulnerability to HIV infection, focusing on how economic insecurity and gender-based violence work together to impede women's ability to negotiate safe sex

(Andersson, Cockcroft, and Shea 2008; Baylies and Bujra 2000; Dunkle et al. 2004; Dworkin and Ehrhardt 2007; Greig et al. 2008; Gupta 2002; Kouyoumdjian et al. 2013). Another aspect of these dynamics is younger women's exchange of sex for gifts from men, or what is commonly referred to as transactional sex. The increasing economic stratification in many African settings, and ongoing monetization of social relationships more generally, is seen as heightening tensions between love and money in intimate relationships in ways that increase a young woman's risk of HIV infection (Hunter 2002; Mojola 2014; Thomas and Cole 2009, 21).[7]

Marriage has also emerged as an important context for the interplay of gender relations, sexual intimacy, and AIDS in Africa. This emphasis on marriage and HIV is in response to two trends: the growing salience of the ideology of "modern," companionate, romantic marriage and the emphasis on marital fidelity in many AIDS prevention campaigns, especially those promoted in the 2000s. A recurring theme in this research is that expectations of trust and marital fidelity have intensified as the ideology of modern, romantic marriage has become more institutionalized around the globe (Ahearn 2001; Collier 1997; Hirsch 2003; Hirsch and Wardlow 2006; Padilla et al. 2007). These expectations, however, are in tension with the reality of men's extramarital sex, even though such affairs would seem to conflict with core elements of companionate partnership.[8] The result is heightened secrecy about extramarital relationships, including both men's efforts to conceal affairs and women's unwillingness to publicly confront their husbands' infidelity. The subtleties of these dynamics have been charted in Africa, especially the way women must negotiate between the social risk of jeopardizing a modern marriage and the biological risk of HIV infection (Parikh 2009; Smith 2009). Such factors combine to make "being faithful" a problematic AIDS prevention strategy for many women the world over (Esacove 2010; Hirsch et al. 2009).

As such research indicates, masculinity has emerged as a central issue in understanding the gendered dimensions of AIDS in Africa, especially how men and women navigate varying ideals of male sexuality. Research explicitly emphasizing masculinity and AIDS in Africa began in the mid-1990s and has made a strong case for connections between dominant ideals of masculinity and the expansion of AIDS, showing how a wide variety of social forces shaped male sexual behavior in ways that fueled the epidemic (Ankrah 1991; Bujra 2000; Campbell 1997; Carovano 1995; Dworkin 2015; Foreman 1999; Obbo 1993; Rivers and Aggleton 1999; Rweyemamu 1999; Setel 1996, 1999). By the turn of the millennium, these issues had become incorporated in global AIDS policy. The annual UNAIDS World AIDS Campaign in 2000 had as its theme "Men Make a Difference," which encouraged involving men more fully in AIDS prevention programs (UNAIDS 2000).

In much of this work, economic insecurity, masculinity, and AIDS are viewed as tightly intertwined. A prominent theme is that persistent urban poverty and unemployment have made it difficult for African men to embody a male provider ideal, establish independent households, and marry formally. The result is that some men attempt to recoup their masculinity by seeking multiple sexual partners, a dynamic that plays a key role in both men's and women's vulnerability to HIV infection (Hunter 2005; Silberschmidt 2001, 2004).

Such work, therefore, strives to place a political-economic frame around men's concurrent (i.e., overlapping) sexual relationships. The role of concurrent partnerships in the African AIDS epidemic has gained a great deal of attention in recent years, with some scholars arguing that these relationships play a key role in creating dense sexual networks that facilitate HIV transmission (Halperin and Epstein 2004; Epstein 2007; Thornton 2008). By demonstrating how the contemporary socioeconomic context is conducive to men's concurrent partnerships, this body of scholarship helps stave off concerns that the focus on concurrency is rekindling racist stereotypes of an African sexual culture of male promiscuity.

Nevertheless, dangers persist when scholars focus attention on men, masculinity, and AIDS in Africa. Amy Kaler (2010) dramatically illustrates these pitfalls in her analysis of the media response to her research on AIDS and men in Malawi. Her earlier study (2003b) revealed that some men in Malawi boasted they were likely to be HIV-positive as a result of having many sexual partners. Media reports of her research, however, framed her findings as evidence that African men actively sought to become infected with HIV to prove their manhood. For Kaler, this media reframing was emblematic of how AIDS in Africa is "filtered through a centuries-old prism of racialized gender knowledge, in which African men are presumed to be irrational, sexually voracious, and uninhibited" (2010, 23).[9]

This cautionary tale makes clear the need to remain attentive to pervasive tropes of African male sexuality that can reframe examinations of the social-structural aspects of masculinity and male power in ways that validate long-standing racist assumptions about African men (Kaler 2010, 33). This attentiveness requires foregrounding how specific social, political, and historical forces have shaped the diverse manifestations of masculinity and male privilege in evidence across the African continent.

It is with these dangers and pitfalls in mind that I take up the story of AIDS in Africa by focusing on how the long-standing AIDS epidemic has shaped masculinity in urban Uganda. The social significance of AIDS for masculinity in Africa remains an area that has not received sustained attention, which is surprising given the severity of AIDS in the region. There are indications that AIDS may be shaping gender and sexuality, including evidence that the toll AIDS has taken on men may be prompting a reassessment of certain masculine sexual norms, such as those tied to multiple sexual partnerships (Hunter 2004). It has also been suggested that AIDS is forcing men to confront their emotions and providing a counter to hard-edged variants of masculinity that conceal emotions in anger and violence (Morrell 2001b). Other research explores how African men's experiences of living with HIV can prompt a critical reflection on dominant masculine ideals, leading some HIV-positive men to advocate for confronting men's AIDS stigma and to mobilize their male peers in prevention efforts (Colvin, Robins, and Leavens 2010; Lynch, Brouard, and Visser 2010; Robins 2008; Wyrod 2011). I place these issues front and center and examine how masculinity is being remade in new ways because of the AIDS pandemic.

THE SOCIAL SIGNIFICANCE OF AIDS

A fundamental assumption guiding this book is that the AIDS pandemic is a social force with the potential to alter how gender and sexuality are lived. This emphasis on the social significance of this disease, however, runs counter to the dominant framing of AIDS. From the start of the epidemic in the early 1980s, a biomedical narrative prevailed, portraying AIDS as a medical problem that should be addressed through scientific, objective, health interventions. A central aspect of this biomedical discourse is the emphasis on individuals as "rational neo-liberal agents" who will respond to the counseling of experts by changing their behavior to reduce their chance of HIV infection or to improve their treatment (Kippax and Stephenson 2012, 789). Failure to adapt one's behavior in response to such scientifically identified, objective risks is framed as irrational, idiosyncratic, and problematic on the part of the individual (Lupton 1999).

Public health initiatives to address AIDS have therefore largely promoted a narrow, medicalized notion of sexuality independent of social relations and reducible to individual sexual behavior. This medicalized sexuality severs AIDS from the social by positing "sexuality as an autonomous domain" that can be managed by individuals responding rationally to objective, scientific sexual health risks (Pigg and Adams 2005, 20). This medicalized conception of sexuality has played a prominent role in the response to AIDS globally, including in Africa. As Colleen O'Manique (2004, 9) argues based on research in Uganda, "The pandemic is still overwhelmingly viewed first and foremost through a biomedical lens, and secondly through a narrow public health lens that focuses on individual sexual behavior."

The biomedical narrative's emphasis on individuals rationally managing HIV risk has been buttressed by framings of AIDS emphasizing individual moral fortitude. In such framings, individualized and puritanical sexual restraint, manifested as abstinence or monogamy, figures prominently as the solution to the AIDS crisis. Like the medicalized sexuality of the biomedical narrative, this puritanical framing emphasizes modifying the risk behaviors of individuals and explicitly condemns individuals who fail to behave "properly," something implicit in the neoliberal model of the individual at the heart of the biomedical narrative.

In the early 2000s, this moralizing frame was integrated into the U.S. global response to AIDS in Africa through PEPFAR, which promoted a simplistic ABC approach to prevention—Abstain, Be Faithful, or use Condoms. Priority was given to initiatives promoting sexual abstinence before marriage and marital fidelity as primary prevention strategies. Condom distribution and education were still funded, but condoms were cast as a secondary form of prevention for those lacking the moral fortitude to abstain or be faithful (Esacove 2013; Patterson 2006).

Yet throughout the history of the AIDS pandemic there has also been a consistent countervailing narrative placing social relations at the center of how AIDS is framed. This narrative emphasizes a nuanced engagement with how social context matters and how inequalities of gender, class, race, and sexuality structure behavior and shape policy in ways that facilitate HIV transmission (Barnett and Whiteside 2002; Farmer 1999, 2005; Hirsch et al. 2009b; Susser 2009; Treichler 1999; Watkins-Hayes 2014). This social narrative of AIDS foregrounds how successful responses to AIDS have often arisen from social, not individual, transformations that have occurred as collectives and communities reacted in locally specific ways to the new threat of the disease (Kippax and Stephenson 2012). Examples include the pioneering of new sexual practices by gay communities in America and Australia that reduced the likelihood of infection, such as selecting partners based on their HIV status; the AIDS Coalition to Unleash Power (ACT-UP) essentially rewriting the rules for AIDS biomedical research; HIV-positive people in Brazil insisting that access to AIDS drugs is a fundamental human rights issue; and the Treatment Action Campaign in South Africa asserting that lack of access to drugs was a form of medical apartheid, forcing action by both the government and global pharmaceutical companies (Brier 2009; Epstein 1996b; Galvão 2005; Power 2003).

Thus, implicit in the social narrative of AIDS is the notion that AIDS as a disease can act as a force to alter social relations. Many of the most successful examples of addressing AIDS—Brazil, Uganda, and gay communities in the United States and Australia—share a similar dynamic. In these places groups and communities developed their own responses to this new disease, and in the process AIDS catalyzed transformations in social relations. In these success stories, groups and communities responded to the new threat of AIDS by creating something akin to a "social vaccine," transforming social relations in ways that reduced the likelihood of HIV transmission and improved access to HIV treatment (Kippax and Stephenson 2012, 796).

The history of AIDS is therefore in part a history of how a novel disease created new forms of social relations. It has often been the groups most stigmatized by AIDS who have played a central role in social change. As Richard Parker and Peter Aggleton (2003, 19) have argued, such stigmatized groups have responded to AIDS by developing "project identities," which emerge when groups of people draw on the cultural materials available to them to "build a new identity that redefines their position in society and, by so doing, seek the transformation of overall social structure." What is implied, therefore, is that HIV/AIDS is not only shaped by the social but also shapes the social: people act in new ways in response to HIV risk and in the process transform social relations (Kippax et al. 2013).

My emphasis on the social significance of AIDS is an effort to make these reciprocal dynamics explicit. The social context shapes the transmission of HIV, especially with regard to the ways social inequalities have produced the myriad context-specific epidemics that compose the global pandemic. In turn, AIDS as an epidemic shapes the social context, in part by bringing the effect of social inequalities into stark relief. In specific times and places, AIDS has also catalyzed new social relations that challenge, and occasionally transform, these inequalities. In this sense, we can conceptualize how AIDS can alter social relations and remake gender and sexual relations, including masculinity.[10]

Uganda is a key site for examining the social significance of AIDS in Africa. Some of the highest HIV prevalence levels in Africa were initially reported in western Uganda in the early 1980s. Ugandans responded to this new threat, viewing it as something they themselves needed to fight. As Robert Thornton (2008) argues in his detailed history of AIDS in Uganda, AIDS was seen as an indigenous disease requiring an indigenous response. This response came from all levels of society and was especially robust at the community level, leading to what Helen Epstein (2007) refers to as "collective efficacy" in addressing AIDS.

Informal and interpersonal communication within families and groups was widespread as Ugandans talked with each other about this new disease, and AIDS became part of social relations across a broad spectrum of society. The net result was changes in sexual relations—from delaying first sex to reducing numbers of sexual partners to condom use—all of which are believed to have contributed to the dramatic drop in HIV prevalence in Uganda in the 1980s (Low-Beer and Stoneburner 2003; Hallett et al. 2006; Stoneburner and Low-Beer 2004).

A crucial component of this response was a form of AIDS prevention Ugandans invented called zero grazing. Zero grazing encouraged men to reduce their sexual partnerships to long-term partners in their immediate social and geographic networks. The phrase "zero grazing" is borrowed from livestock raising and refers to the practice of tying a cow to a peg to limit its grazing to a small circle, or zero. Importantly, zero grazing did not empha-size monogamy or abstinence but simply encouraged men to have fewer sexual partners and to keep these relationships close to home (Thornton 2008, 19). Although zero grazing proved to be an effective, context-sensitive AIDS prevention strategy in Uganda, it also accommodated and reinforced normative notions of male sexuality and masculine sexual privilege.

Nevertheless, zero grazing is believed to have severed links in broader sexual networks, resulting in fewer new HIV infections (Epstein 2007; Thornton 2008). And it is this success story about a social response to AIDS, and the resulting social transformation, that makes Uganda such an interesting place to examine the social significance of AIDS, including the disease's impact on masculinity.

As I discuss in chapter 2, however, this apparent success story is compli-cated. In the early 1990s, Uganda's success made it the recipient of a great deal of international funding for AIDS prevention and treatment, a trend that continues today. This funding supported conventional biomedical and behavioral prevention and treatment efforts that largely supplanted earlier approaches, like zero grazing, that had been rooted in the Ugandan context and the country's indigenous social response to AIDS.

The emphasis on biomedical approaches has, in fact, increased in recent years, not only in Uganda, but in the global response to AIDS more generally. This is due to the new focus on using AIDS drugs to reduce new HIV infections, including giving HIV-positive individuals treatment sooner to reduce their infectiveness and giving antiretroviral medication to HIV-negative people to prevent them from becoming infected, both of which have been shown to be highly effective (Anglemyer et al. 2011; Baeten et al. 2012). This move toward "treatment as prevention" has been framed as a massive turning point in the fight against AIDS, leading some to claim the AIDS epidemic can be drastically abated. This perception is troubling, however, because a biomedical fix can ignore social drivers of AIDS, such as gender inequality and poverty. In this book I offer a correc-tive to any approach that neglects the social dimensions of AIDS. I empha-size the social significance of the pandemic, especially its profound and dialectical entanglement with gender and sexual relations.

AIDS AND THE REMAKING OF MASCULINITY

In an effort to get to know more young people during my fieldwork, I often spent afternoons at a secondary school in greater Bwaise, located up a steep hill along a road lined with mature banana plants. My visits to the school were a welcome respite from the dust and dirt of barren central Bwaise. I chose this school because it had an active after-school club for students that focused on sex education. These "Straight Talk" clubs were popular in Kampala, and the organization that coordinated them was seen as yet another part of Uganda's successful response to fighting AIDS. Each Straight Talk club had an adult "patron," and at this school it was Matthew, a lanky thirty-year-old teacher from the Gisu ethnic group of eastern Uganda. I came to know Matthew well and always found our conversations insightful. He was a devout Pentecostal Christian, yet his sexual politics were complex. This was exemplified by his passion for the Straight Talk club, which promoted frank and open discussions of safe sex for teenagers, including the use of condoms.

Matthew told me that he was contentedly monogamous in his marriage but stressed that Gisu and other ethnic groups in Uganda valorized men with multiple sexual partners. Yet in Matthew's opinion, this had been tempered by AIDS. He explained:

> Most of us men were ruled by our culture. The culture of having many women would give you social standing. Other men would see you as a powerful man. You could manage three women. But now that one has changed. . . . It is no longer the old format of men thumping the chest because they have many women. It's not there. So people have been a bit humbled. They are a bit cautious in going about affairs . . . Everyone understands the problem now. Because every man now knows why the other is behaving like that. Because they meet and talk about these things and say, "AIDS is there, it's real, it has no cure."

In this conversation with me, Matthew addressed the question at the heart of this book: How has the AIDS epidemic shaped men's sexuality and sexual privileges in Uganda? His views also highlighted a recurring tension in my fieldwork: the sense that an "African," or "Ugandan," or in this case "Gisu" culture dictated certain aspects of men's sexuality but that such entrenched cultural norms could shift, or be remade. In one sense,

Matthew reflected the fact that many of the men and women I met articulated a cultural essentialist notion of male sexuality—one that saw men's sexual behavior as determined by, or as Mathew put it, ruled by, a static, unchanged, "traditional" "African" or "Ugandan" culture. This cultural essentialist framing of men's sexuality by African men and women has been noted in many contexts across the continent, and it is often combined with a biological essentialism that frames African men's sexuality as an innate drive that needs frequent release (Hunter 2010; Johnson-Hanks 2006; Nyanzi, Nyanzi-Wakholi, and Kalina 2009; Simpson 2009; Smith 2014; Spronk 2012).

Yet Mathew also alluded to a key aspect of prevailing sociological perspectives on sexuality, namely, that sexuality is not reducible to any cultural essence or natural, innate drive but is socially constructed in historically and context-specific ways. This denaturalizing of sexuality has been a central tenet in sociological theories of sexuality, and sociologists have demonstrated how sexual identities and practices are "intersubjectively negotiated social and historical products" that vary across both time and space (Epstein 1996a, 145; quoted in Gamson and Moon 2004, 48).[11]

While much research in this vein has focused on homosexuality, this perspective on sexuality has also proved useful for understanding how heterosexuality—including male heterosexuality—has been constructed (Ingraham 1994, 2002; Jackson 1996, 1999, 2005; Kimmel 2005; Schwartz 2007). This includes work by feminists specifying a dominant discourse that "sees men as sexually insatiable and male sexuality as naturally an uncontrollable drive" (Hollway 1984, 63). Nicole Vitellone (2000, 152) notes how this framing of the male sex drive as a "spontaneous, uninterruptible, powerful, hydraulic force" has been used to explain the well-documented aversion many heterosexual men have to certain safe sex practices in the context of AIDS, especially condom use.

This discursive construction of the male sex drive is in many respects a global masculine trope and a key facet of the broader construction of heterosexual masculine sexual privilege. Such privilege emphasizes male sexual pleasure, pervasive sexual double standards that give men greater sexual freedom and self-determination (including numbers of sexual partners and expectations of fidelity), and male-dominated decision making in the dominant scripts structuring sexual intimacy (Gagnon 1990; Gupta

2000, 2002; Hirsch et al. 2009a; Rutter and Schwartz 2011; Seal and Ehrhardt 2003). There is evidence from many social contexts, including sub-Saharan Africa, that such discourses do not fully determine men's sexual practices and that heterosexual men often struggle with, and at times critically engage, such discourses (Brod 1995; Dworkin and O'Sullivan 2005; Morrell 1999, 2001b; Ratele et al. 2007; Spronk 2014; Wagner-Raphael, Seal, and Ehrhardt 2001). Nonetheless, these constructions of male heterosexuality remain salient and are often more durable than normative notions of female heterosexuality that emphasize passivity and meeting a male partner's needs (Kimmel 2005; Segal 1994).

Such links between masculinity, sexuality, and male privilege have been a prominent theme in studies of men and masculinity. Sexuality has been understood as a key component of "hegemonic masculinity"—the dominant, idealized form of masculinity that provides a solution to the "problem of the legitimacy of patriarchy" in a particular time and place (Connell 1995, 77). Hegemonic masculinity not only refers to dominant ideals of male sexuality, but also normative gender ideals, such as men as breadwinners and authority figures. It is therefore a valuable concept for understanding how particular normative masculine ideals of both sexuality and gender are intertwined in the dominant ideal of masculinity that prevails in a particular context. While few men fully embody this hegemonic ideal in any given setting, it nonetheless naturalizes men's power over women, and the power certain men have over men who are marginalized and subordinated by race, class, and sexuality.

Sociologists originally conceptualized hegemonic masculinity as a form of social practice, emphasizing that masculine ideals shaped social interactions—that is, the everyday enactments of masculinity—in ways that both subordinated women and created power differences among men (Carrigan, Connell, and Lee 1985). However, much research that followed focused instead on categorizing ever finer distinctions between types of men—black masculinities, white, Asian, Muslim, and so on. This categorical essentialism has been widely criticized because it suggests that all members of a particular social group embody a specific form of masculinity that can be slotted into this overall rigid hierarchy (Aboim 2010; Beasley 2008; Hearn 2004; Lusher and Robins 2009; Pascoe 2003, 2007; Schrock and Schwalbe 2009, 280). It also neglects the original sociological emphasis on practices and processes of masculinity, and the dynamism, diversity, and complexity that emphasis implies.

These concerns about conceptualizing masculinity have also been articulated by the growing number of Africanists examining African masculinities (Cornwall 2005; Miescher 2005; Morrell 2001a; Ouzgane and Morrell 2005; Richter and Morrell 2006). Much of this research calls into question fixed hierarchies of masculine types, stressing instead that historically competing masculine identities "promoted sometimes divergent images of proper male behavior within certain contexts" (Lindsay and Miescher 2003a, 6). It emphasizes that African men cannot be easily pigeonholed into a single category, hegemonic or otherwise, and that there are often multiple, conflicting masculine identities in any given setting (Aboim 2009; Cornwall 2003; Cornwall and Nancy Lindisfarne 1994; Groes-Green 2012; Morrell 1998, 2001b; Morrell, Jewkes, and Lindegger 2012; Simpson 2009; Spronk 2012).[12] This literature also foregrounds the dangers of recycling problematic racial stereotypes about African men as violent, sexually promiscuous, and bound by "traditional" patriarchal beliefs, even if Africans themselves often frame male sexuality in these terms. It highlights the variability and mutability of African masculinities, past and present, as well as the ambivalence many African men exhibit toward dominant, hegemonic masculine ideals (Spronk 2014).

To address such conceptual issues, one recent trend in masculinity theory is to see the boundaries between masculine types as more porous, especially with respect to how hegemonic masculinity can incorporate elements of marginalized or subordinate masculinities (Demetriou 2001). Identifying these hybrid masculinities has revealed how hegemonic masculinity can adapt to changing contexts while still preserving and perpetuating gender and sexual inequality (Bridges 2014; Bridges and Pascoe 2014). Another trend has been to focus on what Douglas Schrock and Michael Schwalbe (2009) have called "manhood acts," the strategies men enact in their efforts to claim male privilege (see also Schwalbe 2014). Manhood acts are diverse and vary according to the resources available to different individuals and the skill and creativity with which individuals utilize such resources. This includes more troubling manhood acts—compensatory manhood acts—in which men attempt to claim an identity as a member of the privileged gender group by emphasizing aspects of hegemonic masculinity, including violence or sexual conquest (Connell and Messerschmidt 2005; Schrock and Schwalbe 2009; Sumerau 2012).

What these trends in masculinity theory share is an attempt to recover the original emphasis on social interactions and social processes in the early masculinity literature and in so doing (re)align it with sociological perspectives on gender more generally (Schrock and Schwalbe 2009, 279). Of particular relevance here is the canonical interactionist, or "doing gender," perspective that emphasizes the centrality of everyday social interaction in the production of gender relations. This perspective highlights the fundamentally interactional quality of masculinity (and femininity), framing it not as a characteristic of individual men but as a property of the dynamic system of relationships that composes the field of gender and sexual relations (West and Zimmerman 2009, 114).

I draw on these insights to conceptualize how masculinity is lived in a place like Bwaise. I am particularly interested in how men understand and describe themselves as accountable to hegemonic masculine ideals, the paradoxes such ideals create for them, and the strategies and manhood acts that men employ in their efforts to embody masculinity, especially in the context of their intimate relationships.

I also build on these insights to specify how these processes play out in context: the way masculinity is practiced in a particular time and place. I focus on how three different aspects of masculinity are interrelated: masculinity and work, masculinity and men's authority over women, and masculinity and sexuality. I focus on these three aspects because implicit in much of the masculinity literature is the idea that hegemonic masculinity usually encompasses ideals of a male economic provider, male authority over women in the home, and ideals of male sexuality equated with sexual virility, freedom, and control. These three core ideals typically buttress each other, and such reinforcing dynamics are part of the durability of hegemonic masculinity.[13] I foreground the analysis of these dynamics and processes, examining how social interactions between these three domains of gender and sexual relations—work, authority, sexuality—are shaped and mediated by the practice of masculinity (figure 1.4).

This framework not only helps us understand the robustness of hegemonic masculinity, but it also provides a way of thinking about how masculinity is remade. As material and economic conditions, ideologies and

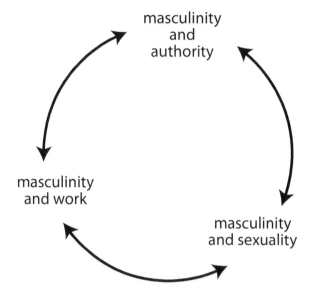

Figure 1.4. Masculinity as a social process.

discourses, and institutions and organizations change, there are reverberations for each of these aspects of masculinity—and the relationships between
them. My interest is in understanding how such social forces alter the established social interactions that link these aspects of masculinity and in the
process remake masculinity by changing the way it is enacted in everyday
life.[14] Are changes related to one aspect of masculinity, such as growing
unemployment for men, always compensated for in other domains, such as
a shoring up of men's authority in the home? And when do changes in one
aspect of masculinity undermine other aspects, creating reverberations in
social relations that can destabilize hegemonic masculinity more generally?

Remaking masculinity is a central theme of this book, and my emphasis on it draws on approaches to gender that recognize that gender ideals
and practices are not static but continually redefined. However, the ways
they are redefined typically, though not always, preserve men's status,
authority, and privilege over women (Fenstermaker, West, and
Zimmerman 1991; Ridgeway 2009, 2011; Ridgeway and Correll 2004;
West and Fenstermaker 1993). Cultural beliefs and practices about gender
are resilient, even in times of significant socioeconomic change. This

theme of continual change and persistent inequality guides my analysis, especially the extent to which remaking masculinity either alters the gender/sexuality status quo or simply reproduces it in a new form.

My emphasis on these three aspects of masculinity as a social process also emerged from my fieldwork and my reading of the history of masculinity in Uganda. My fieldwork revealed the constellation of masculine ideals that compose hegemonic masculinity in the contemporary urban Ugandan context. I discuss these ideals in detail in chapter 2, including their historical roots, but they can be sketched here as follows. First, with regard to masculinity and work, there is a male provider ideal primarily embodied by men working to provide for most of their family's material needs. Second, there is an ideal of male authority, especially the notion that men are superior to women and have authority over women and children in the home. Third, there is the ideal of male sexuality that centers on masculine sexual privilege, which encompasses both men's control over the terms of sex and their privilege of having multiple sexual relationships if they so choose.

A crucial component of my fieldwork was not only identifying these ideals but also observing how the changing broader social context is impinging on these ideals and remaking how masculinity is practiced. There are, in fact, forces at work in urban Uganda that are undermining and destabilizing each of these ideals. With respect to the male provider ideal, chronic male underemployment has made being a provider elusive for many men—a particularly frustrating experience given rapidly growing economic inequality in urban Uganda. Simultaneously, women are increasingly earning money that sustains families. With regard to men's authority in the home, I see relatively new discourses of women's rights as the primary contextual shift challenging this ideal. As for the ideal of male sexuality, the prolonged AIDS crisis has challenged notions of masculine sexual privilege in ways that are unprecedented.

Importantly, these social forces are not only impinging on each of these masculine ideals, but they are also altering the interrelationship between the ideals, with significant ramifications for how masculinity is practiced and remade in everyday social interaction. A key assumption of my analysis, therefore, is that we cannot understand the impact of AIDS on the practice of men's sexuality and masculine sexual privilege in isolation. We need to remain attentive to how AIDS has shaped men's sexuality in relation to changes in the meaning and practices of the male provider ideal and men's authority within the home. In each empirical chapter of this book, I focus on one of these three aspects of masculinity (chapter 3, work; chapter 4, authority; chapter 5, sexuality). I reveal how these aspects are intertwined and the implications such entanglements have for the remaking of masculinity in the age of AIDS.

MASCULINITY IN THE EVERYDAY LIFE OF AN AFRICAN SLUM

Like many African capital cities, Kampala is a study in contrasts. As the only true metropolis in Uganda, this city of over a million is a confounding mix of gleaming office towers, rambling traditional markets, leafy elite residential enclaves, and sprawling slums. Most of the country's ethnic groups rub shoulders and interact with expatriates from all over the world. It was precisely this dynamic and diverse milieu that led me to locate this study in Kampala.

Although Kampala's most attractive feature is its many hills, the majority of the city's residents make their homes in modest communities in the city's flood-prone valleys. I conducted my fieldwork in the poorest of the city's five divisions, Kawempe Division, home to approximately one-third of the city's population (Uganda Bureau of Statistics 2006). Most families are in debt, have limited prospects for economic mobility, and are surviving on incomes of one or two dollars a day.

Bwaise (pronounced BWEYE-say) is the dense heart of Kawempe Division and was the focus of my fieldwork (figure 1.5). Three miles from the city center and covering an area of one square mile, Bwaise is a low-lying section of Kawempe, operating much like a self-contained town. It is considered an undesirable place to live because it lies at the confluence of two rivers that have become enormous sewage canals. During the two rainy seasons, the canals back up and spew sewage from surrounding hills onto Bwaise's streets. Many residents have built concrete barriers around their homes, but these provide little protection during the inevitable floods.

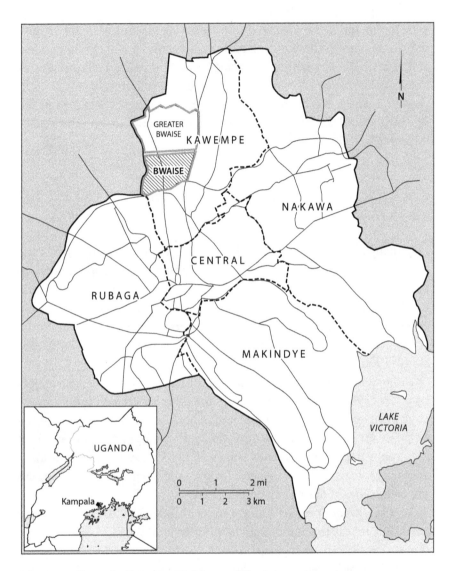

Figure 1.5. Kampala, Kawempe Division, and Bwaise.

Figure 1.6. Housing in Bwaise.

Bwaise was a better neighborhood in decades past. Throughout the neighborhood, substantial old homes previously occupied by more well-to-do families have decayed and are now rarely occupied by a single family. Most of the recent housing is crude and rudimentary, built as cheap, basic shelter. Squatters fill the remaining spaces, cobbling together makeshift homes of mud and wattle. (See figure 1.6.) When I began my fieldwork in 2004, at least fifty thousand people called Bwaise their home (Uganda Bureau of Statistics 2006), and the neighborhood initially seemed to me like a former middle-class town resettled by the urban poor.

Bwaise, therefore, has a well-deserved reputation as a slum—a term residents did not shy away from when describing their community. Many of my informants were second-generation residents who doubted they would ever leave, and there are, in fact, good reasons to live there. During the day, the main commercial intersection is jammed with people doing business at the long strip of storefronts that include furniture showrooms, cell phone shops, pharmacies, butchers, hardware stores, and barbershops (figure 1.7). In the evening, Bwaise's many raucous bars and clubs ensure

Figure 1.7. Business in Bwaise.

that nightlife is always boisterous. Life is difficult in Bwaise, but there is also opportunity, and for many residents this dynamism and energy make up for otherwise harsh living conditions. Over the course of my fieldwork I, too, grew increasingly accustomed to the squalor and more drawn to the excitement of Bwaise and the resilience of its residents.

While Bwaise is well known as one of Kampala's more notorious slums, it is by no means unique. Each of the five city divisions has neighborhoods that are similarly challenging places to live; in 2012, an estimated sixty-two slum communities existed throughout the city (Kampala Capital City Authority 2012). A few of these areas first emerged in the early twentieth century, but most, like Bwaise, became slums after 1950. The fringes of the city are no less bleak, suffering from the same lack of planning and infrastructure. As in Bwaise, families often live in one-room homes and share communal latrines, living in their own version of urban squalor at the city's edge. Thus, while conditions in Bwaise are unquestionably difficult, they are also representative of what life is like for the many Kampalans who struggle to get by in comparable communities across the city.

Research Methods

Because Bwaise was one poor community among very many in Kampala, my fieldwork in the community allowed me to trace the cultural implications of the AIDS epidemic for masculinity in urban Uganda. My aim was to gain a holistic sense of everyday life in Bwaise, especially how men and women navigated masculine ideals in the context of precarious work, women's changing roles in society, and the omnipresence of AIDS. This was a task especially well suited to the ethnographic practice of observing, and ideally participating in, the minutia of everyday life. Participant observation reveals subtle interactive processes that reproduce, and at times subvert, gender and sexual relations. I conducted my research for twelve months in 2004, with extensive follow-up research for three months in 2009 and one additional month of fieldwork in 2015. Together, these periods of fieldwork provided a rich, longitudinal aspect to my research, allowing me to examine how many of my informants' lives progressed over an entire decade.[15]

Much of my fieldwork was carried out in classic ethnographic fashion, involving unstructured time in Bwaise talking with men and women in shops, markets, drinking joints, dance clubs, on the streets, and, especially, in their homes. Being present in the community provided insight into how residents discussed and framed their everyday challenges and how their concerns were inflected by gender and sexuality. I complemented this research with fieldwork at three strategically chosen sites that allowed me to better understand how masculinity was being remade by the nature of work, the promotion of women's rights, and the impact of AIDS.

To learn firsthand about the nature of work, I spent five months as an apprentice carpenter in a small carpentry workshop in Bwaise, working one to two full days a week on average. Carpentry was seen as men's work in Kampala and was one of the main occupations for the first wave of men who became permanent Kampala residents in the early twentieth century (Mair 1934). In Bwaise, hundreds of men work in carpentry workshops large and small, churning out overstuffed chairs and sofas, king-size beds, and intricate armoires. The workshop where I apprenticed was relatively small, owned by one man who employed three to four full-time carpenters. As a modest but somewhat successful business, this workshop was emblematic of the ways many men survive in Kampala's economy, providing me with a window on how economic conditions are intertwined with masculinity and intimate relationships.

My fieldwork also confirmed that Uganda's reputation as a leader in women's rights activism in Africa was indeed deserved. Many women's organizations were active in Kampala, and some of the most interesting activism was focused on a rights-based approach to preventing domestic violence. I became involved with the most dynamic of these organizations, the Center for Domestic Violence Prevention (CEDOVIP), created in 2003 by a coalition of local organizations in the Ugandan women's movement, in collaboration with the regional NGO Raising Voices and supported by international donors. CEDOVIP's staff was composed completely of Ugandans. Their work addressed domestic violence in Bwaise and Kawempe Division from a community perspective, involving local leaders, religious groups, the police, and healthcare workers (Michau 2007). For nine months, I worked closely with CEDOVIP staff and volunteers in Bwaise to examine how men and women in the community responded to their projects.

To understand the nature and impact of AIDS prevention and treatment programs in Bwaise, I volunteered one day a week for nine months at the main government health clinic in the area. This modest compound was an active site for HIV testing, AIDS support groups, and HIV prevention workshops. I spent my days in the company of several personable female nurses, observing them as they administered HIV tests and AIDS counseling. During my fieldwork at the clinic, I was fortunate to witness the formation of the Bwaise Positive Men's Union, a unique, grassroots AIDS support group for men, created by HIV-positive men from the community.[16] For six months, I participated in their weekly meetings, attended their events, and became an honorary member.

During the three months of follow-up fieldwork in 2009, I again spent time hanging out in Bwaise, reconnecting with friends and informants, and revisiting all my key field sites, including the carpentry workshop, CEDOVIP, and the health clinic. Because I felt I needed a better sense of how masculinity is navigated in intimate relationships, I added a new component to my research. I spoke with nineteen cohabiting couples who represented a diverse sample of relationships in Bwaise, young and old, monogamous and polygamous, Muslims and Christians, and HIV-negative and HIV-positive individuals. I spoke at length with them about their expectations for ideal partners and relationships, power dynamics within their relationships, and their ideas of proper sexual behavior in the age of AIDS. Together, the couples provided rich information on how masculinity is negotiated, and occasionally reworked, in intimate relationships.[17]

Each of these facets of my ethnographic fieldwork proved essential to gaining a holistic understanding of how masculinity was lived in Bwaise. As this book reveals, masculinity, work, rights, and AIDS were deeply intertwined in the lives of my informants, something that became most evident in my longitudinal research with my closest key informants. Throughout this book, I provide detailed portraits of several informants to bring these dynamics into full relief.

I complemented my fieldwork and participant observation with numerous in-depth interviews that lasted one to two hours. During the two main research periods, I conducted formal interviews with a total of 116 residents, including 19 individuals who were interviewed in both 2004 and 2009. Ten of my informants became friends with whom I interacted extensively during both fieldwork periods, interviewing them formally and informally many times. I strove to interview a wide range of individuals to capture the demographic diversity of Bwaise with regard to ethnicity, religion, and education (see Appendix tables A.1 and A.2). With few exceptions, my interviewees and other informants lived in the greater Bwaise area, and those who did not commuted to Bwaise regularly for work or other reasons.

In all these interviews, I asked about the challenges of living in Bwaise, conceptions of masculinity and femininity, attitudes toward women's rights, marriage and relationship ideals, sexual history, and views about

AIDS. I also conducted four group discussions with similar themes. The groups had eight to twelve participants each; two groups were composed of men; one was composed of women; and one, both men and women. Nearly all verbatim quotes in this book are taken from my interviews, group discussions, and informal conversations that I recorded and transcribed.

I carried out my ethnographic fieldwork and interviews in both English and Luganda, the language of the Baganda and a lingua franca throughout Kampala. Formal Luganda language training before and during my fieldwork allowed me to conduct fieldwork and the majority of interviews in Luganda, with occasional assistance from Baganda research assistants. The Baganda are the largest of Uganda's approximately thirty ethnic groups, representing 17 percent of the country's population. Kampala is located in the southern part of Uganda, in Buganda, the home of the Baganda people.[18] Most residents of Bwaise are Baganda, and my research therefore focused on the Baganda and Ganda culture while recognizing that the cultural fabric of Kampala was significantly more complex. Unless noted otherwise, all individuals quoted in this book were Baganda.

After my 2009 fieldwork, I remained in close contact with several of my key informants. Through phone calls and email, I stayed informed about the lives of several central characters in this book. In 2015, I returned once more to Bwaise and reconnected with many of my friends and acquaintances and conducted interviews with ten of my main informants. In the epilogue, I reflect on the arc of their lives, as well as changes in Bwaise as a community, over the course of more than a decade.

Locating Myself in Bwaise

There was another, more fundamental reason I was drawn to ethnography. As a relatively privileged, white middle-class American man, I had little knowledge of what it meant to live in a place like Bwaise. Ethnographic fieldwork allows for, and in fact requires, prolonged, intimate immersion in life in a particular place. For me, this provided an education about a world that was in many respects incommensurable with my own. The immersive nature of fieldwork helped me to gain a better understanding

of how my own distinct and privileged subject position shaped my interactions with Bwaise's residents.

As described in the opening vignette, my entry into the field was largely as a familiar trope in Bwaise and Kampala—the Western AIDS researcher. On the referral of a friend at the local health clinic, I first came to Bwaise to visit Christine, the dynamic community AIDS counselor. As she would later tell me with some pride, I was not the first Western researcher who had visited her home, although those other visitors had not returned. I was impressed with Christine's dedication to fighting AIDS and her willingness to discuss her own intimate relationships. In retrospect, I see I was also relieved that people in Bwaise were so open to talking with me about sensitive topics like sex and HIV.

As I would come to learn, however, this openness was complicated. The intensity of AIDS in Uganda and the magnitude of responses to the disease meant that nearly everyone I met in Bwaise was quite knowledgeable about AIDS, from basic virology and prevention techniques to the effectiveness of AIDS drugs. Interactions with me, therefore, were opportunities for residents to demonstrate their fluency in AIDS knowledge to a seemingly powerful white foreigner. These dynamics were no doubt exacerbated in the early part of my fieldwork when I often described myself as conducting AIDS-related research, slipping comfortably into this established role for a white man.

In time, I learned to avoid this terminology, stressing instead that I wanted to learn what it was like to live in Bwaise in order to get past what I came to see as a prevailing AIDS script. When residents deployed this script, it typically combined an emphasis on sexual "responsibility" (fidelity and monogamy) with competency in AIDS knowledge as markers of sophistication as modern urbanites. This script was also used to disparage other residents, for example, the ways men were critical of women and especially how women criticized men. The script figured prominently in the testimonies of HIV-positive people about their lives, especially the way men who were open about their status described coming to terms with being HIV-positive as a redemption story.

My prolonged fieldwork in Bwaise mitigated but did not eliminate these issues. As my fieldwork progressed, I became more savvy about getting beyond this AIDS script. My constant presence in Bwaise meant I was no longer fitting neatly into the AIDS researcher role, especially among people I interacted with on a daily basis. Although I lived in a neighboring community during my fieldwork, I became a regular fixture in Bwaise. This was especially true after I began my carpentry apprenticeship in the heart of Bwaise, where I was ostentatiously on display, dressed in one of the workshop's bright-blue jumpsuits. I also began to spend more and more time socializing in Bwaise with informants, some of whom were slowly becoming friends.

Thus I believe I transitioned from appearing as another AIDS researcher to someone interested in understanding everyday life in Bwaise more generally. By the end of my first year of fieldwork, I found that many residents I met for the first time were already well aware of my recurring presence in Bwaise. This opened up opportunities for discussions about surviving in Bwaise that were broader than AIDS, and I felt that people often saw me as a conduit for voicing their frustrations about the persistent problems they faced as members of the urban poor.

Yet this new identity posed its own problems and challenges. For one, my persistent interest in people's intimate relationships meant I was becoming a repository of highly personal and, in some cases, combustible information. I was especially concerned that women would be reluctant to share problems in their relationships with me, and at times I chose to have a female Ugandan research assistant talk with women alone. Less expectedly, I found that familiarity also posed certain issues when talking with men, especially younger men in their twenties. This was not only because I was a white foreigner but also because I was a married man. My wife, also white and American, accompanied me to Uganda during my fieldwork and spent time at my field sites in Bwaise on numerous occasions. My key informants, therefore, were all aware that I was married, and for the younger men this added to my status, even though I did not have children. Several young men were especially eager to craft images of themselves as on a similar trajectory to male adulthood. The better I came to know them, the more actively they seemed to be managing their image of themselves to me, especially whether or not they were "faithful" to their girlfriends. They would explicitly state that they saw me as a model for their relationships, and it was often only through mutual friends that I would fully understand how they navigated masculinity, intimacy, and AIDS in their lives.

ORGANIZATION OF THE BOOK

This book emerged out of my interest in understanding the sociological significance of a great tragedy of our time—the African AIDS crisis. When I began this project, it was clear that AIDS would leave deep and long-lasting scars on societies across sub-Saharan Africa. What was less evident was how an event of this magnitude was altering social relations, especially gender and sexuality. This book is organized around this central theme and is structured to provide an understanding of how masculinity has been remade in urban Uganda in the context of AIDS.

Understanding the contemporary contours of masculinity in the context of AIDS requires historical perspective. In chapter 2, I trace the roots of the masculine ideals I found to be central to life in Bwaise. As this chapter reveals, conceptions of masculinity, and femininity, have been continually remade in the past century. A recurring theme in these remakings is the intertwining of work, authority, and sexuality. I also chart the social history of AIDS and show how HIV became ever more entangled with gender and sexual relations in Uganda throughout the second half of the twentieth century.

In chapter 3, I turn to how masculinity is lived in Bwaise, examining how masculinity and work were intertwined. I begin with the attention to work because, as all my informants repeatedly told me, work and earning money were at the core of the key masculine ideal of being a family provider. My informants' insistence that masculinity was rooted in work and earning money grounds this book in the political economy of masculinity in Bwaise. My fieldwork, including my work as an apprentice carpenter, revealed that employment opportunities were largely precarious and poorly paid, making it difficult for most men to fulfill the provider ideal. I explore the links between this male provider ideal, precarious work, and male sexuality. I show how this gender ideal was related to expectations about men's sexual behavior in ways that reinforced men's entrenched sexual privileges. Masculine sexual privilege was not simply about sex; it was also deeply intertwined with other gender ideals. By focusing on the material conditions of masculinity, this chapter also underscores how the Ugandan government's economic policies, which have not addressed the needs of the urban poor, have contributed to the social context of poverty and underemployment in which men and women navigate masculinity, sexuality, and AIDS.

In chapter 4, I examine masculinity in Bwaise in light of the promotion of women's rights in Uganda. I draw on my research with cohabiting couples who revealed the complex and often contradictory effects women's rights discourse has had on conceptions of masculinity. Of particular importance was the difference between the ways rights were mobilized to challenge men's authority as decision makers in the home and the much more muted impact women's rights has had on men's sexual privileges.

Both chapters 3 and 4 reveal a core theme that emerged from my fieldwork in Bwaise: the salience of masculine sexual privilege in the ways masculinity was lived in Bwaise. In chapter 5, I build on these insights and focus specifically on AIDS and masculinity. Through a detailed discussion of the lives of several key informants, this chapter reveals that while the context of AIDS has troubled masculine sexual privilege, it has not fundamentally undermined it—a surprising finding given Uganda's alleged success in addressing AIDS.

In the concluding chapter, I situate my findings about Bwaise in the broader literature on masculinity, intimate relationships, and AIDS in Africa. There are striking and important similarities between what I observed during my fieldwork in Bwaise and dynamics in many other urban African contexts. I also elaborate on the more conceptual contributions that emerge from my research, including the importance of examining how sexuality is tied to the reproduction of gender inequality.

I bring the book to a close by exploring the significant and timely implications for AIDS policy that emerge from this study, especially given the recent increase in HIV infections in Uganda. This disconcerting trend indicates that a true AIDS success story requires a more significant and sustained engagement with masculine sexual privilege and the way in which this privilege is intertwined with gender inequality.

2 The Making of Masculinity in Urban Uganda

At the cusp of the twentieth century in southeastern Cameroon, a series of events unfolded that would alter human history. The simian immunodeficiency virus was able to make the leap from a chimpanzee to a human, becoming the human immunodeficiency virus. The transfer most likely occurred when humans, butchering chimps for bush meat, cut themselves, allowing the virus to enter their bloodstream. This transfer had almost certainly happened many times in the past, but at this moment the virus gained a foothold in the human population and continued to spread, first across sub-Saharan Africa and then eventually around the globe. Many factors contributed to making this momentous series of events possible, among them colonial road and railway construction, the development of colonial cities, and perhaps the use of reusable syringes in colonial medical campaigns (Pepin 2011). What was certain was that by the late 1970s the virus was responsible for one of the world's first mass AIDS outbreaks, in southwestern Uganda, making southern Uganda, including Kampala, an epicenter of the African AIDS pandemic (Doyle 2013).

Understanding how this new peril has shaped life in Uganda requires historical perspective on gender, sexuality, and intimate relationships in this region. That is the aim of this chapter. I examine how work, authority in the home, and sexuality have all been intertwined in different ways across the twentieth century in Uganda and how the relationships between these domains of social life were shaped by notions of masculinity.

My discussion focuses on the Baganda, the largest ethnic group in Uganda. While Uganda and Kampala are ethnically diverse, Kampala is in the center of Buganda, the home of the Baganda people (figure 2.1). The Baganda have been, and remain, the majority of Kampala's residents. They have been the dominant ethnic group in southern Uganda since the eighteenth century, a status bolstered by their role as the key political mediators in the British colonial system of indirect rule in Uganda. For several centuries, therefore, the Baganda have been the prevailing cultural force in the region, with migrants to Buganda and Kampala pressured to assimilate to the customs and practices of their Ganda "hosts" (Parkin 1969). The Baganda share many similarities with the other interlacustrine Bantu ethnic groups that stretch from Burundi, Rwanda, and northern Tanzania to southern Uganda. These Bantu ethnic groups have had comparable centralized political structures, with kings or paramount chiefs, that limited the influence of patrilineal clans. Compared to the Nilotic and Nilo-Hamitic ethnic groups of northern Uganda and western Kenya, they have a less pronounced patriarchal culture, with more limited control over women (Southall 1960). Ganda women, in particular, have historically had forms of agency and independence that continue to play an important role in gender and sexual relations in Buganda and Kampala. The social life that I observed in my fieldwork was, therefore, inextricably tied to the culture of Buganda, which has shaped how masculinity is lived in Bwaise.

THE PRECOLONIAL ERA AND THE KINGDOM OF BUGANDA IN THE NINETEENTH CENTURY

The vibrant, cosmopolitan, and rapidly growing metropolis of Kampala that I experienced during my fieldwork is in many respects a relatively recent phenomenon. Strategically chosen by the British for its close proximity to the *kibuga* (capital) of the kingdom of Buganda, which had been the center of power in the region for several centuries, Kampala was just

Figure 2.1. Main ethnic groups in Uganda.

emerging as a colonial city a century ago. It was officially designated a township only in 1906.

The kingdom of Buganda had a sophisticated hierarchical structure. At its apex was the *kabaka* (king) who ruled over a complex network of hereditary clan heads and appointed chiefs. For the bulk of the population, life revolved around individual families cultivating their small plots of lands, or *maka* (homesteads), in villages of 30 to 80 maka (Southwold 1965). For young Ganda men there was no male initiation ceremony and so a crucial step toward male adulthood was finding a promising piece of land for his maka, typically in a village some distance from his father's village. A man could then embark on his central passage to manhood, namely, finding a woman to marry. Rituals surrounding marriage included a formal introduction ceremony between the families (*okwanjula*), a wedding ceremony (*embaga*), and the crucial payment of bridewealth (*omutwalo*) to the bride's family.

The man could then bring his wife to his maka, symbolizing his new authority over her. However, unlike most other ethnic groups in the region, the Ganda wife remained part of her own family's clan and could return to her father or brother if her marriage proved unsatisfactory. Nonetheless, marriage marked a woman's transition to female adulthood, a process that required the additional step of producing a child who, in this patrilineal society, would become part of her husband's lineage. Procreation was also an essential component of masculinity: an impotent man was not considered fully a man (Kisekka 1973, 153).

There was clear division of labor along gender lines in Buganda. The principal duties of the wife involved providing for her family's daily necessities, including cultivating her garden, cooking, cleaning the home, and caring for the children (Roscoe 1911). Men were not involved in agriculture, except for the very infrequent clearing of land. Instead they built houses, made cloth, hunted, fished, labored on public works, attended to the chiefs, and occasionally went to war (Southwold 1965, 106).

Women, therefore, played the central role in subsistence agriculture—the backbone of life in precolonial Buganda. In reality, women, not men, were the family providers, supplying the essentials for their families' survival. Women's work, however, was restricted to the domestic sphere, the maka and the home. Unlike societies in West Africa in this period,

Ganda women were not involved with trade. Thus there was no precolonial precedent for women in the market economy. In their comprehensive history of women and work in Uganda, Grace Kyomuhendo and Marjorie McIntosh (2006, 67) argue that a woman's primary identity in this period was as wife and mother who was "expected to stay within the domestic context." This identity was central to a gender and sexuality status quo that dictated women were to be submissive and deferential to men and faithful and sexually available to their husbands.[1]

Men, in contrast, were the heads of households and decision makers who provided a family's shelter, clothing, and protection. In this sense, men's *ekitiibwa* (honor, respect) had what John Iliffe (2005, 170) refers to as a householder aspect that required establishing and properly maintaining a home and family.[2] Yet, in many respects, men's householder responsibilities were limited, especially given women's central role in providing food for the family. Men, however, did have the responsibility of acquiring material possessions needed for gift giving, an essential part of the many ceremonies of family life (Mair 1934). This was especially true of the marriage ceremony, which entailed high expectations of gift giving from the husband's family, including cloth, beer, cowry shells, and livestock. Gift giving was a key way a man could exhibit his wealth, creating links between masculinity and the notion of the man as dispenser of material goods—a notion that intensified greatly in the twentieth century. While women controlled any surplus produce they grew in their gardens, their opportunities to acquire material goods were very limited because they were excluded from warfare and the market economy. In this regard, a wife was "completely dependent on her husband for clothing and other material goods," even if the provision of material goods and gifts was often considered a show of a husband's grace as much as of his duty as a "proper" man (Richards 1964, 257, 264).

While this gender division of labor was the foundation for male identity as household head, masculine status was also tied to men's social mobility in precolonial Uganda. One of the distinguishing aspects of the kingdom of Buganda was its basis in class, not caste. Compared to neighboring kingdoms with rigid caste systems, Buganda had a much greater degree of individual social mobility (Mamdani 1976, 30). The kabaka appointed his many chiefs from the ranks of relatively ordinary men who secured their office and the associated ekitiibwa not by inheritance but by "talent and courage" (Iliffe 2005, 168; see also Gibbs 1965).

This social structure allowed ordinary men to become chiefs, and it also gave men with ambition the opportunity to improve their lot. Because the Baganda were only moderately patrilocal, a man might choose to leave his ancestral land and seek favor with a powerful appointed chief and establish his maka on the chief's estate. An individual could use the relative freedom from hereditary clan allegiances "to seek his own advantage by changing his allegiance from village to village and from chief to chief" (Southwold 1965, 100). In this sense, a man's social standing and status came not only through hereditary lineage but also through hard work and skillful political maneuvering. Greater political centralization in the kingdom "increasingly opened positions of power and wealth to men of talent," which made men's social mobility culturally valued, a dynamic that only intensified in the twentieth century with the proliferation of occupations for men (Fallers 1964, 159). A masculine competitive spirit suffused social life in Buganda, and ekitiibwa was its currency.

This emphasis on men's individual accomplishments in the precolonial period meant that men's status was achieved, and masculinity often turned on the ability to build political alliances and gain access to the material resources that came with them. Thus masculinity and male status have long been tied to political power and wealth in Buganda. With the monetization of the economy in the colonial period, the association of masculinity with wealth intensified. By midcentury, a rural man's ability to be economically self-reliant was a leading masculine trope. Martin Southwold (1965, 101) notes, "In modern times, the individualism of Ganda life has perhaps been accentuated by the fact that every man now makes a living in his own gardens, and is not economically dependent on any chief or landlord, let alone his clansmen or kinsmen." The correlation between masculinity and earning money became especially pronounced in urbanizing Kampala, and by the time of my fieldwork it was the main preoccupation of the men I came to know.

Throughout the twentieth century, this link between masculinity and money became ever more entwined with men's identity as heads of households. A man increasingly proved his masculinity through his own achievement in a competitive milieu, diligently earning the money required to support himself and his family. The corollary of this association of men's status and economic achievement was that a man's inability to earn money became a personal failing, a factor that helps explain the intense demoralization that poor men in Bwaise often expressed to me. It also lies at the heart of why many men who were unable to economically achieve masculine status found women earners threatening to their identities.

While there were clear paths for men to achieve status and authority in relation to other men, men's authority over women was assumed, with the exception of elite women.[3] Marriage to a dutiful and deferential wife who produced obedient children was at the center of the householder dimension of all men's ekitiibwa. Young, unmarried women had some independence, but marriage marked a new phase of life in which a woman was subordinate to her husband. This transition was symbolized in the marriage procession when the bride "was expected to weep loudly at losing her freedom" because she was "passing into the power of a man who could treat her just as he liked" (Mair 1934, 84). The husband as household head was a commanding authority figure who "expected deference and often abject humility from his wife and children," while his wife's sphere of authority was restricted to her kitchen, banana grove, and children (Richards 1964, 257).

This is not to suggest that wives had no influence in their households. An honorable wife—a woman who listened to her husband, properly welcomed visitors in her home, and raised children who respected their elders—was seen as having *empisa* (character) and earned her own form of ekitiibwa, or respect. With empisa and ekitiibwa came some say in household decision making and some counterbalancing of men's authority in the home. As Lucy Mair (1940, 14) notes, while a wife was expected to obey her husband as his subordinate, there was "a definite conception of dignity of the household"; "the husband should listen to his wife's opinions; if he pays no attention to her it is said, 'He does not know she is his wife.'" In this regard, the relationship of husband and wife mirrored the broader political structure and was akin to that of a chief and his peasant (Mair 1934, 96; Southwold 1973, 171). Thus men's *obuyinza* (authority, power) was defined in more managerial terms in the past, while I found that in Bwaise *obuyinza* often had a harsher, more domineering connotation, which may reflect the particularly fraught nature of gender relations in contemporary urban Uganda.

Other aspects of marriage in precolonial Buganda complicate any notion of gender and sexual relations in Buganda as resolutely patriarchal. The most common form of marriage was based on mutual attraction and premised on a woman's consent. A "proper" marriage, therefore, was one in which a woman freely chose to accept or decline a marriage proposal and in which her family was paid the full bridewealth (Doyle 2013, 48). Individual choice and agency in marriage also extended to divorce. Unlike women in neighboring societies, Ganda women enjoyed the right to leave their husbands if they neglected to provide properly or were sexually inept or if the woman fell in love with another man (Doyle 2013, 49). A man's authority in his home, therefore, was earned to a small degree. A stingy husband, or one unable to obtain material goods, could find his wife had left him and returned to her own family (Richards 1964, 260). Bridewealth, however, had to be repaid to make divorce official, requiring that a wife's family support her decision and return the initial payment.

As the kingdom of Buganda became more centralized, polygyny also became institutionalized. Whether as spoils of war or gifts to seal client-patron relationships, women were increasingly used as objects of exchange between men in the kingdom. As Nakanyike Musisi (1991, 772) argues, these political developments were tied to the rise of the institution of polygyny because, "as women became signs and objects of prestige and class, polygyny stratified men. The more wives a man had, the higher his status on the political and social ladder. . . . [W]omen became a commodity to be accumulated and carefully guarded by the wealthy and powerful men."[4]

While polygyny became a highly regarded male ideal, few common men were able to marry more than one woman. The bridewealth a prospective husband was obligated to pay to his wife's family was relatively low among the Baganda, but it was still prohibitive for most common men (Musisi 1991, 785). Although a young man's father often provided much of the bridewealth payment, the demands for animals, cloth, and beer could be onerous such that "a man frequently spent twelve months begging among his relatives and friends [for] the amount asked" (Roscoe 1911, 88).

Thus in the precolonial era multiple wives became an important marker of male status, which, as my fieldwork reveals, remains largely true in

Bwaise today. However, the financial difficulty of formally marrying more than one woman has meant that monogamy has long been a common and unremarkable part of Ganda men's sexual relationships. Most men in pre-colonial Buganda spent much of their adult lives in monogamous marriages since only older men were typically able to afford a second wife. Yet all men retained the privilege of starting another relationship that could lead to marriage—a privilege women unequivocally did not share.

Ostensibly, both men's and women's extramarital affairs were strongly condemned by official regulations of the kingdom, which punished adulterers with death or torture. However, the ethnographic literature provides many examples of how such punishments could be averted and the guilty party absolved of any wrongdoing (Doyle 2013, 55; Sacks 1979, 212). This was especially true for men, and there was a conspicuous disconnect between stringent regulations regarding adultery imposed by the kingdom and the masculine status that such affairs accorded men. As Mere Kisekka (1973, 153) writes in her discussion of the precolonial roots of contemporary Ganda masculinity and sexuality, "*Okubaliga* (extramarital love affairs) are recognized as almost an essential part of masculinity; a man who is faithful to his wife only is suspected of having little sexual strength. Men's fantasies move around *amaanyi* (sexual strength)." Amaanyi and men's multiple sexual partnerships were a theme in my own fieldwork, attesting to the long-standing connections between sexual privilege and the Ganda conception of masculinity.

Although a distinct sexual double standard constrained precolonial Ganda women generally, some women were not so bound by such restrictions. Among elite women, for example, abambejja, princesses or daughters of royal men, were permitted to engage in "sexual conspicuous consumption," having sexual relationships with any man they wished whenever they wished (Musisi 1991, 774). Their sexual freedoms were severely limited in other respects, however, and until the nineteenth century they were forbidden from marrying or having children. In this sense, as Musisi (1991, 774) argues, abambejja occupied "an ambiguous gender position—elevated in some respects, circumscribed in others."

Certain nonelite Ganda women were also less bound by patriarchal control. *Banakyeombekedde*, which can be translated as "women who live alone," were independent female householders who lived without men, either because they never married, or were divorced, or deserted their husbands. These economically self-sufficient women enjoyed significantly more sexual freedom, including having affairs with whomever they desired (Davis 2000, 33; Doyle 2013, 56; Obbo 1980). Economic self-sufficiency and sexual freedom were, therefore, linked for these women—a theme that would become a recurring tension in gender relations in the twentieth century, especially in Kampala. The word *bakirerese* referred to "restless people," and female bakirerese were transients who established temporary sexual relationships with men who could support them (Davis 2000; Obbo 1980). When they grew tired of the relationship, they simply packed their belongings and moved on. While banakyeombekedde and bakirerese evaded much of the regulation and surveillance endured by married women, they were stigmatized and marginalized as unmarried women with too much sexual freedom (Davis 2000).

Key aspects of contemporary notions of masculinity in Bwaise find roots in this much earlier era. Male adulthood was premised on establishing a household through formal marriage and then providing certain material necessities for the family. Men's social mobility meant that male status also had a significant achieved dimension, making political power and wealth key markers of masculinity. Men's authority over women was assumed, although wives did have some influence in decision making and the ability to leave and divorce a neglectful or abusive husband. Finally, there was a distinct sexual double standard, with men carefully controlling and regulating women's sexuality while they themselves enjoyed the privilege of considerable sexual latitude. This was particularly evident in the male status associated with polygyny and the leeway afforded men who had extramarital relationships.

THE COLONIAL PERIOD AND THE UGANDA PROTECTORATE, 1894–1962

In 1894, a mere three decades after the first European explorer, John Hanning Speke, arrived in Buganda, the British government assumed control of Buganda as the centerpiece of their Uganda protectorate. The first few years of British rule were tumultuous, leading the British to pursue a policy of mediated, indirect rule. The Baganda were given the central role of intermediaries between the British and the general population, making them the most powerful of all the protectorate's ethnic groups (Southwold 1965).

Colonialism also brought the privatization of land, the introduction of cash crop farming, and new types of migration that together had a significant impact on gender and sexual relations in Buganda. The British fostered an economy focused on small-scale farmers who owned their own land and produced cash crops for export. They introduced cotton and coffee, and it was on thousands of small farms that these crops were cultivated, accounting for the vast majority of the protectorate's earnings (Mamdani 1976, 47). In contrast to neighboring Kenya, Uganda had few large agricultural plantations controlled by white settlers, and unlike southern Africa, there were no mines that drew male labor away from family farms. Thus throughout the colonial era Uganda remained predominantly rural, and even by 1959 only 3 percent of the population was urban (Kyomuhendo and McIntosh 2006, 13).

The advent of cash crop farming greatly altered work in Buganda, providing both new opportunities for earning an income and new reasons for why access to cash was a necessity. Cash crop farming expanded men's participation in the market economy, and at the same time the availability of commercial goods, the monetization of bridewealth payments, and new requirements for men to pay taxes increased men's need for cash. For rural men, this meant much more time in their fields in order to pay for both necessities and luxuries (Southwold 1965, 106).

Initially, cotton and coffee cultivation were simply an extension of women's existing agricultural work, with men controlling the profits. Many Ganda women, however, took issue with this arrangement and demanded greater control over the money generated from the crops they grew. Audrey Richards (1954a, 21) attributes women's demands for better treatment to "a gradual change in the status of women in Buganda," a shift C. W. Hattersley (1908) had described as a new "suffragette" mentality influenced by Christianity. Threatened by the prospect of their wives' greater economic independence, Ganda men reluctantly reframed cash-crop farming as men's work. It was only then that men began laboring in the fields themselves, although many Ganda men loathed this idea. These men preferred to employ migrant laborers, resulting in an unprecedented influx of migrants to Buganda (Richards 1954a).[5] Thus, in the span of approximately two decades, 1910 to 1930, a potentially dramatic challenge to men's identity as the money earners was averted through a reconfiguration of the gender division of agricultural labor.

Colonialism also spurred the slow but steady growth of Kampala. Some men chose to migrate to urban areas in search of employment, hoping to earn enough money to return to the countryside, purchase land, and build their own maka (Southwold 1965). Unlike other parts of colonial Africa, men's options for wage labor in the protectorate were quite limited. Kampala, therefore, drew men seeking paid employment. While men were not stigmatized for living in the city like women were, they had limited options for earning cash. Colonial officials discouraged permanent urban settlement, and policies were enacted to ensure that clerks, administrators, merchants, and shopkeepers were either European or South Asian men, dramatically limiting African men's prospects for steady, long-term, wage work.[6] Much of the male urban migration in the early twentieth century was therefore temporary. Men struggled to secure a niche in the market economy somewhere above the few urban women traders but well below European and South Asian men.

After World War II, urban migration remained relatively modest, as did opportunities for wage labor.[7] By the late colonial period, elite and well-educated men were being groomed for leadership roles in an impending independent Uganda, but less educated men struggled to earn consistent income. Thus by the end of the colonial period an urban male identity as family provider was in place but only to a limited extent. Without consistent wage labor, there was no strongly defined male breadwinner ideal (Kyomuhendo and McIntosh 2006, 89).

Nonetheless, this was a period when it became the husband's responsibility to earn cash as the family income earner (Kyomuhendo and McIntosh 2006, 83). Men's traditional occupations had become largely obsolete by the 1930s. As Mair (1934, 123) notes, "Instead, men are now not bread-winners—that is still the woman's function—but earners of money to provide the household with clothes and the new 'necessities of life' which European contact has created." For Mair (1934, 146), men's precolonial displays of wealth and status through gift giving were now channeled into money earning, and "economic acquisitiveness" was a new marker of masculinity. The image of a man as a self-sufficient laborer who earned money for his family's needs was solidifying.

As Iliffe (2005) argues, during this period in Uganda, and in much of Africa, men's honor was being rechanneled into a Christian, Westernized notion of modern respectability that turned on economic self-sufficiency, aligning men's dignity and men's work in unprecedented ways. Paid employment, previously stigmatized because it lacked the reciprocal claims of patronage, became a new avenue for men's advancement and self-fashioning, especially for younger men willing to migrate to cities like Kampala (Iliffe 2005, 211). Urbanization was therefore central to new forms of African masculine respectability and status. The model of a modern, economically self-sufficient urbanite was emerging as a new embodiment of male ekitiibwa.

With these opportunities came intense competition among urban men. Work opportunities were limited and insecure, a reality that became more acute in Kampala beginning in the 1950s (Iliffe 2005, 294). Urban unemployment emerged as a novel form of masculine dishonor and humiliation and would become a leitmotif for much of urban Africa in the late twentieth century. Towns and the urban masculine honor they fostered also became central to new intergenerational tensions, as young men sought to free themselves from their fathers' authority, especially by earning the money that allowed them to become independent, married householders. Such tensions often focused on increasingly high bridewealth payments as older male patriarchs struggled to defend their authority and control (Iliffe 2005, 222, 267).

Women also explored urban migration in the first half of the century. However, in the 1920s and 1930s the women who came to Kampala found they had few socially acceptable ways of supporting themselves (Kyomuhendo and McIntosh 2006, 57). They primarily survived by selling staple produce, making food, brewing alcohol illegally, and, less frequently, engaging in sex work. This continued to be the case through the late colonial period as women gradually expanded their range of urban income-generating options.

The emergence of independent, single, urban women, or *abakazi be tawuni* (town women), in this period caused anxiety among men, including both Ganda elites and colonial officials (Davis 2000; Ogden 1996). Ganda men were concerned that economically independent urban women posed a threat to male authority, and British officials did not want women competing with men (who needed cash for taxes) for the limited work available in the city. Largely unsuccessful efforts were made to inhibit women in urban areas, stigmatizing not only independent town women but also married women seeking to participate in the market economy (Davis 2000; Kyomuhendo and McIntosh 2006, 90). In 1955 and 1956, for example, native authorities in Kampala drastically cut beer permits, rounded up women of alleged ill-repute to send them back to their fathers, and passed an ordinance that treated unmarried women as minors up to the age of thirty (Southall and Gutkind 1957, 193–94).

Given that the emerging male income-earner ideal rested on a weak economic base, especially in Kampala, it is not surprising that women's efforts to participate in the market economy troubled men. As early as the 1920s, there was already growing apprehension among Ugandan and British men that women were no longer under their control. In this period a powerful new ideology of gender relations arose, redefining "proper" womanhood. This "domestic virtue model" combined existing, largely Ganda gender norms with the Victorian patriarchal mores of the British (Kyomuhendo and McIntosh 2006, 79–80). The key elements of this model emphasized that a "good" woman was a wife and mother whose duties and work were within the household. She was submissive to male authority, not a decision maker, and could use, but not control, land and property.

The strength of this gender ideology lay in part in the fact that it combined Ganda and British norms of gender and sexuality. In many respects, however, it marked an intensification of patriarchal attitudes compared to the precolonial period, emphasizing the need for women to limit their activities to the domestic sphere and remain submissive to men (Kyomuhendo and McIntosh 2006, 80). This model of gender relations was deeply appealing to both Ugandan and British men and, as Kyomuhendo and McIntosh (2006) argue, remained the core gender ideology throughout the twentieth century.

Thus, in contrast to changing notions of male dignity and respectability, there was substantial continuity in ideas of female honor throughout the colonial period. Elite women saw their status decline dramatically, but for most women ideas of female respectability and "proper" womanhood were remarkably consistent, not only in Buganda, but also in most colonial African societies (Iliffe 2005, 263). African men, whose honor had been destabilized and challenged by colonialism, defended ideas of female honor centered on "fertility and industry under protective male dominance," with marriage and motherhood remaining at the center of proper womanhood (Iliffe 2005, 263).

It is important to stress, however, that there was often a disconnect between this official, public domestic virtue ideology and the actual sexual conduct of women, as well as men. The ideology did not deter women from continuing to carve out new income-earning strategies in the city, including those bold sexual entrepreneurs who explored a variety of approaches to sex work that challenged norms of female sexuality. In addition, as discussed in more detail below, men often dispensed with Protestant norms of men's sexual decorum, obliging wives to conceal their husbands' extramarital affairs and additional wives. The domestic virtue model, therefore, went hand in hand with the subterfuge, concealment, and discretion that characterized many sexual relationships in the colonial period.[8] These more flexible aspects of sexual conduct continue to this day and no doubt shaped what my own informants did, and did not, disclose to me with regard to their sexual relationships.

Colonialism also ushered in a significantly more complex sociopolitical landscape in Buganda, with the kabaka, Ganda chiefs, Christian missionaries, and colonial officials each pursuing their own agendas. Of particular concern for all was how the social upheaval wrought by colonialism affected marriage and sexuality. Their interests would often diverge and result in an increasingly chaotic and unpredictable social landscape with regard to intimate relationships. The prime example of this confusion was the proliferating categories of marriage, which were codified in three separate marital codes: customary law, the colonial Marriage Ordinance, and the laws of Christianity and Islam (Doyle 2013, 106). Couples were forced to choose between a customary ceremony or a civil or religious one, with civil and Christian marriage deemed incompatible with customary marriage, especially its allowance of polygamy.

Christianity took hold quickly in Buganda—by 1921 more than half of Baganda were Christians—and estimates of official polygamous marriages declined (Doyle 2013, 115). By the 1930s Christianity was central to social status and regarded as "an integral part of the superiority in the social scale whose material indications [were] a corrugated iron roof, a motor bicycle, and a suit of European clothes" (Mair 1934, 102).[9]

Among the newly Christianized Ganda elite, however, there was reluctance to embrace monogamy. Both missionaries and colonial officials feared alienating Ganda elite men and attempted to sidestep this issue by declaring a second, customary wife a concubine. This meant polygamous men could not be prosecuted for violating the Marriage Ordinance (Doyle 2013, 109). Official polygamous marriage was also becoming less common among ordinary men, a trend Mair (1934, 101) attributes to the growing expense of marriage and family, not disapproval of polygamy. Like their elite male peers, ordinary men still exercised privilege by increasingly having one official wife and another less formalized relationship with a second woman (Richards 1954b). Despite apparent enthusiasm for Christianity among the Baganda, Christian teachings were viewed by most Ganda men as "a set of arbitrary rules to be disobeyed when that [could] be done with impunity" (Mair 1934, 281).

Ambiguity about proper legal marriage was compounded by other changes that came with colonialism, including commercialization of the economy that created new opportunities for some women to earn money, either as rural cash crop farmers or in the urban markets. The result was new ways for women to live independently of men, especially in Kampala (Doyle 2013, 123). Women's strategies for income earning in Kampala were most often an extension of their rural domestic work, including food and drink preparation and small-scale trade in produce. Some women engaged in sexual entrepreneurism, ranging from single transactions typically associated with prostitution in the West to the longer-term *malaaya* variant, which combined sex with domestic duties such as cooking and washing clothes in return for gifts and monetary support from men (Halpenny 1975; Southall and Gutkind 1957; White 1990). Urban women's sexual innovation only heightened the recurring concerns Ganda chiefs, missionaries, and colonial officials had about women's freedom and autonomy.

Concerns about female sexuality crystallized in colonial campaigns addressing sexually transmitted diseases (STDs). Throughout the first half of the twentieth century, colonial authorities regularly claimed there was an impending sexual health crisis among women, whether it was high rates of syphilis, declining birthrates, disconcerting numbers of abortions and premature births, or sterility (Summers 1991; Vaughan 1991). Many colonists considered that these problems were caused by unbridled female sexuality unleashed from traditional patriarchal authority. Not surprisingly, the male Buganda elite embraced this notion, which resonated with their own anxieties about the impact of colonialism on men's authority over women. As Megan Vaughan (1991, 139) argues, "In these circumstances, the chiefly elite of Buganda were enthusiastic in their reception of the idea that what their country was experiencing was an 'epidemic' of a sexually transmitted disease, caused by the 'promiscuity' of uncontrolled women."

Syphilis eradication campaigns were especially prominent and initially focused on medical interventions. In the period after World War I, however, Christian missionaries became the key players in new anti-STD efforts. Unlike many colonial administrators who saw "traditional" Ganda sexuality being eroded by colonialism and Christianity, the missionaries viewed Ganda sexuality as primitive and innately sinful, with polygyny as the epitome of its immorality (Vaughan 1991, 135). With missionaries leading the syphilis campaigns, "it was no longer a medical response to an epidemic. It became a moral crusade" (Summers 1991, 795). Using supposed rampant sexually transmitted diseases as the pretext, Christian missionaries endeavored to introduce a new ideology of gender and sexuality based on monogamy and companionate marriage as the ideal form of intimate partnership. Ultimately, these campaigns were not successful. For Vaughan (1991, 140), they reflected "a very European preoccupation with sexuality, and particularly the sexualized nature of power. For the British in Buganda, as elsewhere, a perceived crisis of control over female sexuality stood for the much larger problem of control over the sexualized African, both male and female." Thus, while Ganda and other men found ways of subverting constraints on their sexuality and preserving masculine sexual privilege, women bore the brunt of sexual surveillance and expectations of sexual restraint.

The anti-STD campaigns are also noteworthy for how they foreshadow the ways the AIDS crisis would be addressed many decades later.

Interventions initially biomedically oriented quickly became moral campaigns, prefiguring AIDS prevention policies toward the end of the millennium (Epstein 2005; Lyons 1999; Vaughan 1991). These public health campaigns were also part of a more general medicalization of health, especially sexual health, that would continue throughout the twentieth century in Buganda and Kampala.

Even with the many colonial interventions, by the mid-twentieth century trends toward increasing marital instability and a more permissive sexual culture were intensifying, especially in Kampala. With Christian marriage tightly linked to social status and prestige, more expensive church weddings and higher bridewealth payments were becoming the norm, making an official Christian marriage a less viable and attractive option for many men. Marriage was also becoming less attractive to young men because it was increasingly difficult for men to recover their bridewealth payments in the case of divorce; by the early 1900s native Ganda courts were unwilling to mandate the return of bridewealth even in customary marriages. Yet bridewealth remained the key marker of official marriage, as it does to this day. The combined effect of high and nonrefundable bridewealth payments was that "the economic risks of marriage . . . greatly increased for the husband at the same time as its actual cost . . . [which] created a strong deterrent to contracting any marriage at all" (Mair 1940, 32).

These factors—high bridewealth payments, difficultly obtaining a divorce, and Christian opposition to polygamy—also contributed to shifts in men's overlapping sexual relationships. As Richards (1954b, 392–93) notes, based on research in a village near Kampala in 1952, official polygamy was uncommon (only 8 percent of men) because "the Baganda marry once, usually with a great expenditure on ceremonials, and then contract subsequent informal unions (usually in another village) concurrently with the main marriage." Richard also remarks, with some frustration as a researcher studying sexuality, how adept Ganda men had become at concealing these additional relationships.

The consequences of such changes for marriage and intimate relationships in Kampala have been vividly, and famously, described in Aidan Southall and Peter Gutkind's urban ethnography, *Townsmen in the Making* (1957), which captures postwar life in Kampala. By midcentury, Kampala was a burgeoning metropolis that in many respects resembled the city I encountered during my fieldwork, including the growth of urban slum communities housing both new migrants and an increasingly large permanent urban population. Life in two such slums is the focus of *Townsmen in the Making*. It chronicles gender and sexual relations in Kampala at a period when contemporary urban life had just coalesced, making the book a key precursor to my own ethnography of the Bwaise slum a half century later.

Southall and Gutkind found a wide range of intimate relationships in these slum communities, from short-term sex work to temporary *mukwano* (lover) relationships and longer-term cohabitation to official marriages sealed with bridewealth payment. Formal marriage was the exception, however; marriage was typically defined in more nebulous terms, with cohabitation and the birth of a child sufficient for social recognition as a married couple. Southall and Gutkind (1957, 165) describe such "free marriages," which involved no ceremony or bridewealth payment, as appealing because they provided stability and security but also allowed men and women to easily end their relationships "with a certain seal of respectability."

While such relationships were an extension of the long-standing emphasis on individual choice in marriage formation and dissolution, for Southall and Gutkind the force truly propelling these dynamics was more contemporary in nature. It was rooted in tensions over shifting gender and sexual relations in an urban context with limited income-earning opportunities for most men and women. These tensions were at the heart of relationship instability, and conflicts between husbands and wives were often intensified by women's growing economic and social independence. Importantly for the themes I underscore throughout this book, Southall and Gutkind argue that these tensions in gender and sexual relations turned on the ways work, men's authority, and sexuality were intertwined:

> Underlying the flexibility and uncertainty of the present marriage system is the jockeying for position of the two sexes in relation to the redefinition of their respective roles. . . . [T]he African woman has come to expect more freedom, less drudgery, and a more equal personal relationship in marriage. . . . [T]he opportunities for earning a living in the urban area of Kampala have given women the economic independence which allows them to assert these claims effectively. Some men also want educated wives who

can give them companionship[,] . . . but much stronger and more general is the male desire to retain the domestic and agricultural labour of women, and to maintain the inferior social status of women, which accords to men the freedom to pursue their own private lives unhampered by new obligations of monogamy and marital fidelity. (1957, 88)

In these Kampala slums at midcentury, therefore, women had become increasingly vocal about their objections to polygamy, men's extramarital affairs, domestic violence, and inability to provide for the household, while men had become defensive and anxious about such shifts—all of which is strikingly similar to tensions I observed in intimate relationships during my fieldwork in Bwaise. Divorce and separation became convenient solutions to these problems for some women, especially given the relative informality of marriage and the acceptance of women living independently in Kampala.

While tension and overt conflict is a prominent theme in Southall and Gutkind's ethnography, equally important is their emphasis on the paradoxes urban life created for men and women. Both men and women were grappling with normative ideals of masculinity and femininity in a context of rapid social change, but the paradoxes they faced were not the same. Women contended with expanding the boundaries of "proper" womanhood and exploiting the new opportunities provided by city life while still maintaining their empisa, or character, and identities as "good" women. Men, in contrast, were preoccupied with maintaining the boundaries of male privilege and authority as they experimented with new domestic arrangements that accommodated women's greater economic and social independence.

Yet Southall and Gutkind (1957, 62) seem largely unimpressed with men's strategies for addressing such paradoxes: "Most African men refuse to adjust themselves either in town or country to a new conception of the female role in the home which would make a compromise possible. . . . [T]his situation favours a sequence of temporary marriages, with rights jealously guarded and few commitments made on either side, rather than any more permanent type of union." Marriage retained its value as a marker of adulthood and a symbol of social status, but this informality represented a partial and incomplete solution to the paradoxes men and women faced navigating a complex, shifting social terrain of gender and sexual relations—all of which, again, was strikingly similar to my field-work in Bwaise five decades later.

By the late 1950s, marital instability and tensions within marriage were occurring in a blossoming liberal sexual culture in Kampala, typified by a growing nightlife scene that provided new opportunities for socializing, often across class and generational divides. This included a growing culture of sex work facilitated by both men's sexual privileges and the many unattached urban women. Because ties between urbanities in Kampala and their rural counterparts remained strong, these urban attitudes toward sexuality extended well beyond the capital. Thus a confluence of social forces produced a distinctly permissive sexual culture in Kampala, and much of Buganda, as Uganda gained independence in 1962 (Doyle 2013, 137).

It is almost certain that it was in this colonial period that HIV first arrived in Buganda. The patterns of sexual behavior that solidified in this period in turn determined the scope and severity of the AIDS epidemic in Kampala, Buganda, and the greater region (Doyle 2013, 16). With the turmoil and unrest that followed in the 1960s and 1970s, an environment emerged that proved tragically effective in facilitating the transmission of HIV.

INDEPENDENT UGANDA AND THE EMERGING AIDS CRISIS, 1962–1986

Initially, there was continuity between life in the late colonial period and Uganda's early postcolonial period, which began with Uganda's independence in 1962. The changes that did occur were particularly evident in Kampala as urban migration continued to increase. Between 1959 and 1969, the population of greater Kampala more than doubled, from 147,000 to 333,000 (Kyomuhendo and McIntosh 2006, 119). This growth coincided with the official consolidation of greater Kampala in 1968, whereby the city of Kampala was merged with the municipality of Mengo (formerly the kibuga) and three neighboring townships. Kawempe Township, which included Bwaise, was one of the major additions, and throughout the 1970s and 1980s unregulated urban development would transform Bwaise from a periurban area to one of the densest slums in Kampala.

For men, the early independence period provided new employment opportunities. With the British administrators largely gone, educated men found consistent work in government positions. Economic growth also spurred an increase in male urban wage labor more generally, creating the conditions for the emergence of an urban male breadwinner identity. But urban migration created new tensions among men that would become amplified by the end of the century, including both greater socioeconomic stratification and increased urban unemployment as migration outpaced job growth (Kyomuhendo and McIntosh 2006, 119).

The early 1960s also saw greater numbers of women migrating to Kampala, either alone or with their husbands. The new government employed nationalistic rhetoric that encouraged a more active role for women in public life. Such rhetoric, however, was rarely matched by concrete action and conflicted with the persistence of the domestic virtue model. Women in this period were, therefore, caught between two sets of norms, and poor urban working women in particular were still viewed with uncertainty and ambiguity (Kyomuhendo and McIntosh 2006, 133).

In the late 1960s, independent Uganda began to unravel, and for most of the next two decades the Ugandan state would be characterized as failing or nearly failed. National stability was based on an inherited export-oriented economy tied to the vagaries of the global cotton and coffee markets. Although agricultural productivity increased in the first years of independence, declining prices for export crops caused an economic crisis for Uganda. This economic volatility affected the legitimacy of Uganda's nascent independent government, led by Milton Obote, who served as prime minister and president throughout the 1960s. During Obote's rule, conflicts stemming from colonial ethnic divisions also created continual instability, especially ethnic tensions between northerners (including Obote's Lango ethnic group) and southerners (especially Baganda).

Obote responded to the growing instability by becoming increasingly autocratic, abolishing all traditional kingdoms, nationalizing private corporations and banks, banning opposition political parties, and declaring a state of emergency. He also strengthened the power of the military and used both military and police forces to terrorize his opponents and civilians. These events set the stage for the 1971 coup by Idi Amin, Obote's commander in chief of the army. While initially viewed as something of a liberator from Obote's final years of tyrannical rule, Amin quickly became unpredictable and repressive. Throughout the 1970s, Amin's government grew suspicious and intolerant of any form of opposition, and Amin's policies produced repeated crises as a weak state became more and more fragile (Hansen 2013). By the late 1970s, Amin had become infamous the world over for despotic suppression of dissent, including terror campaigns in which hundreds of thousands of people are believed to have been murdered (Amnesty International 1978; Ullman 1978).

Amin also instituted radical economic policies as part of his "economic war," emphasizing Ugandan self-reliance, independence, and an end to economic interference by those deemed to be foreigners. In 1972, Amin expelled all citizens of South Asian descent, who, although a small minority, played a central role in trade and business. Amin gave South Asians ninety days to leave the country and then turned over their shops and factories to Ugandans with limited business experience. Amin also dictated trade policies aimed at reducing foreign imports and increasing domestic agricultural production. Collectively, these policies had a disastrous impact on the economy, stifling legitimate trade and producing periods of hyperinflation.

What emerged in this extended episode of instability was a new informal economy—magendo—based on illicit and semilegal trade.[10] From Mombasa on the Kenyan coast through Kampala, north to Sudan, and west to Kigali in Rwanda, a "great artery of corruption" emerged that involved a high-stakes game of smuggling goods (Southall 1980, 632). The military played a central role in controlling the magendo economy, using violence as part of its currency. As Tony Barnett and Alan Whiteside stress (2002, 133), this new network not only facilitated illicit trade, but also disease, because "illicit markets, secretive transport and the human interactions that tied such a system together were a risk environment *par excellence* and fertile ground for the development of an epidemic of HIV/AIDS."

Amin was finally ousted with help from the Tanzanian army in 1979. However, his successor, Obote, in his second term as president, was once again brutal and did little to stabilize the country. Violence increased, especially in the Luwero Triangle of Buganda north of Kampala, which was the center of anti-Obote resistance. As older Bwaise residents told me, the Ganda population of Bwaise increased in this period as people fled rural

Luwero for the relative safety of Kampala, making Bwaise poorer and more densely populated. It was not until the rebel leader Yoweri Museveni came to power in 1986, after his National Resistance Army waged a protracted guerrilla war, that the country started on a path toward reconstruction and began to address what had become a severe AIDS crisis in Uganda.

For most Ugandans, life during the Amin and second Obote periods was at best precarious and at worst desperate. Under such conditions, gender and sexual relations were strained in unprecedented ways. There were few opportunities for men to fulfill the provider role in any conventional sense, and what had been an emerging male urban breadwinner ideal became much less pronounced. The men who prospered were those who exploited opportunities for corruption, smuggling, and illicit trade. Men who participated in magendo trade had incomes drastically inflated compared to women, who largely did not directly participate in the magendo economy, which heightened women's insecurity and dependence. "Women gained access to economic resources, often, but not uniquely, through sexual relationships with men," according to Barnett and Whiteside (2002, 13), and this created a social environment conducive to the spread of HIV.

Links between masculinity and violence also became more explicit in this period, as typified by the tyrannical excesses of Amin and Obote. These links were particularly overt during the Amin regime, both in terms of Amin's methods of rule and in terms of his own identity as a ruler. Alicia Decker (2013) argues that particular conceptions of masculinity were central to how Amin's militarized state functioned and were rooted in Amin's long military career. His leadership instilled a notion of manhood prioritizing strength, courage, and virility; he had five official wives and many other sexual relationships that he flaunted (Kyemba 1977, 163). Amin modeled a masculinity that was militaristic, highly sexualized, patriarchal, and misogynistic.[11]

Thus women in this period of postindependence turmoil had to contend with new embodiments of masculinity that shaped gender and sexual relations in ways that were often dangerous and sometimes deadly. Persistent conflict and civil unrest placed Ugandan women at greater risk of sexual violence; rape and sexual abuse of women were commonly reported during both the Amin and Obote regimes. State surveillance of women, and female sexuality in particular, also increased and played a central role in Amin's recurring Keep Uganda Clean campaigns. Inaugurated in Kampala in 1973, these campaigns were ostensibly about cleaning up and beautifying the city, but in actuality they were another of the regime's tactics of social control. Amin infamously decreed regulations on women's attire, banning iconic seventies fashions such as miniskirts and hot pants. Women who failed to comply were harassed and molested on the streets or rounded up and dragged before judges (Davis 2000, 56).

Intimate relationships were a key battleground in these campaigns. Urban women, in particular, became symbols of immorality and social decay (Decker 2010). Single women, it was suggested, should be forced to leave the city because they lived without a man's supervision. Divorced and married women were accused of being promiscuous and leading men to infidelity. In 1977, the Venereal Diseases Decree was introduced, allowing inspection of anyone suspected of having syphilis or gonorrhea, and urban women were often singled out and stigmatized as disease vectors. Like colonial syphilis campaigns, Ugandan women's sexuality was once again the primary preoccupation and blamed for the spread of sexually transmitted diseases. Amin's repressive campaigns against women deemed too independent were based on a more extreme version of the domestic virtue model and were especially focused on ways women's sexuality was perceived to defy male control and supervision (Kyomuhendo and McIntosh, 2006).

However, Amin's economic and social policies also had contradictory effects on women, including some surprising benefits. Under the Amin regime, poor women engaged in unskilled labor were able to earn money outside the home and provide for their families while maintaining their dignity as "proper" women. Kyomuhendo and McIntosh (2006, 152) see this dynamic as having important implications: poor working wives "earned and spent money, became decision makers, and developed confidence," all of which strengthened their position at home and weakened the economic basis of their husband's authority.

The complexity of the social and moral terrain in Kampala during this period has been vividly captured by the Ugandan anthropologist Christine Obbo (1980). Like Southall and Gutkind's (1957) ethnography of Kampala slums two decades earlier, Obbo's ethnography of two Kampala slums in the 1970s reveals a social milieu conducive to experimentation and innovation in gender and sexual relations, especially with regard to women's self-sufficiency and sexual autonomy. She describes how severe urban unemployment in this period forced many men to rely on, and contend with, women's expanding income-generating activities in the informal economy, including beer brewing, food preparation, sex work, and petty trade. This resulted in strained and conflict-ridden intimate relationships. A constant complaint of men in these slums was that "women these days are not controllable," and men feared that women's financial independence would inevitably lead them to want greater sexual independence as well (Obbo 1980, 9, 48).

Obbo stresses that some urban women's strategies for survival, therefore, inadvertently challenged the gender status quo and placed these women at the vanguard of social change. The urban space provided new possibilities for more independent lives, and such women drew on long-standing Ganda identities of unmarried women to achieve their goals. Some of these women were modern variants of the banakyeyombekedde, supporting themselves, sometimes owning property, and exercising freedom in their sexual relationships. Modern bakirerese, in contrast, were dependent on men but refused to settle down. They prided themselves on conspicuous consumption of urban fashions, and as they shuttled between Kampala and rural areas they become rural trendsetters, linking city and countryside through "fashionable styles of dress, and new ways of cooking" (Obbo 1980, 96). These two categories of vanguard urban women, while quite different, were similarly stigmatized as abakazi be tawuni, or town women, and often scapegoated as the cause of the social and moral disorder of the 1970s and 1980s (Davis 2000; Obbo 1980).

Married women often strove to distinguish themselves from this vanguard and deployed very different strategies for gaining greater independence. The majority of married women Obbo interviewed described their marriages as successful in part due to their strategic use of deference, including traditional signs of submission such as kneeling when greeting their husbands. Such tactics helped to assuage men's concerns about losing their authority in their homes, especially those homes where women were taking on a more active role in income earning. This bargain was often tacitly acknowledged by men, with several men saying that it allowed them to "feel that we are in control of women who are no longer controllable" (Obbo 1980, 147).

For Obbo, Ugandan women's struggle for economic independence in this period was at the center of transformations in gender and sexual relations, including changes in normative notions of femininity and masculinity. What bound the women in her study together was their common goal of striving for dignity, which, these women maintained, had "as its minimum condition economic independence from men[,] . . . [for] with economic independence, social and sexual independence were possibilities too" (Obbo 1980, 150).

Like Obbo's more complicated perspective on gender relations during Amin's rule, Doyle (2013), too, recommends a reexamination of the narrative portraying Ugandan sexual relations in the 1970s as unusually violent, desperate, and disordered. Heightened economic insecurity, inequality, and violence in this period did contribute to the spread of HIV, especially among certain groups such as young women. The virus, however, had already taken root before the worst period of economic decline, and the broader patterns of sexual behavior in the 1970s were not new, Doyle argues, but instead an intensification of shifts that began in previous decades. In addition, Doyle (2013, 331) contends, the conventional narrative overestimates the extent of social disintegration in the Amin period, obscuring how "sexual culture changed during these years as much due to new forms of aspiration as desperation."

Like the dynamic urban sexual culture of the 1950s described by Southall and Gutkind (1957), Kampala in the 1970s was a time of sexual experimentation and innovation for men and women. However, also like the 1950s, women, much more than men, had to weigh the appeal of new forms of sexual aspiration and entrepreneurism against engrained notions of sexual restraint. In addition, and more ominously, women were now making these calculations in a social context with intensified forms of sexual violence and predation, accompanied by a new sexually transmitted virus that was establishing deep and tangled roots.

YOWERI MUSEVENI'S UGANDA, 1986–2016

Coming to power in 1986 after two decades of conflict, civil war, and state collapse, the Museveni government faced the daunting task of rebuilding the country's economy and administrative capacity and the citizenry's faith in the state. By the early 1990s, the new government had made considerable progress in achieving these goals. For men, the relative political and economic stability of the Museveni era resulted in greater emphasis on the male provider ideal, especially in urban areas like Kampala.

However, in the late 1980s and early 1990s, the Ugandan economy remained in dire condition. Museveni's compliance with the neoliberal economic restructuring programs of the World Bank and the International Monetary Fund (IMF) further compounded the socioeconomic problems for most ordinary Ugandans (Musisi 1995). The structural adjustment policies imposed by these institutions limited state spending on agriculture subsidies, social services, and government employment. This exacerbated the plight of most Ugandans by reducing opportunities for civil service employment in urban areas, increasing costs for services like health care, and making cash crop farming less profitable. Thus for many men fulfilling the ideal of family provider remained elusive.

Rising gross domestic product (GDP) rates in the 2000s indicated some positive changes, but prospects for ordinary Ugandans did not improve significantly. Economic growth was coupled to mounting inflation that placed new stresses on urban residents in particular. In 2011, rising food and fuel prices contributed to an annual inflation rate of over 20 percent, the highest level in eighteen years (Ojambo 2011). When Museveni's political opponent Kizza Besigye staged "walk to work" protests in Kampala in 2011 to draw attention to intensifying inflation and economic stratification, they were violently suppressed by the government, resulting in at least nine deaths (Kron 2011). Many elite Ugandans have prospered since 2000, and a small urban middle-class has emerged. The contrasts between the expanding elite and middle classes and the poor masses are now strikingly evident in Kampala, heightening male-male competition and tensions in places like Bwaise as ordinary men struggle to provide for their families.

During the Museveni era, women's paid work has expanded in important ways. More women from all social classes now work in a greater diversity of jobs, including occupations conventionally viewed as men's work (Kyomuhendo and McIntosh 2006, 226). While wage or salaried work has remained limited, ordinary women have come to dominate urban market trade, and some educated women have gone into larger-scale businesses, including international trade (Kyomuhendo and McIntosh 2006; Musisi 1995).[12]

The first decade of Museveni's presidency was a period of rapid, and in many ways radical, changes for gender relations in other respects. Women's political participation and certain aspects of women's rights were promoted by the new government. These changes had implications for notions of men's authority over women and were a stark departure from both the Amin and Obote regimes (Tripp 2000; Tripp and Kwesiga 2002). In particular, the Museveni government dramatically increased women's involvement in government at both the local and national levels: in 1986, a seat was reserved for a woman on all levels of the local council system, and in 1989, after pressure from women activists, thirty-nine seats in parliament (one for each district) were reserved for women (Tamale 2003a). Thus the Museveni regime took steps to institutionalize new notions of gender equity that gave unprecedented government support to women's political and civil rights.[13]

The Museveni government was also supportive of women's organizing in the 1980s and 1990s. While women's activism, broadly defined, started as early as 1946 with the formation of the Uganda Council of Women, it was during the first decade of Museveni's presidency that women's organizations proliferated (Mills and Ssewakiryanga 2002). By the early 1990s, Uganda was recognized internationally as having perhaps the most dynamic women's movement on the African continent. Comprising academics, NGOs, and a few supportive politicians, this women's movement advanced a far-reaching agenda emphasizing gender equality and broader notions of women's rights. This included advocating for the inclusion of explicit rights for women when the Museveni government undertook a rewriting of the Constitution in 1995 (Tripp 2000). The Constitution states, "Women shall have the right to equal treatment with men and that right shall include equal opportunities in political, economic and social activities" (Republic of Uganda 1995, 30).

By the early 1990s, international development agencies began taking an active role in supporting Uganda's local women's organizations. This allowed local NGOs addressing women's rights to extend their reach, and by the late 1990s, they were influencing policy on national, regional, and continent-wide levels. The net effect has been that new discourses of gender equality have entered the public's imagination, especially in urban areas like Kampala. Unlike previous discourses on gender equity, which retained older ideas of gender difference, the gender equality advocated by women activists poses a direct challenge to ideas of men's authority as assumed and natural. In chapter 4, I provide a fuller discussion of the complex contemporary terrain of women's rights in contemporary Uganda.

During the second decade of the Museveni era, a significant backlash against women's advancement emerged. Political support for women's issues began to wane and attempts to pass new legislation extending women's rights failed. The two most notable defeats were the Land Act (1998), focused on improving women's property rights, and the far-reaching Domestic Relations Bill, aimed at revising divorce laws, increasing domestic violence protections, and strengthening women's sexual autonomy in intimate relationships.[14] These gender tensions were not limited to the public sphere but also began to suffuse relationships between men and women more generally. Many men felt increasingly threatened by what they perceived as women encroaching on men's duties and responsibilities. As Kyomuhendo and McIntosh (2006, 245) note, "In the face of such challenges to male identities, many men demanded that, when women were at home, they conform to the requirements for submissive behavior to their husbands, fathers, and other male relatives." Kyomuhendo and McIntosh's interviews with a broad sample of Ugandan women in 2003 indicate that women's economic independence was, once again, a central aspect of tensions in marital relations. At least a third of their interviewees describe the extensive ways men attempted to supervise, limit, or prohibit their wives' or girlfriends' income-generating activities—dynamics that were also a major theme in my own fieldwork.

That women are still seen as competition for limited income-generating opportunities compounds feelings of insecurity for many men. In response to such pressures, some men withdraw from family responsibilities, further undermining men's authority and exacerbating male insecurity. The results are strained and contested gender relations that make intimate relationships and marriages unstable—all of which echoes what Southall and Gutkind (1957) chronicled at midcentury. Ordinary men struggle, often in vain, to shore up a faltering sense of status in a context in which

women's work and new discourses of gender equity and equality are perceived as threatening their authority and identities.

It is perhaps not surprising that in this milieu sexual relations are also
contested terrain. These tensions are tied to an increasingly complex
moral landscape of competing ideas of "proper" sexual relationships, from
notions of romantic love and companionate marriage, to the focus of conservative Christian groups on monogamous male-dominated households
to Muslim protests against any attempt to regulate polygynous marriage.
AIDS has complicated these dynamics further by heightening scrutiny of
sexual behavior, making men more suspicious of female sexuality and
women more critical of men's sexual privileges.

Sexuality has not, however, been a significant focus in efforts to advance
gender equity and equality in Uganda. While the Museveni government
received praise for its proactive measures to address AIDS in the 1990s,
sexuality was never an aspect of the government's promotion of gender
equity. Women activists have also been leery of emphasizing women's sexual rights in their efforts to promote gender equality. Those few activists
who have linked sexuality to debates over gender bias and inequality have
often been the subject of conservative vitriol (Tamale 2003b). A few wom-
en's NGOs focused on domestic violence prevention have campaigned to
end sexual violence, especially marital rape. More recently, some of these
same NGOs have made explicit links between AIDS and unequal sexual
relations, stressing connections between the sexual dimensions of gender-
based violence and women's vulnerability to HIV infection.[15] However,
the bulk of women's activism has steered clear of sexuality, with efforts
focused instead on women's political participation and women's equal
access to education, employment, and healthcare.

More recently, these dynamics have shifted to a certain extent. In 2010,
the Domestic Violence Act, which contained significantly enhanced penalties for many forms of gender-based violence, including sexual violence
against women, was passed. This act prompted an unprecedented national
debate about the sexual aspects of women's rights, especially in relation to
marital rape (Abramsky et al. 2014). Also in 2010, the Prohibition of
Female Genital Mutilation Act was passed, which outlaws all forms of
female circumcision. Then in 2015, the Ugandan Supreme Court ruled 6
to 1 to ban the repayment of bride-price in the case of divorce; a ruling

intended to make it easier for women to divorce. It is important not to overstate the impact of these advances. The Domestic Violence Act has been criticized by prominent female judges for lack of dissemination or meaningful implementation (Goitom 2013). The bride-price ruling has drawn censure from some female activists for tacitly endorsing all other aspects of bridewealth exchange (Akumu 2015). Nonetheless, all three developments are notable for moving beyond an emphasis on individual civil and political rights for women, for addressing power imbalances in intimate relationships, and for making sexuality more central to women's rights activism.

Tensions and controversies about sexuality, however, have been most dramatically thrust into public discourse in relation to homosexuality. In 2005, the Ugandan Constitution was amended to ban gay marriage, making Uganda one of only a handful of countries to change their constitutions to outlaw same-sex marriage. This was followed by the Anti-Homosexuality Bill, introduced in 2009 and signed into law in 2014, which significantly increased penalties for anyone suspected of engaging in homosexual sex and for actions seen as promoting homosexuality. For the first time, it also explicitly included lesbianism in illegal homosexual activities. While the Ugandan Constitutional Court struck down the new law in 2014 on a technicality and President Museveni grew increasingly concerned about the economic fallout from the law, a more extreme new version of the bill was introduced in 2015.

As discussed in chapter 1, I see this bill as a symptom of the current heightened tensions in gender and sexual relations and part and parcel of attempts to shore up male privilege in a context where it is being threatened on many different fronts (see also Tamale 2003b). It is likely no coincidence that in 2014 another controversial bill was signed into law: the Anti-Pornography Act creates broad new regulations on acts deemed illicit and immoral. Reminiscent of the Idi Amin era, the act has been interpreted as justifying new scrutiny of women's attire, with special attention on banning miniskirts. In 2014, the Ugandan Women's Network, a coalition of NGOs focused on women's issues, organized a public protest against harassment of women in the wake of the Anti-Pornography Act. Thus long-standing tensions around gender and sexuality have become public in new and dramatic ways.

In recent years Museveni has begun to show more autocratic tendencies. As Aili Tripp (2010, 194) has argued, the Museveni government is currently best described as semiauthoritarian, combining "elements of democratization with illiberal rule." Under Museveni's leadership, the Ugandan state has vacillated between a pro-rights regime (especially with regard to women's rights in the late 1980s and 1990s) and one increasingly inconsistent on individual civil rights and freedoms (especially rights to political expression, freedom of speech, and freedom of assembly). Museveni has astutely used a commitment to neoliberal economic reforms as a way to assuage Western donors' concerns about rights abuses (Tripp 2010). Relatively robust economic growth in Uganda in the past decade has provided convenient cover for a regime that has become bolder in asserting its continuing claim to power—a claim often made at the expense of rights, including women's rights.

As men and women in Uganda strive to make sense of new social conditions, gender attitudes and norms often lag behind. As Kyomuhendo and McIntosh (2006, 265) argue, the domestic virtue model has continued to constrain women. Many Ugandans still believe that women are solely responsible for maintaining the household and raising children, need to remain submissive to men and defer to their decisions, and should not compete with men in the public domain. As Kyomuhendo and McIntosh also note, domestic virtue thinking has stifled changes in notions of masculinity and deterred the development of new ways of being a "proper" man that could help ameliorate gender tensions. Both men and women continue to draw on entrenched gender attitudes and beliefs to make sense of new material conditions (see also Ridgeway 2011). Yet these changing material conditions, especially women's increasing roles as money earners, may eventually alter gender ideologies.

·   ·   ·   ·   ·

It was in this context of heightened gender tensions that I began my fieldwork in Uganda. As we have seen, these tensions are part of a long history of how women's contributions to their families and the nation have been reconciled with the tenacious gender ideology of men as authorities in the public sphere and the home. Throughout the twentieth century, men's

identities as authority figures became slowly intertwined with the notion
of the man as the money earner, even while the male breadwinner ideal
based on wage labor remained less pronounced in Uganda. Women
increasingly found paid work to supplement their long-standing unremu-
nerated agricultural and domestic labor, and for much of the twentieth
century the domestic virtue model provided the ideological basis for
accommodating women's work with men's authority. But it did not eliminate gender tensions.

By the start of my fieldwork, these tensions had become especially pronounced, which helps explain why men's identity as family providers was
such a poignant topic for my informants. What this book reveals is that
gender tensions were also deeply intertwined with sexuality, including the
ways some men sought to shore up an embattled masculinity through
their intimate relationships. This dynamic has a long history in Uganda,
but the AIDS epidemic created a new context in which men and women
negotiate sexual intimacy, making links between gender inequality and
sexuality more complex, and often more dangerous.[16]

THE RESPONSE TO AIDS IN UGANDA

The severity of AIDS in Uganda was matched by the success of the country's early response to the epidemic. In the early 1990s, Uganda was the
first country to show a significant and sustained decrease in HIV prevalence—an especially notable trend given the rapid rise in HIV prevalence
in many southern African countries in the same period. This success is
typically attributed to two factors: (1) the proactive role of the Museveni
government in addressing the disease and mobilizing a broad "multisecto-
ral" response; and (2) the openness and willingness of ordinary Ugandans
to talk about the epidemic and establish indigenous grassroots organizations to provide care for the sick (Kinsman 2010; Kippax and Stephenson
2012; Stoneburner and Low-Beer 2004). This openness is believed to have
catalyzed a rapid, deep, and broad awareness of this new sexually transmitted disease. It also helped disseminate new strategies for altering sexual
behavior, especially reducing the number and frequency of sexual partnerships (Low-Beer and Stoneburner 2003, 2004; Hallett et al. 2006).

Given the legacy of public health interventions to promote sexual health in Buganda, it is not surprising that ordinary Ugandans responded to AIDS in this way. As Doyle (2013, 384) argues, openness to addressing AIDS among the Baganda and the neighboring Haya and Nkole ethnic groups emerged out of the region's history of interventions for STDs: "From the beginning of the twentieth century right through to the 1970s the historical record in both Buganda and Buhaya is littered with campaigns to improve public morality. . . . In a direct sense they achieved little obvious success, but this series of attempted reforms must have familiarized many Ganda, Haya, and Nkole to the concept of safer sex, and habituated them to external interventions in the most private aspects of their lives."

As discussed in chapter 1, an especially notable Ugandan AIDS prevention initiative during this period was the "zero grazing" campaign. Beginning in the late 1980s, this AIDS prevention strategy sought to decrease multiple sexual partnerships, especially longer-term concurrent relationships. Zero grazing did not promote monogamy or fidelity but instead encouraged Ugandan men in particular to have sex with a small number of long-term partners. This strategy is believed to have helped break up sexual networks in Uganda, especially those networks of concurrent, overlapping partnerships that are now recognized as particularly efficient routes for HIV transmission (Epstein 2007; Epstein and Morris 2011a; Halperin and Epstein 2004; Thornton 2008).[17]

It is critical to understand that zero grazing was not a challenge to but an implicit endorsement of men's sexual privilege of having multiple sexual partners. The pragmatic zero grazing strategy was valuable during this early period of extremely high HIV prevalence in Uganda. Its value is limited in addressing the particular challenges of AIDS in the twenty-first century, including the rise in new HIV infections in Uganda since 2005.

As the AIDS epidemic in Uganda began receiving greater attention from the West in the early 1990s, a new biomedical phase of AIDS prevention came into practice to complement and then supplant local efforts (Kinsman 2010). New efforts to control HIV infection placed a greater emphasis on individual behavior change, rooted in the assumption that sexual behavior was best conceptualized as a rational, individual act and that an individual could learn to "responsibly" manage HIV risk. While ostensibly drawing on Uganda's successful local initiatives, the newer strategies soon focused more on the generic ABC prevention message: Abstain from sex, Be faithful to your partner, or use Condoms. This approach was simplistically focused on individual behavior change, failing to incorporate recognition of the social context of sexuality, which was at the heart of the zero grazing campaign's success and a serious mischaracterization of the complex, multifaceted Ugandan success story (Thornton 2008).

This shift to an ABC approach was coupled with increasingly puritanical moralizing in AIDS prevention programs during the 2000s. Paralleling the Christian syphilis campaigns of the early twentieth century, AIDS prevention was recast as a moral crusade by local and international conservative Christians. There was a marked increase in a more religiously inflected approach to AIDS prevention, which labeled premarital sex immoral and emphasized abstinence for young people, especially young women. As noted in chapter 1, this shift was due in large part to the creation of the President's Emergency Plan for AIDS Relief by the George W. Bush administration in 2003, which encouraged conservative, faith-based approaches to AIDS prevention in which sex should be limited to monogamous marital relationships. This shift in AIDS prevention coincided with the expansion of evangelical Christianity and the rise of Pentecostalism, which gained considerable momentum in Uganda during the 1990s and 2000s (Epstein 2005). In 2004, for example, Uganda's First Lady, Janet Museveni, an evangelical Christian, proposed a national census of virgins in an effort to promote abstinence. During the same period, the conservative preacher Martin Ssempa led thousands through the streets of Kampala in an "abstinence pride" march to counter what Ssempa described as permissive messages in AIDS prevention programs.[18]

Echoing earlier Christian STD campaigns, these religiously oriented AIDS prevention initiatives framed the containment of sexuality within monogamous, "faithful" marriage as the key to AIDS prevention. As such, they promoted an ideology of gender and sexuality that was linked to patriarchal nuclear families. Sexual relations occurring outside the context of this "proper family" were deemed immoral, obscuring how gender power relations within marriage could fuel HIV transmission (Hirsch et al. 2009b).

By the close of the first decade of the twenty-first century, criticism of the PEPFAR approach to AIDS prevention had become institutionalized.

The Obama administration removed much of the religious emphasis in PEPFAR guidelines and also began the process of having countries take ownership of their own AIDS programs. These events coincided with the rise of a more strictly biomedical approach to AIDS prevention: the new treatment-as-prevention strategy that now dominates approaches to addressing HIV/AIDS. "Treatment-as-prevention" refers to using antiretroviral AIDS drugs either as prophylactics for those who are HIV-negative (referred to as pre-exposure prophylaxis, or PrEP) or, for those who are HIV-positive, as a way of reducing their infectiousness. Clinical trials have shown both approaches to be highly effective in reducing HIV transmission, prompting new optimism that the global AIDS pandemic can be significantly abated (Anglemyer et al. 2011; Baeten et al. 2012).

Uganda's response to AIDS is now being reshaped by this new emphasis on biomedical interventions, resulting in concern that the core elements of Uganda's success in fighting AIDS—rooted in a social, not a biomedical, response—are being eclipsed again (Kippax and Stephenson 2012; Kippax et al. 2013). I extend these critiques and emphasize the importance of keeping gender relations at the forefront of efforts to fight AIDS.

3 Providing in Poverty

Even after several months of fieldwork in Bwaise, I found the congested area overwhelming, at times even intimidating. During the day, the throng of people, trucks, cars, and motorcycles was intense, and as a white man I always felt conspicuous because very few *bazungu* ever ventured into Bwaise. It was only for a few hours, in the dead of night, that I could easily walk through Bwaise's main intersection. The loud vehicles that usually crowded the streets were absent. The shops had shuttered their steel doors, and even the nightclubs were quiet, with all but the most dedicated patrons at home. Perhaps a bicycle taxi peddled past or a disoriented goat ambled by, but otherwise, for this brief time, the streets of Bwaise were still and empty.

A little before sunrise, the fleeting calm was broken as business began again in Bwaise. In the maze of homes behind the commercial streets, residents began to stir, opening wooden shutters, washing with water from yellow jerry cans, and sweeping the dirt from the front of their homes. As the sky turned from black to pink to yellow, the mosques issued their first call to prayer. Before long it seemed all of Bwaise was on the move. Along the dirt paths and narrow roads winding past the houses, residents were up and about, cooking porridge and drinking strong, sweet tea. Matatus passed on their first runs for the day, dropping off passengers and then quickly filling up again with residents headed to the city center. Men selling *rolex* (eggs in chapatti) had set up their grills to provide a quick breakfast for commuters, a greasy treat I often indulged in at the start of my day. Trucks reappeared, some stopping outside the main market to disgorge their first load of matooke, dumping the bright green bundles on the orange dirt of the street. Clouds of dust, mixed with exhaust fumes, polluted the air. Together with the smell from open sewers and the ubiquitous garbage, Bwaise's chaotic streets regained their distinctive stench.

During my fieldwork I was especially interested in learning how men made a living on the streets of Bwaise, and by eight o'clock in the morning I found that the main commercial intersection at the heart of the community was bustling. Dozens of *bodaboda* (motorcycle taxi) men assembled on one corner, starting a long day of waiting as they competed for customers. Behind them, across the open sewers that line all of Bwaise's streets, the corner was crowded with butchers in one-man stalls specializing in intestines and organs. Across the street was a collection of auto repair shops where I watched men in soiled jumpsuits labor over dissected cars and trucks. Men with white pickup trucks for hire shared this corner with private taxi drivers, who, like the bodaboda men, specialized in waiting for infrequent customers. At the bottom of the male transportation hierarchy, bicycle taxis congregated across the street near a large mosque.

Across from the bicycle taxis, on the most congested corner, I often just stood to take in the action, carefully dodging cars, trucks, and motorcycles. A music shop selling cassettes had a prime location, but the main draw was the market tucked behind the commercial strip. The entrance was narrow, and much of the market activity spilled onto the sidewalk, especially the sale of bulky items like matooke. Adding to the congestion were the metal workshops where men wielding acetylene torches blocked the sidewalk as they fashioned large doors and gates. Wedged between two metal shops was a milk distributor where men filled three-foot aluminum canisters with milk and then loaded them on bicycle taxis for delivery.

While I was focused on men's work, I found that women were by no means absent from Bwaise's commercial strip. Some worked the counters in pharmacies, office supply stores, hair salons, or the many mobile phone stores. Others prepared and served the food sold on Bwaise's streets, in the few official restaurants and the many informal ones operated out of homes. When the large matooke trucks made their daily deliveries, many of the bulk buyers were women. In the two markets, I noticed that the preponderance of sellers were women, as were their customers, but all the market managers I met were men. Educated women worked as teachers in Bwaise's schools and at the health clinic, but many of the more common jobs were not options for women: carpenters, mechanics, butchers, bus drivers, motorcycle taxis, and construction workers were always men.

As day turned to night, I watched Bwaise undergo yet another transformation. Some of the businesses along the main roads closed, but many merchants stayed open, hoping to profit from Bwaise's lively nightlife. During the evenings, the main intersection remained clogged as people strolled the streets, enjoying the cool evening air. The auto mechanics and metalworkers were gone, replaced by street hawkers vying for spots in the informal night market. Men and women displayed their wares on blankets and small tables, using kerosene lamps to illuminate their merchandise and joking with passersby to spur a sale. Some of the butchers remained open, competing with men and women on the street selling grilled meat and fish for late-night snacks. For some, the night included a trip to one of Bwaise's nightclubs, and these revelers helped keep Bwaise's streets busy well into the night. But by two or three in the morning, I found that the streets were quiet once again.

·   ·   ·   ·   ·

Bwaise had a reputation as a rather sordid place, not only prone to flooding, but also rife with prostitution, drinking, drugs, and, to some extent, crime. While other areas of Kampala were also known for nightlife and prostitution, Bwaise was something of a poor man's version. In addition to the three larger nightclubs, there were innumerable small drinking joints, mostly serving homemade *amalwa* (beer) and *waragi* (gin). *Enjaga* (marijuana) and *miraa* (khat) were readily available and readily consumed, and cocaine, speed, and even heroin were rumored to be on offer. The nightlife, drugs, and alcohol combined with the general squalor of the area to give Bwaise its mostly deserved rough-and-tumble reputation.

But Bwaise was more than just an entertainment district for those of modest means; it was also a thriving commercial center. During my first visits to Bwaise, I was struck by the sheer quantity of business. Bwaise was a dirty and chaotic place, and the drinking joints with their alcoholics were certainly part of life, but I soon realized that business took center stage.

While far from the glamorous employment possibilities in the city's office towers, Bwaise still presented options for making money and remained a draw for ordinary men and women who hoped to capitalize on all they thought it offered. Yet nearly all the men I met in Bwaise were frustrated by their slim prospects for earning money, which in turn limited their ability to fashion themselves as respectable family providers and thus respectable men. Women were frustrated as well, both by men's inability to provide and by their own constrained options for generating income. Work was therefore a central concern for all adult residents of Bwaise, and it was fundamental to tensions in gender relations.

In keeping with my informants' repeated and vocal concerns about men and money, in this chapter I foreground the links between the material, economic conditions that structure work in Bwaise and the ways masculinity is lived. This chapter provides an important starting point for understanding the contours of masculinity in this community. It also illuminates a central theme of this book, namely, the interdependence of work and masculine sexual privilege during Uganda's prolonged AIDS crisis.

THE POLITICAL ECONOMY OF MASCULINITY AND SEXUALITY IN THE SHADOW OF AIDS

My focus on the entanglement of masculinity, sexuality, and work emerges from both the literature on masculinity and research bringing a political-economic focus to AIDS and sexuality. In much of the masculinity literature, work lingers as a master narrative, with the implicit assumption that men and masculinity are made through work. For example, in his study of American masculinity, Michael Kimmel (1996) creates a historical typology of masculinities based on types of work, from the "genteel patriarchs" of the late eighteenth century to the modern "marketplace man" of the twentieth century. Kimmel has also famously connected the modern, self-made masculine identity to men's need to incessantly prove themselves to other men, especially through work. Chronic employment insecurity is now a leitmotif in masculinity studies, including the assumption that changes in work regimes that produce male unemployment and job insecurity result in a "crisis" of masculinity (Faludi 1999).

This trope of masculinity in crisis is now a global one. Given that many urban African settings have labor markets and work opportunities best described as extremely uncertain, it is not surprising that we find similar concerns about chronic male unemployment producing a crisis in African masculinity (Ferguson 2006; Haram and Yamba 2009). As Andrea Cornwall (2003) notes, to be a man in southwestern Nigeria is now "more than a day's work." Many men, she observes, are unable to provide even the basics for their families, which leaves men vulnerable to accusations, by both women and other men, that they are "useless" (Cornwall 2002, 967). Adam Ashforth (1999, 57) likewise indicates that men in the Johannesburg slum of Soweto are often viewed with contempt, noting, "it would be scant exaggeration to say that most women consider the fathers of their children to be useless."

This focus on masculinity and work in Africa dovetails with recent research that provides a political-economic analysis of AIDS. A large body of research shows how political and economic forces have shaped AIDS epidemics across the globe, from the structural violence of development projects in rural Haiti and the emergence of a tourism-centered economy in the Dominican Republic to the effect of neoliberal social policies on drug users in the United States (Farmer 1999; Padilla 2007; Bourgois 2009). Of particular relevance here are studies on the intersection of economic insecurity, gender relations, and AIDS. A rich literature now traces how entrenched gender inequalities interact with poverty to place African women at risk of HIV infection (Baylies and Bujra 2000; Campbell, Nair, and Maimane 2006; Kalipeni et al. 2004; Mojola 2014; Susser 2009). Recently, more attention has been given to how masculinity and economic insecurity interconnect with AIDS, focusing on the ways chronic male underemployment and growing economic stratification shape men's sexual behavior, often in ways that heighten both men's and women's vulnerability to HIV (Higgins, Hoffman, and Dworkin 2010; Nyanzi et al. 2004; Smith 2006).

Mark Hunter (2005, 2010), for example, argues that the high value the South African men he studied placed on having multiple sexual partners filled the void left by their inability to establish independent households, marry, and provide for their families—all long-standing markers of adult manhood. Hunter's insights are echoed in research by Margrethe Silberschmidt (2001, 2004), who describes men in rural Kenya and urban Tanzania as "disempowered" by socioeconomic changes. Men's precarious and uncertain work, Silberschmidt argues, has meant that many men suffer from feelings of inadequacy, and this has become linked to "aggressive sexual behavior with multiple partners" (2001, 668).

Tropes of male disempowerment and masculinity in crisis are problematic because they may neglect the persistence of male privilege in times of economic uncertainty. Nonetheless, this literature demonstrates that AIDS and sexuality need to be analyzed in relation to those economic conditions that structure social interactions within intimate relationships. This chapter is grounded in this key assumption and demonstrates how men, as well as women, remade masculine sexual privilege in the context of both precarious work and HIV/AIDS.

EVERYDAY SURVIVAL AND TENSIONS OF GENDER IN BWAISE

Surviving in Bwaise was stressful for nearly everyone I met, and residents typically exhibited the signs of irritability and anxiety that come from living with persistent economic insecurity. As they discussed their money problems, men and women in Bwaise revealed another central axis of tension: gender relations. Talk of financial concerns and gender relations often went hand in hand.

The nearly universal refrain I heard from men talking about their problems was *obutaba na ssente* (being broke). Even working men in Bwaise stressed that *obutaba na mulimu* (unemployment) always loomed. Steady incomes were elusive, and without it men described the frustration of being unable to fulfill what they saw as their responsibilities, paying for food, rent, and their children's school fees. All men in Bwaise were preoccupied with economic matters, and they made clear to me that their identities as men were predicated on earning and dispensing money.

This tight coupling of masculinity and earning money was apparent in a conversation I had with Henry, an extroverted, forty-five-year-old manager of a hardware shop. Henry's shop was in a prime location near the main commercial intersection in Bwaise. Unlike many storefronts, it was filled with merchandise, including hammers, saws, metal piping, electrical wiring, plastic buckets, brooms, and mops. Henry did not own the business and was paid just forty dollars a month as the manager, not nearly enough to support his wife and five children. Nonetheless, he took pride in running such a well-stocked shop in the heart of Bwaise.

Like many men and some women I met, Henry's notion of what made a man in Bwaise combined essentialist, taken-for-granted aspects of manhood with those that could not be assumed but instead needed to be earned.

> It is nature that makes us men. . . . So as men we have *obuyinza* [authority, power], and we are the family heads who are responsible for planning for the whole family. But the hardest part of being a man in Uganda is the level of income. . . . You have to work as a man to fulfill your naturally given responsibilities. . . . Men here generally try to prove their manhood using their finances. We have a saying that "a real man has money, and if he does not have money he is not a man." [With money] you have a say. Then you can say something in a meeting. But without cash you just have to sit down even if you have all the wisdom. But when you have cash it is as if your wisdom is from heaven!

For men in Bwaise, money was not only the source of their problems but also the solution—both their curse and salvation. Money gave men the ability to provide for the material needs of their family, and by fulfilling those responsibilities their authority was reaffirmed.

Men often discussed the pressure they felt to earn money and solve every problem their family faced. Ali, an unemployed thirty-two-year-old single man, expressed these anxieties this way:

> Under these conditions here in Uganda, you will find many men regretting they are men. You start asking yourself why you were created a man. So whenever you sleep, you are thinking about the children, the wife, and

asking yourself, "What am I supposed to do, especially when work is not stable?" The women actually have an advantage because they were created differently. . . . If a woman realizes that her partner cannot help her, it is simpler for her to go to another man so that he can provide for her and look after her. But you don't have that option. And eventually you become desperate, and you will always be worried.

Other men echoed this sentiment and also stated that men are underappreciated and "women are never satisfied." Yet, while many men were vocal about the burden of their responsibilities, few were willing to question the status quo of masculine privilege.

Several women I met in Bwaise agreed that men should be responsible for all of a family's material needs. Some said an ideal man should "be responsible for everything all the time," "be responsible for every concern in the home," and "if you have a man, everything depends on him." Nearly all women recognized that poverty made it difficult for men to live up to this provider ideal, but their sympathy was limited. As one fifty-year-old woman told me, "Some stupid men think that some types of work are not worthy of their age, job standards, and so on, so they decide to pick pockets and break into houses and steal money instead of working for it." In Bwaise, a job and hard "honest" work were key markers of a responsible man; men who found alternative routes to money had to tread carefully.

An example of this policing of respectable masculinity was the deployment of the label *muyaye*. The term is used to describe a disreputable teenager or young adult (usually a male) who is a thug or petty thief and probably into drugs as well.[1] For adult men, it was an especially profound insult to be called a muyaye.

Such tensions in everyday gender relations came through clearly in a discussion I had with a group of women. All the women framed their problems squarely in relation to the men in their lives—men they viewed as largely failing to fulfill their role as the family provider. "A real man should be able to fulfill all his obligations at home, including paying children's school fees and providing food, and look after his wife, as well as any medical needs for the family," one woman began. "He should be able to fulfill all these responsibilities and also show us all love." "[But] you will never experience peace at home when the man is poor," said a second woman. "The men fear responsibilities at home, and so they leave those responsibilities for the woman," added a third.

This recurrent criticism of men reflected many women's frustration that they were required to rely on men, yet were themselves ultimately responsible for their families' everyday survival. Some of these women were so exasperated that they decided the best course was to earn money themselves. However, they recounted challenges raising the necessary capital to start their own businesses and stressed that working heightened tensions between them and their male partners. " In most cases, when a woman gets a job and begins to work, the man stops fulfilling his financial responsibilities and just leaves it all for the woman," said the first woman. "When we work as women and get our own money, the men take it from us," added a fourth woman. "At times he comes and borrows it, but he never pays it back. Other times, he just grabs the money without your knowledge or consent. And when you ask about where the money went he says he doesn't know. . . . These men are just *abayaye,* hooligans." The other women laughed in agreement. "But you just have to keep quiet and let it go," she said, "or else you will suffer the consequences."

Men in Bwaise repeatedly told me that unemployment and poverty made it difficult to provide for themselves and their families. Women in Bwaise also saw poverty as central, but they tended to blame men for their problems. What bound these attitudes together was the notion of the man as the primary economic provider. Gender relations were fraught with the tensions that came from surviving in such a difficult urban environment, and it was in relation to this central achieved aspect of masculinity that these tensions were most often framed.

Although the urban male economic provider ideal is a recurring theme in much of the literature on gender relations in contemporary Africa (Agadjanian 2002; Cornwall 2003; Hunter 2010), there is also a history of women contributing financially to their families in Kampala and in the surrounding region of Buganda (Mair 1934; Richards 1954a). Kampala has long been a place where women have pursued opportunities to earn money, often in ways not available in rural areas. As Musisi (1995) notes in her discussion of women working in contemporary night markets in Kampala, women have played a vital role in urban economic life since the colonial period. In Bwaise, I found working women everywhere, as modest charcoal vendors, food hawkers at the night market, and office workers for the city council. Men have never been the sole economic providers; there has always been negotiation between men and women over who is contributing financially to a family's well-being.

What my fieldwork reveals, therefore, is that the contemporary urban environment has made these negotiations especially tense. Given the acute poverty, I assumed men would be eager to have their girlfriends or wives earn money. However, the idea of employed women elicited anxieties in most of the men I encountered. One especially wary man told me, "If I am employed, my wife does not need to go out to work, because she may be attracted to men she meets and because she would be on display. To avoid all this, it is better she stays at home." These men were not only articulating their fears about women's sexuality but also tacitly acknowledging the threats posed by men's sexual privileges. Many men took a conciliatory position, supporting women's work outside the home as long as they did not encroach on men's authority. One man put it succinctly: "A woman can work, but decisions are still made by the man."

Embedded in these concerns was the notion that if a woman is capable of taking on the male provider role, then the benefits and authority normally accrued to men should be accorded to her as well. This was a troubling predicament for many men. Mohamed, a furniture showroom manager, told me, "The biggest problem in families is when as a man you are not employed. That is a very big problem at home. . . . If you do not have money and not even a job there can never be any joint decision making at home. Your wife and children will hate you, and they will not listen to anything you tell them to do because you didn't bring any money home." For such men, it was a short and slippery slope from women working and having a greater voice in decision making to women no longer respecting men's opinions to men losing their dignity altogether.[2]

Obbo (1980) notes that working women in Kampala have long triggered anxieties among many men. Her research in the 1970s shows that for decades men have accused working urban women of becoming "big headed" and "arrogantly" challenging conventional notions of male authority (8). The contemporary tensions and negotiations over women working that I observed are a continuation of a long-standing trend, but today these conflicts occur in a context in which women's increasing access to education allows some women to not only provide supplementary income, but actually compete with men as primary providers, which raises questions of authority in the household. Novel ideas of women's rights and gender equity have also gained legitimacy and frame these negotiations in new ways, as discussed in detail in the following chapter.

In the remainder of this chapter, I examine how male sexuality is intertwined with work and the male economic provider ideal. Are significant sexual privileges afforded to those men in Bwaise who succeed in fulfilling the provider ideal? How does this ideal shape the sex lives of men who struggle to meet it? What are the implications for those men who attempt to evade the provider ideal? And how are these dynamics connected to the persistence of masculine sexual privilege in the age of AIDS? I explore each of these questions and reveal the four main ways work and male sexuality were interrelated in a place like Bwaise.

WORK AND SEXUALITY AS A
PERFORMANCE OF MALE STATUS

As my fieldwork progressed, I learned that not all men in Bwaise were struggling financially. A few had capitalized on the business opportunities that this urban environment presented to become relatively well off—and this was the very much the case for Julius.

In 2009 a friend who worked as an AIDS counselor at the local health clinic suggested I talk with Julius. When we first met, it was immediately apparent that Julius was different from most other men I had met in Bwaise. I found him in the clinic courtyard, dressed in a starched, striped business shirt and dress shoes, leaning against the hood of his white Toyota pickup. Over six feet tall and with a large, solid belly, Julius projected confidence and was quite imposing.

We got into his pickup and drove to his home on the northern edge of Bwaise, a substantial, two-story, U-shaped building that looked more like a commercial property than a home. One side fronted the main road, and there was a well-stocked housewares shop on the ground floor perfectly positioned to capitalize on the constant traffic. I was impressed. At fifty-two, Julius had clearly accomplished a great deal to afford this home. As he would tell me, he had built a successful business selling used auto parts, slowly growing the business over two decades. For a man with only a primary school education, this was quite an achievement and the kind of success many men I met in Bwaise only dreamed about.

We climbed a narrow staircase to reach a large second-floor living room packed with furniture, children's toys, piles of clothing, and a large TV set. His wife Jacqueline, forty-six years old and an Anglican like Julius, was waiting for us, dressed casually in a loose white blouse and slacks. Jacqueline, I would learn, had a cowife, Pamela, who was one year younger and lived in a nearby house. Julius also had a third wife, but she died in 2005. He had children with all these women and was responsible for eighteen sons and daughters in all.

As I got to know Julius, it was clear he connected his success as an economic provider with his sexual privileges. For Julius, men, unlike women, had a right to multiple wives or girlfriends if they had the means.

> What we know from our nature as men and women is that a woman should have one man. But a man can be with several wives if possible. A man can be with his wife, or three wives, or any number of women so long as he feels they are enough for him. . . . I think the number would be according to a man's *amaanyi* [sexual strength]. It is his right to be with any number of women he chooses. No one can stop a man from having the wives he wants.

When I asked him what he would do if he learned his wife had a relationship with another man, he said, "I couldn't even discuss it with her or give her any chance to explain. I would just tell her to leave and we would separate. Because I married her to be with me alone, not to get some other man."

Julius and Jacqueline had been married for twenty-five years, and they both spoke of Jacqueline as the first, or senior, wife. They had taken all the steps to be officially married, including an introduction ceremony, paying bride-price, and a church wedding. Jacqueline made it clear to me that she had become quite adept at negotiating aspects of Julius's authority in the home, and she proudly told me how she had convinced Julius to let her start the successful shop on the ground floor of their home. Jacqueline had been less successful, it appeared, negotiating Julius's sexual privileges. This was especially evident in how she felt when Julius decided to take Pamela as his second wife, a decision he made without consulting her. "At first, it really hurt me and was difficult to accept. But over the years I've slowly become used to it," she told me when we talked alone. "What can I do about it really? [laughs]. Because if I complain about it directly he begins to question the kind of person you are, even though it was his behavior that caused the problem. So there are things you just need to love because your partner loves them. You have to get used to it because he loves having the second wife."

I met Pamela when Julius and I drove to his second home. This house was even more impressive. It was a true two-story, four-bedroom home with orange brick and white siding in the style popular with Kampala's aspiring middle class. With its sizable front yard and well-manicured green lawn, the home would not have looked out of place in an American suburb. Pamela was waiting for us in their living room, which was filled to capacity with upscale furniture. She was dressed elegantly in a flowing dark blue dress, projecting confidence and composure.

When I spoke with her alone that afternoon, I learned that Pamela, like Jacqueline, carefully negotiated Julius's authority in the home, acknowledging that he was the ultimate decision maker. "Because he is the one with *obuyinza*, and he is owner of the home, you just have to keep quiet," she told me. "It is God who gave men that *obuyinza* . . . you have to be below your husband."

Pamela seemed less content than Jacqueline, though. She claimed that she was Julius's first wife, having been together longer than Julius's twenty-five-year marriage to Jacqueline. Yet Pamela's claim on being first wife was tenuous because they were not formally married and had not even taken the first step, the introduction ceremony. When asked what she most wanted to change in her relationship, she said she wanted to have an official wedding ceremony, but she had made little progress over the many years they had been together.

These concerns about marriage dovetailed with other frustrations Pamela felt about negotiating Julius's relationships with other women. Like Jacqueline, Pamela said she had no say in Julius's decision to have multiple wives. "Of course it didn't make me happy. It couldn't possibly make me happy," she told me. "Whenever a man gets another family he changes the way he behaves in your home. It changes how you're able to feed your family. It affects your living standard. All of life changes."

Jacqueline's and Pamela's inability to challenge Julius's sexual privileges, especially given his economic success, was emblematic of the tight coupling of the male provider ideal and masculine sexual privilege in urban Uganda. Yet this dynamic proved to be more complicated in this family. Julius began a relationship with his third wife in the late 1990s, and in 2005 this woman died from AIDS. By the time of her death, Julius knew he too was HIV-positive, which left some doubts about who infected whom. Both Jacqueline and Pamela were uninfected but now had to contend with the fact they were in a serodiscordant relationship with Julius.

Julius was reluctant to disclose his HIV-positive status to Jacqueline and Pamela; it was only after his third wife's death that he discussed it. "It is not good to talk about [being HIV-positive]," Julius told me, "because it is not good to say so and so has this type of disease . . . you keep it a secret." Jacqueline and Pamela said that they were angry with Julius when they learned he was HIV-positive, but, like their concessions on Julius's authority and sexual behavior, they decided it would be best to forgive him and just move forward. Like Julius, Jacqueline thought it was best to keep this problem a secret and said she had not even told her mother.

Pamela was taking a similar approach to dealing with HIV in their relationship, but her anger at Julius was more palpable. "I did fight with him when he decided to get those other women," she told me. "The way that situation was I knew he could get AIDS." When he finally disclosed his status, Pamela said, she considered divorce but eventually forgave him.

Julius, in turn, portrayed himself to me as an innocent victim. He was convinced that his third wife had infected him, not the reverse. He was, however, concerned that his positive status would be interpreted as caused by what others might label improper behavior. This worry emerged when I asked him how many sexual partners he had in his life.

That is a question that is hard to answer. But I hope you are not going to consider that the main reason I am infected? I became HIV-positive due to my third wife. I married her when she was HIV-positive. So I can say that she is the one who made me sick. . . . People will say that a man with more than one woman is *omwenzi* [a womanizer], yet he is not if he just has his wives. His wives are staying at their homes with the husband, and then people call that man a womanizer? And then there is another man with only one wife who is not faithful at all, perhaps sleeping with four women in one day, which most men would not like. So for me I have my two wives. I also had the third one, but after that I couldn't go and look for any other women. That's the good thing [about polygamy] and an advantage for the Muslims. Yet [Christian men] say that they have one wife, but they have so many women outside their marriage. So my view is like the Muslims, that I had only my wives who are legally married. But I am not woman-hungry.

I was sympathetic to Julius's plight. He was a man paying a high price for largely conforming to normative expectations of masculinity. He simply had "policies that were similar to those of Muslims" and was now vulnerable to accusations of being irresponsible, selfish, and a threat to his wives. He struggled with disclosing his status to his wives, and that too was something I found common among positive men in Bwaise who feared their wives would leave them and they would die alone (Wyrod 2011).

Importantly, this problem with HIV serodiscordance had prompted some changes in Julius's relationships. Julius was eager to stay with his wives, and this provided Jacqueline and Pamela with new leverage in their relationships. Both women proudly told me that they were now using condoms consistently with Julius. This was indeed a major accomplishment, because Julius had told me he detested condoms. In this sense the presence of HIV in their relationships allowed both Jacqueline and Pamela to assert more control over their sexual relations with Julius.

Pamela went further with her newfound leverage. After Julius disclosed his status, she pressured him to have an official introduction ceremony, a major step toward formal marriage. In 2009 he finally acquiesced and they completed the ceremony. When I asked Pamela why she thought Julius agreed to the introduction ceremony now, she said, "It's due to the period we have been together, but then the AIDS issue also happened. OK, first you have to get angry because of the fear of AIDS, but then I forgave him about it. So I think that made him agree." HIV, therefore, allowed Pamela to achieve something she had not been able to negotiate in nearly two decades of cohabitating. She used her leverage to improve her social status by setting her relationship on the path to a wedding ceremony.

With regard to their own sexual health, the gains Jacqueline and Pamela made were important but ultimately limited. Julius was adamant about how much he disliked condoms. "We try to do what is advised, but I have never been comfortable with condoms. It makes me feel bad, and I think that someday I will run away from my wives," he told me. "So sometimes I agree to use condoms, but I hate them so much. It's not my wives but me who doesn't want to use them."

The safety Jacqueline and Pamela had negotiated was therefore tenuous. It was possible that Julius would eventually seek unprotected sex with another woman, as he himself implied he might do. It was also possible that Jacqueline or Pamela would acquiesce and agree to unprotected sex with Julius, risking HIV infection in order to secure status as the favored wife. So Julius's sexual privileges were still playing a big role in his wives' vulnerability to HIV infection. Both Jacqueline and Pamela were well aware of this; they frequently tested for HIV and said they were not sure what else could be done to ensure their safety in their polygamous family.

This view into Julius's life reveals how his success in fulfilling the male economic provider ideal worked in synergy with masculine sexual privilege in urban Uganda. Succeeding as a provider allows men to establish and exert control over multiple sexual relationships, and those sexual relationships can in turn be a performance, or demonstration, of male economic status. In this sense, men like Julius provide a template for other less successful men in Bwaise. While most men knew that much of what Julius had attained was beyond their reach, they could still strive to claim aspects of masculine sexual privilege, including the status that comes from having multiple sexual relationships, even if it would be difficult to maintain them.

Julius also reveals how such synergistic dynamics have been complicated by HIV/AIDS. The danger of AIDS, it appears, did not deter Julius from having multiple relationships, even though this was a concern of his wives. It was not until Julius knew and disclosed that he was positive that HIV affected his relationships, altering the power dynamics in subtle ways. The fact that he was an HIV-positive man provided new leverage for his HIV-negative wives—leverage they used to temper aspects of masculine sexual privilege, especially with regard to practicing safe sex. I observed similar dynamics in the other serodiscordant couples I came to know but only in cases like this one when the man, not the woman, was HIV-positive. Yet, in the end, this effect of AIDS was limited and, as in Julius's case, did not substantially challenge men's sexual privileges (Wyrod 2013).

Julius's financial success was elusive for all but very few men in Bwaise. In this sense, he was an outlier among the men I came to know. I now turn

Figure 3.1. Kimombasa section of Bwaise during the day.

to examine the life of a man on the opposite end of the socioeconomic spectrum who lived in an area of Bwaise known as Kimombasa.

WORK AND COMPENSATORY SEXUALITY

Kimombasa was the most notorious section of Bwaise, a rough-and-tumble area that I initially avoided in my fieldwork (figure 3.1). At night Kimombasa was a haven for those seeking cheap alcohol, cheap drugs, and cheap commercial sex.[3] Over the course of my fieldwork, Issa, a true denizen of Kimombasa, became one of my closer informants. His life reveals how precarious work was linked to what I refer to as compensatory sexuality in a place like Bwaise.

A wiry twenty-seven-year-old full of energy, Issa lived in the middle of Kimombasa in a dilapidated, half-built house with a dirt floor and no electricity or water. Initially, I was somewhat intimidated by Issa's streetwise persona and omnipresent crew of male companions. With the help of a mutual friend, I eventually summoned the nerve to introduce myself and quickly learned that Issa was charming, gregarious, and very much the center of his male clique's entertainment. Issa and his friends spent a lot of time at his sister's house, which was next door to the home of my closest friends in Bwaise. Eventually, some of my most enjoyable times in Bwaise were in this home. After a long day of fieldwork, I looked forward to sitting in front of their old television, listening to the endless banter of young men fueled by cigarettes, alcohol, and large amounts of khat that Issa and his male friends chewed habitually.

Issa's clique also provided a window onto how interactions among men both buttressed and subtly critiqued normative notions of masculinity. Sex was a frequent topic of conversation, especially since everyone knew I was interested in AIDS. Issa and his friends often portrayed women, especially young women, as the driving force behind the epidemic. As Issa provocatively said one evening:

> With women it is really hard to have a relationship because you can't trust any woman in Bwaise. As you see, the place is busy, so any woman, at one moment she's yours, and then the next minute she's not yours. . . . So every time a woman slides away from you she goes around the corner and another man gets her.

A friend animatedly rebutted Issa:

> But it is very hard to find a man in Bwaise with only one girlfriend! There are very few who have one girlfriend or wife! You find that most of the men, they leave their wife and go to the next corner and find another good-looking girl. And a man feels he has to stop and talk to a good-looking girl like her! So you find that you can't trust a man, or a woman, in Bwaise.

Another evening, it was clear that this khat-fueled banter perpetuated notions of both sexual privilege and a powerful, insatiable male sex drive. One of the men present that night was nicknamed Sniper, and Issa joked, "He earned that name because he never lets a woman pass by without taking a shot at sleeping with her. And he'll be going out looking later and he won't let a lady pass. But he better watch out for AIDS!" Everyone laughed at this gallows humor. Sniper just smiled and nodded proudly.

It seemed Issa's primary occupation was enjoying Bwaise's nightlife and avoiding work whenever possible, and he relished his reputation as a committed libertine and free spirit. He was adept at supporting his social life through the kindness of others, and I often found myself unable to resist his requests for assistance. When Issa did work it was in sporadic fits that often involved short-term opportunities to trade goods, such as used auto parts. Although perpetually in need of money, Issa nonetheless described such work as an annoyance and was perturbed that so much effort resulted in so little pay. "My life has been too difficult," he told me early on, "and so I just drink and go clubbing to forget it all."

Issa and his family had an unusual background, something Issa claimed contributed to his woes. He and his sister were part Musoga (an ethnic group bordering Buganda to the east) and part South Asian descent, or what Ugandans referred to as Muhindi. Being part Muhindi was something of an outsider identity in Uganda, and many men like Issa complained it excluded them from patronage networks that provided employment. This had been true for Issa, and while his family had been more prosperous two generations back, they now had few resources to exploit.

As Issa and I became friends, he proved to be an excellent guide to Bwaise's more decadent side, especially the clubs and nightlife that made Bwaise notorious throughout Kampala. A key venue was the Lion's Club, the center of gravity for many teenagers and twenty-somethings. When the club was in full tilt, the dance floor was packed with young people writhing feverishly to the sounds of Ugandan favorites like Chameleon and Ziggy D. With the pumping music, flowing alcohol, and youthful adrenaline, the atmosphere was charged, to say the least.

One of our nights at Lion's proved more adventurous than I was expecting. At 11 P.M., my wife and I met up with Issa and several of our mutual male friends. Once inside, Issa asked me for money for the first of several rounds of drinks, and at the bar he flirted aggressively, and unsuccessfully, with the female bartender. Issa then provided the entertainment for us, telling us he had to recently cut back on his excessive drinking and marijuana smoking because he was starting to hear voices in his head. He also bragged about his frequent sexual escapades with women he met at the clubs, describing his many one-night affairs, including the two times the women he had sex with robbed him in his sleep.

After Issa's story, we moved to the dance floor packed with sweaty bodies bouncing to the local hip-hop booming from the walls of speakers. Black lights, the main source of lighting, had the unfortunate effect of making my wife's white T-shirt, pale skin, and white teeth stand out so that she was even more conspicuous. Like some other men in the club, Issa started grabbing at women to dance. Quite a few complied, seeming unfazed.

As the night wore on, more and more youthful bodies jammed the dance floor and the sexual tension rose. My fascination with Lion's was starting to wane, and I was concerned that my wife was getting too uncomfortable. At one point, two young men stood inches from us, gestured suggestively at my wife, nudged each other, and studiously ignored me. With that, we looked for Issa to make our escape, and he cleared a path for us through the bodies. Issa thanked us for the evening and returned to the dance floor, quickly engulfed by his fellow revelers.

A few days after our night at Lion's, I talked with Issa more and gained a better sense of what drove his need for escapism. Issa and his crew had planned to give me a tour of Kimombasa. We began at an alley behind the main market and entered a labyrinth of buildings half devoured by the swampy ground. Most of the buildings doubled as informal drinking joints, with courtyards enclosed by tall papyrus mats that provided much-needed anonymity. A large sewage canal ran through Kimombasa, and in the evenings its banks were lined with young, female prostitutes and the men who were their customers.

As we sauntered through Kimombasa, our conversation turned to what it was like surviving as a man in Bwaise. Issa's cheery demeanour soured. "A real man in Bwaise is somebody who has got money, has got a house, has got a job, a business," he said. "That's a real man. Because when you don't have a house in Bwaise, and you have no work and no job, then you are not a man. You'll just be like one of the crooks in the street." One of Issa's friends chimed in, sounding even more demoralized. "To be a man in Bwaise, you survive just by suffering. We have no jobs. We are just surviving. There's nothing. No hope. You suffer a lot," he said. "I would like to lead a better kind of life. You want to be like any other kind of man and own a place and be able to sustain yourself. I admire those men who can lead such a life. But the ability for us to do that is so, so limited." Issa turned to me and added, "If you have no one helping you, you find that you're just a failure."

To leaven the mood, Issa decided it was time to visit a miraa dealer in Kimombasa to restock his supply. We entered the back of a shop, and inside we found Fina, a young woman who often sold khat to Issa and who handled the transaction with this group of lively men with aplomb.

By this point we had wound our way back toward Issa's sister's house, and we stopped in front of one of the many "lodges" (brothels) in Bwaise

Figure 3.2. Exterior of a lodge in Bwaise.

(figure 3.2). In case anyone was unclear what services this establishment provided, the entrance was flanked by a life-size statue of a curvy woman with blouse unbuttoned, breasts exposed, and pants partly unzipped. Issa's friends had left us, and it seemed like this was a good opportunity to ask Issa if he thought much about AIDS. "I fear AIDS, but then again I'm used to it now. Because I don't know if I am alive or not alive, positive or not," he told me. "I don't want to go for a checkup because I know it will just make me scared. And it will make me lose whatever time I have and just make my life shorter." Issa then turned to the statue of the prostitute, saying, "She's so beautiful isn't she? Every time I pass by her I'm afraid she'll be gone and with another man!" With that, Issa was ready to relax at home. "We've been working hard the whole day together. So we're going home, we'll rest, we'll chew our miraa, and we'll wait for another day."

While Issa was adept at downplaying his frustrations about work, it remained a prominent source of angst for him, especially, I would learn, in relation to his daughter and former wife. Issa relied on drinking, clubbing, and casual sex as an escape from the drudgery of other aspects of his life, and in this sense he was representative of how some of his male peers dealt with the frustrations and challenges of being a man in a place like Bwaise.

When I returned to Bwaise in 2009 and visited Issa at his house in Kimombasa, I was disheartened to see it was in the same dilapidated state. Issa shrugged this off, but now, at the age of thirty-two, he seemed more sensitive about how he was perceived as an unemployed man. He was especially concerned that he would be dismissed as one of Bwaise's abayaye. We went into his dank bedroom, and Issa lit a candle so I could see a picture of his daughter. This was the first time he had talked to me about her. Now eleven, she was two years old in the photo. "She lives with my ex-wife, her mother, now," Issa said. "I really do miss her, and that's why I keep her picture here near my bed. I see her in the picture and know she is out there somewhere."

As we talked about his daughter, it became evident to me that his relationship with his ex-wife had left Issa scarred. "I don't think I will ever trust any woman again. I think the problems started because I didn't have work. Every time she would see me she would just feel bad, wondering why am I just at home," he said. "Even if I would get another wife it is going to be the same. When I have no money to feed her she will just have to go [with another man]. . . . I now prefer to go and get somebody, she stays for one day, two days, and then she goes. I think that is the best this way I am living now and I'm used to it now." Issa told me his wife left him in 2003 for a German man who had considerably more financial resources. "He's won," Issa said, adding that he felt there was little he could have done to prevent it.

Issa still found solace in Bwaise's nightlife, and he boasted about his girlfriends. He had also grown more fatalistic about the dangers of AIDS:

Really I don't worry much about AIDS because I know there are so many sicknesses out there. I don't think I will die of HIV. If I was to die of AIDS, I would have died a long time ago, like ten years back [laughs]. . . . With AIDS, even if you are sick you can get something to help you to push on. So I think it is like any other disease, like the flu or heart disease. . . . I don't have any symptoms or anything that are disturbing me, so I think I survived it.

Toward the end of my fieldwork, Issa and I found ourselves back in front of the lodge near his sister's house where the statue of the prostitute, blouse open and pants unzipped, was still standing guard. Issa noted that another new lodge had opened right behind his house, and it seemed to be doing brisk business. He started talking about his dreams for the future.

When you come back, if I am still alive I think I will open up a lodge like this one. I hope I will be able to show you my own place like this. I think I will call it Night. Because every day these places are full. People they don't stop doing it. [Laughs] I like the name Night because it's in the night when there are so many possibilities, unlike the daytime. I like the night because it's when I have my freedom.

When I got back in touch with Issa two years later, I learned that his Night Lodge was still a dream deferred. He had, however, fathered two more children with women from two different short-term relationships. One of the mothers was raising their child on her own and the other woman had abandoned their child, leaving her with Issa's sister. Issa himself was uninterested in staying in contact with these children or their mothers. His first child was also no longer in his life, having moved to Germany with her mother and stepfather.

Like nearly all men in Bwaise, Issa was frustrated with his options for earning money. His response, however, ran counter to the ethos of hard work that most men in Bwaise professed. In many respects, Issa's lifestyle was one that many residents of Bwaise would criticize. Yet he defiantly channeled his contempt for the vagaries of life in Bwaise into a license to indulge in the pleasures he would say other men desired but feared to pursue so openly and consistently.

Issa therefore illuminates the ways some men became defeated by the provider ideal and turned to escapism, including sexual escapism, to compensate. He implied that Bwaise's nightlife, especially the thriving commercial sex work, was fueled in large part by these dynamics of compensatory sexuality. Thus failing or struggling to fulfill the provider ideal had important consequences for male sexuality in Bwaise because men were as likely to draw on their sexual privileges when the provider ideal seemed elusive as when it had been achieved.

Julius and Issa are two extreme examples of how precarious work, the provider ideal, and masculine sexual privilege are intertwined. Most men I met in Bwaise fell between these extremes. They looked at a man like Julius as a model of a successful man whose accomplishments were evidenced in part by his intimate relationships. Yet many men also felt some camaraderie with a man like Issa who struggled to find some pleasure in the shadow of being a failed provider—although few shared his fatalism and seeming indifference to the dangers posed by HIV. To illustrate these more nuanced dynamics, I turn to my experiences apprenticing in a carpentry workshop and discuss how my coworkers negotiated masculinity and sexuality in relation to this strenuous but poorly paid work.

THE VIEW FROM A CARPENTRY WORKSHOP

During my fieldwork, I was eager to gain an up close and visceral perspective on men's precarious work in Bwaise. Summoning the courage to actually approach a business, however, was another matter altogether. As a white American walking the streets of Bwaise I was certainly a curiosity but one that people could place—a researcher, a development worker, or perhaps a Christian missionary. But I knew that asking to apprentice as some kind of manual laborer would seem bizarre. I nonetheless persevered and decided to focus on working in a carpentry workshop.

Early on in my fieldwork I stumbled on what seemed like the perfect place. The Kibira workshop was tucked into the densely packed, ramshackle homes located right behind Bwaise's main commercial intersection. Kibira was typical of the many small carpentry workshops throughout Kampala that employed fewer than a dozen men (figure 3.3).

Carpentry, like metalwork and automotive repair, was one of a handful of semiskilled occupations for men in Kampala. Throughout the city, men

Figure 3.3. A typical carpentry workshop in Bwaise.

worked in carpentry workshops large and small, churning out elaborate king-size beds of mahogany, intricate armoires, and more mundane tables and chairs. While it was physically demanding work, carpentry was seen as a profession that, if mastered, could lead to steady income. In this sense, carpentry was a respectable type of work capable of producing a respectable man. However, it was beset by the same problems of most work in the area: it was for the most part irregular and poorly paid.

Eventually, I found the nerve to enter the dark interior of the Kibira workshop and approach the owner, Dennis. He was intrigued and open to my working with them, saying they had many men who apprenticed in the workshop. He was no doubt excited to befriend an American man who might provide connections or new capital, but he also seemed eager to introduce a muzungu to the craft of carpentry.

Our workshop was a modest affair, more like a shack than anything else. The walls were half-rotted wood panels; raw ceiling beams supported the simple corrugated-metal roof. The main work area was a blackened worktable in the rear of the shop surrounded by a sea of wood shavings that were occasionally gathered up by scavenger boys. Within this small, 15-by-30-foot space, several men made their living. Most days there were four or five of us in the shop, including Dennis, thirty-one, and Rafik and Medi, the two full-time workers, both in their early twenties. All three had only a primary school education.

My work as an apprentice was physically demanding, and I was often winded after the first hour. By noon I was frequently drenched in sweat. But Rafik and Medi were usually oblivious to the heat, just finding their rhythm in the long day's work. They moved smoothly and steadily, all their motions efficient. Their concentration was intense, and they often waited until late in the day to break for lunch.

As I would come to learn, both Rafik and Medi derived pleasure from this type of hard work and from mastering the craft of carpentry. In a week they could transform huge slabs of hardwood into a simple but pleasing king-size bed. They were proud of their finished products, which they often described as beautiful. Both saw carpentry as a special category of manual labor that allowed men of modest means to earn some admiration. "In this job people give you respect. Everywhere we go people admire the furniture we make," Rafik told me. "That's why I respect my job. I'm proud to be a carpenter, I really am proud."

While I expected to be relegated to mundane work like sanding, my coworkers took my apprenticeship more seriously. On my first day, after receiving my own blue work smock, Dennis took me to the worktable in the rear of the shop. My task was to use a small, very sharp chisel to carve out an intricate pattern in a sheet of plywood (figure 3.4). Overcompensating for my jitters, I feigned confidence and started quickly chiseling away at a slab of wood. My technique, or lack of it, elicited laughter from everyone, and Dennis chuckled, "Genda mpola. Mpolampola [Go slowly. Slowly, slowly]."

As I would hear again and again during my apprenticeship, it was vital to work slowly, smoothly, and steadily. No doubt this approach came in part from practical considerations; raw materials were expensive, and even our simple manual tools were dangerous. Yet it also reflected how a confident and professional carpenter should work and, by extension, the

Figure 3.4. Author during carpentry apprenticeship.

proper way a man exhibits and applies his strength and skill. In this sense, carpentry work encapsulated many assumptions about masculinity: a man should draw on his assumed male power to produce useful things that generate the money he needs to provide for his family.

When Dennis checked in on my progress during my time in the workshop, he often stressed that tasks like sawing and drilling require using your amaanyi. If harnessed properly, the smooth and steady application of this amaanyi could transform resilient materials, like dense *mvule* hardwood, into beautiful and useful things. It was clear Dennis associated such amaanyi with men, and because I too was a man I possessed such strength. Dennis told me, "The amaanyi I have as a man is different from that of a woman. The way we were created, our nature is different. As you know, the woman's nature is different. So even the actions and work men and women do can never be the same. They are supposed to differ. Much as we can all talk and breathe we are still different in some ways." Dennis's use of the word *amaanyi* was quite typical of how I heard others use it, especially its association with perceived gender differences and notions of men's innate strength, power, authority, and, often, virility.[4]

Thus, as my apprenticeship continued, I realized I was being schooled not only in the craft of carpentry but also in this notion of male power and its proper application. Occasional admonitions from my coworkers about moving too quickly or being too hyperactive were as much about proper male comportment as honing my skills as a carpenter.

These issues coalesced poignantly when it came to learning how to plane. A heavy metal object that felt satisfying in my hand, the plane had a razor-sharp blade that shaved and shaped even the thickest wood. Its use required both strength and control, and if wielded properly there was little risk of injury. Yet the force required to plane correctly meant a novice like myself was a danger to himself and his coworkers. Mastering the plane, which I never did, was emblematic of acquiring the knowledge and experience of the proper application of amaanyi.

Such understandings of "appropriate" male work were continually reinforced by the space of the carpentry workshop itself. Only once during my apprenticeship did a woman enter the rear of the shop. Men, however, found the space welcoming and would often stop by simply to hang out. The workshop's location in the heart of Bwaise meant a steady stream of male visitors, especially unemployed men with time on their hands. Both out of boredom and to keep up appearances, many of these men would pitch in on a project for an hour or so and then saunter back to the streets.

Through my apprenticeship, therefore, I came to appreciate how this semiskilled carpentry work exemplified idealized notions of how men should hone and wield their assumed strength. Carpentry encapsulated the idea that men's amaanyi, if channeled and applied properly, was uniquely productive not only of useful things but also of respectable men. The labor of carpentry exemplified not simply a working-class masculinity; it also reflected dominant ideas that men and women were complementary but essentially different and that men possess certain powers and attributes that give them responsibilities and privileges. Women could and did support men's work, but it was ultimately men who possessed the amaanyi to sustain a family. My coworker Medi summed up this paradigm: "Just look around this place. There are no women here, even though we have vacancies for them. But they can't even come here because they know they can't do such men's work."

However, in urban Uganda this semiskilled labor was no longer sufficient to guarantee that a carpenter could fashion himself as a respectable man. The actual business of carpentry was precarious, which often frustrated my coworkers and complicated their intimate relationships. Dennis acknowledged that his business was uncertain and he often lacked the capital to purchase the expensive raw materials, but he maintained that it allowed him to fulfill his obligations as a provider. He evaluated other men by a similar yardstick, saying, "*Omusajja ddala* [a true man] must have a job, and he must be hardworking." He continued, "But if you are a kind of man who doesn't work and you simply sit around and wait, then you cease to be a man. Those men are very many in Bwaise. They may think of themselves as men, but for those of us men who are working we don't see them that way." Dennis seemed confident that his Kibira workshop allowed him to pass this masculinity litmus test in Bwaise.

Neither Rafik nor Medi, however, romanticized carpentry work, and both were quick to note that there was an overabundance of carpenters in Bwaise, and Dennis could easily replace them. Typical for this kind of labor in a Bwasie, Rafik and Medi were paid only after pieces were sold, and fair compensation was left to Dennis's discretion. As dedicated and hardworking young men, Rafik and Medi found this routine exploitation at Kibira difficult to tolerate.

Thus, while there were opportunities for the resourceful, the hard work of carpentry did not translate into steady income for most men. Even the ambitious and diligent were guaranteed nothing, and young men were often exploited by older men. This made for tension between this idealized form of male semiskilled labor and the money it actually generated. Besides, the semiskilled carpenter was hardly the paradigm of contemporary urban masculinity in cosmopolitan Kampala. For young men like Rafik and Medi, the work of carpentry both reinforced the male provider ideal and was an emblem of limited social and cultural capital.

WORK AND SEXUALITY AS A PRAGMATIC PROBLEM

Carpentry had always been central in Dennis's adult life, and after a dec-ade working as a carpenter's assistant he eventually amassed the capital to build the Kibira workshop. Dennis told me that he started to think more seriously about marriage and family in his early twenties. As a teenager, he had a few girlfriends, but at nineteen he decided to stop having girlfriends, and sex, altogether. For four years he abstained from sex. Then he found the woman he would marry, and they began living together and quickly had a child. By the time I apprenticed at Kibira, Dennis and his wife, both Anglicans, had been together for seven years and had four children.

I often talked with Dennis about his sex life as a married man, and he repeatedly claimed he had had no sexual partners other than his wife once they started living together. His motivations were practical, he said. Temptations were natural, but he had to resist.

> It happens, and I think about getting a girlfriend on the side. Sometimes I am able to put a brake on that. Because it might be that the woman I've admired will ask for $50, but I have only $25, so I just give up. But naturally it happens because it's just a natural thing. So it's up to you to control your-self. You can decide to control your body or to go on with the idea. You have to consider the strength of your wallet. Yes, but it's not easy.

Without the extra money another relationship required, Dennis implied, he had been able to control his urge to have a girlfriend outside his mar-riage. In addition, he suggested that the demands of contemporary urban life made additional relationships impractical and less of a status symbol for men. "A man used to show his manhood with many women. But that is no longer applicable today," he told me. "It used to happen with our grand-fathers because, for them, they could have eight to ten women to show that they were men. But now that does not make sense. You just can't have six women when you don't have the money to sustain them."

It was not only money that shaped Dennis's attitudes toward intimate relationships; AIDS was clearly a significant factor as well. "It is not good these days to have a girlfriend outside your marriage," he stressed. "These things would have been good if it was not for AIDS. But with AIDS it's become a very bad practice. That's why I can't be some kind of lover with many girlfriends. . . . Because the moment you leave this girlfriend's house there will be another man waiting to enter and have sex with her!"

When Dennis and I talked about AIDS, he seemed truly frightened by the disease and how it could affect his family. "I first of all looked at my family and the children and then decided that I will have to give up certain things. If you are [HIV-]positive, you will always be worried of how you will leave your children," he told me. "The fear of death is always there. You always are worried about it."

When discussing other men in Bwaise, Dennis vacillated between reserving judgment on other men's sexual behavior and being critical of men with several lovers, "I think some men want to have more than one woman just because of their nature, as *omwenzi* [a womanizer]. . . . But we are all still human beings. So you may find that one man may be interested in sleeping with two or four women in one day. Yet personally, I can't be bothered with that. So I think it's just one's nature." Looking around Bwaise, with its growing number of brothels, Dennis said that some men had become too accustomed to AIDS. He repeatedly emphasized that the costs, financial and medical, were simply too high to have sex with anyone but this wife.

When I returned in 2009, the Kibira workshop was more weathered but still open for business. Dennis's life had changed little. He and his wife now had a fifth child. Dennis said that business was much worse and the stress of struggling to provide for his family had taken a toll. From what I could tell, money now preoccupied Dennis completely, and he said his family often had only one meal a day. Even with a new child, he felt nothing good had happened to him since the time I was an apprentice in his workshop. "It is only money that brings a change," he said. "It is the key to a man's life." The financial vice was indeed tightening for Dennis. I met the son of his landlord and learned Dennis was six months behind on rent, and the landlord was now threatening to tear down the Kibira carpentry workshop, destroying Dennis's livelihood in the process.

When I asked Dennis if there had been any changes in his personal life, he again emphasized that money had determined his options.

> I'm still only with my wife. There's no other woman, not even back in my village. Because if I get another wife, since I don't have any money, it's just not cost-effective. You must use up a lot of money to sustain more than one

wife. So it's better to just leave other women altogether and remain with one woman. But when you have money, then you can get any number of wives you feel like, be it five women or even more . . . if you have the money! [Laughs]

It was also evident that his financial problems had affected his relationship with his wife. "When there is poverty at home, someone who is hungry is very angry. What kind of happiness is that?," he asked. "She's hungry, and you are telling her to go to bed? If there is no food, there is no sex, no love. There just isn't." From my conversations with Dennis, it seemed money was now the only frame through which he viewed his life. Dennis did not talk much about AIDS, as he had when I spoke with him five years earlier. In fact, I found it difficult to engage with Dennis at all, and I struggled to get past the increasingly bitter shell he seemed encased in. Of course, any bitterness was certainly justified, especially when interacting with a relatively affluent American like myself.

Overall, Dennis's earlier concerns about AIDS, combined with his nearly single-minded attention to money and his increasingly modest income as a carpenter, seemed to make the idea of an extramarital relationship, or another wife, unattractive to him. Unlike Issa, Dennis's money problems did not lead him to shore up his masculinity through sexual relationships. Money, it appeared, had the opposite effect for him, especially given the continuing threat of AIDS.

In many respects, Dennis's approach to dealing with sexual relationships in a place like Bwaise was a very old story in Uganda. The historical and ethnographic literature emphasizes that in precolonial Uganda the expense of formal marriage meant most men spent the bulk of their lives married to one woman (Mair 1934; Musisi 1991). Dennis was making similar pragmatic economic decisions.

Although Dennis did not mention it explicitly, his practical approach of limiting his sexual partners was a key aspect of Uganda's indigenous zero grazing AIDS prevention strategy. Approximately two-thirds of the men I interviewed in 2004 claimed to be monogamous and told me they had only one sexual partner in the past twelve months. Yet, while I found Dennis convincing, I was less sure about many of these other men. When I elicited more detailed life histories from them, I found their relationship histories significantly more complex. As in precolonial Uganda, the pragmatic approach to men's sexual relationships went hand in hand with recognition of the male status associated with having multiple sexual partnerships, an issue Dennis himself alluded to. This was true for the zero grazing strategy as well, because it encouraged men to reduce the number of sexual partners but left intact—or actually tacitly reinforced—the notion that men had a right to multiple sexual partners if they so chose.

While Dennis was more representative of men I met in Bwaise than either Julius or Issa, his strictly pragmatic approach to sexuality was not typical. I now turn to my final example, my coworker Rafik. Rafik's story is the most complex example of how work, sexuality, and AIDS intertwine and in many ways represents best how most men I met in Bwaise grappled with the paradoxes posed by work and sexuality in the context of AIDS.

WORK AND SEXUALITY AS A RESERVOIR OF PRIVILEGE

For a young man with modest means, Rafik had succeeded in crafting a stylish, even trendy image for himself. His look was inspired by London deejays, and he often wore a tight black shirt with just enough Spandex to hug his torso. In his jeans and wraparound sunglasses, Rafik could have passed as a university student. With his attractive face and lean but muscular build, Rafik knew he was a good-looking young man and occasionally boasted to me that many young women were drawn to him. He moved easily among the various male cliques in Bwaise, from the club set to the more reserved men like his coworkers at Kibira.

As I became friends with Rafik, I saw that he was diligently cultivating another image, that of a serious, mature man on the cusp of respectable adulthood. During my second day at Kibira, Rafik, an Anglican, volunteered that he had a steady girlfriend, Margaret, immediately adding proudly, "I don't cheat. I'm faithful to her." Part of what Rafik found so alluring about Margaret was that she had completed some university-level training as a nurse, which was significantly beyond his primary school education. Employed at the main national hospital, she earned a small but steady income, which Rafik found attractive rather than threatening. He said she was the kind of woman he could build a future with.

Rafik lived in a small, one-room apartment in his father's family compound two miles north of Bwaise. When I met Margaret one afternoon at Rafik's house, it was immediately evident that she was different from most young women in Bwaise. She wore the tight stylish jeans favored by college women, and her hair was carefully coiffed in a trendy cut. She was soft-spoken, articulate, and very comfortable with English, unlike Rafik. As the three of us talked, Rafik fawned over Margaret, calling her baby and sweetheart. I asked them what they envisioned for their future, and Rafik quickly exclaimed, "I want to be with her, to have a big house, to have the money and a big place, you know! That's why I keep to only one lady. I want her to trust me." I was admittedly caught up in Rafik's romantic vision of his future with Margaret. As I said my goodbys that afternoon, I left them snuggling on Rafik's small couch, feeding each other bits of a chocolate bar.

Rafik was still enamored with the Bwaise club scene, including the Lion's Club, but continually stressed to me that he was nearly ready to move on to what he saw as a more adult stage of life centered on marriage, a house, and children. Rafik also wanted me to know that he was critical of some of his male peers for pressuring him to act in ways he now saw as problematic. "Some guys say, 'When you have good money you have to stay with five ladies. You have to be a man, you know as a city man.'" I was surprised when Rafik told me how much he had learned from me about relationships. "As a good man you have to stay with one lady," he said. "Like you, Robert, I want to be like you. That's what I like. That's why I want to be with one lady."

Rafik also made clear to me that he was knowledgeable about AIDS, which he equated with being a sophisticated, mature man. "I fear AIDS," he told me. "If I go for a blood test and the doctors say, 'Rafik, you are HIV-positive,' that's not good. You will have failed. You failed your girlfriend, and you'll lose your girlfriend. You even lose respect for yourself." Rafik stressed his fluency in AIDS prevention messages, from condoms to faithfulness to regularly testing for HIV. He said he had tested twice with previous girlfriends and portrayed himself as something of an AIDS prevention counselor to his peers.

Rafik's relationship with Margaret entailed both benefits and risks. As a man from a modest background and with limited education, Rafik was attracted to Margaret in part because she was a notch above him in the social hierarchy. Margaret could help him attain higher social status, but it was exactly those qualities that could prove to be liabilities. Rafik knew his charm and good looks provided only limited protection from the competition of more affluent men who might be attracted to Margaret. His repeatedly voiced concerns about his housing were emblematic of his anxiety that a young woman with nursing credentials could do better than him.

In 2009 when I returned to Bwaise, I learned more about Rafik and Margaret's relationship. I had no trouble reconnecting with Rafik because he was now running a cell phone repair shop at the main intersection of Bwaise. As I approached the tiny shop, I saw Rafik standing out front, looking much bigger, with a thick torso and fuller face. Still stylish, he was wearing a hip plaid shirt, jeans, trendy dress shoes, and mirrored, aviator-style sunglasses that gave his look an edge.

He was very eager to tell me how his life had progressed since we last met. He excitedly told me he now owned a car, parked right next door, a major status symbol. Rafik had more to show me that afternoon in his new neighborhood, a pleasant section of greater Bwaise, up above the fray where the air was clearer and there was more vegetation. He was renting half of a small, new, one-story house surrounded by green space.

As we relaxed on his ample and comfortable couch, I asked Rafik how exactly he had managed all this. He said it all began with his decision to leave Kibira for another carpentry workshop. Within a year, he was able to amass enough capital to start his cell phone repair business with his friend. I was happy for him but remained unsure how he afforded everything and suspected he might be receiving some help from relatives.

Although Rafik's work life had progressed since my prior fieldwork, his intimate relationships had proven more complicated. Not long after my initial fieldwork, Rafik revealed to me, Margaret had left him. I immediately assumed it was because she had found a more upwardly mobile man, but Rafik said that was not the case. To my surprise, he said it was his fault she left because he was "jumping around [having sex] with too many other women," and Margaret could no longer tolerate it. It was then that I heard Rafik's new mantra, "But Robert, now I've changed my life."

He told me that when we worked together at Kibira, Margaret was his serious girlfriend, even his fiancée, but he was also intimately involved with two other women. He tried to hide these affairs from Margaret but suspected she knew all along. Their serious conflicts began, however, when Margaret offered to use her earnings as a nurse to rent a bigger house that they could live in together. "She said to me, 'Come and stay in my house.' But I said, 'No. I cannot stay in your house—a woman's house. I cannot be married by a woman [*okufumbira*]. I'm the one to marry you [*okuwasa*]!' She insisted, but I said, 'No, I refuse.'" In Luganda, Rafik was making the distinction between *okuwasa*, the active form of the verb "to marry," and *okufumbira*, the passive form meaning "to be married by" or "to be married to." In conventional usage, only a man would be described as actively marrying (okuwasa), whereas a woman would be described as passively married to a man (okufumbira).[5]

For a man from a modest background struggling to make a living with limited skills and social capital, the idea of living in his girlfriend's house struck a nerve. "If she marries you [okuwasa], as a man you cannot make decisions in the house. She can even decide to bring in another man because the house is hers," he said. "When people see you living out of a woman's house, they will say you are too lazy to work. And as a man you cannot be respected if you do it." Margaret, hurt and angered by his decision, then confronted him about his other relationships. As Rafik recounted it, she said, "You're just a *muyaye*. You've lied to me about us and other women. You don't love me." Margaret ended their relationship.

Rafik was clearly saddened by all that had transpired but insisted it was his fault for "jumping around with other women and not being serious." Rafik was nonetheless eager to tell me about his current main girlfriend, Rose, one of the young women he had been seeing behind Margaret's back. I had the chance to meet Rose a week later when the three of us had lunch at Rafik's home. Dressed in tan corduroy pants and a crisp, colorful blouse, Rose immediately introduced herself to me, making clear her English was excellent. Although just twenty-one, she projected confidence and seemed educated well beyond her four years of secondary school. It appeared to me that Rafik had once again been drawn to a woman who would help him craft a more upwardly mobile persona.

That afternoon, Rafik described how their relationship had evolved. "When I was with Margaret, I was also with Rose, but it was a confidential affair," he confided. "So when Margaret and I started having problems,

Rose covered over the problems we had.... She was patient with me, because I was very unfaithful to her. She knew about those other women but still loved me." Rafik then told me how much I had "changed his life." I found this odd, given that Rafik had not originally disclosed his relationship with Rose to me, but he said that he had learned a lot from me about relationships and planning for his future. Rafik also wanted to make it clear that he was thinking differently about AIDS, that AIDS prevention efforts stressing fidelity were now shaping the future he envisioned with Rose. "The most important thing in preventing AIDS in Uganda is to stop from sleeping around with many women," he said. "You find a girl, get a relationship, and be with just her."

These concerns dovetailed with another development in Rafik's life. Rafik's family was Church of Uganda (Anglican), but he had now become a born-again Christian and was a member of the large and powerful Jesus Life Church. Located at the southern edge of Bwaise, Jesus Life was a megachurch, popular with people from all over Kampala. Some members of parliament were even rumored to be regular attendees.

One Sunday I accompanied Rafik to a service at Jesus Life Church. Inside the cavernous structure were row after row of folding chairs, perhaps two thousand in all, neatly leading up to the grand, three-tiered stage. Much of the service involved a long, improvised homily on marriage. Couple after couple were invited to the stage to pledge their faithfulness to each other, and the preacher loquaciously extolled the virtues of marital fidelity. The homily was periodically interrupted by an energetic band playing lively, Congolese-style pop songs. Rafik seemed to especially enjoy this music, dancing more vigorously than most of his fellow congregants, in a way I found oddly reminiscent of his nights at the Lion's Club.

After the service, I asked Rafik why he converted. He replied:

When you come here you see families who are university graduates. You see families that have good marriages. That's why I like the people who are *balokole* [born-again Christians] and that's why I tried to believe in Jesus.... Because last time you were here in Uganda, I didn't know Jesus. I had many girlfriends and I would go to clubs. But I don't want to go to clubs anymore because I have got Jesus, which is a better thing. With Jesus you save your money, you get one girl, you make your money, and you save your money. That's why I want to be a *mulokole* [born-again Christian].

In many respects, Rafik had channeled his abundant passion and enthusiasm for clubbing into religion. It all fit neatly with the redemption story
he created for himself after Margaret left him:

> Before, when I was with Margaret, I had three other girlfriends outside our
> relationship. But today I have only one girl. That's why now that you've
> returned, Robert, you see I have a car, I have a good house, I have a job.
> That's why I am born again. I changed my life. Because God helped me.

For Rafik, masculinity, work, money, sexual relationships, and religion
were all woven together.

Rafik was eager to portray his relationship with Rose as on the cusp of
marriage, but the more time I spent with them, the more I wondered
about their future. One afternoon I visited Rose in the beauty shop Rafik
had financed for her. It was one of many tiny shops lining one small street
off Bwaise's main commercial avenue. Rose presented herself to me as a
mature woman ready to marry, saying she believed Rafik was the right
man for her. "He's a very good man generally and different from the men
in Bwaise," she said.

There were, however, lingering concerns, and they emerged when we
talked about AIDS. "I do worry about AIDS," she said. "I can be faithful,
but I don't know what my partner will do. I don't say I don't trust him. I
do. But I should not trust him 100 percent." She continued, "These
men can be so controlling. You can be yelled at for simply turning off the
television. . . . Love in Africa is hard. If you find out someone doesn't love
you it's better to just quit the relationship and get someone else who will."

Four months after I returned home, I phoned Rose for an update. I was
only partially surprised when she said she had broken off her relationship
with Rafik: "The major thing was that I caught him with a woman in what
I used to call our bed. With this, I wasn't ready to lose my dignity fighting
over such a man, so I decided to let him go. This in spite of the fact that he
was my first real boyfriend."

Rafik seemed caught in the pull of conflicting notions of male sexuality.
He was eager to be seen as having a serious, modern romantic relationship
based on trust and monogamy. His emphasis on fidelity was buttressed
by the threat of AIDS and by prevention approaches that upheld monogamy as the best, most "responsible" strategy. In 2009, he found further

encouragement in this regard through his conversion to evangelical Christianity. Yet, ultimately, Rafik remained reluctant to fully embrace monogamy, and the allure of relationships with multiple women remained strong, likely fueled by his male peers and the models provided by older men, including his father, who had two wives. His work as a carpenter and small businessman further complicated matters, making him eager to settle down with more educated women but then frustrated when he struggled to provide for them financially. Rafik's often passionate discussions about how he was working through these issues offer special insight into the paradoxes of masculinity, sexuality, and AIDS confronted by many men in Bwaise. He even explicitly stated that my own identity as a married American man affected how he portrayed himself, both in how he managed my image of him and in how he grappled with different models of masculinity.

Both Margaret and Rose initially accommodated Rafik's desire for other sexual partners, and both eventually reached their threshold of tolerance. For Margaret, these tensions were exacerbated by Rafik's refusal to accept her offer to rent a house for them. Rose, in turn, began to view Rafik as too similar to other uneducated and financially unstable men in Bwaise, and his affair confirmed her suspicions. Rose, in particular, expressed something of a fatalistic attitude about men in Uganda, suggesting that the sexual privileges afforded to men were entrenched, making it unlikely she could ever have the type of intimate relationship she desired. The ways Margaret and Rose navigated male sexuality in their intimate relationships were, therefore, intertwined with the precariousness of men's work, including the insecurities such work created for a man like Rafik as he strove to embody conflicting ideals of masculinity. Women's toleration of men's infidelities, up to a point, has a long history in Buganda. As discussed in chapter 2, wives and girlfriends have been active participants in helping men craft an image of a "modern" Christian monogamous family since at least the 1920s (Peterson 2012). This dynamic underscores that women, not just men, can play key roles in reshaping the contours of masculine sexual privilege, a theme that recurs in the following chapters.

Rafik's struggles with work and conflicting ideals of male sexuality were common among men I met in Bwaise. When his relationship with one woman became complicated and problematic he began another concurrent relationship to, as he put it, "cover over the problems." It was this dynamic in particular that I came to realize was a facet of the relationship histories of many men I met in Bwaise—a dynamic largely missed by conventional sexual behavior surveys. The right to have multiple sexual partners was a reservoir of privilege that men could draw on when their relationships became stressed, often due to financial problems. This was especially common when a couple's children entered school and the financial responsibilities for men increased. It is important to underscore that these types of concurrent, overlapping, long-term relationships are now recognized as especially effective ways of transmitting HIV.

PRECARIOUS WORK AND THE REMAKING OF MASCULINITY IN THE CONTEXT OF AIDS

In this chapter I present the four main ways work and male sexuality are interrelated in Bwaise: sexuality as a performance of male status, compensatory sexuality, sexuality as a pragmatic problem, and sexuality as a reservoir of privilege. These dynamics are, in turn, a reflection of three broader themes regarding how masculinity, work, and sexuality are entangled with AIDS in Bwaise. First, a central component of hegemonic masculinity in Bwaise is the male economic provider ideal. Men and women repeatedly stressed that a "proper" man in Bwaise proved his manhood by earning the money that sustained his family. This ideal was mostly uncontested, although Issa was an articulate and insightful critic of the economic conditions that make this aspect of hegemonic masculinity unobtainable for so many of his male peers.

Second, the nature of work in a place like Bwaise buttresses masculine sexual privilege—a dynamic made evident in different ways by Julius, Issa, and Rafik. Julius's financial success reinforced his assumed sexual privileges as a man, especially the privilege to have multiple sexual partnerships. Issa provided an interesting complement to Julius. Demoralized by falling short of what a proper man should be, Issa was frustrated by the precarious and uncertain work that was available to him. While he appeared to revel in a rejection of the male economic provider ideal, he divulged to me his feelings of failure and inadequacy for not being a proper husband and father. Issa excelled, however, in finding other ways of shoring up his embattled masculinity, especially through his sexual relationships—a dynamic I refer to as compensatory sexuality. In this sense, Issa provides the clearest example of the dynamics both Hunter (2005) and Silberschmidt (2001) have also highlighted, namely, that the sexual domain becomes an arena in which men exercise their gender privileges when they feel frustrated by their economic options.

Julius and Issa illustrate how men exercise their male sexual privilege both when they fulfill and when they fail to fulfill the male economic provider ideal. These same dynamics shaped Rafik's intimate relationships, although in a different way. All three men reveal that masculine sexual privilege has remained largely unquestioned, especially by men. Precarious and uncertain work may make it difficult to embody aspects of such privilege, but that has not undermined and in fact often reinforces it.

This chapter also demonstrates the limited impact AIDS has had on masculine sexual privilege. This third theme—the persistence of masculine sexual privilege in the age of AIDS—was the key issue animating my fieldwork, and this chapter makes clear that precarious work is central to this persistence of privilege. This is indeed a surprising finding given Uganda's AIDS success story and the expectations that I had for social change in Uganda. Men's poorly paid and uncertain work may elicit feelings of a crisis of masculinity for individual men, but it prompts remakings of masculinity that buttress masculine sexual privilege, even with the looming threat of HIV.

That is not to dismiss the important new dynamics that have emerged in the context of AIDS, such as the subtle power shifts in Julius's serodiscordant relationship. Julius's HIV-positive status provided a new opportunity for his HIV-negative wives to assert more control over the terms of sex, especially the use of condoms. These social implications of HIV discordance are receiving greater attention globally, and there is a growing literature examining the interplay between gender, living with HIV, and the balance of power in relationships (Bunnell et al. 2005; Davis and Flowers 2011; Orengo-Aguayo and Perez-Jimenez 2009; Persson and Richards 2008; Stevens and Galvão 2007).

Another facet of these new dynamics is illustrated by Dennis and other men who approached their sexual relationships as pragmatic problems.

For Dennis, this involved not a rejection of men's sexual privilege of having multiple relationships but instead a pragmatic distancing because of his limited finances. The dangers of AIDS worked in tandem with these economic concerns and made the idea of an extramarital relationship, or another wife, unappealing, even while Dennis acknowledged that money, male status, and multiple sexual relationships still went hand in hand. As discussed in detail in chapter 6, Hunter (2005) makes a similar observation and suggests that AIDS in South Africa has led to heightened scrutiny of men's multiple sexual partnerships, making them less attractive to some men.

It is important to reiterate that the complexities of masculine sexual privilege in urban Uganda mean that Dennis's pragmatic monogamy is in many respects unremarkable. As discussed above and in chapter 2, monogamy has long been part of the range of acceptable male sexual relationships in Kampala and Buganda. Precarious work and AIDS made this long-standing option more attractive to Dennis. His views reflect the fact that monogamy is just one choice among several for "appropriate" male sexual behavior and that monogamy and masculine sexual privilege coexist in a place like Bwaise. However, it is also important to stress that how Dennis distanced himself from masculine sexual privilege without disavowing it reflects the lingering influence of Uganda's zero grazing approach to AIDS prevention. Zero grazing stressed reducing sexual partners but not monogamy, thereby tacitly reinforcing masculine sexual privilege.

This effect of AIDS on masculine sexual privilege was not at all evident in Issa's life as he became increasingly fatalistic about whether he had been infected with HIV. The effect of HIV was only modest in Rafik's life, even with his fraught ruminations on the dangers of AIDS. Rafik strove to show me his fluency in AIDS prevention messages and talked about his dedication to approaches based on fidelity. Yet he repeatedly vacillated between drawing on the reservoir of masculine privilege by having multiple sexual relationships and disavowing it. He was, therefore, emblematic of the many other men I met in Bwaise who grappled with contradictory and conflicting ideals of masculinity and male sexuality in the context of AIDS.[6]

The tension between competing ideals of male sexuality is a theme in other research on intimate relationships in Africa. Shanti Parikh (2007) highlights how in southeastern Uganda denial and secrecy regarding men's extramarital affairs have become primary ways men and women maintain the appearance of "modern" companionate marriages, even as male multiple sexual partnerships remain a hegemonic aspect of masculinity. As Smith (2006, 136) notes, based on research in Nigeria, the consequences for women can be dire, because "emerging ideals and patterns of marriage unfold in a context of continuing gender inequality, such that expectations about fidelity, romantic love, and intimacy are placing women at risk of contracting HIV from their partners." I return to these issues in chapter 6.

This chapter illustrates that AIDS has had limited impact on masculine sexual privilege, in part because such privilege has been reinforced by the context of precarious work. In contrast to precarious work, the promotion of women's rights in Uganda has been viewed as something that could challenge or moderate masculine sexual privilege in the age of AIDS. In chapter 4 I examine women's rights in detail, exploring how they have affected the negotiation of male sexuality in intimate relationships in Bwaise.

4 Women's Rights in the Remaking of Masculinity

Visiting Isaac and Edwina's home provided a pleasant escape from Bwaise's ever-present noise, mud, trash, and traffic. Perched on a gentle slope on the periphery of Bwaise, in an area much less congested than central Bwaise, their home was part of a cluster of low-slung, one-story buildings. Plaster walls, slightly bronzed by Kampala's orange soil, propped up simple tin roofs.

Like their neighbors, Isaac and Edwina made their home in a small section of one building. A feeble wooden front door led into a small room subdivided by a hanging sheet. One window struggled in vain to stave off the dankness, and the unpainted, gray walls were colored only by a thin layer of grit. Half the space was consumed by a queen-size bed, and the rest was filled with a red couch and matching armchair that seemed to be sinking into the concrete floor from years of use. A makeshift wooden coffee table completed the furnishings that cramped their tiny home. Two old calendars decorated the walls, as well as a faded poster I recognized immediately from a local domestic violence prevention organization.

When we met in 2009, Isaac was fifty and Edwina was forty-two. They had been together for twenty years. Both Catholic, they had four children together, the oldest a fifteen-year-old girl and the youngest a six-year-old boy. Isaac was a small, lean, energetic man with a handsome face; Edwina had a larger, more solid frame and striking high cheekbones. Isaac had worked most of his life as a casual laborer on house construction projects, but now such work was inconsistent at best. Edwina sporadically supplemented Isaac's income by selling sugarcane from their home. Their combined income barely paid the rent and provided the basics for their family. While Isaac and Edwina's struggles were typical of many families I came to know, they were grappling with an additional issue in their relationship: Isaac was HIV-positive, and Edwina was HIV-negative. A mutual friend told me they had devised their own strategy to deal with this challenge, and I met with them so I could learn more.

Over the course of two days, I spoke with Isaac and Edwina together and individually. Isaac tested HIV-positive in 2003 and believed he was infected by a partner in another, more informal long-term relationship that overlapped with his relationship with Edwina. Isaac was quite frank when discussing the relationships he had with other women during his two decades with Edwina. When Isaac learned he was infected, Edwina was pregnant and had tested negative. Isaac, however, was slow to disclose his status to Edwina, telling me he was preoccupied by his fear that she would leave him. After approximately two years, a serious illness finally prompted Isaac to tell Edwina he was HIV-positive.

When describing their current predicament as an HIV discordant couple, both Isaac and Edwina held Isaac responsible for the problems they now faced. "I am the one who made the mistake," Isaac told me. "After realizing that I had made the mistake, I really had to consider the needs of my family." He also criticized his male peers: "That is why you still see AIDS. Because a man is not able to tell a woman that he is HIV-positive. Then he keeps on loving other women."

Initially Edwina considered ending the marriage, but her concerns for their children led her to stay with Isaac. Living with discordance was especially challenging for this couple because Edwina did not want to use condoms, fearing they could break or provide inadequate protection. Edwina said she found broaching this subject with Isaac difficult. Both she and Isaac agreed that the husband was the head of the household and the ultimate decision maker. "It's the man who is the head of the family because it is the man who has *obuyinza*," Edwina said. She was nonetheless determined to devise a strategy that could protect her from HIV infection, so she demanded that they stop having sex completely.

Edwina was emboldened, in part, by ideas of women's rights. "Women's rights are a good thing," she said. "Because now women have a voice that needs to be recognized. I can say to my husband, 'Let's not do that. Let's do this instead.' And sometimes the men listen." Like most men I met in Bwaise, Isaac was ambivalent about women's rights. He was concerned it made some women too assertive and "spoiled" them. "It is good, but sometimes it becomes too much," he told me. "Some women have divorced men because of these powers given to them . . . they separate because of those freedoms. It should be limited. That's why the number of prostitutes is increasing every day. A married woman should always be only with her husband."

Edwina said Isaac initially recoiled at her suggestion that they stop having sex; only the intervention of a male relative forced his hand. Isaac finally agreed, grudgingly, to Edwina's demand, under the condition that he could still have sex with the woman who infected him. Given Isaac's health problems, I was surprised he made sex such a priority. When I talked with the couple together, Isaac implied he only took advantage of this aspect of the agreement on occasion. Alone, however, Edwina insisted that this was not at all true, that Isaac was frequently visiting this woman, as well as another woman he saw more casually. Unhappy but resigned to accept this situation, Edwina tried to make the best of it: "Because we no longer have sex together I just tell him to go and have it with that second wife, or maybe the other woman will be interested [laughs]."

Edwina's frustration with Isaac shaped her views on men generally. "With AIDS, it is good for a man to have just one wife," she said. "But there are those who still think a man can have as many sexual partners as he wants. The men still hold those views. It's not right, but they do it because of their *amaanyi*, the *amaanyi* that they say was granted to them by God. For all these things, men will say they are superior to women and that as a woman I can't stop him from doing something."

Edwina had nonetheless persevered, and for four years she and Isaac had completely abstained from having sex with each other. She was forthcoming with the details of their arrangement. "The good thing is that I made a gap between the two of us. He sleeps here, in the chair, and I sleep on the other side with my children [between us]," she said. "He knows this is best, and he does it. I think he feels good about it." When I asked him why he consented to this arrangement, Isaac emphasized the need to look after their children: "I am HIV-positive. I got it, and my wife is HIV-negative. If I spread it to her, where will this leave our children?"

The couple's lack of sexual relations appeared to be protecting Edwina from HIV infection, but it also changed the nature of their relationship. Edwina was now ambivalent about her marriage: "I am no longer interested [in the marriage]. I am here just for the sake of the children. I do love him, but the other bedroom love is now gone, but I still like him."

These changes were also evident in how Isaac described the relationship. When I asked him whether their marriage was still strong without sex, he said, "She is now my sister." Their agreement remained a sensitive issue for Isaac, and he refused to discuss the specifics of it with me, especially the fact he was not allowed to sleep in his bed with his wife. After my prodding, he eventually addressed the issue indirectly. "Do you know what a bedroom is? It is a place where secrets are kept," he said. "If you quarrel and if she refuses to have sex with you, you leave the bed and sleep somewhere down on the floor. But it is not a matter of shouting to inform everyone that your wife has refused to have sex with you." Isaac saw himself as making a difficult sacrifice for his children. Although he thought most other men would likely be unwilling to maintain a marriage without sex, he felt there were some men who would make the same decision. His other relationships no doubt provided physical and emotional comfort for him—a luxury not afforded to Edwina.

·   ·   ·   ·   ·

For over two decades, women's rights in Uganda have been actively promoted by the state, a dynamic women's movement, NGOs, and international development agencies. Women's rights have also been viewed as an essential component of Uganda's AIDS success, facilitating women's ability to negotiate safe sex and challenge the sexual privileges accorded to men (Epstein 2007; Epstein and Kim 2007). Given this salience of women's rights, it is important to understand exactly how they have shaped the ways masculinity is practiced in Bwaise. Has the promotion of women's rights limited men's authority over women? Or have the ways that women's rights have been framed and interpreted constrained how they challenge hegemonic aspects of masculinity? What are the implications for sexual relationships, especially for men's sexual privileges in the context of AIDS? And how does the context of precarious work discussed in chapter 3 matter to the ways women's rights are understood and enacted?

Isaac and Edwina's relationship reveals some ways these dynamics play out in urban Uganda, even if Edwina's ability to negotiate such an agreement was unusual. Isaac became infected with HIV pursuing sexual relationships that largely conformed to normative masculine expectations. Having multiple sexual partners made Isaac vulnerable to infection, probably in ways he himself did not fully grasp. Testing positive then created something of an existential crisis for him, something I found common among HIV-positive men in Bwaise (Wyrod 2011).

When Isaac eventually disclosed his status, he was eager to maintain his marriage because of the care it afforded him and because he was concerned about his children. Living with discordance then provided Edwina with new leverage in her marriage—leverage she used to negotiate a sexual agreement that protected her from HIV infection. Edwina was further encouraged to act by relatively new notions of women's rights, or as she put it, the fact that "women now have a voice that needs to be recognized . . . and sometimes the men listen." In addition, her sexual agreement with Isaac was premised on his recognition that her demand to stop having sex was a legitimate one and should be respected. In this sense, AIDS and women's rights worked synergistically, if modestly, to give Edwina more confidence to exert agency in their relationship. Isaac, however, agreed with Edwina's demands reluctantly, and he did not frame his decision in terms of women's rights. Instead, he aimed to portray himself as a responsible family provider concerned primarily with his children's well-being.

What made their agreement especially interesting was that even though Edwina enacted newfound agency, Isaac still insisted on maintaining his perceived male sexual privileges. Edwina voiced criticism of her husband's sexual behavior and resentment that he had brought HIV into their relationship. While Isaac acknowledged some aspects of this critique, he never questioned his right to maintain his other sexual relationships. Sexuality was, in fact, a means for Isaac to shore up his masculinity after abdicating some control in his marriage. Through their agreement, therefore, both Isaac and Edwina renegotiated certain aspects of men's rights and authority but simultaneously reinforced core features of male sexual privilege. Not being able to have sex with his wife was clearly stigmatizing for Isaac, a fact that might well make it difficult to maintain their agreement over the long term. Edwina had thus relinquished her own sexual pleasure for a safety that was tenuous.

In the remainder of this chapter, I draw on my research with nineteen cohabiting couples to present the more complete range of ways women's rights matter to gender dynamics in intimate relationships (see table A.2 for more information on my sample of couples). I focus on three relationships, each of which reveals an important aspect of how relationship power dynamics change when women's rights come home. The last relationship I discuss is emblematic of how most men and women I came to know in Bwaise grappled with women's rights in their long-term relationships.

Intimate sexual relationships are an important, and typically overlooked, arena for the production of local meanings of women's rights (figure 4.1). They are a crucial forum of social interaction in which ideas of women's rights are rebuffed, reinterpreted, and strategically redeployed. In this sense, intimate relationships are not only central to "doing gender" (West and Zimmerman 1987) but are also key to the ways women's rights are framed, invoked, and contested. As a century of feminist scholarship makes evident, the ostensibly private and personal domain of sexual intimacy and family relations is in fact deeply politicized in ways that sustain gender inequality. It is necessary, therefore, to examine the microscale social interactions in intimate relationships in order to see how women's rights become meaningful in specific social contexts and what the implications may be for how masculinity has been remade in the context of AIDS.[1]

WOMEN'S RIGHTS IN UGANDA

To understand the dynamics I observed in intimate relationships, it is helpful to begin by examining the institutionalization of women's rights

Figure 4.1. A young couple in Bwaise.

in Uganda. Chapter 2 presents a broader history of women's activism in Uganda. Here I focus on the institutionalization of women's rights. There are three primary aspects, or layers, of rights discourse comprising the complex terrain of women's rights in contemporary Kampala: the current government's promotion of women's rights, the role of the Ugandan women's movement, and the continued relevance of much older Ganda notions of rights and women's social status.

In Luganda, "human rights" is translated as *eddembe ly'obwebange* (personal rights) or *eddembe ly'obuntu* (rights of humanity). *Eddembe* can mean rights, and it can also mean freedom (as in *eddembe ly'okwogera*, freedom of speech), liberty, peace, or simply leisure (Murphy 1972, 65). Notions of eddembe were important in the precolonial kingdom of

Buganda, where rights were conferred according to communal member-ship, family ties, and individual achievement. Although it does not refer to human rights in the modern sense, eddembe continues to shape under-standings of rights among the Baganda today.

Ideas of rights were evident in precolonial Buganda; it is important to emphasize, however, that contemporary notions of equality and shared power do not easily map onto the hierarchical structure of politics and power among the Baganda. As Mikael Karlstrom (1996) discusses in his analysis of democracy in Buganda, eddembe ly'obuntu is not necessarily synonymous with Western notions of intrinsic individual rights and freedoms. Instead, it is rooted in a hierarchical system of clans and king-ship and indexes "an understanding of freedom as guaranteed by a rightly ordered polity, a society where both rulers and subjects conform to stand-ards of civility which are inseparably ethical and political" (Karlstrom 1996, 490).[2] The implications of this model of power for gender equity and equality are significant. As Karlstrom notes, a single leader at the apex of the social hierarchy is "echoed at other levels of social organization as well: every household has a single (prescriptively male) head" (491). In my fieldwork I found that certain aspects of these long-standing notions of rights and power among the Baganda remained salient today and oper-ated to largely but not exclusively impede the institutionalization of wom-en's rights and gender equality in Bwaise.

Contemporary women's rights discourse galvanized in Uganda in 1986 when Museveni's National Resistance Army seized power after a protracted guerrilla war. Museveni was inspired by socialist notions of economic and social equality and encouraged women to participate as soldiers in his rebel army. Once in power, the Museveni government considerably increased women's political participation in government (Tripp 2010, 2). This was not so much an ideological commitment to women's rights as a politically strategic move to solidify women's support for Museveni's party (Goetz 2003). Nonetheless, the Museveni regime placed issues of gender *equity* on the national agenda and gave legitimacy to claims that women should have the same political rights as men.

The Museveni government, however, never promoted a broader agenda for women's rights and empowerment that challenged patriarchal aspects of the gender order. From the 1990s to the present, the government has largely focused on providing greater equity in opportunities for individual women's advancement, especially in the realm of politics and to a lesser extent in education. This emphasis on individual women's rights, as opposed to broad-based social change, was bolstered by the large influx of Western development aid since 1986. Most development initiatives targeting women, especially those funded by the U.S. government, have also focused on promoting gender equity in government programs and policies and rarely directly address systemic social-structural issues undergirding gender inequality.

The Ugandan women's movement, in contrast, has promoted a more far-reaching agenda emphasizing gender *equality*. During the rewriting of the Ugandan Constitution in 1995, women activists successfully advocated for the inclusion of language stressing a full range of women's rights (Tripp 2000). The women's movement has also pursued a wide array of others issues, including women's landownership and changes in marriage laws, thereby moving closer to a more expansive conception of women's rights rooted in notions of economic and social rights (Ahikire 2003; Tamale 1999). The main way such ideas of gender equality have been disseminated in urban Uganda is through local and international NGOs whose work has addressed women's empowerment and community development. Such organizations are active in the Bwaise area, and many of my informants had some direct interaction with at least one.

During my fieldwork in Bwaise I investigated how this complex and dynamic terrain of women's rights is understood by ordinary men and women. I found that a new configuration of gender relations is evident in urban Uganda—one that accommodates some aspects of women's rights while retaining previous notions of men's authority over women (Wyrod 2008). The majority of men I interacted with in my fieldwork were receptive to expanded women's rights, so long as these did not undermine their authority within the home. For such men, women's rights should be limited in scope and not synonymous with equality between men and women.

Discussions of gender equality sometimes provoked quite combative and reactionary responses. As one man told me during a discussion I had with men in Bwaise, "A man will always remain a man, and superior to a woman. But because of this current storm of equality the women have now surpassed us and they are higher than us."[3] However, some women

I met and a small number of men linked women's rights to gender equality and, in the process, challenged entrenched notions of a masculinity rooted in male superiority. Nearly exclusively, the strongest advocates of gender equality I met were working with Center for Domestic Violence Prevention, the local NGO I volunteered with during my fieldwork.

Though most men and women I interviewed in Bwaise supported aspects of gender equity, gender equality was much less palatable. Men expressed concerns about women "climbing on" or "ascending over" men or asserted that in "any given society there has to be a head." Equality seemed to be interpreted as a zero-sum game in which someone has to be "bigger" than someone else (Wyrod 2008, 817).[4] Gender equity appears more compatible with Ganda ideas of politics and power because it does not contradict the notion that a single person should be at the head of any given level of society. In addition, the Ganda emphasis on individual achievement and social mobility, although conventionally related to men, may make certain aspects of advancing women's status through gender equity more culturally acceptable than the notion of men and women sharing power.

Both men and women saw the government as the main advocate of women's rights, which had important implications for how women's rights were debated and wrestled with in everyday life (figure 4.2). Tension over women's rights focused largely on a limited agenda that promoted gender equity, while systemic challenges posed by notions of gender equality were rebuffed by most men and many women. Criticisms of women's rights discourse, therefore, occurred on many different fronts, including critiques of the government's politically motivated promotion of women's rights, overreaching by Ugandan women activists, and neocolonial meddling by Westerners. This was often voiced in a variety of ways, from the president "spoiling" Ugandan women to women activists making women "big headed" to women and some men "acting like whites" in their support of women's rights and gender equality. Yet it was also clear that people viewed women's rights, in whatever variant, as at least partially woven into the fabric of contemporary gender relations. This chapter takes this recognition as its starting point to explore how women's rights were rebuffed, mobilized, and, much more frequently, carefully negotiated in intimate relationships.

Figure 4.2. A family outside their home in Bwaise.

WHEN WOMEN'S RIGHTS COME HOME

Samuel and Sophie: Rights Rebuffed

Reaching Samuel and Sophie's home required burrowing deep into the oldest and densest residential section of Bwaise. Their compound was one of the original homes in Bwaise, which over the decades had become surrounded by *buzigo* (modest one-room houses for rent). The narrow, snaking alleys that led to their home were rather suffocating, and arrival at their small courtyard provided much-needed space and air.

Samuel, a fifty-two-year-old Catholic, had lived in Bwaise his entire life, having inherited this home from his father. Sophie, thirty-eight and Muslim, was also born in Kampala. When she was sixteen her grandfather, Samuel's good friend, arranged her marriage to Samuel. Both Samuel and Sophie had a year or two of secondary school education, and they had raised five children together, making them fairly typical of families in Bwaise. Their only money came from modest rental income for rooms in their compound. As I would come to learn, this small compound comprised most of Sophie's world.

When interviewed together, Sophie let her husband answer my questions. Samuel described their marriage as a happy one, and both agreed the man was the leader in the home. Samuel was quick to qualify this, however: "She also has some authority. . . . We share the power, so if she says no to something, I leave it. Because she can also be the leader in the home." Samuel acknowledged that their financial problems produced stress in their relationship, and in a rare interjection, Sophie made clear she was eager to work but did not have the capital to start a business.

When I spoke with Samuel alone, he again strove to portray his marriage as harmonious. He described himself as the authority but said that he listened to, consulted with, and trusted his wife. When asked specifically about his attitudes toward women's rights, Samuel replied, "It is good, giving them rights. Because it isn't good to harass your wife. So women's rights, it stops men from beating and abusing them. This gives a woman freedom, so, yeah, it's good. . . . Let us also be like whites. Like, do you think you can beat a white wife? How can you beat her? The police will come for you." Samuel continued, saying that a woman could now even be the leader in a home, "free to make any decision she likes." "Yes," he added, "let them be equal. It's a good thing!" Knowing Samuel was likely tailoring his answers for me, I pressed him further. He conceded he was not fully comfortable with the changes he perceived, and he shifted from talking about violence against women to women earning their own money.

> Yes, we men are somewhat beleaguered now. We used to be with a lot of power, which isn't the case these days. Now the wife might have much more money as compared to you. Are you aware of these changes? You are her husband, but she has much more money than you. So don't you think that such a wife can do whatever she feels like? . . . [But] there is always someone

who is better than others, so the man remains above the woman. However small the power he has over her now, the man still remains above the woman.

Although Samuel's insistence that men ultimately remained superior was typical of men I met in Bwaise, as we continued to talk I realized Samuel was not so typical after all. There was a profound disconnect between his endorsement of certain ideas of women's rights and the reality of his relationship with Sophie. For Samuel, having a much younger wife presented potential problems—problems he had worked hard to contain throughout their relationship. "Young women are faced with so many challenges because they are not settled," he told me. "It is so hard to control them!" When I asked if Samuel trusted his wife, he replied confidently and proudly:

Ah, ah, ah, that is not a problem! That's because she is always at home all the time. People in the area don't even know she exists! [Laughs] She doesn't even know where markets and shops are. Ah, ah, ah, no, she doesn't. And whenever I give her money, she just gives it to our children to go and buy food. She doesn't go there to the market. She doesn't even know that area or even any of the shops. . . . So can you say that she is a bad woman? No! She's a good woman, and that's why she is not just walking all around!

Thus it emerged that Samuel was in fact very controlling and took pride in keeping his wife under close surveillance during their long relationship.

When Sophie was interviewed alone, she used the opportunity to vent her frustration and did not hide her contempt for her husband.[5] "Ha, my husband! The only thing I like about him is that he has supported me all the time we've been together. Only that and nothing else," she said. "I find myself just having to stay and live with him. I have to stay with him, but there is no such thing as love." When asked who made the decisions in the home, Sophie replied somewhat impatiently, "Well, obviously it's my husband. He has more power than me."

Perhaps not surprisingly, Sophie supported the idea of promoting women's rights, saying, "It is good. That means they are helping the woman, so that women are not being violated. It also helps the woman to make her own decisions." However, she did not feel women had the same rights as men: "The man is always different. He possesses more power and the women have less power. The men are always above the women." While it was difficult to determine for certain if Sophie thought this perceived gender status quo was acceptable, she did make it clear that she was unhappy and felt fairly powerless in her own relationship.

Sophie saw working as a big part of the solution to her problems, and she was clearly frustrated that she had few options. "I spend most all of my time around this house. I rarely go out," she confided. Her ambitions were modest and amounted to selling produce or other food items in the nearby market, but Samuel was not supportive.

In addition to earning money, Sophie was preoccupied with family planning and her sexual health in general. When I spoke with the couple together, Samuel insisted that he had been faithful to Sophie since their marriage, and he bristled at the notion of using condoms. "I'm not a womanizer, so we don't need to use condoms. We are both mature," he said. "And family planning? No, we don't go into such things." Surprisingly, Sophie interjected, "I do use family planning. I decided to. It was me. Me alone." Samuel appeared unfazed and replied, "I don't know about those things."

When alone, Sophie elaborated, saying that her decision to use contraceptive injections secretly was motivated by Samuel's refusal to use condoms. "I talked about them and he got angry so I gave up on that," Sophie said. "He rejected the condoms, even recently when asked about them, saying he didn't want to know anything about them. He refused to use them, again saying he was only interested in going live [having sex without a condom]."

Condoms were also attractive to Sophie because of the looming threat of HIV. She said she had remained monogamous in her marriage and had no evidence that Samuel had ever been unfaithful in twenty years of marriage. When I spoke with them together, Samuel was adamant that Sophie was his only sexual partner and said he even took special precautions, like only drinking alcohol near his home to avoid temptation. "I've decided [to remain monogamous], not because I'm Catholic, but that is what I decided in my heart," he told me. "I don't have any other sexual partner. Likewise, she doesn't have any other partner. So where will we catch AIDS?"

Nonetheless, suspicions seemed to linger for Sophie. "You know men's ways, he may have one and he refuses to show you," she said when interviewed alone. "He can't let you know. You may get angry, but if he has already made the decision, often you are left with no option because he has simply decided it is so." Sophie also said neither she nor Samuel had ever taken an HIV test, something Samuel confirmed when I spoke to him alone. While Samuel said he had no interest in testing, Sophie felt differently.

> I have never tested. Testing is not a simple task. It is easy to give out the blood sample, but waiting for the results, umm. When they tell you that you are positive, it's like you die instantly. I will test, but it is a sacrifice. The health workers have come here repeatedly to test us, but I told them to give me some time. Yes, I am planning to test, but I am scared. I am very scared.

According to Sophie, dealing with HIV was a burden she would have to carry alone; Samuel would never consider testing with her, and if he had the test alone he would not disclose his results. "He is not a kind of person who makes time to talk with me about these or other issues," Sophie said. "He has never talked about it. He can't accept dealing with it." Samuel confirmed this when I was with him and asked if he ever talked with Sophie about preventing HIV infection. "I rarely sit down with my wife and have a conversation," he said. "I don't have the time. I'm always look-ing for money. Actually, I think it's bad to talk too much to your wife because then she will only suspect you have another wife or girlfriend."

Sadly, four months after completing my fieldwork I learned from a close friend that Sophie had died. My friend was a community health worker who had known Sophie well. She said Sophie had tuberculosis, and although no HIV test was done she suspected Sophie was in fact HIV-positive. Before she died, Sophie told my friend repeatedly she thought Samuel had infected her. My friend also reported that during the last few months of her illness Samuel had moved Sophie from the main house to a room deep in their compound where she could not be seen.

The story of Samuel and Sophie indicates how easy it can be to appear to conform to certain notions of women's rights, something Samuel likely felt compelled to do when speaking with me. Women's rights influenced this intimate relationship in only the most limited way, primarily serving as a way for Samuel to project an image of himself to me as a man versed in the new discourses of gender equity. In a relationship defined by a large age difference and a semiarranged marriage in which Samuel was firmly in control, it was a simple matter to espouse such ideas, knowing he was not compelled to practice them. He knew women's rights did little to challenge the gender status quo in his home—a status quo that Samuel suggested he was quite content with and that served his needs well.

Sophie expressed support of aspects of women's rights, yet she was a realist. Her male-dominated marriage made it impossible to gain leverage from the prevailing limited notion of women's rights as gender equity. While she found areas where she could demonstrate her agency and independence, notably with family planning, her life was profoundly constrained by her husband. Thus in the context of this relationship it was not surprising that Sophie was ambivalent about women's rights, viewing them as something theoretically beneficial but largely irrelevant to her daily existence.

Wilfred and Phoebe: Rights Mobilized

Nearly every morning and late afternoon, Wilfred stood in front of his home presiding over a large, blackened wok. For an hour or two, he methodically plopped tan batter into caramel-colored oil, waited patiently for the deep-brown fried maandazi to float to the surface, and then scooped them out of the wok. Once he had a batch of several dozen, he filled a plastic tub with the cakes and delivered them to his clients in and around Bwaise. If all went well, the maandazi generated $2 to $3 in profit a day.

I first met Wilfred, a Catholic in his mid-forties, with some secondary school education, in 2004. In contrast to Samuel, Wilfred was a more typical example of how men in Bwaise attempted to accommodate new notions of gender equity and equality while still retaining their authority over their wives and families. His home, deeper in the more residential section of Bwaise, was a five-minute walk from the Kibira carpentry workshop where I apprenticed. Only ten feet wide and twenty feet deep, it was akin to a narrow, one-story townhouse nestled between two storefronts, constructed of orange bricks partially covered with tan plaster. The concrete foundation raised the house only a few inches off the dirt and provided minimal protection from the regular floods. Punched through the front of his home were two large square holes where he hoped to install windows some day. A steel grate draped with a white sheet served as the door.

In the past, Wilfred had found additional work with Plan International, an NGO that funded sanitation, education, and sexual health programs in Bwaise. This work provided a modest stipend, as well as occasional workshops that exposed Wilfred to notions of women's rights, gender equality, and development. However, the NGO ended their program unexpectedly during my initial fieldwork, leaving Wilfred with only the money from his maandazi to provide for his wife and two young children. Wilfred admitted that being the provider was a struggle, and he stoically suggested this was just the burden men faced: "In Uganda a real man has to be responsible for looking after his family and providing all that's needed in the family."

Wilfred was quite proud of his relationship with Phoebe, a thirty-three-year-old Catholic with a year of secondary schooling to whom he had been informally married for seven years. "They won't give you any respect as a man without a wife," he told me, "even if you are fifty years old." Wilfred had four children from relationships with three women during his twenties, relationships he did not consider serious. His current relationship was different, however; for him it was emblematic of his maturity as a respectable man.

Wilfred's views on masculinity and gender relations were complex. When I asked him if men and women were equal, he strove to balance women's rights and empowerment with his notion of male authority.

> Now a woman can do anything that a man can do. For instance, in the past times there were no women doctors, but now there are women doctors. So biologically they are not equal, but in work they are equal. Which is a good thing. Considering the rate at which the world is moving, it's good because it brings development.

Wilfred's distinction between biological sex and gender was somewhat unusual for men in Bwaise, as was his moderate openness to notions of gender equality. This was a departure from the government's emphasis on gender equity, and I suspected it reflected Wilfred's involvement with Plan. When I then asked Wilfred if men and women were equal in the home, he replied:

They are not equal in the home but the reality is that there are now challenges that arise where a woman surpasses the man because she has more money than a man. The woman might want *okulinnya ku musajja* [to dominate the husband],[6] and eventually the man won't be able to question the time at which the wife comes back from work, even if it is 11:00 P.M.. . . And another thing that is coming up nowadays is that women have started *okuwasa abasajja* [to marry men]![7] If a young man does not have money, an older woman may marry him!

Wilfred also expressed concerns about how changing gender relations affected an important aspect of manhood—owning property.

Culturally, in the past, it was the man who was supposed to have power over his property. But as things are changing, more problems are coming up. There are many laws enacted in favor of the woman, giving her powers, including over property. That's why you see that there are many challenges in families.

As much as Wilfred viewed greater opportunities for women as promoting development, it was disorienting to come to terms with a world in which women now married men, were doctors, and whose daughters may inherit their land.

For Wilfred, certain aspects of such changes were positive. For example, he claimed to be critical of domestic violence as an outdated, excessive, and inhumane exhibition of men's authority. "In the past, men wanted to prove that they had power, and that's the reason why they beat their wives," he told me. "But as the world has kept on developing, now men have learned that we are all human beings." In other respects, however, Wilfred was still grappling with how these changes affected the meaning of manhood in Uganda.

What it means to be a true man has started changing recently with the coming of equality of men and women. Now women make their own money, they have built houses, bought cars, and they own businesses. Generally, a woman will look at herself and see that she can provide for herself with all that a man should have provided. So it has reduced the things that constituted a real man.

Wilfred's views were typical of how many men in Bwaise understood shifting gender relations. I was intrigued by his attempts to come to terms with a changing society, and when I left Uganda in 2004, I was hopeful he and his family could find modest happiness in Bwaise.

When I returned in 2009, I had no trouble finding Wilfred. He was living in the same house, and on my first visit I found him in his usual spot frying maandazi. The years had not been kind to Wilfred. His potbelly was much more pronounced, his face was puffy, and he seemed sluggish and tired. He explained that his work was largely unchanged, but his family life was drastically different. He and Phoebe were now separated. Their two children were still living with him, as was Phoebe, but they considered their informal marriage officially over. I was disheartened to hear the news. Wilfred and Phoebe still wanted me to interview them but individually, and I suspected both were eager to tell me their versions of why their marriage had unraveled.

When Wilfred and I spoke, he said their troubles began two years after I had first met him. He and Phoebe had become embroiled in a conflict over their home, which Wilfred owned, and which included an adjoining storefront that was now a modest bar. For a man like Wilfred, this property was a considerable asset, worth several thousand dollars. In 2006, Wilfred took out a large bank loan using this property as collateral. Unfortunately, he defaulted on the loan. The bank would have seized his home if Phoebe had not intervened and saved their property with her own money.

Phoebe had been working for years and had amassed significant savings. She started small, selling charcoal, tomatoes, and banana leaves, and then received an infusion of capital from cattle that her family sold back in her natal village. Phoebe used this money to expand her business, first selling bananas and then moving up to waragi, the potent, locally brewed gin. It was Phoebe who had set up the simple bar in their adjoining storefront—a business that proved quite lucrative and that allowed her to occasionally earn more than Wilfred.

When Phoebe covered Wilfred's loan she did so under one condition—that Wilfred would sign a written agreement stating she was now the owner of the property. Wilfred consented, saying he did not think she would ever use this agreement against him.[8] However, at some point Phoebe decided she wanted to end their relationship and was determined to sell the property and leave him. Wilfred's concerns in 2004 about women with money and property challenging men's authority now seemed prescient.

I learned that Phoebe had been quite savvy and strategic about securing control over the property, and she was not afraid to make their conflict increasingly public. She first went to a local legal aid NGO, the Uganda Association of Women Lawyers (FIDA), then to the police, then to local government officials, and finally to court. Wilfred eventually decided to concede ownership, settling out of court and allowing Phoebe to receive most of the money from the sale of the property. In his mind, Wilfred did what was honorable and also prioritized the needs of his children.

"I could have sold that house without her consent. She would just see that she was being sent away," he told me. "But we had an agreement. And I also realized that my children were involved. So then I had to settle the matter, for the children." Other men, he said, would have resorted to violence and never agreed to any settlement: "You hear some people kill their wives. Do bad things. They cut off their heads and do whatever. But in my mind I couldn't think about such things ... I've been a community resource person. I learned about people's legal rights. So I had a bit of knowledge, I was a bit knowledgeable. That's why I approached things in the simple way I did." Wilfred's depression, however, was palpable. After all, he had lost his wife, his property, and his children and would now be forced to rent and live alone.

By selling the property and ending the marriage, Phoebe had ostensibly forced Wilfred out of his own home—an extreme thing for a husband to do to his wife, let alone a wife to do to her husband. Wilfred gave me no indication of why his wife would have taken such a drastic step. Instead, he portrayed himself as a victim of a deceptive and empowered wife. Phoebe was eager to give me her side of the story, but she was leery of provoking Wilfred by speaking with me. After several canceled interviews, we eventually met in her simple bar next door to their home during a time she knew Wilfred would be off selling his maandazi.

Phoebe wanted to make clear that a confluence of factors had led her to end their marriage. "He was harassing me, he doesn't pay school fees for the children, he doesn't buy food for the children," she told me. "He also has other women outside our marriage, including the mothers of his other children. I also fear AIDS because he has so many other women. So I decided to leave him." Phoebe described chasing away one of Wilfred's girlfriends and said she was concerned "he still has his *malaaya* [prostitute]."

Phoebe's list of accusations—neglect, infidelity, and domestic violence—was denied by Wilfred but certainly plausible given what I knew about relationships in Bwaise. Phoebe no doubt saw me as a potential resource for herself and her family, like nearly everyone I interacted with my field-work. And gaining the sympathy of an American muzungu might lead to some kind of support from me now or in the future. What exactly had transpired in their relationship between my periods of fieldwork I could not know for certain, but Phoebe wanted to make it clear to me that she saw her relationship problems interwoven with AIDS. She asserted that the violations she endured were particularly egregious because they heightened her risk of HIV infection.

I pressed Phoebe for the main reason she wanted to end the relation-ship with Wilfred. "The major factor was taking away my money," she said. "Because when he gets his money, he takes it for gambling. So it was not because of the AIDS issue that made us separate, but it is the money issue." She described where Wilfred gambled: a notorious gambling den tucked in an alley behind Bwaise's largest club. Tall papyrus reeds shielded the gamblers, most of whom were older men with money to lose, from prying eyes. A man like Wilfred could easily have gotten in over his head. "When I realized that he started taking away my money," Phoebe said, "I had to respond. It was one thing to take away my money, but when our children do not have school fees, anything to eat, medical care, it wasn't just a women's issue anymore."

Once Phoebe had given up on the marriage, she was adept at mobiliz-ing the resources she needed to sell the property. One of them was FIDA, the legal aid NGO; she was proud to tell me that hers was one of FIDA's most high profile cases. "Whenever they get white visitors from abroad, like Europe, they call me so I can talk with them about my case," she said. Phoebe had few regrets about her decision, even though she intimated that others might view her actions as too extreme. Of the nineteen couples I interviewed in 2009, this was the most dramatic example of a woman challenging her husband's authority. Women initiating divorce or separa-tion, it should be noted, has a long history among the Baganda. However, the contemporary context of women's rights, and the associated resources now available to women, facilitated Phoebe's actions in new and unprecedented ways—a point Wilfred himself alluded to when I spoke with him.

Significantly, Phoebe did not explicitly refer to *eddembe ly'abakyala* (women's rights) when telling me how she responded to the problems in her marriage. She did not emphasize that her eddembe were being violated by Wilfred's alleged violence and financial neglect or that she had a right to sell their home. Instead, Phoebe repeatedly spoke of *emirembe* (peace), saying her actions were necessary to restore some peace in her life. "I did not have emirembe in my marriage," Phoebe told me several times. "So I decided to sell off the house because there wasn't emirembe at all. But I am free now. I have a little emirembe and I am no longer quarreling." Phoebe did not portray herself as the victor in her battle with Wilfred but instead said, "I am saving my life. I did these things simply because I want *obulamu* [life, well-being]." In this sense, Phoebe was similar to most women in the couples I studied in that she strategically drew on the resources that came with the promotion of women's rights while simultaneously downplaying aspects of women's rights discourse that could be perceived as clashing with established ideas of "proper" femininity and womanhood. Yet Phoebe was also an outlier among women in Bwaise because of the extent to which she was willing to challenge her husband's authority (especially over land issues) and her skill at mobilizing the resources she needed to accomplish her goals. If Sophie and Samuel were at one end of the gender-power spectrum, Phoebe and Wilfred were at the other.

Phoebe expressed sympathy for Wilfred, knowing full well this outcome was most likely devastating for him. "If I had a bad heart, I wouldn't still give him my money. But I take care of him because he is the father of my children," she told me. "[When I stay here], I cook food for him. I wash and iron for him. I make his bed. I do all that because I have a good heart. And I don't want domestic violence happening all the time." Wilfred was more ambivalent about the end of his marriage and the prospect of a future alone. "I was thinking there would be peace in my marriage," he told me. "Everything was going to be good, and there would be peace, there would be development."

Wilfred and Phoebe's relationship was fraught with tensions over women's changing roles in society and the status of men's authority. These changes allowed Phoebe to extricate herself from a relationship she viewed as highly problematic, and in a way that provided some financial cushion. Wilfred, in contrast, largely saw himself as a victim of, or perhaps noble martyr to, these changes. Persistent financial problems heated their conflicts and brought them to a boil, eventually ending the relationship. In a densely packed community like Bwaise, the troubles this couple faced were likely well known and no doubt interpreted in many ways. For men like Wilfred, and more reactionary men, this was a cautionary tale of how men were losing out in this new era of more equitable gender relations. For some women, this was likely interpreted as a success story of how a woman could confront a feckless husband and win. Most women, however, would probably have an ambivalent take, sympathetic with Phoebe's struggles to provide for her children but wary of tactics that directly confronted her husband's authority in the home.

Wilfred's and Phoebe's relationship underscores the extent to which urban poverty shapes relationship dynamics, including the ways women's rights discourse is framed and mobilized. For Phoebe, the fundamental problem in her marriage was Wilfred's failure to embody the male provider ideal. Emboldened by both her own capacity to earn money and by resources now available to women, Phoebe was willing and able to take drastic action—action she felt was best for herself and her family. While many men and some women see women's rights as threatening to marital harmony, in the context of poverty and chronic male underemployment this threat is significantly amplified. Men's precarious work, women working, and relatively new notions of women's rights combine to produce gender trouble. Even in relationships like this one, where the man was somewhat open to ideas of gender equity and equality, these tensions can destabilize, and in this case end, already stressed intimate relationships. Importantly, although Phoebe complained about Wilfred's alleged sexual behavior, it was his inability to fulfill the male provider ideal that ultimately prompted her dramatic and decisive action.

Musa, Madina, and Rashmi: Rights Negotiated

As a purveyor of traditional medicine, Musa possessed special knowledge he worked hard to exploit to earn a living. While his expertise was limited, his friends often referred to him as *musawo* (doctor), which brought a proud smile to his face. His makeshift pharmacy was in the dense center of Bwaise, in what appeared to be an abandoned storage shed. Most mornings Musa could be found in the dilapidated structure mixing small vats of his specialty—a thick, purple cough syrup. After filling brown bottles and affixing his custom label, he would load up his backpack to peddle his wares throughout Bwaise.

Musa, a Muslim, was in his early forties, with a stocky build and a bit of a belly. With only two years of secondary school education, Musa knew his options for earning money were limited, and he diligently tried to capitalize on his tiny niche market. Unfortunately, his work as a musawo generated a meager income of about a dollar a day. He had been with his first wife, Madina, for over a decade, and they had two children together. She was Muslim as well, and although she was only twenty-eight years old her solid frame and full face made her look more like a middle-aged woman. When I first met Musa in 2004, he discussed a short-lived affair with another woman and said he would like to have another wife if only he could afford it. In 2006, he had taken that step and had informally married his second wife, Rashmi, an energetic and youthful-looking twenty-four-year-old Muslim, and they had one child. While Musa claimed to be happy splitting his time between his two households, he was clearly struggling to support both families.

I spoke with Musa alone about what he viewed as an ideal marriage. His response was harmony, peace, and mutual understanding. Musa claimed that both wives largely met these expectations, and there was little quarreling. He saw his first wife as more ideal, though, because they were formally married and he had paid her bride-price. "She is better than the other one," Musa told me. "This one does everything I ask, knowing that her bride-price was paid." Thus Musa's notion of marital harmony combined an emphasis on collaboration with an assumption that the husband should be respected as the authority in the home. For Musa, this authority required reinforcement in certain circumstances: "You may tell [your wife] to do something and she instead quarrels with you, and when you are upset you can beat her."

Musa's views on women's rights reflected this tension between domestic harmony and threats to male authority.

It's good to observe the rights of a woman. It even brings happiness in the home. . . . The problem is that when the women heard of the rights granted by the president some of them misunderstood it. They tend to go beyond their limits. So everything you do to her she will think of reporting to the police because she has her rights. So you keep questioning her moral character and whether rights mean misbehavior.

Musa's views on women's rights were fairly typical for men in Bwaise in that he sought a balance between the promotion of certain aspects of rights and the defense of men's role as leaders in the home. Interestingly, his concerns about women's alleged (sexual) misbehavior suggested that he saw women's rights as potentially giving women greater sexual freedom. This tacit acknowledgment of the socially constructed nature of women's sexuality (and sexuality generally) was voiced by many other men, especially given perceptions of women's increasing economic independence. Musa was grappling with the meaning of gender equality in a similar manner.

Men and women would be equal, but some women go beyond their limits. The reason they are not equal is that it is the man who got the woman and married her and brings her to his home and he looks after her. But there are certain instances she will abuse you because she has her rights. It brings peace in the house, but at the same time there are some who misuse it.

What separated Musa from a man like Samuel was that his grappling with the meaning of women's rights had real consequences in his relationship. His relationships were sites in which the meanings of rights were still congealing, and for his wives the right to work and earn their own money was of central importance.

Madina was born in a village west of Kampala. Her sister had helped arrange her marriage to Musa when Madina was sixteen. When I spoke with her alone, Madina strove to project an image of herself as a polite, well-mannered, and dutiful wife. "I totally agree to do what my husband wants me to do," she told me at first, "and that's what makes him happy." She then added, "But let me tell you this, for whatever we have discussed, I try to lead him in what we can do. . . . The man has more power in the home. But he listens to me."

Madina's views on women's rights were complex and echoed her husband's concerns about rights threatening harmonious marriages.

> Women's rights. On one side it is a good thing, but on the other side it is aimed at undermining men. . . . The good thing about it is that they gave us a voice—that if he does something wrong I will go to the police and report him. That is the difference that is there, but the rest is bad. Most of the women are now stubborn. That's why you see that families are breaking up day and night. Because the women now have a voice, they feel they can speak all the time. . . . [Such behavior] is impossible because that is what our culture dictates. That is the natural way of our culture, and it must stay that way. That's how it is supposed to be. I personally want it that way, when the man is the one who has more power and authority [in the home]. That's always good.

Madina's relationship with Musa, however, was complicated by the fact that she was working, selling goods in downtown Kampala, making more money than Musa. This was a point of pride for Madina, and she claimed it meant she had a large say in the important decisions they made as a couple. However, she was also very concerned about exercising this power within the established bounds of female decorum. To her, women who suggested men and women were equal were poorly raised, and such disrespect was a clear indication the woman lacked empisa, character. She was therefore diligent about remaining tactful in the way she exerted her power in her relationship. "I do not get upset, but I just sit with my husband, and I tell him that what you have done is wrong," she said. "But I don't ever say a word or even comment on whether anything is right or wrong in front of visitors."

Madina's work outside the home was something she had fought for in her relationship, and fought for intensely. Three years before I met Musa and Madina, their relationship had gone through a crisis. Madina had purchased an expensive television with her own money, and Musa had taken it from their home without consulting her. As Madina suspected, Musa had given the television as a gift to another woman—to Rashmi, the woman who would become his second wife. Furious, Madina left Musa and returned to her parents' home in her village. She seriously considered divorcing Musa, but her parents advised her to be patient and wait for Musa to realize his mistake. The strategy was successful, and Musa did seek her forgiveness.

The intriguing twist in this story is that Madina used this crisis to demand her husband's permission to work in downtown Kampala (but she did not demand Musa break off his relationship with Rashmi). Madina had, in fact, been secretly running a business in the city center selling her own hand-sewn clothes for two years before the television incident. She never told Musa because she believed he would have forbidden it, and the television crisis provided Madina's opportunity to force Musa's hand. "I decided to stay in the marriage because he knows I am working and he can't beat me up. He fears to harm me. And also when I am working I am able to support myself," she told me. "I have *eddembe* because of having my own money. So, so much."

When I asked if she still considered leaving Musa, she replied, "The reason I don't think about it anymore is because every type of support I need, I can get it myself now. So I thought it would be a waste of time, and I decided to use my self-sufficiency to protect my reputation and the *ekitiibwa* [respect] I have as a married woman." Madina was striving to strike a balance between maintaining her empisa (character), gaining and exercising eddembe (rights), and earning ekitiibwa (respect), from her peers and husband. It was a delicate balance to maintain, but in the context of her relationship she appeared to be succeeding, and this balance had reestablished a degree of harmony in her relationship with Musa.

Madina was fairly typical of many women I met in Bwaise who were striving to capitalize on the new possibilities presented by women's rights within the limits of established notions of proper femininity. When I spoke with Musa alone, he talked about slowly coming to accept such changes in their relationship, especially those related to Madina's work. "You get used to it," he told me. "Especially if she is not the kind of women susceptible to bad *empisa*." This is not to suggest that Musa had become completely comfortable with Madina, or Rashmi, working outside the home. He valued their contribution to the household finances and recognized to some degree that women had a right to work, but he felt their independence needed to be monitored carefully. "You keep running personal investigations about their behaviors at work," he told me. "But generally you find that all your expectations are wrong. Because you will see that whenever she finishes work she comes directly home."

While notions of women's rights created suspicions among men like Musa, especially the suspicion that his wife was being wooed by another man while she was working, he suggested that he had come to have new respect for Madina. He saw her as rather difficult to control now, or "big headed" as he put it, but emphasized that she had maintained her good character and did not neglect what Musa saw as her wifely duties. Thus, in Musa's eyes as well, Madina appeared to have succeeded in her attempt to claim new forms of eddembe, and even ekitiibwa, while maintaining her empisa. The couple had reached a compromise, without infringing on Musa's sexual privilege.

These dynamics were tied to ongoing apprehensions Madina had about her relationship that surfaced most palpably with respect to AIDS. Madina was concerned, even fatalistic, about becoming infected with HIV.

> I am concerned about AIDS because the other wife may be promiscuous. After all, my husband snatched her when she was with another man. Most of the women I see these days have many partners. But what I do is every three months I go and get an HIV test to see how my life is progressing. So one day when God denies me his grace and I get a problem with HIV, I will know right away and be able to start the medication as soon as I need it.

Madina was uncertain about Musa's status because he refused to use condoms and to test for HIV with her. "He will never say no outright, but he simply refuses to ever test," she told me. "The only thing that could force him to go for testing at this point is if I tell him that am going to divorce him if he doesn't test [laughs]." When I spoke with Musa alone, he acknowledged that both his wives were quite worried about AIDS. He claimed to have tested with them and shared his test results with them, something both wives emphatically denied. The context of AIDS, therefore, made it more difficult for Madina to negotiate Musa's sexual behavior and privileges, even if the consequences were potentially life threatening.

Madina's cowife, Rashmi, was grappling with similar issues, and her status as the second, younger wife created its own complications. When interviewed alone, she said:

> Women's rights, it's a good thing. . . . Now we can work in all places. And even the world has developed because of this. So, yes, I need to work. Yes, yes, yes. Because when you work, you can get money and your *eddembe*. And when you have money, you can have *eddembe*. But no money, no *eddembe*.

Rashmi expressed some ambivalence about whether men and women should be viewed as equals: "We are all equal. . . . In general, I would say I have rights to do this and that, but still the man has more rights than me." But she clearly stated that women earning their own money had significant implications for relationship dynamics.

> It is the man who leads you. When you are at home, there should be a leader who leads you, who takes on all the responsibilities at home. That is why he is better than you. . . . But it should be changed! Because also we women, we also have responsibilities. . . . It has changed. The one who has money is the boss. In order for a woman to be the leader at home, she should have money. But for a man, even if he doesn't have money, he can still lead the home.

For Rashmi, work was a central preoccupation, and she saw her marriage as beneficial in this regard. Polygamous men, she said, were under financial pressure to allow their wives to work in order to provide for two or more families. Rashmi herself had benefited from this: Musa had provided the capital for her to start her own hair salon. This support from Musa was, in fact, one of the qualities Rashmi liked most about him: "You know what we like most about men is when you get a man who gives you *eddembe nga eryoobuntu* [human rights]. My husband gives me rights. But there are those men who refuse to let their wives to go and work. But mine gives me my rights and I go and work." Unlike Madina, Rashmi did not refrain from using starker terms to discuss the implications of women working.

> There are times when the man goes to work and he doesn't get any money. Then it is up to you, the wife, to look after a home. You can also pay the rent to the landlord. So you're doing what? You're now acting as a husband. You take on the responsibility because the husband cannot. . . . When such a time comes, for those of us who are working, we can act as husbands.

Rashmi went even further: "If I get money when he has not gotten any, I can build my house and I'll take him from a rental house to my house." As Rashmi knew, this would be a dramatic deviation from conventional gender norms, which dictated that a man married a woman and brought his wife to his own home.

When I spoke with Rashmi and Musa together, Rashmi was equally assertive. As with Samuel and Sophie, family planning emerged as a critical relationship issue. Rashmi revealed that she was using contraceptive injections, a decision that, like Sophie, she had made on her own. I was actually taken aback by just how assertive Rashmi was in discussing this issue with her husband present.

> I can tell him to wait until we get more money and then I can resume having children. . . . So I need to first increase my earnings to the level of being able to properly dress two children. So that is why I tell him I won't have more children. I can only manage one child. A second child! Ha! [Laughs] Not until I notice a change in this household. Then I can be forced [to stop using contraception] but not until I realize there is a change.

While Rashmi spoke with a great deal of confidence about her right to use contraception, it emerged that the issue was more complex and difficult for the couple. Rashmi said the injections were causing serious complications, including excessive bleeding and, most problematically, a decline in her libido. She pointed out that this was a very difficult relationship issue, and Musa interjected, "If she doesn't have the appetite and you do have it, you simply go ahead with the action. At times she regains the appetite along the way as you have sex." Rashmi laughed nervously and said she feared this problem might drive Musa to get another wife.

In her interview alone, Rashmi discussed these issues in greater detail and conceded that her control over when to have sex was sometimes limited.

> He can't force me to have sex when I don't want to. I might come back very tired, and he can also see that. I say no I don't want to [have sex] and he accepts. . . . [But] sometimes we get misunderstandings, like when I refuse and he forces me to have sex. It happens. . . . That is what I would like to change, just for him to listen to me whenever I tell him that I am not in the mood.

I was deeply troubled by Rashmi's suggestion that Musa had committed what I would consider marital rape. I did not ask Musa directly about this accusation, uncertain what consequences such probing would have for Rashmi. Yet when I spoke with him alone he confirmed there was a limit to his tolerance of Rashmi's use of family planning.

> It will become a big problem if I keep telling her [to stop using family plan-
> ning] and she still refuses. . . . In fact, you might think about it and at times
> you react with anger to show her that it is not a good thing to do. If she
> knows what is good for her she will stop using the injections so that we can
> have another child.

Musa linked these problems over family planning with Rashmi's work.
"She is so preoccupied by her job. She will tell me that if she gets pregnant
she won't be able to go to work," he said. "She really is just so much taken
up by the money." Musa seemed to be losing patience with Rashmi and
suggested that he might take action in the near future to limit her control
over family planning and to rein in her attention to her hair salon. Like
Madina, Rashmi was proactively asserting her agency in her marriage, but
unlike Madina, her approach placed her at greater risk of a backlash.

Rashmi shared Madina's concerns about AIDS but was slightly less
fatalistic about becoming infected.

> Before I started using family planning, I told him about condoms and he
> was very angry about it. He asked me, "How could a husband use condoms
> with his wife?" . . . I am very worried about AIDS. But so long as I am faith-
> ful, and if my husband is faithful too and doesn't get another partner, and if
> my cowife is faithful, then there is a chance we might survive it.

Rashmi also complained about Musa's unwillingness to consider testing
together for HIV. Like Madina, therefore, there was a sense of frustration
and powerlessness in how Rashmi talked about her vulnerability to HIV.
This was a stark contrast to her assertiveness about working and even her
more cautious insistence on controlling the couple's family planning.

Overall, the context of a polygamous family provided interesting, and
rather unexpected, opportunities for Madina and Rashmi to reframe
notions of women's rights. Both women were leery of more expansive
notions of women's rights rooted in gender equality, and each strove in her
own way to balance ideas of rights with "proper" wifely comportment and
maintaining marital harmony. However, both women emphasized the
centrality of a woman's right to work. In this way they reframed the discourse of rights to focus on women's economic security. This is not to suggest that women in Bwaise were in any sense money hungry; their preoccupation with money was rooted in the relentless financial pressures

families in Bwaise felt as they struggled to provide the basics for themselves and their children. The financial and emotional demands of maintaining a polygamous marriage made Musa receptive to certain aspects of how his wives reframed women's rights. He enabled Rashmi's work and more begrudgingly came to accept Madina's work. Yet, in both relationships Musa remained conscientious about containing the implications of women's rights, striving to retain his position as the ultimate authority in the home.

Sexuality was the key domain in which Musa pushed back in his negotiations over women's rights. His decision to have an affair with Rashmi and the ensuing television controversy may have been prompted in part by Madina's growing financial independence. What was clear was that he now tolerated her working in town because he closely monitored her behavior, in what bordered on stalking, and was confident about her empisa.

These tensions were more explicit in Musa's relationship with Rashmi. Musa was clearly growing impatient with Rashmi's focus on work, especially because he considered it linked to her insistence on using family planning. Rashmi recounted times when Musa forced her to have sex, and Musa insinuated he would ultimately assert control over their sex life and fertility if necessary. The threat of AIDS only magnified these tensions over sexuality. Musa's reluctance to explore options other than fidelity, and his refusal to test for HIV with his wives (according to Madina and Rashmi), was another area in which Musa asserted his control over sexuality in negotiations over women's rights, women's work, and women's agency. This relationship, then, illustrates how women's rights discourse can be reframed and strategically redeployed in the home, in the process subtly reshaping some relationship dynamics and ideals of masculinity while reinforcing others.

WOMEN'S RIGHTS AND THE REMAKING OF MASCULINITY IN URBAN UGANDA

What this examination of the intimate politics of women's rights reveals is that women's rights have been integrated into everyday gender relations and the personal lives of women in a limited sense. The government's promotion of gender equity dominates how rights are understood, marginalizing more substantial connections between women's rights and gender equality advocated by the Ugandan women's movement. In addition, the postcolonial political context means that women's rights can be dismissed as Western cultural imperialism. Ideas of women's rights can be invoked, but their limited institutionalization means they are not normative. Any aspect of women's rights discourse that truly challenges the ideal of male authority is negotiated intensely, and often resisted, by both men and women.

What is also evident is limited synergy between women's rights and challenges to men's sexual privileges. This is most apparent in Samuel and Sophie's relationship, where all aspects of women's rights were essentially spurned by Samuel even while he sought to project an image of himself as a man conversant in the language of rights. If Sophie was in fact infected with HIV by Samuel, her experience is a dreadful illustration of the inability of women's rights discourse to meaningfully affect women's sexual health. Yet the extremes of this relationship make it atypical in many respects, for few relationships I encountered in Bwaise were so thoroughly male dominated.

Overall, of the nineteen couples (nineteen men and twenty-one women) who participated in my couples research, four men were critical or dismissive of women's rights (e.g., Samuel), four supported them with qualifications (e.g., Wilfred), and eleven displayed marked ambivalence (e.g., Musa). None of the women were completely negative or dismissive of women's rights, five were strongly in favor, and sixteen were ambivalent, especially about whether the man should still be seen as the ultimate authority in the home.

Given that most men and many women expressed ambivalence about women's rights, the relationship between Musa and his two wives provides the clearest illustration of how most of the families I came to know in Bwaise grappled with women's rights and masculine sexual privilege in the context of AIDS. Especially with Rashmi, Musa's negotiations over women's rights turned on an assertion of his control over sexuality. Both Rashmi and Madina associated rights with work (as opposed to sex), which enabled Musa's assertion of his control over sexuality. Rashmi, for example, knew that challenging Musa's control by using birth control injections would potentially threaten the relationship, and HIV heightened her concern. Both Madina and Rashmi felt they had few options to negotiate greater sexual safety in their relationship with Musa.

Contrary to what one might expect, AIDS largely constrained women's agency in the sexual domain, working in conjunction with both men's and women's limited and circumscribed adaptations of women's rights. Since by and large women's rights were not interpreted in relation to ideas of women's sexual autonomy or challenges to men's sexual privileges, rights were not a resource women could easily draw on to negotiate AIDS and sexual intimacy.

This is not to suggest that women's rights had no effect, as Edwina's negotiation of her sexual agreement with Isaac indicates. AIDS provided Edwina with new leverage in her relationship—leverage she used to negotiate a sexual agreement to protect herself from HIV infection. This agreement certainly came with caveats. Edwina gave up on the possibility of sexual pleasure with Isaac while conceding Isaac's privilege of finding physical affection in the arms of other women. Yet the presence of HIV in their relationship, and to a lesser extent the circulation of notions of women's rights, did allow Edwina to assert her sexual agency in new ways.

In the other four serodiscordant couples I spoke with in which the men were HIV-positive, the women also gained new leverage, though they used that leverage in different ways. One woman prioritized sexual safety, as Edwina had; two women prioritized their social status and demanded that their husbands marry them formally;[9] the fourth woman vied for more emotional support and loving expression from her husband. I also spoke with two discordant couples in which the women, not the men, were HIV-positive. This also influenced the relationship dynamics but in the opposite way: the men's power was largely strengthened and their control over decision making intensified.[10]

These shifts in gender power dynamics are an important facet of how the AIDS epidemic has influenced the remaking of masculinity in urban Uganda. HIV is glaringly evident in the relationships of serodiscordant couples and can prompt negotiations between partners that challenge aspects of masculine sexual privilege, especially a man's right to determine the terms of sex. Other research in Kampala has also found that discordance can destabilize gender norms and power dynamics (Bunnell et al. 2005). This included HIV-positive men agreeing to sexual contracts with their wives. One man allowed his wife to find a new male partner provided she continued to care for him (see Smith 2014, 156, for a related example from Nigeria). Such findings are not limited to sub-Saharan Africa; other research has revealed that living with discordance prompts critical engagements with gender norms, with women exerting greater agency in their relationships and men becoming more critical of normative masculine ideals (Orengo-Aguayo and Perez-Jimenez 2009; Persson and Richards 2008; see also Davis and Flowers 2011).[11] These findings resonate with research on masculinity and health more generally, especially those studies that indicate that subtle reworkings of masculinity can emerge in response to significant new health problems (Creighton and Oliffe 2010; Emslie et al. 2006; O'Brien, Hunt, and Hart 2005). The long history of Uganda's engagement with AIDS, especially the openness to talking about HIV and addressing it as a national problem, no doubt facilitated Edwina's negotiations with Isaac. Similar subtle remakings of masculine sexual privilege, one can assume, have occurred in many other discordant relationships in Uganda.

I expected the Ugandan context of women's rights to be an equally if not more powerful catalyst in remaking masculine sexual privilege. This, however, was not the case. Overall, I found that women's rights are having a more limited impact on gender power dynamics in relationships in Bwaise than I had anticipated. There are complex navigations and negotiations of masculinity and women's rights, but they are limited in scope. The dominance of the government's framing of women's rights as gender equity is not to be underestimated in its ascendancy. This framing explains why nearly all the women I spoke with did not want to disrupt the gender hierarchy and engaged with women's rights discourse in relation to strategic, instrumental gains in their relationships. Their focus was largely on the resources they could utilize to achieve their pragmatic goals and how they could claim agency in the moment. This was even true for Phoebe, notwithstanding the dramatic effects of her actions in her relationship.

Importantly, this gender equity framing of women's rights does little to challenge men's sexual privileges—a theme in all three relationships. In fact, threats to the ideal of male authority posed by women's rights often led men to shore up their masculinity by emphasizing their masculine sexual privilege. This underscores the extent to which gender inequality and sexuality are intertwined and how sexual dynamics in heterosexual relationships can, and often do, reinforce gender inequality.

Yet this story of women's rights and incremental renegotiations of the patriarchal bargain (Kandiyoti 1988) does not imply that no meaningful remaking of masculinity is under way. The terrain of women's rights in urban Uganda is complex, and these couples clearly illustrate the varied and creative negotiations of women's rights in everyday social interactions. Other research in Uganda highlights similar dynamics, with Shanti Parikh (2009) arguing that women's rights discourse is prominent enough that some women can occasionally feel compelled to publicly confront their husbands about extramarital affairs in order to appear to be modern women who know their rights.

Elsewhere in Africa, this theme of women carefully balancing their reputation as "proper" dutiful wives with new notions of women's rights and more equitable relationships is also evident, including Daniel Jordan Smith's (2014) research in Nigeria. In South Africa, Mark Hunter (2010) describes very similar negotiations over women's desire to earn their own money and men's attempts to defend their authority in the household. He also finds that women were least able to rework relationship dynamics with regard to sexual matters. Also in South Africa, Shari Dworkin and colleagues (Dworkin et al. 2012, 112) find that many, but not all, men were hostile to women's rights altering power dynamics within intimate relationships, which made rights in the private realm "a site of solid contestation and struggle." Money was central to such struggles, with women's income earning typically a threat to men who struggled to embody the male economic provider ideal (Dworkin et al. 2012, 103).

My fieldwork shows that places like Bwaise are ripe for more ambitious promotion of women's rights, as well as deeper exploration of how women's rights could facilitate negotiations over sexual safety in the context of AIDS. As I discuss in detail in chapter 6, HIV prevention programs could, and in rare cases do, act as catalysts, building on the types of negotiations already happening in relationships like Isaac and Edwina's. In addition, the broader landscape of women's rights continues to change and progress in Uganda. As noted in chapter 2, the Domestic Violence Act of 2010 has

spurred national debate on marital rape and may have prompted much more discussion of sexual violence in intimate relationships (Abramsky et al. 2014). While the impact of such legislation cannot be overstated, and it has not been translated into any concrete or specific government policies, it does underscore that the institutionalization of women's rights, including women's sexual rights, continues to deepen in Uganda.

Bwaise's context of urban poverty, however, significantly limits progress on women's rights because poverty considerably heightens gender tensions. While the Museveni government continues to claim to advocate for women's rights, it neglects to address the economic conditions that so fundamentally structure intimate relationships among the urban poor.[12] In order for ideas of women's rights premised on equality to become truly normative, there must not only be a movement beyond rights as gender equity, but there must also be a genuine effort to ameliorate the material and economic conditions in a place like Bwaise that make harmonious intimate relationships not only precarious, but all too rare.

5 The Intersection of Masculinity, Sexuality, and AIDS

The AIDS epidemic has made men's control over the terms of sex and men's privilege of having multiple sexual partners more convoluted and contentious. Yet while AIDS has complicated aspects of masculine sexual privilege, it has not truly challenged it. Given Uganda's success in fighting AIDS—a success believed to be predicated in part on men reducing their sexual partnerships—the persistence of masculine sexual privilege is unexpected at first glance. The relationship between masculinity, sexuality, and precarious work is certainly key to this story, as is the particular history of women's rights. But a deeper exploration of how Ugandans have grappled with AIDS is needed to grasp why the persistence of masculine sexual privilege was predictable.

My efforts to understand AIDS and the remaking of masculinity began at the Bwaise Health Clinic, the primary public health facility for this district of the city. Located near the outskirts of Bwaise, this clinic was the epicenter of HIV prevention and treatment in the area, and I made my first visit very early on in my fieldwork. When the matatu dropped me in front of the clinic, I was surprised to see that it was such a modest facility. A tall wall with flaking green paint, topped with a feeble strand of barbed wire, surrounded the compound. Flanking the entrance, a rusting sign listed services at the clinic, including antenatal care, dentistry, and immunizations. Opposite, a much newer sign with bright yellow letters announced "Counseling and Testing Service." Entering the unpaved, dusty courtyard, I saw that the main structure was an open-air pavilion with a new coat of gray paint beside an older building with dark and dank examination rooms. On the opposite side of the courtyard, two newer buildings faced each other, one containing tables and chairs and the other a small laboratory for on-site blood tests. Outside the laboratory were two long wooden benches filled with women waiting patiently for test results.

As I stood in the courtyard considering just how limited health services could be in Kampala, a gregarious woman in her early forties with large eyes and a wide, bright smile came over to introduce herself. Hope was one of the main AIDS counselors, and she was eager to tell me about their programs. We took a seat between two women on the bench outside the lab, and I learned that this modest facility was doing a great deal to address AIDS. The clinic provided free HIV testing and counseling twice a week, hosted AIDS support groups, organized home visits for the seriously ill in the area, and held HIV prevention programs for teenagers. These efforts were being conducted in conjunction with Uganda's two main AIDS NGOs, the AIDS Support Organisation (TASO) and the AIDS Information Center. Much of the work was done by dedicated volunteers like Hope.

For the next nine months, I spent Wednesday afternoons at the Bwaise Health Clinic, often in the cramped office that Hope shared with her fellow AIDS counselors. These warm and friendly women graciously tolerated my presence, and my time with them was largely spent observing their counseling activities. Although they had limited medical training and there was no full-time physician on staff, these women were providing valuable and in-demand services. I was particularly impressed with the care and compassion they showed to all those who came for HIV/AIDS services. This was especially evident on the day I accompanied Hope on her home visits. She took me to her own neighborhood, where we visited house after house with people afflicted with advanced AIDS. Often her help was more empathetic than medical, sitting patiently while people discussed their problems, sometimes offering an arm massage or back rub to ease the pain.

My regular visits to the clinic also coincided with the weekly meeting of the Post-Test Club, a support group for community members who had taken an HIV test. Primarily composed of residents from the greater Bwaise area who were HIV-positive, the club combined support services with HIV prevention activities. During the group's lively weekly meeting, 75 to 100 of the club's 250 members filled the benches in the clinic's main pavilion, sharing suggestions for coping with HIV and discussing how to encourage others to test and join their group.

Much of what I observed at the clinic over these months was in keeping with my expectations of how Ugandans would address AIDS. With limited resources, ordinary people were working to provide services and support, often with little or no monetary compensation. Uganda was famous for community engagement in addressing AIDS, which was seen as crucial to its success in reducing HIV prevalence in the 1990s. The Post-Test Club was a particularly impressive example of these dynamics, and I found it thrilling to see so many people participating, and open about their HIV status, in such a public forum.

One important caveat was the paucity of men. During my time at the clinic, the vast majority of people who came for services were women. The official roster of the Post-Test Club showed a similar gender discrepancy: only about 10 percent of those listed were men. When I first mentioned this imbalance to the staff and volunteers, who were also almost exclusively women, they confirmed this was the case and said it was something that hindered their work.

Hope told me in one of our first meetings, "The truth is I have some grudges with men. Men are not coming like we expected. They're not coming for testing according to our records. And they are not coming out to the Post-Test Club." She stressed that change is slow: "In Buganda, men make all the decisions about sex . . . and to cut through culture is very difficult from one generation to another." She agreed that more men should participate but was also skeptical, saying that she saw men who were Post-Test Club members, well versed in AIDS prevention messages, who continued to have multiple girlfriends simultaneously or mistresses outside their marriage, and she doubted most used condoms regularly. "It's difficult for men to change their behaviors," she said. "That's why you see men shying away from fighting transmission of AIDS. They tend to be hiding from the truth."

Throughout my fieldwork, many women echoed Hope's opinions. Like Hope, their views often combined biologically essentialist thinking about men's allegedly innate sexual drives and culturally essentialist views about African patriarchal cultures resistant to change. While such women were typically highly critical of men's behavior, how they framed issues of male sexuality also perpetuated the normative notions of male sexuality they found so problematic.

I was eager to hear how men would respond to such criticisms, and at one Post-Test Club event I was fortunate to meet Joseph, a lanky, forty-two-year-old. Much to my surprise, Joseph invited me to the weekly meeting of the new Bwaise Positive Men's Union. I was excited to learn about this support group for HIV-positive men and was grateful to have Joseph's invitation. For the next six months, I participated in all the union's weekly meetings and activities, working closely with the group as they slowly expanded their membership. As an honorary member, I gained better insight into how men themselves coped with living with HIV, how they explained their male peers' reluctance to come to places like the Bwaise Health Clinic, and how they understood, critiqued, and occasionally reworked normative conceptions of masculinity.

ADDRESSING MEN'S AIDS DENIAL: THE BWAISE POSITIVE MEN'S UNION

I was excited to participate in the beginning stages of the new men's union, but I was also unsure of what to expect. I had interacted with small groups of men in other settings, most notably during my carpentry apprenticeship, but I suspected this would be different. When I arrived at the clinic for my first union meeting, I found eight men seated in a tight circle under a mango tree in the back of the clinic. I joined the circle, and the sense of intimacy was immediately palpable—something I had not experienced to the same degree with other groups of men. Not surprisingly, my arrival disrupted the proceedings. I introduced myself and felt obliged to confirm that I was welcome to participate. The men were polite but not especially friendly and agreed I was welcome to stay. Eventually, Joseph arrived and made it clear that he had invited me to attend.

As the meeting proceeded, women occasionally passed our group. Their curious smiles showed that they were surprised to see a group of men organizing something at the clinic. Mukasa, the union's chairman, stressed to me that this group was unique because it was the only grassroots organization started by and for HIV-positive men in the community.[1] Another member stated that the union was important because men, unlike women, had not taken up the initiative to fight AIDS. Men had been "behind the curtains," he said, treating AIDS privately.

Coming in, I assumed the members would regard men as victims and complain that HIV-positive women received more than their fair share of attention and support. Most members, however, echoed the goals stated in the union's constitution, which prioritized educating other men about the dangers of HIV. Joseph had brought a copy of the constitution to the meeting and pointed out the section that read, "The union's main goal is to bring together men living with HIV/AIDS as many are still in shock, fear and denial," with the main objective being "to share facts of living with the killer virus . . . and be at the forefront in this struggle against HIV/AIDS, as a remedy lies in our hands as men." Obtaining more resources for HIV-positive men, such as antiretroviral drugs, was the last of a long list of objectives. It was men's fear of AIDS, and what they saw as the associated denial, that preoccupied union members.

The extent to which members themselves experienced shock and fear was made clear to me during a later meeting, when a thirty-nine-year-old man disclosed his attempted suicide. "I was going to die, and the children were also going to die," he told me. "So why should I waste my time and go on; I should just die." Having grappled with suicidal thoughts and other fears, the union members were dedicated to helping their male peers cope with HIV.

Over the course of my fieldwork, the union slowly expanded its membership from nine to twenty-two regular members. Staff and volunteers at the clinic were supportive of the union, but it received only one, very modest grant from TASO during my fieldwork in 2004. The men were nonetheless committed to their cause. As I participated in meetings and interviewed union members, they continually stressed to me that fear of AIDS paralyzed men in unique ways and that men were unlikely to support each other. Most of the men in the union drew sharp contrasts between the

ways men and women dealt with HIV and AIDS. "Women, they are very, very, very good," Richard, thirty-two, told me. "But men, that is our challenge. . . . Although it is a fatal disease, [men] have some denial. That's why they come when they have already weakened up to the extent of death." Although women were role models to the men in the union, members were adamant that men needed a male-only support group to break through their denial and get them to test.

This reluctance to test was a frequent topic among the members. Most members cited a combination of reasons: men were too busy to attend AIDS seminars, they saw health clinics as women's spaces, they were afraid of being discriminated against when searching for work, they feared their sexual partners would leave them, and they feared having to deal with the consequences of being HIV-positive alone. One union member found men's denial disturbingly ironic: "Men are the ones who cause AIDS, but men are very few [at the clinic]. They keep on hiding. I say they cause AIDS because men go for many women. And they don't tell their partners that they have AIDS. They keep quiet. They just keep quiet."

When discussing the impact of AIDS in their own lives, most members said that AIDS-related health issues had made it difficult to work and earn money. Several members were experiencing acute financial hardship. Vincent, who had been unemployed for some time, told me, "If you are positive no one will employ you, no one will sympathize with you." In his mind, there was a clear connection between a man's ability to earn money and his reluctance to test for HIV. Several other members described losing or leaving jobs as their health deteriorated, including the member who attempted suicide. He had left his teaching job and was in a predicament other men feared: he was relying on an AIDS service organization for food for himself and his children, dependent on his mother for money, and forced to walk to weekly union meetings because he lacked bus fare.

There was, therefore, a strong association union members made between certain masculine ideals, especially being a family provider, and men's reluctance to participate in AIDS programs offered at a place like the Bwaise Health Clinic. This association emerged in a poignant way as I observed union members prepare to participate in an event focused on involving men in preventing mother-to-child transmission (PMTCT) of HIV. Representatives from the Ugandan university hosting the event had visited the Bwaise Health Clinic and invited the union to participate. This was the union's first public event, and local dignitaries would be in attendance, including the mayor of Kampala. This opportunity energized the union, and for several weeks our meetings focused on the speeches, dramatic skits, and banners the union would create. It was clear to me that the theme resonated with the members and they were eager to promote the idea that men, including HIV-positive men, could play a critical and productive role in healthy pregnancy and childbirth.

The event itself was held across the street from the clinic in a large, open field. A sizable stage had been erected with a banner reading, "PMTCT Health Fair: Male Partner Involvement Can Make a Difference." Union members had set up a table to provide information and decorated it with a banner that read in English, "We are the Ones. Men Living with HIV/AIDS. Give Us Support." A marching band began the proceedings, which included the arrival of Kampala's mayor. The union drama group performed a skit portraying a man who only reluctantly accompanied his pregnant HIV-positive wife to the hospital. This was followed by heartfelt testimony from a union member who described his own similar journey and concluded with a passionate appeal: "I want to encourage all of us men who are here to get determined. Because it is we men who hide our positive status, not the women. We need to get strongly determined to come out and fight AIDS, because if we fight it will be reduced." These courageous union members were not only reaching out to their male peers but also countering the status concerns members faced as HIV-positive men.

Through the course of my fieldwork with the Bwaise Positive Men's Union, I came to see that denial and stigma were central to how union members themselves had experienced living with HIV. In their view, many men equated being HIV-positive with no longer having intimate relationships, being unable to produce children, and not being able to earn money to provide for their families—all key components of masculinity in urban Uganda. AIDS remained so stigmatizing for men in this context because the disease symbolically encapsulated the challenges men in urban Uganda faced living up to local ideals of masculinity. While poverty and unemployment made fulfilling masculine ideals difficult, it was not impossible for many men in Bwaise. But union members emphasized that AIDS

was a challenge of a different order, and coming to terms with a protracted, incurable illness was too troubling for many men to acknowledge.
Male peers would be of little support because they too had been socialized
to be independent, with relationships between men defined more by hierarchy and deference than mutual support and cooperation.

By drawing attention to the links between masculine ideals and men's
response to AIDS, union members voiced an implicit critique of masculinity. They did not question the masculine ideal of men as family providers
yet were critical of how their male peers coped with the pressures associated with AIDS. They were experimenting with a modest remaking of
masculinity centered on a more active role for men in their own and their
female partners' sexual health.

My discussions with union members indicate how the experience of
living with HIV can prompt a reflection on, and occasionally a reassessment of, normative gender relations. Sometimes the members reproduced
the idea that if individual Ugandan men simply took more "responsibility"
for their own sexual health, AIDS could be addressed. However, they also
often stressed how the normative notions of masculinity shaped and constrained men's behavior. In the process, they highlighted those social
structural factors that pose limits to HIV and AIDS campaigns calling for
personal responsibility and individual behavior change.

My involvement with the men's union helped me see the important role
conceptions of masculinity play in the ways men cope with AIDS and
showed me that the social context of AIDS can prompt a reflection on
gender norms. Yet, even while the union catalyzed critical reflection, I
found that several members continued to draw on their sexual privilege to
deal with challenges and crises in their relationships. One example of this
was Joseph, a cofounder of the union and the man who first invited me to
participate in the group. As a man whose adulthood coincided with the
recognition of an AIDS crisis in Uganda, Joseph's sexual history was especially helpful for understanding the links between AIDS and masculine
sexual privilege in urban Uganda.

A Munyankole from southwestern Uganda, Joseph moved to Kampala
in 1980 after he finished secondary school. City life initially treated him
well, and he found work with a construction company. When I spoke with
him about this time in his life, he remembered it fondly and said the

steady income allowed him to have girlfriends and many casual affairs in Kampala while supporting a wife and daughter back in the village.

By 1990, however, when Joseph was twenty-eight, several former girlfriends had died from AIDS. Concerned about his past, he tested and discovered he was HIV-positive. His daughter was spared this fate, but his wife in the village, whom Joseph believed had remained monogamous, died from AIDS several years later. Eventually, with much counseling from TASO, Joseph came to terms with his status. In 1994 he spoke publicly about being HIV-positive for the first time and in 2000 presented his life story at an international conference in Kampala.

In 1997 Joseph met an HIV-positive woman named Sarah through TASO. They started living together and sex without contraception led to an unplanned pregnancy in 1998. Their child, a boy, was born HIV-positive and lived for only four years. After the boy died, Joseph and Sarah separated.

When I first met Joseph in 2004, he was living alone but had a new girlfriend who was also HIV-positive. Joseph said he was more careful with this relationship, always using condoms when they had sex. I viewed Joseph as an example of man who had slowly come to terms with the severity of the AIDS epidemic and had adapted his intimate relationships to fit this new reality. As Joseph said to me at the time:

> Men are different because now some men are faithful to their partners. . . . There are still those men who are used to having many wives. But at least you don't go on the street, or go with these waitresses in bars. Like in the 1980s, we used to go there, buying this woman for 200 shillings, that one for 100 shillings. But these days, OK there are some men who still do that today, but not as it was back then. There is a change. Men have changed.

When I returned in 2009, Joseph was responding well to antiretroviral therapy, and he and Sarah had reunited and were living together in her village outside Kampala. However, Joseph had fallen on hard times. He had no steady income and had reached a point where he could no longer pay the rent for his home in Bwaise. According to Sarah, it was Joseph who had suggested reuniting.

Sarah lived only a few hundred yards off the main road in a two-room, unpainted house constructed of the most inexpensive, hand-made bricks.

While Joseph claimed he was happy living with Sarah, his struggles with money seemed to be taking a toll on their renewed relationship. From my conversations with Joseph and Sarah separately, it was evident they were not very close. Sarah described their relationship as involving little love or communication: "He is a silent man, and I also spend most of my time silent. . . . But there is nothing I can do, I just have to be with him because I have no other partner." They were still sexually intimate, and Joseph even complained to me that Sarah's AIDS medication often made her too interested in sex.

Joseph himself was preoccupied with having another child—ideally a son to compensate for the boy that he and Sarah had lost to AIDS. Sarah, however, had decided to have a tubal ligation and could no longer conceive. Joseph said this was, in part, why he was also seeing another HIV-positive woman in Kampala. He was quite open about this arrangement, and on our bus trip to the village he showed me a photo of his girlfriend, proudly telling me that they had been living together for the last two years.

Sarah said she was well aware Joseph had this other relationship in Kampala the entire time he had been staying with her in the village. "If he decides that he is going to have another wife in the city because he doesn't have a child, that's up to him, but I'm sticking only with him," Sarah told me. "I don't mind. I just live with him the way he is. I just keep quiet because he doesn't spend most of the time with her. He spends most of the time here with me. So I just accept it. It doesn't make me happy but I have no option . . . he could even have other women here in this village. That's what I think, but he won't tell me." A month after completing my fieldwork in 2009, Joseph had again separated from Sarah and went to live with his girlfriend in the city.

Having gained this fuller sense of Joseph, I realized he was emblematic of many men I had met through my fieldwork. Joseph was fluent in AIDS prevention discourse, and as someone living with HIV he was continually confronted with the reality of AIDS. He channeled these concerns into his work with the Bwaise Positive Men's Union, and he also seemed to be committed to having relationships with only HIV-positive women. He was critical of other men for not acknowledging their HIV status. Nonetheless, the masculine privilege of having multiple sexual partners remained a prominent aspect of how he negotiated intimate relationships in the context of AIDS, underscoring that even socially underprivileged men were able to capitalize on masculine sexual privilege. He also made clear to me that women did not have such privileges, especially the right to more than one sexual partner.

> It's better if a woman has only one sexual partner. It minimized the spread of AIDS, especially among those of us who are HIV-positive. For instance, if my wife, Sarah, went out sleeping with just anyone, she will keep on spreading the disease. . . . But the way people look at it around here, a man has a right to more than one sexual partner at a time. It's not his right exactly because it does affect the wife. But sometimes the conditions at home force you to look for a place where you can have more peace.

The persistence of masculine sexual privilege was a recurrent theme in my fieldwork with the union more generally. Of the six additional union members (ages thirty to fifty-seven) who provided me with life histories, three said they believed they became infected when they were living with their wives and had overlapping sexual relationships with one or more women.[2] Like Joseph, their relationship histories revealed just how difficult it could be to sustain relationships in urban Uganda. They all described how financial stress undermined their relationships and how living with HIV only compounded the problems. Overlapping, concurrent sexual relationships for men were an outgrowth of this interplay between economic conditions, feelings of marginalization, and masculine sexual privilege.

THE CONTOURS OF MASCULINE SEXUAL PRIVILEGE IN BWAISE

If you were to follow the road outside the Bwaise Health Clinic south for a mile, you would find yourself at the bustling and chaotic intersection at the center of Bwaise (figure 5.1). Cars, trucks, and motorcycles clogged the streets. Pedestrians warily dodged the traffic. The air was filled with a noxious mix of exhaust fumes, fine orange dust from the dirt sidewalks, and the sickly sweet smells emanating from the open sewers beside the sidewalk. Though it sometimes produced sensory overload, I enjoyed standing

Figure 5.1. Bwaise's main intersection.

at this intersection, engrossed by the frenetic activity. This was the heart of my field site, and over the course of my fieldwork I came to know many of the men and women who made a living from the shops and businesses. I turn now to conversations with a few of these people, to give a better sense of how Bwaise residents were remaking masculinity and male sexuality in the context of AIDS.

I begin with Henry, a forty-five-year-old Protestant with some secondary school education who managed a small hardware store.[3] His ample supply of merchandise was well organized, and he was clearly proud to be in charge. I was introduced to him by a mutual friend, and he was eager to talk with me about relationships in Bwaise.

"I have five children," he told me, then boastfully joked, "They are from different mothers, and that's why I'm a big man!" Henry repeatedly spoke of a close relationship between men, money, and sexual relations in Bwaise.

> Generally men try to prove their manhood using their finances. . . . And if you don't have money you cannot get women to be with you. Women won't even look at you. But if you have the money, then you can get many women and even have a surplus you have to chase away!

Henry also stressed that AIDS made relationships complicated in Bwaise.

> AIDS is a big challenge. . . . We have tried to limit this habit of sleeping
> around with many women, and this thing of trying to get so many wives. . . .
> You have got to be careful because that is the only solution. You have to stop
> having other wives and sex with other women and be with one wife only.
> That's why we beg our wives to show us love. We tell our wives they have to
> show so much love for us, and then we will be able to really run away from
> AIDS. But if the women get weak at that, then we men will just find our-
> selves facing so many temptations.

Henry told me he had been able to resist such temptations in his own
marriage. "For me, those waves of being attracted to another woman normally happen, but you can fight them," he said. Although Henry did not
admit it to me, our mutual friend informed me that for the past few
years Henry did have the occasional brief affair, lasting only one or two
nights.

What I found most interesting about Henry's comments was the connection he made between men's status and the attendant sexual privileges.
For Henry, men in Bwaise gained status largely through earning money,
which in turn provided opportunities for new sexual relationships, further
reinforcing a man's status (i.e., the dynamics of sexuality as a performance
of male status; see chapter 3). AIDS had complicated this calculus, but,
like many other men, Henry implied that women, especially women looking for men's money, were the key problem. In the context of AIDS, Henry
believed that the onus was on women to care for and comfort their male
partners so that they could resist the persistent (and largely unquestioned)
masculine sexual privileges that came with money.

Henry's views on masculinity and sexuality were, therefore, quite typical of men in Bwaise. He suggested that men had innately strong sexual
drives but that the contemporary urban context of precarious work and
HIV had created paradoxes and conundrums for men's sexual relationships. While he did not say so explicitly, his own strategies for dealing with
HIV reflected the lingering influence of Uganda's zero grazing approach
to HIV prevention. Yet he implied that men's ability to practice zero grazing was less dependent on critical reflection on men's sexual privileges
than on women fulfilling their "proper" roles as dutiful, loving wives.

From Henry's hardware store, it was just a short walk down Bwaise's commercial strip to the smaller of two markets, consisting of a cluster of two dozen small cement stalls where male and female vendors displayed their produce, fish, and meat. One afternoon I had the chance to meet the manager of this market, Kalif, a forty-one-year-old Muslim with four years of secondary school education. His managerial position was a coveted one that provided steady income, and Kalif was doing somewhat better than most men I knew in Bwaise, earning about $50 a month.

On the afternoon I spoke with him, the market was fairly quiet, but we still struggled to find a private corner to talk. I began by asking him what he thought it meant to be a man in Bwaise, and he replied, "In my view a real man is someone who is responsible—he's the one who tries to work hard so as to be able to support and sustain his family." Our privacy was soon interrupted by Kalif's coworker, also in his early forties. Overhearing our conversation, he came over to make what he thought was an important point: "In places like Bwaise men prove their manhood by having extra relationships with other people's wives and also sleeping around with school girls. You will find a man who will tell you, 'I am a man because I have more women.' It's how he proves he is a powerful man. That's how you show your amaanyi as a man." Kalif laughed softly, not indicating if he agreed or disagreed, then politely shooed away his coworker.

Our conversation then turned to Kalif's relationships. He claimed to be happily married for eighteen years. He said he appreciated all the cooking and cleaning his wife did, as well as the money she earned to help pay for school fees. Kalif found his marriage sexually satisfying too, but the couple did quarrel occasionally. Kalif said that the quarreling caused him to start having sex with another woman, and for at least the past year he had a steady girlfriend in addition to his wife. "The reason I got another woman is because women are quarrelsome," he said. "They quarrel with you whenever you come home. So whenever you go home and she argues with you, you can turn to the second woman for comfort."

Kalif was adamant that two women were enough, both because of his limited finances and because of the threat of HIV. "What I know is that AIDS has really made my infected brothers and sisters suffer. Some of them have died," he told me. "That's why I really fear AIDS, and that's why I'm no longer getting new sexual partners and I no longer sleep around with many women. I don't have many women anymore." Unlike some men and many women I spoke with, Kalif thought other men had made similar decisions: "Because of AIDS most men are now using condoms, and many men have changed their sexual behavior in that they don't sleep around with women. Many of them are reducing their number of sexual partners. Most of them are changing. The majority are, actually."

Like Henry, Kalif noted the link between money, men's status, and men's sexual relationships, emphasizing that money was a prerequisite for additional relationships. However, he foregrounded another prominent theme in my fieldwork, namely, that most men in Bwaise understood themselves as having the privilege of starting another sexual partnership if their relationship with their wife or girlfriend had become contentious (i.e., compensatory sexuality; see chapter 3). Kalif indicated that AIDS had complicated these dynamics somewhat, and like Henry, he drew on zero grazing as his main strategy and suggested that many of his male peers had done the same.

Moving deeper into Bwaise's residential interior, there was an assortment of older and newer houses, along with one of the defining features of Bwaise: the twenty-foot-wide sewage canal running through the center of the district, bisecting it into eastern and western halves. During the dry months, the stone embankments proved high enough to contain the thick brown muck filled with trash. In the rainy season, however, water poured into Bwaise from the surrounding hills and the canal frequently broke its banks, flooding the center of Bwaise with raw sewage (figure 5.2).

Crossing this canal along one of the rickety pedestrian bridges, the housing remained dense and equally run-down. It was in this section of Bwaise that David lived. David was a thirty-two-year-old Catholic with only a primary school education who was a generation younger than Henry and Kalif. His home stood out as one of the more substantial and well maintained in the area. Inside were several spacious rooms, including an uncluttered living room, making the home feel much less claustrophobic than others in Bwaise. David shared this house with his aunt and ten of his relatives' children, including those of one brother who had died from AIDS.

Figure 5.2. Bwaise during the rainy season.

David had moved to Bwaise five years earlier from the town of Masaka in the Rakai district southwest of Kampala. Rakai had been hit especially hard by AIDS and was considered the original epicenter of Uganda's epidemic. Life in Bwaise had treated David fairly well. Both he and his aunt had managed to become successful traders, selling coffee, beans, and corn in Bwaise's smaller market. More than other Bwaise residents I knew, David maintained strong connections to his hometown, where his wife of seven years still lived with their two children. As he freely divulged to me, he had a second long-term relationship with another woman who also lived in Masaka. David claimed to make a profit of $10 to $15 a day, which was considerably more than many other men I knew, but he said this was barely enough to support his wife, children, long-term girlfriend, and the many dependents he was helping look after in his Bwaise home.

With his penchant for hip-hop-inspired track suits and a New York Yankees knit cap, David projected a slightly hardened, streetwise persona that likely provided some protection in his interactions with Bwaise's tougher young men. City life also seemed to have shaped his sense of what constituted success for a Ugandan man, especially the connection between masculinity and money. When I asked David what kind of man he respected, he replied:

> To me a real man is the one who has a lot of money. He has buildings in the city, land in the city, he drives a car, and owns plots of land in the city. . . . And a man with several women is in the same category. Because only a man with enough money can support several women. That's why I would like to have two wives. That shows I am capable of sustaining them. But I don't need another girlfriend here in the city now. No, I don't want that. When you don't have enough money, they are very expensive and they consume a lot of money [laughs]. . . . I would eventually like to have a woman here in the city as well, but since I still have only a little capital I don't want to waste it on her.

David said ideally he would like to marry his long-term girlfriend in the village when he had enough money, and then he would have two wives. I asked how his first wife would feel about this. He replied matter-of-factly, "I will have decided about that, and I don't care if she is happy or not. I am the one who decides what to do because I'm the man." Nor was his Catholic faith an obstacle for him: "My religion does not prohibit it. Or maybe it does. I don't know exactly because I have seen many Catholics having more than five wives. You hear that some even have up to ten wives."

As a man from the Rakai district, it was not surprising that David was concerned about AIDS. "I worry about AIDS very, very, very much," he told me. "I worry about *okukwanakwana* [having multiple sexual relationships]. So even if I get more money I will still have only two wives." He added that he had already lost nine uncles and one brother to the disease. Due to what he perceived as the looming threat of AIDS in his life, David said his life was different from that of previous generations.

> There has certainly been change in my life because of AIDS. Because in the past, before AIDS came, people used to enjoy life very much. But now you get scared and you give up on that joy and excitement, including being with other women. . . . I know if you have a sexual partner, say, for example, you have a wife who you don't fully trust, even if you are faithful you will be scared that she will go out and get involved with another man. So you will fear that she might get another person and then she will infect you.

The way David implied that women were to blame for the spread of HIV echoed Henry's and Kalif's remarks. Yet David was also critical of his male peers.

> To me, men have not changed in Bwaise because of AIDS. They have actually increased being *omwenzi* [womanizers] and *okukwanakwana* [laughs]. There is no big change even in the village either. It really is only you, as an individual, who will be scared and take a stand to change yourself personally. But communities and men generally have not changed.

David saw himself firmly in the category of those men who decided on their own to conduct their sexual relationships differently because of AIDS. He proudly told me he had taken an HIV test several times, and so had his wife. While wary of AIDS, he remained optimistic his future would be different from that of his many uncles whose lives had been cut short by the disease.

Thus, although David was a generation younger than Henry and Kalif, he too was attempting to navigate between the dangers of AIDS and the expectations of masculinity. In David's mind, he had plotted a sensible, pragmatic course that balanced maintaining multiple intimate relationships with protecting himself and his female partners from infection. Compared to Henry and Kalif, David was in certain respects more frank—even blunt—about sexual relationships as emblems of male status and the extent to which HIV had placed a damper on men's sexual pleasures. And while he too emphasized zero grazing as his primary prevention strategy, which is significant given that it was introduced before he became an adult, he was much more pessimistic than Kalif that this signaled any real shift in the meaning of manhood at a community or societal level. While David would not put it this way, he underscored how men's sexuality has been remade in the context of HIV by strategies like zero grazing but remade in a way that preserves masculine sexual privilege. In this sense, he illustrated the dynamics of sexuality as a pragmatic problem, as discussed in chapter 3.

This theme of remaking masculinity in the context of AIDS emerged in a discussion I had with a group of eight men working in Bwaise.[4] We began by talking about how men showed they were true men in Bwaise and initially the men focused on the importance of providing for a family. Before long, however, the conversation turned to sexuality.

"I also have something to important to say," said the first man. "The other way we prove we are men is having many women as sexual partners. Don't you all agree with me?"

"Yes," replied most of the men.

"How do you keep to only one woman?," the first man continued. "You are supposed to have about four wives, and that's a true man."

"That thing sometimes happens because religion dictates it, but there are also some of us who are not religiously permitted to have many women," said a second man.

To my surprise, the discussion then quickly transitioned to the merits and drawbacks of having extramarital relationships.

"If a woman is your official wife, you can expect her to give you children. But those other women we sleep with are just there as parasites on us," said a third man.

"A wife helps in many other things, for instance washing your clothes while you are away, unlike these other extramarital partners who are not beneficial at all," said a fourth man.

"So why don't we give up on them if they are not good at all?" asked a fifth man.

"We all know that we men have sexual desires so when we need sex the women help us, be it the official wife or the woman outside the marriage. Because naturally there will be a time when you desire sex, just like you will feel thirsty and need water to drink," said a sixth man.

For these men, AIDS further complicated these already complex relationship dynamics, and they all stressed it was something they worried about a great deal.

"In order to really get sexual satisfaction you need to have tested and both found that you are HIV negative," said the third man. "Then you both can truly enjoy each other. But sometimes you will be gripped by lust and sleep with a woman. And when you realize what you just did you will lose all the joy you got from sex from the fear of HIV infection."

"Generally there is less excitement and enjoyment because of AIDS," said a seventh man. "We have tried to change our relationships by making personal decisions not to sleep with other women, but then we end up going back on those decisions."

"Because of AIDS we do use condoms with other women we sleep with but not with our wives," added the first man. "There is no way you can use a condom with your own wife unless you are also sleeping with a prostitute. And in addition, even with any other woman you will only use the condom on the first encounter. But you cannot keep using the condom all through on the subsequent times you sleep together. The more you sleep with her, the more you forget about condoms."

This group of men provided a window onto how men themselves framed male sexuality, combining biological essentialist notions of male sexuality as a demanding natural urge and cultural essentialist expectations of what constitutes of real man. Yet what was most illuminating was the fraught collective ruminations about the costs and benefits of normative notions of male sexuality, especially in the context of AIDS.

A core theme in all these discussions I had with men was the dilemmas men faced as they enacted, and attempted to remake, normative notions of masculinity. Having multiple partnerships remained a privilege (if not a right and social expectation) in most men's eyes—a privilege that accorded pleasure, social status, and escapism, especially in the context of chronic poverty. Yet men were well aware of how such sexual relationships heightened their vulnerability to HIV infection and their partners' vulnerability as well. For many men, this was indeed a quandary that was difficult to resolve, making intimate relationships even more tenuous, crisis prone, and difficult to sustain. As the group discussion reveals, these dilemmas could prompt some critical reflection on normative notions of masculinity among men. Overall, however, I found such reflection focused largely on ways of preserving masculine sexual privilege in light of contemporary threats to it, which made the HIV prevention approach of zero grazing an especially useful strategy in remaking such privilege in the age of AIDS.

Finally, in a context in which "being faithful" has been heavily promoted as an effective and "responsible" form of AIDS prevention, I found that men also had a strong incentive to conceal their enactments of masculine sexual privilege. Approximately two-thirds of the men I interviewed in 2004 claimed to be monogamous and told me they had only one sexual partner for the previous twelve months. Only four of the twenty-seven married men I interviewed (15 percent) said they had a concurrent, non-marital partner in the previous year.[5] While I did not dismiss men's claims of monogamy, all such self-reported data merits some suspicion, especially in a context in which monogamy and marital fidelity have received such emphasis in efforts to reduce HIV transmission. As noted in chapter 2, there is a very long history of Christian men claiming to be monogamous in order to maintain social status while they, and their wives, hid their extramarital partners. Concealment was probably more likely when talking to an American man like me, and it became clear in my fieldwork that men's sexual histories were often more complicated than they first revealed.

A particularly interesting example of these dynamics was Edward, a young man whom I came to know well over the course of my fieldwork. We first met in 2004 when Edward was twenty-six years old and living with his informal wife, Betty, a twenty-two-year-old Muslim, in the heart of Bwaise. They had been living together for a year in a clean and cozy one-room space attached to Betty's mother's home and appeared to be a happy couple. Edward, a Seventh-Day Adventist, did not drink or smoke and avoided Bwaise's club life, something Betty said she appreciated. Betty was more socially outgoing, drank beer occasionally, and was especially fond of playing pool with men at the nearby club, a habit that concerned Edward but that he nonetheless tolerated.

The couple was struggling financially, however, and while both had several years of secondary school education and spoke English well, neither had a steady income. Edward was striving to create a career for himself in development work; he had succeeded in making some connections, including an NGO devoted to helping urban youth, but this work was largely unpaid. Betty supplemented their income with occasional work braiding hair, but Betty's mother was largely supporting the couple.

Although Edward's NGO work provided little in the way of steady income, it was central to his identity. He was well versed in the language of development, including AIDS prevention programs, women's empowerment initiatives, and addressing the problems of "at-risk" urban youth. Edward's interest in improving his community was genuine, a quality I admired in him, and he also took satisfaction in how this work helped him build his reputation. "People know me. I've been educating them," he told me. "Almost all of Bwaise knows me. People say, 'This is Edward, he's a peer educator working with Plan International, Family Planning of Uganda, the Uganda Youth Development Link. He has been educating people to get out of their problems.'"

I was impressed with the depth of Edward's knowledge about AIDS and sexual health. He was quite fluent in the biology and epidemiology of HIV, as well as the panoply of AIDS prevention approaches promoted by various organizations, including marital fidelity campaigns, condom promotion, HIV testing and counseling, and even links between domestic violence and women's HIV infection. Through such fluency, Edward was striving to cultivate an identity for himself as an educated, modern, urban young man well versed in the discourse of development, including the dangers of AIDS.

This was especially evident to me when Edward talked about his relationship with Betty and discussed being a role model for his male peers: "One thing I'm sure of is when you have one partner and your partner does too, then others start admiring your ways, admiring your character." While Edward told me that he was "faithful" to Betty, he empathized with some of his male peers who were unsure their relationships would last. "Other [men] have multiple partners for the reason that other girls disappoint them," he told me. Edward repeatedly emphasized, however, that he was different from other young men. Betty joked that Edward was more like an old man because he was not interested in clubs, drinking, and dancing. Edward took pride in this, seeing it as an emblem of his maturity and his ability to resist the influence of his peers.

When I left in 2004, I was fairly optimistic about their future together, but when I returned in 2009, I was initially dismayed to find Edward and Betty's home abandoned. The construction of a new road and a large church had increased flooding near Betty's family home and the water had slowly eaten away at the foundation. Through Edward's twenty-seven-year-old cousin, Peter, a good friend of mine, I learned the couple had relocated to a small, clean, two-room house on higher ground in greater Bwaise.[6]

In the intervening years, Edward had worked hard to develop his own independent community-based organization in Bwaise. The focus was on helping at-risk youth in Bwaise, especially homeless young people and female sex workers. As I saw for myself, Edward would often venture into the seediest sections of Bwaise and Kimombasa at night to talk with young female prostitutes and let them know about organizations that could offer them support and services. I admired Edward's commitment to improving the lives of young people in Bwaise, yet his work remained an unpaid labor of love. He had been able to find some work with the local city council office, but it was poorly paid and seasonal. Betty was also only working occasionally, as a hairdresser, but her mother was no longer providing as much financial support.

In my conversations with Edward and Betty together, both stressed that they were committed to each other and hoped to be formally married soon. Over the course of conversations with Edward and Betty alone, however, I learned that their relationship was not on solid ground. Their financial problems had started to cause tension, and their relationship had deteriorated to the point that Edward was now spending some nights at his cousin Peter's home in Bwaise. In addition, for several years Edward and Betty had been struggling to conceive their first child, an issue that had caused a rift in their relationship. The fact that the couple did not have the money for a thorough medical exam only exacerbated their problems.

After many conversations with Edward alone about his relationship, he conceded that his informal marriage was in crisis. He emphasized how much he cared about Betty and seemed genuinely confused about how to proceed. It was evident to me that Edward was also motivated to stay with Betty because of the status being in a serious relationship provided; he was thought of as *omwami* (a husband) and not simply *omusajja* (a man). Edward insisted that he was not interested in having two girlfriends, or wives, simultaneously; the key dilemma for him was whether to stay with Betty or find a new woman. He was striving to portray himself to me as a faithful husband in a very difficult position, and several times he solicited my advice. "Would you leave that person and just go?," he asked me. "Would you ask for an opportunity of getting another partner? What would you do?"

When I spoke with Betty alone in their home, she was depressed and somewhat taciturn. To my surprise, Betty told me the main issue for her was not children but Edward's sexual behavior: "I think he is keeping a secret from me—having a second partner. I can't guarantee that he has another partner, but you know the way men behave. . . . I have asked him

about it and he told me that he doesn't have anyone else. . . . I think it has just happened recently and he rarely stays with her." Betty was also preoccupied with the possible health implications if her suspicions were correct. When I interviewed her alone and together with Edward, Betty became most animated when asking me about discordant couples. She wanted to know how couples managed that issue and how the negative person dealt with the possible social stigma of people assuming he or she was actually HIV-positive. When I asked her if they were taking any precautions, she acknowledged that they were not using condoms because they were trying to conceive. "But I told him that if he goes to other women, he should insist on using condoms," she added. "I fear that he may be teaching people in the community about using condoms when he is not using them himself."

While Betty was interested in testing for HIV with Edward, they had never done so. Betty herself had tested negative recently and told Edward, and he assured her he tested regularly. However, Betty claimed he had never shown his test results to her, which Edward disputed when I spoke with him alone. These problems had made Betty unsure if she still wanted to have a family with him.

I was having trouble reconciling Edward's and Betty's descriptions of their relationship and decided to turn to Edward's cousin Peter for his perspective. I got to know Peter well in my initial year of fieldwork and felt quite close to him. I explained the inconsistencies, and Peter eventually confided that Edward was concerned about how I perceived him. "He does not want you to know about the problems in his marriage," Peter told me. "And he really does not want you to know about his other girlfriends."

The complexity of Edward's life became more apparent to me a week later when Edward, Peter, another more affluent male cousin, and I took a trip to their family's village three hours outside Kampala. As we left Bwaise, Edward first stopped by a small cosmetics shop. His cousin honked the horn, and a young woman with a round face came running out. She and Edward giddily greeted each other while holding hands, and Peter winked at me, mouthing, "She's one of his girlfriends." When we reached the village, another young woman was waiting for Edward. While Peter and I spent the day touring the fields, Edward escorted this young woman around the property, walking with her hand in hand fifty feet behind us. At the end of the day, right before we left, Edward introduced her to me: "She is my very good friend. We talk every day." On the ride home, Edward's cousins repeatedly alluded to Edward's girlfriends, jokingly referring to him as "a star." Edward assiduously ignored their comments and took any opportunity to change the topic.

Later, when I asked Peter if Edward did have another girlfriend, he said, "That woman at the cosmetics shop, she is his girlfriend. Also the one we met in the village." Peter was adamant that these were sexual relationships: "He sleeps with the one in town. And the one in the village is in town now, and she slept with him today. . . . So now you just find that chain of relationships. Why is he keeping them connected? I don't know."

I was not surprised that Peter was critical of Edward; Peter had largely avoided relationships with women altogether, focusing instead on his studies. He had graduated from the leading university in Uganda, nearby Makerere University, on a full scholarship, but even after completing his studies he remained leery of relationships. His reasons were complex but had much to do with his failure to find decent work and his family's experience of AIDS. "Back when we met in 2004," he said, "my decision to not have a girlfriend was due to my personal experiences with HIV. . . . I lost my father, two uncles, and an aunt, and my mum is positive. . . . But now what is keeping me away [from relationships] is money. . . . It is how little that I am earning that is totally too stressful. And the fact that I have a university degree, the girlfriend or wife will have very high expectations of me."

Peter's perspective shaped his assessment of his cousin's sexual behavior.

> I've been speaking to [Edward] about it. Telling him to maybe stabilize his relationships. Then he was telling me, "You know, they say *omusajja okusaj-jalaata.*" Meaning in English that a man has to show his manhood, and should have those multiple partners. And he was telling me, "You don't understand, Peter. Do you know women? Peter, you don't know who women are!" So I think again he has the knowledge, but I don't know what's keeping him back. He's not using any of the knowledge. He's giving it to other people and telling them to use it.

Peter conceded that Edward and Betty were facing serious problems, including both their fertility challenges and the fact that Betty's family had

stopped supporting the couple. Peter believed their relationship was ending and did not understand why they had continued as long as they had,
adding, "It shows the risk of, how do they call it, concurrent relationships."
He complained that Edward's girlfriends and wife often called him for
advice and said he felt like "a marriage counselor to a very big-headed
young man." Peter felt Edward was already well informed from his seminars and workshops: "Anything I can possibly tell Edward he already
knows. What I am going to inform him about? Nothing." He did little to
hide his exasperation with his cousin, saying, "He's so much frustrating,
and disappointing."

I found Peter's assessment of Edward rather harsh. What Edward's
intimate life revealed was how men made decisions as their relationships
began to falter. He felt he was caught between competing pulls of marital
fidelity, a desire for children, and the allure and status of new, multiple
relationships. His concern that a marriage needed to produce children
was unremarkable given the long-standing link between marriage, sexuality, and biological reproduction in Buganda.

Indeed, Edward seemed to be strategically drawing on masculine sexual privilege in the short term to address his dilemma (i.e., sexuality as a
reservoir of privilege; see chapter 3). His extensive knowledge of AIDS
seemed to have only modest impact on his decisions, given that he had
likely created a network of overlapping sexual relationships and that he
and Betty were not using condoms. Eventually, I would learn that in 2012
Edward left Betty and married the woman from the village, and soon after
they gave birth to a baby boy. Many couples I met in Bwaise followed a
similar trajectory whereby relationship pressures over money and family
intensified to the point that the man, and occasionally the woman, began
exploring other relationships. There was much starting, stopping, and
overlap in relationships in Bwaise, all exacerbated by poverty and the persistence of masculine sexual privilege.

This interplay of urban poverty and normative notions of masculinity
cannot be overstated when examining men's sexual behavior in a place like
Bwaise. My descriptions of Henry, Kalif, David, and Edward could be mis-
read as simply reproducing highly problematic stereotypes about African
men's alleged sexual promiscuity and innate voracious sex drive. My analysis throughout this book counters such racist clichés by revealing the

complicated and often fraught ways men grappled with prevailing norms of male sexuality in the face of precarious work, new notions of women's rights, and the looming presence of HIV/AIDS. The ways men wrestled with the conundrums they faced as they strove to have meaningful intimate relationships is a thoroughly contemporary sociological story, filled with contradictions, paradoxes, and insecurities.

The fact that many men I came to know drew on and remade masculine sexual privilege as they navigated the contemporary social context is unsurprising. So too is the fact that some men prioritized monogamous relationships, as men in Buganda have for centuries. While most of these men enacted what I refer to as pragmatic monogamy, a small number of men I met were more committed to monogamy as an ideal. These were largely born-again Christians whose monogamy typically went hand in hand with patriarchal authority as household heads. I also met a very small number of men who linked monogamy and more equitable gender relations, striving to build relationships that were equal partnerships. These few men tended to be in their early twenties, and most worked in the domestic violence prevention program I volunteered with. These men also often struggled maintaining their relationships, and one young man I came to know well saw his hopes frustrated when his wife left him for a man with more money. Taken together, this broad spectrum of men's intimate relationships in Bwaise runs counter to bigoted tropes of African male promiscuity and instead foregrounds the complexity of contemporary social dynamics driving the remaking of masculine sexual privilege in urban Uganda.

WOMEN AND MASCULINE SEXUAL PRIVILEGE: CRITIQUES AND ACCOMMODATIONS

Over the course of my fieldwork, I had many conversations with women about men's sexuality, and through these discussions a central theme emerged. Nearly all the women I spoke with said that masculine sexual privilege, especially men having multiple sexual partnerships, remained a hegemonic aspect of masculinity in Bwaise. Most women were highly critical of men's sexual behavior and said their intimate relationships were

Figure 5.3. A group of women in Bwaise.

often marked by distrust and fear that their partners had, or would have, additional sexual partners. Women often noted that not all men were untrustworthy, but when speaking of men as a group their assessments were generally quite negative. Both women and men, therefore, described sexual relationships in Bwaise as fraught with tensions, conflicts, and suspicions that were only exacerbated by the stress of chronic poverty and the dangers posed by AIDS (figure 5.3).

Of the women I interviewed during my first year of fieldwork in Bwaise, half had in fact decided to forgo relationships with men and to try to survive on their own.[7] All these women were informally married at some point and had children with their former husbands. Nearly all of these relationships ended in divorce or separation, and a few of the women were AIDS widows. All of these women claimed to be monogamous while married but accused their husbands of extramarital affairs, and most said they experienced domestic violence at some point in their relationships. For many, such behavior became intolerable and led to separation; others were abandoned by their husbands.

These women were all struggling financially, even by Bwaise standards. Their financial problems might have been eased if they found a new man to live with, but all were very leery of starting new relationships. A new relationship might bring money, but from their experiences it could also bring unwanted pregnancies, physical abuse, and neglect. For most, the additional dangers posed by AIDS made these relationship risks unacceptably high. One thirty-two-year-old woman, for example, told me that in all three of her long-term relationships she was monogamous, but all her lovers had other sexual partners. Not surprisingly, these experiences left her embittered and resentful of men. She complained to me that men "are never satisfied. However good a woman is, a man would get another woman. They are very promiscuous. Ugandan men are excessive!" When I asked her if some men were different now because of AIDS, she replied, "Oh no! The men never change. We women fear AIDS more than men do. I fear it. The women have completely changed. The women I live with say that if a man wants to make love to her without a condom she would not accept. When a man has had a four-month-long affair he wants a baby. Do you expect such a person to be afraid of AIDS?"

The other half of the women I interviewed were all in long-term relationships. Few were formally married, but all had cohabited with their partner for at least three years, some for decades. All claimed to be monogamous while married, and several said they had only had sex with the men they had lived with over the course of their lives. Most of these women expressed deep ambivalence about their intimate relationships and were unhappy with, or concerned about, their partners. Conflicts over money were common, and nearly all the women were concerned about the possibility their husband had had, or may be having, extramarital affairs.

All of these women expressed frustration about having limited ability to influence their husband's sexual behavior. Some said they were careful not to upset or challenge their husbands for fear of making their domestic life too stressful, which might lead him to look to other women. As one older woman put it, "I try to keep quiet when my husband annoys me so that he will not go away from me and get another woman on the side, and when we have sex he might then already have acquired HIV and I will also

get it accidentally. . . . Men fear family responsibilities and go out with other women who will not demand as much as the woman at his home."

Not all the marriages were quite so bleak. One woman, for example, had married a man ten years her senior and thought of herself as quite lucky. She had remained monogamous during the marriage and was confident her husband was monogamous as well, saying they both found their marriage sexually satisfying. Her husband's monogamy was central to her assessment of his character, although she also had lingering concerns about AIDS. "Maybe if I found him with another women, without AIDS I might not fear it so much. But with AIDS I fear it so much," she said. Most men in Bwaise acted as if AIDS did not exist, she added, and had many sexual partners. "They are no longer fearing AIDS so much. It's just like a fever now. They no longer see it as a serious problem."

The critique of masculine sexual privilege in the context of AIDS was particularly poignant in a discussion I had with a group of women in Bwaise.[8] They expressed a great deal of frustration about how their male partners dealt with the disease.

"The problems with AIDS all begin with denial because your man will not accept that he is responsible for bringing the infection into your house," said the first woman. "He will still blame you, the wife. So he will be able to realize sooner that he is infected and start medication confidentially. And in the process he will be looking healthier than you, so he will blame you for being responsible for the HIV infection."

"We are also worried about getting the infection from the men because you never know how he moves around and who he has slept with," added a second woman. "So you will always be scared, especially when he comes back late because you will think that is the day he has brought HIV home."

"Also, there is no way you are going to refuse to have sex with him. Even if you sense that he got infected with HIV you still have to have sex with him," said a third. "Because you are husband and wife, and as a woman there is no way you can say that I am not going to sleep with him, even if I know that he slept with Jane who might be HIV-positive. Instead you are supposed to continue having sex with him. So there is no way you can protect yourself against it because he is the man and so he is supposed to have sex with you whenever he wants."

"Yes, yes," other women agreed.

The third woman continued, "Yes, he will say, 'I married a wife for sex, so what is the meaning of asking to use a condom?'"

When I asked these women if they or their male partners changed anything in their lives because of AIDS, some responded that AIDS had partially altered their relationship dynamics.

"The earlier generations were worse," a fourth woman began, "because a man would marry and sleep with six women in the same bedroom! But today we can now stop them from doing such things. I put pressure on him until he gives up on those other women."

"We would have changed, but our husbands are not willing to do that," said a fifth.

"We women are not the promiscuous ones," said the third woman. "Generally, women are not unfaithful."

"Yes," agreed a sixth woman, "we stick with one man."

"But our partners have not changed," said the second woman.

"But some men have changed because some of them also fear AIDS just like us," said the fifth woman. "Some do stick to one partner and when they sleep with other partners they use condoms."

"Even the number of women they slept with has now reduced," said an eighth woman. "Those who used to have many women now have fewer."

These women suggested that AIDS has prompted a critique of masculine sexual privilege among many women. Yet their comments indicated that while the context of AIDS has resulted in some renegotiation of this privilege, its core elements remained in place. Discussing these issues with a group of women no doubt amplified their critiques. Many women had a more accommodating position on masculine sexual privilege when I spoke with them alone. They typically voiced concerns or frustrations with the men in their lives but balanced this with varying degrees of acceptance of the sexual status quo. A prime example was Esther, a nominal Catholic in her early thirties with three young children.

I first got to know Esther during my follow-up fieldwork when I began frequenting her small restaurant located along Bwaise's main commercial strip. Her space was only ten feet wide and twenty feet deep, but the stools that lined the walls were often filled with customers. Like other regulars, I was drawn by both the tasty food and Esther's vivacious personality. Dynamic, confident, and somewhat sassy, Esther had no problem managing this business by herself and seemed equally comfortable bantering with her male and female customers.

Esther had been married to an older Catholic man for over a decade, and he also had a second wife. Esther said she was grateful her husband was supportive of her restaurant and appreciated the freedom and independence he had provided her, allowing her to run it over the past four years. Esther's assertiveness, and her success at managing her own business, did bring her some scrutiny. Some people joked that she behaved more like a man than a woman, while others gossiped that her husband gave her too much freedom and that she may have younger boyfriends on the side. Esther brushed off such rumors and maintained that she was happily married and faithful to her husband.

When I asked Esther her opinion of men in Bwaise generally, her comments echoed those of the women above.

> However much you try to care for a man, however much you try to look after him, he will still never have just one woman. Even when he tells you that he is only with you he will still have another one at work. So you only really know a man after he dies, because then you will learn that he had other women and children that you never knew about. . . . Ideally, the girlfriend or wife remains faithful to her man out of respect for their husband. But the man does not have to do that. . . . The Baganda say that *omusajja alina okusajjalaata* [a man has to prove his manhood (by having multiple partners)]. I am a good example of this because my husband has two wives!

Esther then softened her critique and indicated she was in many respects comfortable accommodating her husband's sexual privileges.

> Personally, I am very proud of my husband. For example, most men never care when their wife gets pregnant, but my husband is different. Even though his finances are limited, he shows me a lot of care. So I won't talk badly about him. There is no way I can do that! He gives me financial support and I never lack anything, so I have nothing bad to say about him. Even if he goes out and gets more women in addition to me and my cowife I don't care. As long as he hides those relationships from me, it's fine with me.

Esther was quick, however, to link men's sexual behavior with AIDS, especially married men with multiple partners. She had an astute sense of the latest trends in the Ugandan AIDS epidemic, in particular, the high rates of infection among those in long-term relationships.

> People around here think that AIDS spreads very fast in this community. And I think married men are mainly responsible for its spread. Because if a married man is not used to using condoms with his wife he will not use them when he sleeps with another girlfriend. That means he will infect his wife with HIV and when he gets yet another girlfriend he will do exactly the same thing again—no condom. So to me it is the married men who spread the infection more than others because they are used to sex without protection. You cannot convince him to use it. And to me that is the reason why there are a lot of infections among couples.

When I asked Esther if she was worried personally about AIDS, she said it was a major concern for her. Her primary protection strategy was to remain monogamous, but she was well aware of the limitations of this approach.

> I worry about AIDS so much. But the problem is that since we are two wives you never know what your cowife is doing. And my cowife also doesn't know what I am doing. So that's one way I fear I can catch it. And then the man will never stick to only the two of you, even though he has two wives.

Esther shared other women's concerns about men's sexuality, but she was nonetheless willing to accommodate her husband's desire to have more than one sexual partner, so long as he remained attentive to her and her children.

In fifteen months of fieldwork in Bwaise, I rarely encountered women with sexual lives as complicated as those of many men. The long-standing link between monogamy and being a "proper" woman no doubt made women more reluctant to discuss multiple sexual partnerships, especially with an American man. Yet my fieldwork also made evident the social and health risks women with multiple partners faced, making me believe women's claims to monogamy were not dramatically exaggerated.[9] The handful of women who told me they were sleeping with more than one man nearly always asserted they did it out of economic necessity. Both women and men frequently told me that money was the main reason women sought out additional sexual partners.[10]

Overall, women's engagements with masculine sexual privilege in Bwaise were complex. While most women were critical of men's sexuality and felt their options were constrained, they did not see themselves as helpless victims. Instead, they pursued diverse strategies in their continual negotiations, and occasional reworkings, of masculine sexual privilege. Frequently, their critiques also reproduced essentialist ideas of men's sexuality, which simultaneously challenged and reproduced norms of male sexuality—all aspects of the multifaceted and contradictory process of remaking masculinity. Like Esther, many were also willing to accommodate men having multiple partners if such relationships were conducted discreetly and the men did not neglect their families. When these terms were violated some women did not shy away from direct confrontation and ended the relationship, knowing the financial implications full well. In 2013 I learned that this was in fact the case for Esther; she decided to leave her husband not because of his multiple partners per se, she said, but because he stopped providing money for her and her children.

TRACING THE IMPLICATIONS OF MASCULINE SEXUAL PRIVILEGE IN BWAISE

In the course of my fieldwork, I slowly came to see how chronic poverty and masculine sexual privilege could bind people together in intricate webs of sexual relations. Having multiple sexual partners remained a male status symbol, yet sustaining relationships in a place like Bwaise proved difficult. Intimate relationships were often conflict-ridden and for some men emasculating. This, somewhat ironically, often led men to have additional sexual relationships, many of which would also prove conflict-ridden and for some men further emasculating. A much smaller number of women also sought out other sexual partners, usually for financial support but also occasionally for pleasure. The private webs of sexual relations that resulted were, however, often quite difficult for me to observe. One such web became visible to me as it grew increasingly public during my fieldwork. This web illustrates how masculine sexual privilege links individuals into sexual networks and shows how men try to manage and contain the ways such privilege affects their intimate relationships in the context of AIDS.

At the center of this web of relationships was Mohamed, a forty-year-old Muslim with a primary school education. Mohamed was an attractive man with a lean, muscular build who had spent his entire adult life living and working in Bwaise. His main income came from managing a large furniture store just a few doors from Esther's restaurant, and he was slightly better off than most of his male peers. When I first met Mohamed, he had been married to a woman close to his age for fourteen years and also had a second wife of four years who was twenty-five years old. Like most officially polygamous men in Bwaise, Mohamed had two houses, one for each wife and their children. Mohamed's home for his younger wife was a modest, single-room, brick structure with a metal roof in a congested section of Bwaise behind Mohamed's furniture showroom. I knew this house very well because it was immediately next door to the home of some of my closest friends in Bwaise. These families all shared a cramped courtyard, and I often greeted Mohamed's younger wife when she sat outside cooking and doing laundry.

When I spoke with Mohamed about his relationships, he told me he was proud to have two wives since he believed men should ideally have more than one wife. AIDS also played a central role in his decision to have a second wife.

> I got my second wife as a protective measure against AIDS in order for me to be able to change up my sex life and have more variety without going outside my marriage for other women. I really fear AIDS very much and have seen relatives die of the disease, so that's why I took a second wife. The first thing we did when we decided to marry was take an HIV test. . . . You know, the longer you stay with one woman, the more her love for you continues to reduce, even to the point of not wanting to sleep with you. She will only have sex with you when she feels like it. But if you get another woman she will have more time for you because your relationship will be fresh. She'll be more willing to have sex, and so even if the first wife refuses, you will not be affected so much by that.

Mohamed believed this strategy had worked well for him, and he claimed that for at least the past ten years he had not had any extramarital affairs. He was confident that he was sexually satisfying his wives, telling me, "That is not a problem for us. And I'm away from each wife for two days so if she did anything wrong with another man I would be able to see the signs." Mohamed wanted to make clear that he was different from other men in Bwaise.

> Most men have girlfriends in addition to their wives. Most men in fact have many such girlfriends. They want to sleep with every woman that they come across. The majority of the men want to taste each woman they see. There are very few men who are like me. It is hard for many of them. If a man is a true Muslim or Catholic, he won't behave like that, and if he does, he will do it secretly.

In my conversations with Mohamed I found him convincing and tended to believe what he told me about his relationships. What neither of us knew at the time, however, was that his life would become entangled with that of a neighbor, a man named James.

James, a twenty-eight-year-old Catholic, was a lifelong resident of Bwaise and like Mohamed had worked in the area his entire adulthood. The shop where James spent his days as a laundryman was wedged in a narrow corridor off of Bwaise's main commercial street, very close to Mohamed's furniture showroom. For twelve hours a day, James and his two business partners washed and ironed the piles of dirty clothes that filled their tiny shop. The grimy, stuffy space was a rough place to work. Heaps of clothes, in combination with the cramped alley, made the space suffocating. The one redeeming value of this business was that James and his two partners were running it independently, although James's share of the paltry profits amounted to only $5 a week. With almost no formal education, James was resigned to a life of tough manual labor, constantly struggling to provide the basics for himself and his family.

For a man of modest means, James had many responsibilities, including three wives and five children. The marriages were all informal, and he lived with one wife in a nearby section of Bwaise. The other two wives lived in a different part of Kampala, and although he wanted to spend more time with them and their children, he spent enough time with them to consider them his wives. James was vocal about not having sufficient income to provide for his family and told me he was overwhelmed by the responsibilities he had taken on. He felt he was constantly sacrificing for his family: working long hours, skipping lunch to save money, and refraining from any entertainment that was not free.

When I asked James why he wanted more than one wife he had a ready answer: "I want to have more than one woman to ensure that I'm happy in my life. So as a man, whenever you get some money the first thing you think of is getting a woman, so you can enjoy life." Work washing clothes, it seemed, provided just enough money for James to maintain multiple intimate relationships and give him an escape from what he saw as the pressures of domestic life. James said he loved the woman he lived with in Bwaise, was grateful for the children they had together, and liked sex with her the most. Yet he also implied she had driven him to seek other women, saying emphatically, "Let me tell you, the main reason a man gets many women is because of the nature of the woman he has at home. It's her that makes you think of going out for other women because of how badly she treats you."

It seemed James was in over his head. He recognized that his second and third marriages were on shaky ground and that he was having trouble taking care of their needs. Sex was part of his dilemma. He confided, "There are times when the woman really wants sex and yet you don't have the energy. But because you want to keep her you force yourself to do it. You have to sleep with your wives to ensure they don't go out with other men." James acknowledged that the two women who lived outside Bwaise were slipping away. Even the relationship with the wife in Bwaise seemed precarious, which is why he hated that she worked as a waitress. "I'm afraid she will sleep with whoever she serves food to," he said.

When I asked James if he had sex with any women other than his wives, he boasted, "In the last year I probably slept with another twenty women. Sometimes I use a condom with them, but if the woman is too attractive I may take off the condom and have sex without it." I was surprised by this because few men I met in Bwaise had such complicated sex lives.[11] Escapism and comfort were James's motivations, and he stressed that other men were not so different: "Not only in Bwaise, but in Uganda generally, you will easily find a man with more than four women. He might not treat them all as wives, but he will be sleeping with all of them. But the main reason most of the men sleep around is because of the need to relieve stress, so they find some relaxation and a rest from responsibilities in those other relationships." Similar to my discussion of work and compensatory sexuality in chapter 3, James implied that the stress of providing in a context like Bwaise led many men to compensate by starting new relationships, with the hope that those would be more pleasurable and less filled with conflict.

Because his father died of AIDS when James was a teenager, I was curious to know if he was concerned about becoming infected. "I do worry about AIDS. No man can say he doesn't fear it," he told me. "I can't guarantee that I'm HIV-negative because I have never been tested. I fear being told that I'm positive, and I know the moment they tell me I will be completely distressed." For James, AIDS was also a symptom of the confusions and contradictions of contemporary urban life, especially those connected to changing roles for women in society.

> I fear AIDS because we can't do without women. I think you know that! [Laughs] A man needs a female creature to survive. That's what makes you happy first and foremost. . . . But nowadays women are hard to control. This government has given the women a lot of rights and it has neglected the men. A woman now can fool all the men she is sleeping with into thinking she is faithful. Generally, the women we have today are a problem, and that's why we are getting infected.

James said that such changes meant he had to take measures to protect himself. "I have tried to reduce the number of women I sleep with, and whenever I want to have sex I use a condom," he said, contradicting what he had told me before.

While the way James discussed these issues did echo comments made to me by other men, most men in Bwaise would have viewed James's life as a cautionary tale rather than a kind of masculine ideal. He was overextended in his relationships and unable to provide for his wives, children, and girlfriends. He had lost his grip on some of the women in his life and was drowning in family responsibilities. His casual relationships provided temporary comfort, but his male peers likely viewed his behavior as excessive. With the looming threat of AIDS, most men would have seen his behavior as potentially life-threatening as well.

When I returned to Bwaise in 2009, I found that the lives of James and Mohamed had become acutely intertwined. I had hoped to interview Mohamed again, but he was reluctant to talk with me. He only told me that he was encountering problems with his younger wife and believed she was having an affair with a man who worked nearby. Mohamed also made it clear that he did not want me to talk with his wife. Eventually, I learned more from my good friend who was Mohamed's neighbor. For the past two years, my friend told me, Mohamed's younger wife had been having an affair with James. She was frustrated in her arranged marriage to a much older man and was looking for a sexual relationship with someone closer to her own age. Mohamed was afraid of losing this younger wife and determined to end her relationship with James; the tactic Mohamed was accused of using against James was witchcraft.

In contrast to Mohamed, James was eager to tell me his side of the story. We met at his clothes washing business, which had changed little over the years. It was immediately evident, however, that James had changed quite a bit. Much of his bulk had diminished, and he looked gaunt and significantly older. When we sat in the back of his shop to talk, he was agitated and visibly nervous. Before I could ask him a question he stopped the interview, saying he felt the spirits descending on him and knocking on his heart. After resting for a few minutes, he regained his composure and calmly told me about how his life had progressed since we last talked.

> I am not OK at all. There is a man [Mohamed] who claims that I fell in love with his wife, but I haven't done so. So he started to bewitch me. Up to now I have been able to use some herbs to treat myself, but he won't stop bewitching me. . . . What he wants is to kill me so that I can serve as an example to others. He wants to show that he has *amaanyi*. . . . He doesn't trust his wife and people gossip she will go with any man. So now he wants to show other men that he has *amaanyi* by killing me as an example.

James was clearly suffering. He said the demons visited every day, causing his heart to beat so rapidly he was afraid it would burst. They were often preceded by a phone call, and as we talked James repeatedly checked his cell phone for missed calls, holding the screen right up to his eyes and illuminating his face with an eerie blue glow.

If the intent of the bewitchment was to stifle James's love life, it appeared to have been successful. James told me:

> I no longer have girlfriends. . . . I don't have enough *amaanyi* because I am always attacked by these spirits. They don't leave you with enough *amaanyi*

to have sex with those girlfriends. If it wasn't for the local herbs I'm using I wouldn't even be having sex with my wives! . . . Before all these problems, I could have as many women as possible because I had enough *amaanyi*. I could make my herbs for *amaanyi gekisajja* [increasing a man's libido] and I could handle many of them. . . . But because of this sickness, when you are attacked every day, then you cannot have sex with many women.

From the way James spoke, these problems had indeed taken over his life. He was no longer able to work full-time and was now making only $2 or $3 a week. He was grateful that his grandfather was a traditional healer who had taught him some herbal remedies. At one point, he lifted his shirt to show me a special rope belt with knots filled with herbs that he always wore. He also frequently sipped from a plastic bottle wrapped in banana leaf that contained an orange liquid he said helped ward off the spirits.

James was concerned that people might confuse his bewitchment with AIDS. "Sometimes a witch doctor will make it look like someone suffers from AIDS," he told me. "They do that to protect themselves so no one knows a person was bewitched." James stressed that he was not HIV-positive.

> I have tested and even still have the result slips. My children are also HIV-negative. In terms of my cheating habits, I can't deny that I ever cheated on my wives. But I only had sex with a few women without using condoms. I insist on using condoms. . . . So I have checked for all those diseases, including AIDS, tuberculosis, and even malaria. I don't have those diseases. This kind of disease I'm suffering from is more serious and there is no test for it.

James was quite pessimistic about his future and felt Mohamed would not relent until he was dead: "If he fails to kill me by bewitching me he will try and stab me with a knife. And I'm afraid my wives will leave me because I'm always sick."

I left James to his ironing and herbs and felt very unsure about how much longer he would survive. If nothing else, he seemed on the verge of a nervous breakdown. My good friend, who was Mohamed's neighbor and also knew James well, was more cynical and doubted James was HIV-negative. It was common, he said, for people to claim they were bewitched when they learned they were HIV-positive. For men, such framings of bewitchment provided yet another means of obscuring links between masculine sexual privilege and HIV/AIDS. My good friend also said that Mohamed's strategy for containing the damage to his relationships had been costly for him. When it became public knowledge that he might have bewitched James, Mohamed was called before a council of local community leaders to explain himself. He was not required to pay a fine, but the general sentiment in the community was that he was responsible for the bewitching and that this was unjustifiable, even if a man slept with his wife. Some community members were so upset they threatened to burn down his house—a sentiment that seemed somewhat at odds with my own preoccupation with this complex web of relationships as efficient for transmitting HIV.

The saga of Mohamed and James illustrates how the persistence of masculine sexual privilege facilitates the formation of dense sexual networks in urban Uganda today. The ways all the key players in this particular network enacted masculine sexual privilege linked them in a dense cluster of sexual relationships, often in ways they could not have foreseen. Mohamed married a second wife for both social status and intimate pleasure but was also keenly concerned about AIDS. In fact, he saw his second wife as a protective measure against HIV infection and described himself as restraining his sexual privileges in response to AIDS. His younger wife, however, negotiated masculine sexual privilege in ways Mohamed did not expect and surreptitiously sought out another partner who could provide sexual satisfaction. Her choice of a partner, however, linked her and Mohamed and Mohamed's first wife to James's complicated sexual network, putting her at great risk of HIV infection. James, in contrast, while also aware of the dangers of AIDS, nonetheless prioritized having multiple sexual partners and exploited his masculine sexual privilege in ways other men would have likely seen as both excessive and dangerous, given his inconsistent use of condoms.

This saga is also indicative of the ways men themselves try to contain the implications of masculine sexual privilege. When he learned of his wife's affair, Mohamed was determined to keep her and focused his energy on restraining James. If the allegations against Mohamed were in fact true, he had succeeded in forcing James to change his sex life and to limit his extramarital affairs. Yet this strategy came with significant social costs for him. In the eyes of community members, his wife's affair with James did not justify the use of witchcraft. This saga thus illuminates how AIDS becomes entangled with the tensions and anxieties of everyday life in Bwaise. While James told me bewitchment, not AIDS, was his major problem now, the two were intertwined in many ways. James feared, justifiably, that people in the community would assume he was dying of AIDS, making both the disease and the bewitchment symptoms of disordered social relations—a disorder brought about largely by the difficulties of surviving and maintaining intimate relationships in a place like Bwaise.

WHY MASCULINE SEXUAL PRIVILEGE PERSISTS

As my fieldwork reveals, intimate relationships have indeed been shaped by AIDS. While this process has significant implications for masculinity, masculine sexual privilege has been remade in ways that ultimately reaffirm it. Among many men there is a recurring attempt to reconcile the forms of male status conventionally conferred by masculine sexual privilege with the relatively new realities of AIDS that impinge on such privilege. Many men find themselves caught between these forces and struggle to find a strategy for maintaining satisfying and stable intimate relationships. Women too play a key role in these processes, with critiques of men's sexual privileges going hand in hand with accommodations of the persistence of privilege.

Ironically, a key facet of how masculine sexual privilege has been remade involves the nature of AIDS prevention programs. As discussed in chapter 2, Uganda's indigenous zero grazing HIV prevention strategy emphasized that men should reduce their sexual partnerships and did not call for abstinence, monogamy, or marital fidelity. This pragmatic strategy is believed to have played an important role in Uganda's early success. While zero grazing campaigns were not explicitly directed only at men, I argue that men were the implied focus. The recurring emphasis by many of my informants on men reducing the number of their partnerships reflects the lingering impact of this approach.[12] Crucially for my overall argument in this book, zero grazing's emphasis on male partner reduction was a tacit endorsement of masculine sexual privilege, not a challenge to it. Considering this, the persistence of masculine sexual privilege is hardly an unexpected outcome.

Zero grazing campaigns were replaced in the 1990s and 2000s with a more generic, global AIDS prevention strategy. In the 2000s this strategy became increasingly inflected by puritanical, religious discourse that stressed abstinence, being faithful, or, if necessary, using condoms (the ABC approach). Those campaigns largely ignored the gendered aspects of sexual behavior and worked instead to heighten the moral scrutiny of any type of "promiscuous" sexual behavior, male or female. As Parikh (2007) convincingly argues, and as I discuss in greater detail in chapter 6, the net effect in urban Uganda has been to drive much male sexual behavior underground. Men continue to have multiple partners, but they cloak their actions in even greater secrecy—a dynamic with deep historical roots in Uganda.

In contrast to zero grazing, I found that the rhetoric of the ABC approach was frequently explicitly voiced by my informants. Many men and women emphasized that *obwesigwa*, "being faithful," was their primary AIDS prevention strategy. Yet the ABC approach also failed to challenge masculine sexual privilege, instead only promoting a more general sexual puritanism. Men like Edward, discussed in this chapter, and Rafik, discussed in chapter 3, drew on masculinity as a reservoir of sexual privilege, yet felt compelled to cloak their actions and present themselves as faithful, committed partners who had taken "responsible" precautions against AIDS. Women, including both Edward's and Rafik's partners, have strong incentives to be complicit in these processes, keeping extramarital affairs a secret to safeguard their identities as "modern" couples (see also Hirsch et al. 2009). When considered as part of a longer story that includes managing relationships in relation to Christian ideals of monogamy that took hold in the early twentieth century, newer ideals of modern romantic love salient since midcentury, and the contemporary emphasis on gender equity and women's rights, Edward's and Rafik's behavior is actually very predictable. The AIDS epidemic complicates the enactment of masculine sexual privilege but has not posed any fundamental challenge to it. Thus it persists.

A subtext in this chapter is the role that economic factors play in shaping intimate relationships. The vast majority of people I met in Bwaise were perpetually concerned about rent, food, and other basic necessities, which in turn created significant tensions in intimate relationships. This was also an urban context with dramatically increasing economic inequality, pitting rich men and poor men against each other and heightening the sense of male status associated with supporting multiple sexual partners. Chronic poverty and economic inequality worked to buttress masculine sexual privilege, often in ways that were deeply entangled with AIDS.

Finally, this chapter reveals that women's rights have played a limited role in how men enact and women negotiate masculine sexual privilege. As discussed in chapter 4, I did encounter women who drew on rights discourse to negotiate safe sex. By and large, however, ideas of women's rights were not mobilized to challenge masculine sexual privilege. In contrast, notions of rights did figure prominently in women's assertions that they were entitled to earn money outside the home and in their claims that earning power gave them more authority within the home. Thus masculine sexual privilege also persists because of the particular contours of women's rights discourse in Uganda, a discourse that has produced a partial challenge to men's authority while eschewing any similar challenge to men's sexual privileges.

The fact that normative notions of masculinity appear to be lagging behind the social changes occurring in urban Uganda is not surprising and hardly something specific to African contexts. As the sociologist Cecilia Ridgeway (2011) has argued, when people confront changing social contexts they draw on established cultural beliefs about gender and sexuality to frame these new contexts. In the process, gender inequality is reinserted in new socioeconomic arrangements, including those that operate to undermine gender inequality. These dynamics underscore the value of the framework for masculinity as a social process that I presented in chapter 1. The interrelation of work, authority, and sexuality is key to understanding how male privilege persists even as normative notions of masculinity are remade to adapt to a rapidly changing social context.

My emphasis on the persistence of masculine sexual privilege should not, however, be understood as suggesting that masculinity in this context is impervious to change. In many respects, this ethnography reveals just the opposite and demonstrates that masculine ideals are in flux, being remade in new ways in response to growing economic inequality, the continuing AIDS crisis, relatively new discourses of women's rights, and women's expanding role as family providers. Indeed, there is a remarkable array of social forces impinging on normative notions of masculinity in urban Uganda, making this contemporary period similar to the early colonial period in terms of dramatic social change. In my next and final chapter, I examine the implications these shifts have for masculinity and intimate relationships in sub-Saharan Africa more generally, as well as the insights they provide for addressing the AIDS epidemic in all its sociological complexity.

6 Beyond Bwaise

One of the most enjoyable aspects of my fieldwork in Bwaise was when I could make time to just amble through the community, choosing to follow one of many dirt footpaths without much forethought. By the end of my time in Bwaise, such walks often brought the seemingly separate aspects of my fieldwork into conversation. I might begin by passing the house of a couple I knew who were coping with HIV, or perhaps greet a community AIDS counselor on her rounds. As I strolled along, I might see a poster about preventing domestic violence produced by the NGO I volunteered with, or come across one of the young men who conducted community outreach activities for the organization. I nearly always passed the carpentry shop where I apprenticed, or the main commercial strip, where I inevitably had conversations with male friends and acquaintances about the vagaries of work in Bwaise.

On these walks, I realized that what seemed like discrete facets of my fieldwork were deeply interwoven. This book can be read in a similar way, and like my fieldwork itself there are several paths through the chapters. One path traces the story of AIDS in urban Uganda, another reveals a story about the gendered culture of a community, and a third foregrounds the everyday challenges of surviving in an African slum. These paths not only intersect but also more often overlap, and together they provide a sense of how masculinity is lived in a place like Bwaise in the context of AIDS.

I was initially motivated to write this book by a desire to understand the social significance of AIDS in Africa. Uganda's reputation as an AIDS success story made me hopeful, perhaps naively, that I could identify a stark shift in how Ugandans enacted masculinity in the wake of AIDS. This did not prove to be the case; instead I found a subtler and more complex story of how masculinity was remade in relation to the dangers and difficulties posed by HIV/AIDS.

A prominent theme throughout this book is that while AIDS has complicated aspects of masculine sexual privilege, it has not truly challenged it. I found that men, as well as women, reworked men's sexuality in light of the persistent presence of HIV, at times questioning but largely reaffirming the sexual privileges accorded to men. For many men, there were recurring attempts to reconcile the forms of male pleasure and status conventionally conferred by masculine sexual privilege with the relatively new realities of AIDS that impinged on this privilege. Many men described themselves as caught between these forces and struggled to find a strategy for maintaining satisfying and stable intimate relationships. In this sense, men continued to make a claim to an entrenched ideal of masculine sexual privilege that afforded them greater sexual liberties, rights, power, and, often, pleasure. Yet the ways they enacted male sexuality in relation to this ideal were complicated by the context of HIV/AIDS.

Part of the explanation for this persistence of masculine sexual privilege is the nature of AIDS prevention programs themselves. This masculine ideal has never been confronted directly by HIV prevention efforts, and in some cases, such as the early zero grazing campaigns, it has been tacitly endorsed. This was reflected in the lives of many men I met who described how they had chosen to limit their sexual partnerships as a pragmatic response to the dangers posed by HIV. The more generic AIDS prevention strategies that followed in the 1990s and 2000s largely neglected the social context and emphasized individual behavior change as a "rational" and "responsible" response to the risks posed by AIDS. This resulted in concerted efforts by men, and some women, to conceal extramarital and other sexual partners by carefully cultivating a public persona of committed monogamy—a dynamic that has precedents dating to the institutionalization of Christianity in southern Uganda in the early twentieth century. While I did find instances when AIDS catalyzed new negotiations of masculine sexual privilege, such as when an HIV-positive man was in a serodiscordant relationship, these were exceptions to the general theme of the persistence of privilege.

Before I began my fieldwork, I had expected the promotion of women's rights to play an important role in undermining masculine sexual privilege, with women empowered by rights better able to negotiate safe sex and to challenge men's privilege of having multiple sexual partners. This was only true in a quite limited sense, with certain serodiscordant couples again an interesting exception. Instead, I found that women's rights were not primarily mobilized to challenge masculine sexual privilege. This dynamic reflects that the government's framing of women's rights as gender equity has limited how women's rights are understood, and this framing does not address sexuality as a component of women's rights. It also marginalizes more substantial connections between women's rights and gender equality advocated by the Ugandan women's movement, including efforts to address sexual violence such as marital rape.

Thus the second key theme in my fieldwork was that the rhetoric of women's rights was only normative in a limited sense. Where women's rights did matter to masculinity, however, was in relation to the masculine ideal of men's authority over women in the home. Both men and women largely understood women's rights as destabilizing ideas of men's assumed power over women, including as ultimate decision makers in the family. However, many men strove to contain the implications of women's rights, especially when their wives or girlfriends were working and earning their own money. In response, many women engaged with women's rights discourse in relation to strategic, instrumental gains, so as not to disrupt the gender hierarchy within the home. Significantly, the way some men negotiated such threats to their masculine authority was by exercising their masculine sexual privilege, either by exerting control over the terms of sex or by exploring additional sexual relationships. The net result was limited transformative synergy between women's rights, HIV/AIDS, and changes in established ideals of male sexuality.

This issue of threats to male authority was tied to the third key theme: the difficulty of fulfilling the male economic provider ideal. The challenges and frustrations most men in Bwaise encountered in their attempts to embody the male provider ideal had important implications for both male authority and the persistence of masculine sexual privilege. In a context in which women were increasingly participating in the workforce, men who struggled to earn money often felt emasculated, and their claim to authority was only further threatened by notions of women's rights. The result was tensions in relationships that could be difficult to manage, and for some men an escape from these tensions was found in exercising the privilege of having an additional sexual partner, even if a new partnership inevitably created its own problems and tensions. Increasing economic stratification in Kampala also buttressed masculine sexual privilege because of the status accrued to men who could maintain multiple relationships. This dynamic also has a long history in Buganda, most evident in the rise of elite polygyny in the eighteenth century (Musisi 1991). In this sense, the entrenched male provider ideal reinforced masculine sexual privilege for men who fulfilled it and for men who struggled to fulfill it. AIDS has had a limited impact on male sexual privilege, therefore, not only because of AIDS prevention programs and the limited scope of women's rights, but also because such privilege has been reinforced by the context of precarious work and growing economic inequality in urban Uganda.

AIDS AND THE REMAKING OF MASCULINITY IN AFRICA

These three interrelated themes—the persistence of masculine sexual privilege, challenges to men's authority, and a precarious male economic provider identity—are by no means unique to Bwaise. They are evident in a wide range of contexts across sub-Saharan Africa, almost always intertwined in the ways they are in Bwaise. In addition, in those countries severely affected by AIDS, there is a great deal of evidence that HIV/AIDS has remade masculinity in a manner similar to what I observed in Bwaise. Here, I draw on much of the richest research on contemporary masculinities in sub-Saharan Africa to contextualize my fieldwork in Bwaise, revealing the striking similarities that exist in the remaking of African masculinities in the age of AIDS.

In Uganda, there is ample evidence to support the prominence and persistence of the ideology of masculine sexual privilege that I have charted in this book. In the only other detailed study of Bwaise, conducted a decade before my fieldwork, Andrew Mickleburgh (1998) describes how men's frequent inability to provide for their families creates inevitable marriage tensions, something I also found very common in Bwaise. Many men respond to these conflicts by drawing on their masculine sexual privilege of having multiple sexual partners to start a new relationship as they slowly exit their marriage. Importantly, Mickleburgh reveals that masculine sexual privilege is not typically manifested as a preoccupation with maximizing a man's sexual partners but instead as the freedom to start a new relationship as a man's current relationship becomes too conflict-ridden—an important corrective to stereotypes about African male sexual promiscuity. Mickleburgh also sees AIDS as having had a very limited impact on these gender dynamics, with key markers of masculinity—that "men need more than one sexual partner [and] women should not question the sexual activities of their husbands"—remaining (275). These dynamics are not limited to Bwaise; recent research indicates that this ideology of male sexuality, including men's concurrent partnerships, are part of life in communities across the city (Kajubi et al. 2011; Rutakumwa et al. 2015).

In their study of *bodabodamen* (motorcycle taxi men) in southwestern Uganda, Stella Nyanzi and colleagues (Nyanzi et al. 2004; Nyanzi, Nyanzi, and Kalina 2005; Nyanzi, Nyanzi-Wakholi, and Kalina 2009) show that the contours of masculine sexual privilege, and its intertwining with men's identity as money earners, can be very similar beyond Kampala. They describe multiple sexual partners as the litmus test of *musajja wa ddala* (a real man) among bodabodamen and thus a key marker of "higher social status, economic well-being, power, and 'more manhood'" (Nyanzi, Nyanzi-Wakholi, and Kalina 2009, 73). Even though they are working class, their daily access to cash makes bodabodamen relatively better off in comparison to other men, and this facilitates their ability to enact hegemonic male sexuality through multiple sexual partnerships.[1] Money, economic inequality, and male sexuality were, therefore, deeply intertwined among these men, who provide a vivid illustration of what I describe in chapter 3 as sexuality as a performance of male status. While this region of Uganda has been severely affected by HIV/AIDS, only a small number of bodabodamen contested the dominant association between masculinity and multiple partners. As in Bwaise, masculine sexual privilege persisted among these men, even though the majority said the bodaboda lifestyle, especially the connection between quick cash and multiple sexual partners, placed them at high risk of HIV infection (Nyanzi, Nyanzi, and Kalina 2005, 117).

This link between men's multiple sexual partners and men's social status is also a prominent theme in Shanti Parikh's (2007, 2009) research among the Basoga ethnic group in Iganga town in southeastern Uganda. As I do, Parikh describes such partnerships as one aspect of men's "masculine sexual privilege" that has roots in precolonial Basoga society and "remains the norm in Iganga" (2007, 1200). Yet Parikh foregrounds how the contemporary context—in particular, the rise of modern companionate marriage ideals, the growing influence of evangelical Christianity, and emphasis on "being faithful" in AIDS prevention programs—has prompted a heightened need for secrecy in men's extramarital affairs. Similar to my discussion in chapter 2, Parikh notes that this need for sexual secrecy and discretion can be traced to the early colonial period, but contemporary notions of sexual immorality are "heightening men's personal motivation for sexual secrecy to avoid public scorn and domestic conflict" (2007, 1198).

These dynamics create profound paradoxes for Iganga men, similar to those I describe in chapters 3 and 5, because "appearing to have sexual prowess and vitality remains an important aspect of masculine status within many male peer groups, but uncontained public knowledge of his sexual exploits can ruin a man's reputation in the wider community" (Parikh 2009, 192–93). In this sense, Parikh also demonstrates that the impact of AIDS on masculine sexual privilege has been quite limited, primarily leading men to hide their liaisons.[2] Such secrecy, Parikh argues, makes it more difficult for wives to discuss issues of marital fidelity with their husbands and thus heightens married women's risk of HIV infection.

Importantly, Parikh considers how efforts to promote women's rights and gender equality in Uganda both reinforce and complicate these dynamics. On the one hand, women's rights exacerbate feelings of emasculation among men in Iganga who are struggling, and often failing, to be family providers. This additional challenge to men's authority in the home often resulted in men starting another sexual relationship to "repossess traditional masculine authority" (2007, 1204)— the dynamics of compensatory sexuality that I describe as arising from the interplay between perceived threats to men's authority and male sexuality. On the other hand, Parikh argues that the institutionalization of women's rights in Uganda also prompts women to occasionally confront their male partners. The status of "being 'rational' modern women who have the knowledge and desire to protect their bodies and rights" compels some women to "go public" about their husbands' affairs when they are not conducted with adequate discretion (2009, 195). Yet, in nearly all cases, Parikh found the wife's ire was directed not at her husband but at his mistress. This blunted any challenge women's rights posed to confronting the sexual double standard, which echoes my central finding in chapter 4 regarding the limited impact of women's rights on challenging masculine sexual privilege.

Elsewhere in East Africa, AIDS as a paradox of manhood is also a prominent theme.[3] As Margrethe Silberschmidt (2001, 2004, 2005) has persuasively demonstrated, men in both rural western Kenya and urban Tanzania are "caught in very similar and paradoxical situations" where normative notions of masculinity position them as heads of families, yet lack of employment prevents them from fulfilling their economic responsibilities as breadwinners and household heads (2001, 668). This leaves men with "a patriarchal ideology bereft of its legitimizing activities" and for many men "multi-partnered sexual relationships and sexually aggressive behavior seem to strengthen male identity and sense of masculinity" (2001, 657).

Thus Silberschmidt provides one of the clearest illustrations of how men's insecure identities as economic providers is coupled with what I have referred to as compensatory sexuality, especially men's multiple sexual partnerships. Like Parikh, Silberschmidt (2001, 666) notes how the promotion of women's rights can exacerbate these dynamics because men "constantly blamed the government" for advocating equal rights. Importantly, she also concludes that the AIDS epidemic has done little to disrupt these dynamics because neither sticking to one partner nor using condoms is an "acceptable solutio[n] to most men" (Silberschmidt 2004, 50). Yet, while Silberschmidt captures the depth of many men's feelings of insecurity and loss of self-esteem, her emphasis on "male disempowerment" and "men's increasingly marginalized situation" (2001, 657, 669) runs the risk of neglecting how male power, authority, and privilege are remade in times of growing economic inequality, including how some groups of men gain from these processes. In addition, as I discuss below, it may underestimate how more careful and strategic promotions of women's rights can provide a challenge to, and not simply an entrenchment of, masculine sexual privilege in the context of AIDS.

In her insightful ethnography of AIDS among the Luo in western Kenya, *Love, Money, and HIV* (2014), Sanyu Mojola reveals a similar contemporary ideology of male sexual privilege. She also illustrates how this ideology is intertwined with young women's desire to become modern "consuming" women, with tragic results in the context of HIV. Mojola found that sexual activity is a central aspect of manhood (which is common across the globe), but so too is "a belief engrained in the minds of everyone I talked with that Luo men could not be faithful" (107). Yet, as in many other African settings, including Bwaise, enacting this privilege requires money, with those men most able to be providers of gifts and other support most able to establish and maintain multiple sexual partnerships (i.e., the dynamics of sexuality as a performance of male status discussed in chapter 3; see also Hunter 2002; Luke 2003; Poulin 2007). Such men tend to be somewhat older and in many African contexts (including Uganda) more likely to be HIV-positive than younger men. For young women, most of whom cannot find work, sexual relationships with these men are the most promising prospects in their efforts to fashion themselves as modern women, allowing them to acquire the cosmetics, toiletries, and clothes that are markers of the sophisticated Kenyan woman. Sadly, these same relationships are also much more risky for HIV infection, which largely explains why these young women are significantly more likely to be HIV-positive than their young male peers who largely lack the money for maintaining sexual relationships.

In what is a recurring theme in the literature on AIDS and masculinity in Africa, Mojola argues that the primary AIDS prevention approaches—especially the ABCs of Abstinence, Being faithful, or using Condoms—have done little to disrupt these dynamics or challenge men's sexual privileges; thus they persist. The only notable exception is among some fishing

communities on the shores of Lake Victoria where what is known as the *jaboya* system of male fishermen and female fish sellers creates dense sexual networks that facilitate HIV transmission. These communities have been exceptionally hard hit by HIV, and in this context of extreme HIV risk "the specter of AIDS was changing [fishermen's] attitudes toward multiple relationships, and the meaning of having many girl-friends had changed" (Mojola 2014, 180). Yet, while AIDS does seem to have catalyzed a critical assessment of aspects of masculine sexual privilege and "many of these men said they were making changes," the overall impact on HIV transmission in these communities may be limited because "the *jaboya* system still thrives" (180).

An intriguing complication to this otherwise consistent story of the persistence of masculine sexual privilege in East Africa is found in Rachel Spronk's book, *Ambiguous Pleasures* (2012). In her study of young urban professionals in Nairobi, Spronk found that men were fiercely grappling with the meaning of manhood, especially in their intimate relationships. Of particular concern for them was finding ways to reconcile hegemonic aspects of male sexuality, in particular, having multiple sexual partners, which were seen "as the norm for men" (213), with notions of modern love and companionate, monogamous relationships. For these men "multi-partnered relationships and financial success are seen as going hand in hand"; however, these men are also accommodating shifts in the gender order and "want to have more egalitarian relationships with women, characterized by companionship, mutual sexual desire and common interests" (214, 180).

These dynamics were also evident in Bwaise, especially in the lives of younger men like Rafik (chapter 3) and Edward (chapter 5), and I discuss them as one aspect of sexuality as a reservoir of privilege. However, these issues were much more front and center in the lives of the Nairobi men Spronk came to know. This was because for this relatively privileged group the "concurrence between sexuality, consumerism and romantic love [has] become central to self-expression," which "sets this group of young professionals apart from other groups in Kenyan society" (Spronk 2012, 276). The result was much fraught self-reflection as these upwardly mobile men wrestled with shifting, and competing, notions of masculinity that made sexuality such an ambiguous pleasure. Significantly, HIV/AIDS was not a particularly salient aspect of men's ambiguity and uncertainty about sexual relationships. AIDS was a "context of life" for these young professionals, and its association as a "disease of immorality" was understood as "a sign of the times," yet HIV/AIDS did not figure prominently in men's narratives about their relationship dilemmas (98). As in other East African contexts, the AIDS epidemic has not been a significant catalyst in the emergence of alternative notions of masculinity and male sexuality in this privileged milieu.

Across the continent, in West Africa, the social significance of AIDS has been most richly analyzed in Nigeria by Daniel Jordan Smith (2006, 2007, 2008, 2009a, 2014), and very similar themes recur. In research spanning more than two decades in Igbo-speaking southeastern Nigeria, Smith provides a nuanced analysis of how gender inequality and increasing economic stratification are intertwined with masculinity and HIV/AIDS. He describes a similar ideology of male sexuality that combines men's control over sex with the privilege of having multiple sexual partners and charts how it is remade in the context of AIDS. Like my analysis, his study reveals how growing economic inequality buttresses men's pursuit of extramarital partners as a form of "conspicuous consumption" (Smith 2009a, 96) for those men with money (sexuality as a performance of male status in my terms) and as a "refuge from their problems . . . to bolster their masculine identity" (Smith 2006, 236, 237) for poor men who are failed family providers (compensatory masculinity in my terms). In addition to these socioeconomic factors, Smith (2007, 1000) emphasizes that men's work-related mobility and the "peer pressures, expectations, and rewards" associated with men's predominantly male peer groups facilitate and encourage men's contemporary extramarital sexual behavior.

Like Parikh, Smith stresses that notions of modern, romantic love have complicated men's enactment of their sexual privileges. Ideals of companionate, egalitarian relationships are of increasing importance to Igbo men and women during the early years of courtship and marriage. Parenthood, however, instigates a greater emphasis on aspects of masculinity tied to sexual conquests outside marriage in which "perceived extramarital sexual activity is socially rewarded" (Smith 2006, 147). Ideals of companionate marriage heighten the importance of maintaining a public facade of monogamous marriage, and when husbands are "unfaithful" both men and women have incentive to keep men's infidelities a secret. Smith, like

Parikh, sees this dynamic as making marriage a context of high HIV risk for many married women, given both the persistence of gender inequality and the common perception that "condoms symbolize impersonal or promiscuous sex" (Smith 2007, 1002). Thus, instead of AIDS posing a challenge to masculine sexual privilege, "the popular association of the disease with sexual immorality has, if anything, contributed to the complex web of silences and secrets that surround [men's] extramarital sex" (1003).

While Smith's fieldwork in Nigeria corroborates findings from East Africa, his analysis deepens our understanding of men's sexual behavior by revealing how it is linked to men's desire to be perceived as "moral actors." He stresses that the tendency to reduce men's motives for extramarital affairs to a quest for sexual pleasure is problematic because it obscures the complex ways men strive to "do intimacy" in many African contexts (Smith 2008, 226). In his book *AIDS Doesn't Show Its Face* (2014), Smith emphasizes that the long-standing link between masculinity and men's ability to provide materially for a wide range of dependents sets a moral framework for the motives and rewards of men's extramarital relationships. Building on similar insights by Ann Swidler and Susan Watkins (2007) based on research in Malawi, Smith (2014, 77) argues that men's extramarital sexual relationships "need to be understood within a larger context of patronage, wealth in people, and men's roles as providers [and] many men reported that they enjoyed the feeling of taking care of another woman, of being able to provide her with material and social comforts and luxuries." The way men "do intimacy" in extramarital relationships is then buttressed by the support, camaraderie, and feelings of intimacy men typically enjoy when they boast about their affairs in male-only peer group interactions.

Smith, like Spronk (2012), is careful to note that men also express some ambivalence about their extramarital relationships, both because of social expectations that men must ensure that their own family is properly provided for and because of the heightened scrutiny of sexuality in the context of moralizing AIDS discourses. Men, therefore, are navigating a complex, sometimes contradictory, contemporary moral landscape, with male infidelity involving "multiple and sometimes contradictory intimacies" (Smith 2008, 242)—a finding that resonates with my fieldwork in Bwaise. Yet, importantly, Smith (2014, 164) emphasizes that men's extramarital

sexual behavior is ultimately buttressed by the prevailing context of gender inequality, especially a sexual double standard that rewards men's
multiple partnerships and punishes women who are "judged as outside
the boundaries of moral sexual behavior." As Smith emphasizes, and as I
point out throughout this book, this sexual double standard is in fact
deeply intertwined with tensions over women's rights, gender equality,
and women's advancing position in society, especially in the context of
AIDS. Women's sexuality, Smith argues (2014, 164), has risen to the top of
the imagined causes of the AIDS crisis in Nigeria because "men in particular fear the demise of a system of gender inequality that assures a division
of labor and power, defining men's and women's social, economic, and
political roles quite strictly and to men's benefit." Thus, while AIDS has
created paradoxes of manhood for many Nigerian men, it has not fundamentally undermined men's sexual privileges, or the system of gender
inequality of which such privileges are a fundamental part.

Turning to southern Africa, two additional books provide compelling
evidence for the persistence of masculine sexual privilege in the region of
Africa hardest hit by HIV/AIDS. The first is Anthony Simpson's *Boys to
Men in the Shadow of AIDS* (2009), which examines masculinities and
HIV/AIDS in Zambia. In this remarkable study, Simpson followed a
cohort of twenty-four young men at an elite Catholic boarding school over
the course of twenty years. His initial fieldwork was in 1983–84, when the
boys were in their late teens and early twenties. In 2002, he reinterviewed
twelve of these men, now in their late thirties to early forties (eight had
died in the intervening years, most from AIDS). Simpson (2009, 8) demonstrates how these young men were socialized by fathers, brothers,
schoolmates, and teachers in an ideology of masculinity, and "at the core
of the prevailing hegemonic version of masculinity was the demonstration
of male potency in sexual conquest." Such male potency was demonstrated
in men's need for regular penetrative sex, a dominant and aggressive
stance toward sex that meant many of these men would "forego using condoms because of their need to prove their virility by the 'strength' of their
performance" (14), and in repeated sexual conquest manifest in the high
value placed on multiple sexual partnerships. Simpson then reveals how
this ideology of male sexuality shaped their sexual relationships in adulthood, often with tragic consequences for these men and their partners.

While this cohort of men did engage with hegemonic masculinity in diverse ways, Simpson (2009, 15) demonstrates that most conformed to (or attempted to conform to) normative ideals of male sexuality, and "most men in this study engaged in unprotected extramarital sex." Many of these men were unable to fulfill their promise as graduates of an elite secondary school and struggled to be the family breadwinner. This contributed to the prevailing absence of trust and satisfaction in marriages, which Simpson found especially evident in sexual matters, and this facilitated men's infidelity. Most important for the arguments I make in this book, Simpson argues that the AIDS epidemic had little impact on the enactment of this ideology of male sexuality. The men were well aware of the dangers of AIDS, and many said their fear of AIDS prompted them to wed, in the hope that marriage would make them less likely to engage in unprotected sex with other partners (similar to my discussion in chapter 3 of sexuality as a pragmatic problem). However, Simpson (2009, 191) argues, because HIV prevention efforts were limited to the simplistic ABCs and HIV testing, "the existing gender order—men's power and men's claims to power—generally went unchallenged. The campaigns failed to address the contexts of Zambians' lives where women felt unable to protect themselves from the risk of infection from their husbands and where men were rarely challenged about their preference for multiple partners." The toll this persistence of masculine privilege took on this cohort of men was indeed dramatic and tragic; approximately a third had died of AIDS, and many of the surviving men assumed they were HIV-positive (190).

Finally, I turn to the book that in many respects most resembles this one: Mark Hunter's *Love in the Time of AIDS* (2010). This is an exceptionally nuanced ethnography of an informal settlement (or slum) and a working-class township in Mandeni, a town in the South African province of KwaZulu-Natal, where HIV prevalence is among the highest in the world. Hunter reveals how economic inequality, gender relations, and HIV/AIDS intersect, with particular attention to the ways shifting conceptions of masculinity have shaped intimate relationships. He presents a detailed historical account of the *isoka*, the Zulu man with multiple sexual partners. In the early twentieth century, this masculine ideal was tied to marriage and the establishment of an independent household as the true markers of manhood. Since South Africa's economic decline of the 1970s and subsequent persistent poverty and unemployment, men have been less able to establish households or marry formally but still define themselves partially in relation to an isoka ideal. The result, Hunter argues (in an earlier work in the same province), has been the emergence of a modern isoka masculinity in which "the high value placed on men seeking multiple partners increasingly filled the void left by men's inability to become men through previous means" (2004, 389). Hunter, therefore, historicizes this key aspect of masculine sexual privilege, revealing how a man's right to multiple sexual partners was remade over the course of the twentieth century.

As he illustrates in the second half of *Love in the Time of AIDS*, the increasingly precarious nature of work in the postapartheid era has made women more dependent on men, while most men fail to find the steady employment they need to be proper providers. Given the persistence of masculine sexual privilege, as manifested in the modern isoka ideal, these economic conditions simultaneously draw women into transactional sexual relationships with men and motivate men's multiple sexual partnerships.[4] These dynamics, Hunter argues, largely explain why a place like Mandeni has been so devastated by AIDS.

Hunter demonstrates that shifting masculinities are fundamentally intertwined with economic change and inequality—a theme that figures prominently in my analysis in chapter 3. It is this entanglement of gender relations and economic relations—what Hunter (2009, 4) describes as "viewing the economic and intimate as dialectical"—that helps explain how men in contexts like Mandeni, or Bwaise for that matter, can be simultaneously emasculated by economic conditions and able to draw on their sexual privilege to reassert their masculinity. As Hunter (2010, 219) stresses, "The coexistence of male power and weakness cannot be understood through either political economy or gender/intimacy alone; an approach is required that incorporates both."

Importantly, Hunter devotes an entire chapter to examining how this economy-intimacy dialectic is inflected by women's rights. As in Uganda, the promotion of women's rights and the struggle for gender equality have been prominent aspects of national politics in postapartheid South Africa. However, Hunter argues that their effect on power dynamics in intimate relationships is far from straightforward. Some young women insisted

that they used rights "to protect themselves from the risks of sex or to demand more sexual pleasure" (Hunter 2010, 136). Yet, with regard to safe sex, a young woman's desire to use condoms was often trumped by her partner's refusal to wear a condom. More surprisingly, a few financially better off young women drew on the language of rights "to argue that now they—just like men—are entitled to have multiple concurrent partners" (147). The vast majority of women in Mandeni, however, were carefully balancing a desire for more equitable intimate relationships with conventional expectations of being a respectful, dutiful wife. Much like my findings discussed in chapter 4, most women were striving for a more modest reformulation of the patriarchal bargain, with men remaining the household authority. Sexuality was not the domain where such women could easily make strides, and, as I also found, a woman's right to earn her own money was often the priority. As in Bwaise, this complex and partial institutionalization of women's rights ultimately has done little to challenge men's sexual privileges.

Overall, therefore, the story Hunter tells is primarily one of the persistence of masculine sexual privilege in the age of AIDS, as evidenced most vividly by the modern isoka masculinity. Yet the extremely high HIV prevalence rates in KwaZulu-Natal complicate this story. Hunter's fieldwork revealed that "day by day, funeral by funeral, AIDS bears down on the *isoka* masculinity. The symptoms, recognized by even very young children in the township, cannot be more emasculating—and de-masculinizing. Some of the most virile, popular, and independent bodies are steadily transformed into diseased and dependent skeletons, shunned by friends and neighbors" (Hunter 2010, 222). In this sense, Hunter sees the AIDS epidemic as prompting unprecedented scrutiny and critiques of this aspect of hegemonic masculinity, and he notes that some of these critiques have become institutionalized in new programs seeking to transform masculinities. While not dismissive of such efforts, he emphasizes that it is crucial "to recognize how deeply hampered *any* interventions to rework masculinities, and more broadly sexuality, are by the extreme poverty in many areas of the country" (2005, 399). He concludes *Love in the Time of AIDS* by underscoring that while antiretroviral drugs have greatly reduced AIDS deaths in Mandeni, "the social roots of this disease remain stubbornly in place" (2010, 225).

Taken together, these studies from across the continent strongly suggest that my findings in Bwaise about masculinity as a social process are also operating in many sub-Saharan African contexts. The key themes from my fieldwork in Bwaise are prominent in eastern, western, and southern Africa: an ideology of male sexuality rooted in men's privileges of controlling sex and having multiple sexual partners; the multifaceted impact of precarious work and economic inequality on male sexuality; the intertwining of anxieties about women's rights and gender equality with masculine sexual privilege; and, most significantly, the limited effect the AIDS epidemic has had on remaking masculine sexual privilege.

These striking similarities point to the interplay of work, authority, and sexuality as a central dynamic in the remaking of masculinity in sub-Saharan Africa in the age of AIDS. Such generalizations about sub-Saharan Africa as a region overall are often studiously avoided, especially given that a monolithic "African sexuality" has at times been used to explain the severity of AIDS in Africa (Caldwell, Caldwell, and Quiggin 1989; for critiques, see Ahlberg 1994; Heald 1995). Yet this hesitancy presents its own problems by diverting our attention from how growing economic inequality in Africa shapes sexuality, intimate relationships, and African masculinities in similar ways. James Ferguson's (2006) critique of the tendency in anthropology to describe Africans as experiencing "alternative" versions of modernity is especially useful here. As Ferguson argues, "In their eagerness to treat African people as (cultural) equals, Western anthropologists have sometimes too easily sidestepped the harder discussion about the economic *inequalities* and disillusionments that threaten to make any such equality a merely ideal or sentimental one" (34; original emphasis). For Ferguson, these inequalities are often strikingly similar across sub-Saharan Africa today. To this I would only add that so too are the effects of such inequalities on many Africans' most intimate relationships.

REMAKING MASCULINITY: SEXUALITY AND THE PERSISTENCE OF GENDER INEQUALITY

My motivation for writing this book was to understand how the AIDS epidemic—a monumental event for most of sub-Saharan Africa—had affected gender and sexuality in Uganda. Through the course of my field-work and writing, it became clear that this book was also as much if not more about how masculinity was lived in urban Africa. This ethnography of Bwaise, therefore, not only helps us grasp the historical significance of AIDS but also advances our understanding of masculinity as a social proc-ess, foregrounding how it is remade in everyday interactions.

When I began my fieldwork, I initially expected that the men I would come to know would all occupy a relatively similar position within a mascu-line hierarchy in urban Uganda. As residents of a Kampala slum, I assumed that men in Bwaise would see themselves embodying a marginalized mascu-linity defined largely by their status as members of the urban poor. A shared identity as marginalized men, I assumed, would shape their attitudes and behaviors in similar ways and the relationships they had with other men, and women, as well. In some respects, these assumptions proved true. The mark-ers of elite or even middle-class male status, especially wealth and political power, were well beyond the reach of most men I came to know. Most men in Bwaise did understand themselves as marginal, poor men, and this mar-ginality did inflect their attitudes, behaviors, and interactions.

Yet, as my fieldwork progressed, understanding men in Bwaise as a homogeneous group proved less useful. Examining masculinity in Bwaise in this way not only obscured the diversity of men but also the different ways men attempted to embody, and at times critiqued, a variety of mas-culine ideals. It also concealed the complex and diverse ways women navi-gated masculinity, from their often vocal criticisms of men's behavior and privileges to their accommodations of, and maneuvers within, the gender status quo. A perspective on masculinity rooted in a rigid hierarchy of masculine identities missed masculinity as a social process and the intri-cate, and to some extent fluid, assortment of masculine ideals that ani-mated how masculinity was lived in Bwaise.

By changing my perspective to one focused on how men, and women, were remaking masculinity, I was better able to understand this diversity in the lived experiences of masculinity. This included how men understood themselves to be accountable to hegemonic masculine ideals, the different ways they attempted to embody these ideals, the ways such actions were assessed by other men and women, and the complex role male sexuality played in these reworkings of masculinity.

As I listened to men talk about how they felt accountable to masculine ideals and observed how such ideals shaped their interactions with men and women, I came to appreciate how complicated it could be for men to enact and negotiate masculine ideals. The net effect was that men's lived experiences of masculinity was often one of frustration and confusion—a dynamic significantly exacerbated by HIV/AIDS. Men often engaged with the three core masculine ideals that constituted hegemonic masculinity in an interrelated way in response to changes in the broader social context. In this sense, the masculine ideals tied to work, authority, and sexuality were interdependent, with men triangulating among them in their efforts to do masculinity properly. This was also the case in how men were evaluated as sufficiently and appropriately masculine by other men, and women as well.

These dynamics were especially evident in men's sexual relationships, and I see the range of intimate relationships presented in this book as one of its distinctive contributions. In their relationships, all the men I met grappled with being accountable to a male economic provider ideal in a context of chronic underemployment and increasing economic stratification. Many of these men responded to these constraints by agreeing, often begrudgingly, to their wives' and girlfriends' desire to earn money. Yet they also remained vigilant in trying to contain the gender ramifications of sharing provider responsibilities, and this was often done through actions meant to reassert the man's authority in the home. The promotion of women's rights typically heightened such tensions and further complicated men's attempts to embody the male authority ideal.

This interdependence of hegemonic masculine ideals, however, was most striking in relation to sexuality. Repeatedly through the course of my fieldwork, I learned how men could draw on masculine sexual privilege as a resource to compensate for concerns about fulfilling the male economic provider ideal and maintaining their authority in the home. Sexuality was a domain in which men could shore up those aspects of their masculine identity that they perceived as being threatened on other fronts. In this way, challenges to men's gender privileges, and to gender inequality more generally, were undermined as men reasserted their sexual privileges—an apt illustration of what Schrock and Schwalbe (2009) have termed "manhood acts."

These dynamics related to masculine sexual privilege were the most complex aspects of how masculinity was being remade in Bwaise. This was true for several reasons. First, as noted throughout this book, this masculine ideal turned on the privilege of controlling the terms of sex and, more crucially, the privilege of having multiple sexual partners, if a man so chose. It did not imply that all men needed to have multiple partnerships to be "true" men, because for at least a century in Buganda, and much of Uganda, the spectrum of proper or typical male sexuality has included monogamous men. Yet the privilege of having additional sexual partners has persisted, and in a context like Bwaise manhood acts that draw on such privilege remain powerful ways for men to claim masculine status and exhibit their ability to embody certain aspects of hegemonic masculinity.

These dynamics are further complicated by growing economic stratification that has heightened the male status associated with maintaining multiple sexual partners, whether through shorter-term extramarital affairs or longer-term concurrent, overlapping relationships. These pressures to enact masculine sexual privilege have been countered, in part, by the rise of companionate marriage and, more centrally for this book, the emphasis on reducing multiple sexual partnerships and the promotion of "being faithful" in response to AIDS. However, as stressed throughout this book, the context of AIDS has at most complicated masculine sexual privilege without posing any fundamental challenge to it. Thus it persists.

It is in this contradictory social context that men assert their claim to masculine sexual privilege as they strive to enact normative notions of masculinity. Yet such assertions are not simple and straightforward. Men acknowledge that many forces undermine their contemporary claims to masculine sexual privilege, most significantly, the tenuous male provider ideal, women's rights, and the omnipresence of HIV/AIDS. The paradoxes men faced as they grappled with what it meant to be a man is a central theme in this book and a key aspect of the process of remaking masculinity in a place like Bwaise. Women also played an important role in these dynamics, most evident in how men's female partners described negotiating masculine sexual privilege in their attempts to have fulfilling and harmonious intimate relationships.

The contradictions men described were most pronounced for the younger men I came to know in Bwaise. Several young men articulately described to me the conflicts and confusion they felt enacting masculine sexual privilege in the context of AIDS. It was also among these younger men that I observed how men could hold each other accountable to norms of male sexuality, sometimes in ways that challenged normative notions of masculine sexual privilege. This was most evident in the interactions between the cousins Peter and Edward that I described in chapter 5. Peter's vocal criticism of his cousin's multiple sexual partners was an interesting example of an attempt to reconfigure the terms of what constituted proper male sexuality, and HIV/AIDS played a crucial role in their interactions.

These dynamics regarding men's sexual privileges underscore the importance of moving beyond a rigid hierarchy of masculinities to a focus on remaking masculinity as a social process. The conceptual framework I presented in chapter 1 provides a way of specifying these processes, drawing our attention to the interplay of work, authority, and sexuality. Recognizing this interplay is especially valuable when examining masculinity in the many contexts across the globe where women's roles as primary economic providers and women's rights are less institutionalized. However, this framework is also useful more generally and provides insight into the frequent backlashes against women's gains that coincide with the recurring economic crises in the West. This book's focus on remaking masculinity in the context of heterosexual relationships is also especially helpful in revealing how heterosexuality can reinforce the links between ideals that sustain gender inequalities and ideals tied to sexuality. This is an area of research that is still emerging. As I discuss in the concluding section, the gendered nature of the AIDS epidemic makes such insights crucial for the sexual health of African men and women whose intimate relationships continue to unfold in the persistent, long shadow cast by HIV/AIDS.

THE ECLIPSE OF THE SOCIAL AND
THE FUTURE OF HIV PREVENTION IN AFRICA

My fieldwork in Bwaise revealed to me that although the Ugandan AIDS epidemic has been and remains severe, and the responses wide-ranging

and multifaceted, AIDS does not appear to have catalyzed a significant reworking of how masculinity is lived in a place like Bwaise. Yet my time in Bwaise also made evident that HIV/AIDS has been, and continues to be, deeply intertwined with masculinity in urban Uganda. Nearly every aspect of the disease that I explored—from HIV transmission to testing, disclosure, drug treatment, and AIDS care—was inflected by masculinity and gender power dynamics. This was at times obvious, such as the paucity of men who came for HIV testing at the health clinic, and other times subtle but profound, such as negotiations within certain serodiscordant relationships that allowed women to protect themselves from HIV infection. In addition, while I observed many examples of how hegemonic masculinity continued to facilitate the transmission of HIV, I also witnessed ways Ugandans themselves attempted to change such dynamics, such as the Bwaise Positive Men's Union.

Over the course of my fieldwork, governments and development agencies slowly started recognizing the intertwining of AIDS and masculinity as an important facet of AIDS prevention and treatment policy, not only in Uganda, but globally. This has coincided with more sociologically sophisticated approaches to thinking about AIDS that take fuller account of the structures of social inequality that exacerbate the severity of HIV/AIDS in different contexts (aids2031 Consortium 2010; Farmer 2005). In sub-Saharan Africa, there is also now a better appreciation of how systems of gender inequality in particular are linked to women's heightened vulnerability to HIV infection in many African contexts (Greig et al. 2008; Gupta 2002; Gupta et al. 2008). This has prompted innovative public health interventions aimed at addressing the social drivers of African women's HIV risk, with particular attention to reducing domestic violence and improving women's economic autonomy (Epstein and Kim 2007; Jewkes et al. 2008; Kim et al. 2007; Pronyk et al. 2006).

In recent years it has become clear that addressing AIDS and gender inequality also requires attention to men and masculinity. Careful and thoughtful attention has been given to how programs and interventions could be tailored for men in ways that transform, and not simply accommodate, those aspects of hegemonic masculinity that heighten women's and men's risk of HIV infection (Dworkin 2015; Dworkin et al. 2011; Dworkin, Treves-Kagan, and Lippman 2013; Higgins, Hoffman, and Dworkin 2010).

A very small but growing number of innovative HIV interventions have emerged focused on men and masculinity in Africa, and these are complemented by efforts to work with men and women together, especially couples, to address AIDS and gender inequities (Burton, Darbes, and Operario 2010; Fritz et al. 2011; Jemmott et al. 2014; Kalichman et al. 2009).

In several African countries in the past decade, most notably South Africa, local NGOs have also focused on working with men to critically examine conceptions of masculinity, especially by linking domestic violence prevention to HIV prevention. The work of the Sonke Gender Justice Network is particularly notable. Their One Man Can program in South Africa has been shown to affect men's attitudes toward women's rights and gender equality, leading to greater acceptance of power sharing in intimate relationships (Dworkin et al. 2013). This includes decisions such as men no longer demanding sex, fewer multiple sexual partnerships, and increased condom use.

Thus approaches to addressing AIDS in sub-Saharan Africa have evolved with greater sociological sophistication and increasing attention to how social-structural inequalities create environments conducive to HIV transmission. These promising developments are, however, being eclipsed by a new emphasis on using AIDS drugs to prevent HIV infection. Recent clinical trials and studies have shown dramatic success in reducing HIV transmission when antiretroviral therapy is used to reduce the infectiousness of HIV-positive individuals or when antiretroviral drugs are used as a form of prophylaxis for uninfected people (Baeten et al. 2012; Cohen et al. 2011; Donnell et al. 2010; Karim et al. 2010; Siedner et al. 2014). These significant advances have been lauded as ushering in a new era of AIDS prevention and seen as having tremendous promise for abating, or even ending, the African AIDS pandemic (Cohen 2011; Lancet Editorial 2011). This new emphasis on "treatment as prevention" and pre-exposure prophylaxis has been the subject of much debate, including the concern that these new biomedical advances will require massive long-term financial support and thus compete with and, in certain cases, displace social and behavioral prevention strategies (Bassett and Brudney 2014; Epstein and Morris 2011b; European AIDS Treatment Group 2014; Seale et al. 2011).

The lure of a biomedical fix for AIDS is a potent one that promises to liberate HIV prevention from the realm of messy, complicated social relations, and part of modern biomedicine's more general fascination with discovering magic bullets to cure disease (Brandt 1987). Treatment as prevention and PrEP have brought these tensions to the foreground and raised concerns that AIDS funding will now prioritize biomedical approaches, resulting in few resources for addressing the sociocultural dimensions of HIV/AIDS. At the heart of this issue is the assumption that one can neatly distinguish between the biomedical and social aspects of AIDS. Such a distinction is rooted in what the sociologist Barry Adam (2011, 5) refers to as an epistemological frame of biomedical individualism that obscures the fact that "all biomedical prevention technologies are also social interventions, whether that is explicitly recognized or not" (see also Dowsett 2013). This distinction is particularly problematic with regard to AIDS because the history of the pandemic indicates that the most successful prevention interventions have involved social responses to HIV and AIDS that catalyzed shifts in social norms, social practices, and institutions. As Susan Kippax (2012, 6) argues, the locus of such change is not the individual but communities and collectives. For such changes in social practices to be sustained, therefore, a broader social transformation is required that comes only through collective agency, which illuminates why "grassroots activism has so often been more effective in responding to the epidemic than formal public health programs or interventions" (Kippax et al. 2013, 1373).

The new ascendancy of biomedical approaches to HIV prevention threatens to marginalize sociologically sophisticated interventions that have only recently emerged—interventions that strive to promote the broader social transformations critical to addressing AIDS. In light of my research in Bwaise, this is particularly problematic: my fieldwork reveals that hegemonic masculine ideals are deeply intertwined with HIV in complex ways, especially with regard to the persistence of masculine sexual privilege. My fieldwork also illuminates that the constellation of hegemonic and emerging masculine ideals in Bwaise is dynamic and that men and women grapple with and rework them in multifaceted, and at times contradictory, ways. Such masculine ideals present many paradoxes for men in particular as they attempt to reconcile dominant and emerging ideals of masculinity in their everyday struggles for survival, paradoxes most men are eager to resolve.

There is, therefore, much to be gained by promoting a critical reflection on masculinity, gender power dynamics, and HIV/AIDS in communities like Bwaise. As my fieldwork makes clear, such critical reflections are already occurring among Ugandans themselves. Programs and health interventions can complement and build on these processes. One particularly innovative example has, in fact, been developed by the Kampala-based NGO Raising Voices, and implemented by CEDOVIP, the local NGO I volunteered with during my fieldwork. Called SASA!, this initiative is a community-based approach to addressing the gender power imbalances linked to both HIV infection and violence against women (Abramsky et al. 2012; Musuya 2011). The strength of this initiative is its holistic approach to community mobilization that is designed to catalyze a critical reflection on gender norms among community members, both women and men, and lead to community-led action to address HIV prevention and violence against women simultaneously.[5] While SASA! is focused on transforming gender inequities, it does so by highlighting power imbalances in relationships, as opposed to stressing women's rights and gender equality; this is a decision based on the recognition that "an initial explicit focus on 'gender' is likely to be off-putting to many" (Abramsky et al. 2014, 15). As discussed below, this approach may be particularly effective in involving men and shifting community norms regarding aspects of men's sexual privileges.

SASA! has been rigorously evaluated in what is the first randomized control trial in sub-Saharan Africa to assess the community-level impact of an intervention focused on preventing intimate-partner violence and new HIV infections at the same time. The results were striking. In communities that received the intervention, women reported large declines in experiences of physical and sexual violence. Women's and men's acceptance of a woman's right to refuse sex were significantly greater in intervention communities (28 percent and 31 percent, respectively), and men's reports of concurrent sexual relationships declined by nearly 50 percent.[6] These last two findings suggest the intervention had an important impact on the two key aspects of masculine sexual privilege: men's control over sex and men's right to have multiple sexual partners.

The study indicated that these outcomes were driven in large part by changes in relationship power dynamics, with men in particular reporting greatly increased joint decision making, participation in household tasks, and more open communication, as well as much higher condom use and HIV testing (Kyegombe et al. 2014a).[7] SASA! also seemed especially effective at prompting men to "vocalize the challenges they were facing in securing enough money for household needs" and this in turn helped a man's wife to "be 'patient' and relieved suspicions she may have had about his fidelity and expenditures" (Kyegombe et al. 2014b, 6). This is a significant finding given the recurring theme across many African contexts of how men's feelings of emasculation as failed providers are tied to men's multiple sexual partnerships. While the SASA! trial did not measure the impact on new HIV infections, a very similar community-level study in southwestern Uganda, called SHARE, did find a statistically significant, 33 percent decline in new HIV infections in communities receiving the SHARE intervention (Wagman et al. 2015).

Interventions like SASA! and SHARE are promising approaches to HIV prevention in African contexts, and they should not be marginalized by the growing emphasis on simply getting more AIDS drugs into African bodies. They suggest that while the AIDS epidemic may not have fundamentally remade masculine sexual privilege, it has created a context in which many men may be open to critical reflection on hegemonic masculinity. Long-term community engagement is essential to capitalize on these possibilities because normative gender and sexual relations are not only resilient to change but also complex. My emphasis on masculine sexual privilege throughout this book could be misunderstood as simply advocating male monogamy as the solution to AIDS in urban Uganda. That, however, is not my intention. Throughout this book I provide examples of how the simplistic focus on monogamy and being faithful has driven male infidelity underground and obscured how masculine sexual privilege persists. In my view, the numbers of sexual partners a man or woman has is not the key issue. The key issue is the persistence of men's privileges to dictate the terms of sex and the freedom to choose, on their own, to establish multiple sexual partnerships. These are the issues that require long-term attention and explicit engagement. My emphasis on privilege intends to foreground the multifaceted ways men's power in the sexual domain is manifested, the range of ways men can access or defer such power, and how such privilege creates difficult conundrums as men attempt to embody normative notions of masculinity in the age of AIDS. A simplistic and puritanical attention to monogamy does little to address these complex gender and sexual social dynamics.

The implications of masculine sexual privilege are also intricate in a context like Kampala because of the complexities of women's sexuality. As I have emphasized throughout this book, women in urban Uganda are far from the helpless victims of male power but instead agentic and creative in how they navigate the constraints of normative notions of femininity and masculinity in the context of AIDS. Historically, women in southern Uganda have had some freedom and latitude in their sexual relationships, and unmarried, independent women in particular have been less constrained by an ideal of female monogamy. As Doyle (2013) and Epstein (2007) argue, these aspects of female sexuality have also likely played an important role in the creation of sexual networks conducive to the spread of AIDS in Uganda, from at least the 1950s to the present day.

It would be a mistake, however, to conflate masculine sexual privilege with women's sexual autonomy by suggesting that men and women enjoy equal freedom to pursue sexual relationships of their choosing.[8] Thus grappling with the persistence of masculine sexual privilege must necessarily involve an understanding of the contemporary landscape of gender equality and women's rights. Linking masculinity, gender power imbalances, and HIV prevention (as interventions like SASA! do) is, in my view, a crucial approach and one in need of further development. My fieldwork reveals how a limited or narrow promotion of women's rights as gender equity can prove counterproductive and make intimate relationships fraught with tensions that heighten women's and men's risk of HIV infection. The complexities of male and female sexuality need to be made central to community-level efforts to integrate women's rights and gender equality into HIV prevention programs.

While promoting long-term community engagement with masculine sexual privilege is essential to addressing HIV/AIDS, my fieldwork also makes clear the sobering fact that urban poverty is likely the central force sustaining the AIDS pandemic in communities like Bwaise. If there was one reality that emerged most strongly from my time in Bwaise, it was that

chronic underemployment and growing economic stratification make everyday survival difficult and harmonious intimate relationships unlikely. This reality runs through this book and is entangled with HIV in different ways in each empirical chapter.

It should not be surprising, then, that a recent, robust analysis of Demographic and Health Surveys from twenty African countries found that the urban poor have a significantly higher likelihood of being HIV-positive than urban residents who are not poor, with urban poor women at a particularly increased risk of infection (Magadi 2013). Such connections between AIDS and economics are not new, and much attention has been given to how neoliberal economic policies have undermined the capacity of African states to adequately address a health crisis on this scale (Craddock 2004; Ferguson 2006; Heimer 2007; Hickel 2012; Lurie, Hintzen, and Lowe 2004; Schoepf 2004; Schoepf, Schoepf, and Millen 2000).

More recently, as African states have become more active in addressing HIV through testing, counseling, and drug treatment, neoliberal ideologies of individual self-reliance and responsibility have also become more salient in AIDS policy (Decoteau 2013b; Richey 2011, 2012). This is especially true in relation to African men, who are increasingly the target of individualistic behavior change interventions that turn on men being more "responsible" for their sexual behavior (Colvin and Robins 2009; Colvin, Robins, and Leavens 2010; Decoteau 2013a). This kind of superficial engagement with changing men and masculinity can further marginalize and demonize impoverished African men. Such programs and policies provide convenient cover for state economic strategies that prioritize GDP growth without addressing increasing economic stratification or any true commitment to ameliorating poverty.

These political-economic aspects of AIDS loom large on the horizon in Uganda today. President Museveni now appears resolutely focused on staying in power, and some of the signature accomplishments of his presidency, from addressing AIDS to promoting women's rights, seem to no longer be a priority. His vanishing commitment to civil rights more generally has been particularly dramatic as his regime becomes increasingly autocratic. The economic needs of the urban poor are lost to these political machinations, and people in communities like Bwaise are left to endure underemployment, inflation, and yawning disparities in economic opportunities on their own. It will be these conditions that largely shape how residents of communities like Bwaise remake masculinity as they strive for meaningful lives and harmonious intimate relationships against the persistent and all too familiar backdrop of AIDS and urban poverty.

Epilogue

Kampala in 2015 was a city markedly different from the one I experienced when I began my fieldwork in 2004. Over the course of a decade, Kampala's charm as a vibrant but still manageable capital city had been trampled by unregulated growth. In retrospect, the signs were evident during my fieldwork in 2009 as many main arteries became clogged with cars, minibuses, and motorcycles and shoddy new hotels and office towers began sprouting up in central Kampala. By 2015 the city had become close to unmanageable, with weekday traffic choking intersections far out into the suburbs, motorcycle taxis commandeering the sidewalks, and pollution hanging over the city even in the rainy season.

More pernicious than the traffic and congestion, however, was the fact that these huge changes were driven by economic forces that benefited only the few. For those with money and political connections, Kampala had undoubtedly become a boom town. This was most evident in the proliferation of new buildings, from a handful of thirty-story downtown towers to the forests of five- to ten-story concrete hulks that had grown thick in areas close to central Kampala. Many were upscale apartment buildings or shopping centers, including a new luxury mall that overflowed with Ugandan elites and expats.

The vast majority of the Ugandans I spoke with were quick to criticize these developments, telling me that they experienced the economic growth as a painful increase in the cost of living. Feeble attempts by the city to address the urban quality of life, such as new ordinances barring street vendors, were for many Kampalans indicative of the prioritization of elites over the needs of the vast majority of city residents. This increasing economic inequality was only exacerbated by the uncertain political climate. President Museveni was determined to stay in power, and the looming 2016 presidential election was driving a steep decline in the Ugandan shilling. Overall, there was a great deal of unease about the economic and political climate, and a palpable, disgruntled edge seemed to be sharpening. The Museveni regime was clearly concerned with this combustible atmosphere: throughout the city massive new armored vehicles were in position to crush protests and urban unrest.

Given the transformation of Kampala, I was not sure what to expect on my return to Bwaise. A major change had already occurred by 2009: the construction of a highway along Bwaise's southern border. That road was not yet open in 2009, but it had already worsened Bwaise's perpetual floods, making some sections unlivable. In 2015, I feared that the new highway traffic would have further eroded Bwaise's quality of life, adding more noise and pollution. Thankfully, that was not the case. I was also pleasantly surprised to learn that the main drainage canal along Bwaise's southern border had been dredged during construction of the road. This mitigated the impact of flooding and allowed new residents to build modest homes all along southern Bwaise. This section, which was in the heart of my field site, was now more densely populated than in 2009 and similar to how I first encountered Bwaise in 2004.

What the new highway did create, however, was terrible traffic. Starting at seven in the morning and lasting well into the evening, the cars and trucks pouring on and off the highway snarled Bwaise's main intersection, engulfing the lone traffic policeman charged with maintaining some order (figure E.1). This intersection had been my favorite vantage point for observing Bwaise's daily rhythms, but by 2015 even snapping a photo there proved dangerous.

In many other respects, the changes in Bwaise were more modest, especially compared to many other sections of the city. Along the main road

Figure E.1. Bwaise's main intersection in 2015.

there was now a four-story building housing a Kenyan chain supermarket, although the supermarket had been closed for health violations. But behind the storefronts the core sections of Bwaise that I knew best had changed very little. On my first visit back, I easily wove through the residential labyrinth, passing familiar landmarks like the tiny clothes-washing shop, the woman selling produce from her stoop, and the make-shift pharmacy where a friend still made his herbal cough syrup. Even many of the shallow sewage streams followed exactly the same course, encircling the homes of friends in the manner they did since at least 2004.

A few businesses appeared to be thriving in Bwaise, most notably the "lodges." One establishment, which was a neighbor to the home of my closest friends, had added a second story and a high-quality stucco facade. Nearby, a similar Bwaise institution had expanded dramatically, adding a three-story, hotel with a large walled courtyard. On the nights I stayed in this hotel, it was indeed doing brisk business and seemed an ideal hidea-way for affluent men's discreet affairs. Other businesses had not fared as well, and unfortunately the Kibira carpentry workshop was among them.

I was disappointed to learn that Dennis had gone bankrupt and lost his business. The site of the workshop was now empty, and I searched in vain in the dirt for a scrap of wood, a nail, or a screw as a memento from my days as an apprentice. As some consolation, a nearly identical carpentry workshop was now directly across the dirt road, with half a dozen men busy crafting beds, tables, and chairs.

The most significant change in greater Bwaise was at the location where I first began my fieldwork. The Bwaise Health Clinic had been razed, and on the site a twelve-story, modern hospital, Kawempe General Hospital, was under construction. The $12 million hospital was being built by the Chinese state-owned conglomerate China National Aero Technology. It was one of several new hospitals in the city with ties to Chinese businesses or the Chinese government. Kawempe General, therefore, reflected the growing Chinese presence in Uganda and the deepening ties between the Museveni government and China—a development that is the focus of my current research.

More centrally for this book, the construction of Kawempe General was emblematic of the shift in the response to the AIDS epidemic in Uganda, from one rooted in a community-based approach to a much more medicalized strategy emphasizing drug treatment. While everyone I spoke with in Bwaise recognized the benefits of the new, modern hospital, the demolition of the Bwaise Health Clinic meant the end to the many vibrant community health programs headquartered there. The two-hundred-plus members of the Post-Test Club no longer had a place for weekly meetings, and outreach visits to homes of HIV-positive people had ceased. The same was true for the remaining members of the Bwaise Positive Men's Union. When I met with two members, they told me the group was still active but smaller and no longer had a regular space for meetings.

My return in 2015 also allowed me to see how the lives of my closest friends and key informants had changed over the course of a decade. I had no trouble reconnecting with everyone I hoped to see because nearly everyone had remained rooted in Bwaise in some way. By and large, their lives were quite similar to when I first met them in 2004, and I was happy to see that most were marginally better off. I was especially interested in how the lives of the younger men I knew well had progressed and how they had navigated a course to male adulthood.

Perhaps not surprisingly, the developments with Issa, who I discussed in chapter 3, were some of the most fascinating. I was relieved to see that he looked healthier, with a fuller and more muscular chest and stronger upper arms. The slightly mischievous glint was still in his eyes, but he was calmer and more relaxed. With some pride, he told me these changes reflected his new clean-and-sober lifestyle. Continued medical problems, especially with his liver, had forced him to give up smoking, drinking, and his beloved khat chewing. His life since my last visit had not been without adventures, however. For several years, he disclosed to me, he had trafficked cocaine from Kampala to Nairobi. This was a lucrative venture for him, but after some colleagues were imprisoned he decided the risks were too great.

Although Issa amassed enough money to purchase land in the neighboring town of Jinja, he lacked the resources to do anything with it. So he still lived in his dilapidated house in the middle of Kimombasa. The house was more weathered, made worse by his current occupation, raising a brood of guinea fowl that he sold for $15 apiece. To keep his birds secure, he had placed their coop in the front room of his house, making the interior a health hazard. Issa now lived out of one room with his current informal wife, a woman I had not met before. His said his new lifestyle also applied to his love life, and he only had sex with his wife. I remained concerned about his health, especially his HIV status, but when I asked him if he had any new health concerns he only said that he and his new wife were fine. Two of our close mutual friends said Issa was not telling me everything. They were adamant that both Issa and his new wife were HIV-positive. I was disheartened to hear this and hoped it was not true.

While the prospect of Issa being HIV-positive was disturbing, I was intrigued to see that he seemed to have entered a period of relationship stability. This was also the case for several other younger men I knew well. My former coworker at the carpentry workshop, Rafik, was a particularly interesting example. As in 2009, I was again surprised to see that Rafik had reached yet another rung on the hierarchy of male adulthood. He now had his own used electronics shop in the center of Bwaise, a few hundred feet from his much smaller old cell phone repair place. A sign reading Rafik Electronics hung over the entrance, and a neat row of TV sets, refrigerators, and other appliances ran out toward the street. He specialized in

European brands, which sold for much more than new Chinese models, and on the days I visited business was steady.

Rafik was proud of his business but much more eager to introduce me to his family and show me his new home. He had upgraded his sedan for a large van, and we drove it north about five miles. Here, at the northernmost fringe of Kampala, Rafik had bought property and constructed an impressive two-bedroom home. It sat on a slight rise, and the small veranda overlooked this edge of periurban sprawl. His wife, an outgoing young woman who spoke English well, had our lunch prepared and introduced me to their two little girls. Later Rafik and I chatted alone. He told me his relationship with Rose ended because she did not want children, glossing over Rose's allegations of unfaithfulness. He said he was now focused on his life with his new wife, building his business and soon, he hoped, having a son.

Like Rafik, Edward (chapter 5) described himself as committed to his new wife, the woman I met in 2009 during my visit to his family's village. Edward's financial fortunes had also improved, and his networking had finally resulted in good contract work with two NGOs, as well as grants for his own community-based organization. In a pleasant open field in Bwaise, Edward now had an office constructed from two large shipping containers that were donated by an international NGO. It was here that he organized weekly workshops for young female sex workers from Bwaise, providing seminars on sexual health and income-generating activities such as hairdressing and making leather shoes and belts. On one afternoon I watched as three dozen young sex workers sat attentively through a two-hour seminar on preventing sexually transmitted diseases. At the seminar's close, Edward's wife arrived, and I finally had a chance to meet their son, a quiet, shy toddler.

Rafik and Edward had both achieved a degree of financial security and found partners who were ready and able to begin families—a combination that seemed to produce relationship stability. Only time would tell how these families would weather their future challenges, especially the upcoming burdens of school fees, and how greater or less financial success would affect Rafik's and Edward's current professed commitment to be faithful to their current partners. Interestingly, Peter, Edward's cousin, had made tentative steps in a similar direction. He remained much more cautious of relationships than his male peers but was on the cusp of moving in with a young woman he had dated for several years. As I saw for myself, his girlfriend was a smart, engaging, and stylish young woman, and in my view a great match for Peter. At thirty-three, he had just completed a master's program in community health, and he was hopeful this credential would finally provide the financial stability he saw as necessary for this budding relationship to succeed.

I certainly understood Peter's concerns, especially that a lack of money would likely derail any relationship, but I was eager to see him take that next step to male adulthood. Peter was still living with his mother, Christine, the woman I described in the first pages of this book. In some respects, Christine's life had changed only modestly, but she seemed less fulfilled. With the closure of the Bwaise Health Clinic and the end of the HIV/AIDS programs she avidly participated in, Christine was at a loss about what to do with herself. In addition, she no longer received the small stipend from visiting HIV-positive residents in the community. She was spending most of her days caring for her elderly mother and claimed to be considering a move to Amsterdam, where relatives could help her find work.

Most surprisingly, Christine confided to me that she had finally gathered the courage to take an HIV test—something she had never done because she simply assumed she was positive after her husband died from AIDS decades earlier. The test, and several follow-up tests, confirmed she was in fact HIV-negative. Christine was clearly still processing this revelation, a task made more difficult because her identity in the community was so closely tied to being HIV-positive. She had not shared this information with her children, even her son Peter. While I was extremely happy to hear the news, it was a reminder of the strangeness of AIDS and the deep, often bizarre ways HIV has insinuated itself into communities like Bwaise, producing fear, stigma, and uncertainty in lives that are already so marked by precarity.

From my vantage point in 2015, the future of Bwaise looked unclear. To address the new congestion, a large roundabout was planned for the main intersection, as well as a new north-south road. Both would displace many homes and businesses in central Bwaise—a trend in city planning that was playing out in other Kampala slums as well. I doubted these developments would alleviate the traffic problems, and I was certain they would do nothing to address the pressing needs of community residents, such as flooding and sanitation, let alone the systemic poverty and unemployment. My friends and acquaintances were often vocal about these disparities, and their views reflected a growing embitteredness about the escalating economic inequality.

Thus the conditions that I first observed in Bwaise over a decade ago—underemployment, men's emasculation as household heads, the weak institutionalization of women's rights, and the persistence of masculine sexual privilege—remain largely unchanged. As I hope this book demonstrates, these conditions are deeply intertwined with and facilitate the transmission of HIV. Compared to other regions of the world, HIV prevalence remains distressingly high in Uganda, especially Kampala. Perhaps the wide dissemination of antiretroviral drugs will be enough to reduce HIV incidence eventually, but the social conditions remain firmly in place to sustain the AIDS epidemic for decades to come. In communities like Bwaise, these social conditions will persist until the government becomes truly committed to alleviating the structural inequalities that define the lives of the urban poor—a commitment that in 2015 was not remotely evident.

Acknowledgments

This book would not have been possible without the generosity of many, many Ugandans. To my friends and acquaintances in Bwaise who greeted my questions and queries with patience, I am grateful. Pledges of anonymity prevent me from including names, but there are several individuals who deserve special mention. My coworkers at the Kibira carpentry workshop welcomed me as an apprentice and mentored me in much more than just the craft of carpentry. Another friend opened her home to me, sharing not only her shrewd insights on life in Bwaise but also meals and friendship; I feel privileged to have remained friends and to now be considered part of her family. At a community health clinic, one staff member took me under her wing and greatly facilitated my research. The clinic was also home to a support group for HIV-positive men who welcomed me as an honorary member and freely shared the intimate details of their lives.

I am especially thankful to the staff and volunteers at the Center for Domestic Violence Prevention and Raising Voices who provided unfettered access to their work in the Bwaise area. Their innovative and successful programs are a great inspiration and continue to motivate me as I strive to make my research relevant to residents of Bwaise. Lori Michau and Dipak Naker of Raising Voices were particularly welcoming. They provided not only intellectual stimulation and feedback on my work but also abiding friendship. At various points my fieldwork was also facilitated by three talented Ugandan research assistants: Barbrah Nanyunja, Julius Lwanyaaga, and, most important, John Paul Matovu. I am also grateful to the Makerere Institute of Social Research for providing my institutional affiliation.

This book began when I was a graduate student at the University of Chicago, and my experience at Chicago would have been significantly less rich had it not been for the guidance of Leslie Salzinger. Leslie introduced me to ethnography and deepened my understanding feminism, and her support remained unwavering long after I completed my PhD. Saskia Sassen, Jennifer Cole, and Andrew Apter all shaped my thinking in ways that set the foundation for this book. My initial year of fieldwork was supported by a grant from the National Science Foundation, and when I returned to Chicago to write, my fellow sociology graduate students Marc Sanford and Sanyu Mojola were particularly helpful and provided much-needed camaraderie. My dissertation writing group was also indispensable in this period, especially Phaedra Daipha's sharp yet always encouraging insights as a fellow ethnographer.

I was fortunate to be awarded a postdoctoral fellowship at the University of California, San Francisco's Center for AIDS Prevention Studies. This postdoc, funded by the National Institutes of Health, placed me at what felt like the center of the global response to the AIDS pandemic. Susan Kegeles and Willi McFarland ensured my time at UCSF was endlessly stimulating, and I benefited tremendously from the insightful feedback on my work provided by John Ziegler, Vincanne Adams, Shari Dworkin, and especially Megan Comfort.

It was at the University of Michigan where this book finally reached maturity. As an assistant professor in the Women's Studies Department, I was fortunate to design and teach a new course on the global AIDS pandemic with David Halperin. Collaborating with David was a highlight of my time at Michigan, and my thinking about AIDS is significantly deeper, broader, and more sophisticated because of his influence. I also benefited immensely from a book manuscript workshop sponsored by Women's Studies. This workshop came at a crucial point in my writing, and I am indebted to Peggy McCracken, Abby Stewart, Elizabeth Cole, Manisha

Desai, Amy Kaler, and especially Sarah Fenstermaker for their truly astute feedback and excitement about this project. It was also a privilege to have Derek Peterson read my manuscript; his deep knowledge of East African history helped me see what was truly new and novel in my ethnography.

My final stage of manuscript writing was a much more gratifying experience due to the meticulous and incisive editing assistance I received from Tamie Harkins. It was such a pleasure to have Tamie as a conversation partner at this stage, and her passion for this book helped me make it over this significant writing hurdle. At the University of California Press, I am tremendously grateful for Naomi Schneider's keen interest in this project from our first meeting. The comments from two anonymous reviewers were extraordinary; this book is significantly better because of them. It has also been a pleasure to work with Will Vincent, who regularly reminded me just how exciting it is to have this book published. Sheila Berg's meticulous editing in the initial stages of production was immensely helpful. She streamlined my writing and created more space for my informants to speak for themselves.

Finally, I would like to thank my family, especially my parents, Nora and Martin, who were steadfastly supportive during a process that at times must have seemed mystifyingly lengthy. My brother, Christopher, first introduced me to Africa, and my sister, Patricia, always made me feel like writing a book was important. I am also indebted to David Rinaldo and Suzanne Gelber Rinaldo for their equally gracious encouragement.

My greatest debt is to my wife, Rachel Rinaldo. It is no exaggeration to say this book would not have been possible without her unfailing support and enthusiasm. Equally crucial have been her insights on every aspect of my research and writing, stretching back well over a decade. This book and my life in general are infinitely more rich and meaningful because of her. It is deeply gratifying to be able to share this book with Rachel and our son, Nathaniel.

Appendix

Table A.1   Demographic Characteristics of Interviewees, 2004

	Percentage	Number
Gender		
Male	73	50
Female	27	19
Age		
Under 18	4	3
18–30	38	26
31–40	29	20
41–50	25	17
51 and older	4	3
Ethnicity		
Baganda	75	52
Basoga	8	6
Bagisu	4	3
Banyoro	2	1
Batoro	4	3
Bakiga	2	1
Banyankole	3	2
Iteso	2	1
Religion		
Catholic	35	24
Anglican	20	14
Evangelical/Pentecostal	17	12
Muslim	28	19
Education		
Some primary	15	10
Completed primary	13	9
Some secondary	23	16
Secondary O-level	23	16
Secondary A-level	13	9
Some tertiary	11	8
University degree	2	1
Total	100	69

Table A.2 Demographic Characteristics of Participants in Couples Research, 2009

	Percentage	*Number*
Gender		
Male	47	19
Female	53	21
Age		
18–30	50	20
31–40	15	6
41–50	28	11
51 and older	7	3
Ethnicity		
Baganda	75	30
Basoga	3	1
Banyoro	3	1
Batoro	6	3
Banyankole	5	2
Kakwa	5	2
Muhaya	3	1
Religion		
Catholic	35	14
Anglican	18	7
Evangelical/Pentecostal	15	6
Muslim	32	13
Education		
Some primary	22	9
Completed primary	10	4
Some secondary	28	11
Secondary O-level	20	8
Secondary A-level	10	4
Some tertiary	5	2
University degree	5	2
HIV Status		
Negative	73	29
Positive	27	11
Total	100	40

Notes

1. REMAKING MASCULINITY IN BWAISE

1. HIV prevalence in Uganda is believed to have peaked at 20 percent in the early 1990s and was 7 percent in 2012. HIV prevalence peaked at 30 percent in Kampala in 1992 and was 9 percent in 2012 (Uganda AIDS Commission 2012).

2. According to the Uganda AIDS Commission's 2012 Country Progress Report, the number of new adult HIV infections (HIV incidence) increased by 16.4 percent from 2007 to 2010. National HIV prevalence (total number of people infected with HIV) also increased slowly and steadily, from 6.4 percent in 2004 to 7.3 percent in 2011. This prevalence increase, however, likely partially reflects the growing number of individuals receiving antiretroviral therapy and thus living longer.

3. The law permits the mandatory testing of pregnant women and victims of sexual violence and enables courts to order the release of an individual's HIV status without her consent.

4. Like many other African countries, older men in Uganda are more likely to be HIV-positive than younger men. Because longer-term relationships between younger women and older men are not uncommon in many sub-Saharan African contexts, this may in part account for the higher HIV prevalence among younger women (Wyrod et al. 2011).

5. Historians of East and southern Africa have also revealed how attempts to regulate and control African sexuality were part and parcel of colonial governing

strategies, from efforts to ban female circumcision in Kenya (Thomas 2003) to campaigns to eradicate syphilis in Uganda (Summers 1991; Vaughan 1991) to the promotion of female contraception in Zimbabwe (Kaler 2003a).

6. The bulk of Stillwaggon's critique is directed at the frequently cited work of the demographers John Caldwell and Pat Caldwell (1987; Caldwell, Caldwell, and Quiggin 1989), who argue that there is a distinct African sexual system characterized by higher rates of casual sex and weak marital bonds. As Helen Epstein (2007) notes, the Caldwells' work has perpetuated stereotypes of sexually promiscuous Africans, something that has been contradicted by empirical research (see Wellings et al. 2006).

7. Transactional sex is not uniquely African. The intertwining of love, sex, and money is prevalent in the West as well (Illouz 1997; Stillwaggon 2006; Zelizer 2005). Sociologists have also stressed that transactional sex is not simply the sexual exploitation of young women but also involves women's agency and culturally established courting practices. Such practices are best understood in the context of unequal ties of dependence that characterize many social relations in sub-Saharan Africa (Poulin 2007; Swidler and Watkins 2007).

8. Such blatant contradictions and problematic heteronormative assumptions have made notions of romantic love and companionate marriage the subject of criticism by many feminists and queer theorists (Butler 1990; Kipnis 2003; Povinelli 2002, 2006; Warner 2000). Given this criticism, it is not ironic that modern companionate marriage often facilitates men's extramarital sex.

9. Colvin, Robins, and Leavens (2010) and Decoteau (2013a) discuss how tropes of African men's irresponsible sexual behavior also become entangled with notions of neoliberal citizenship that stress individual responsibility and self-actualization, as evidenced in some South African AIDS programs and policies.

10. Elsewhere, I have used the phrase "the dialectics of gender and health" to capture this notion of the reciprocal relationship between gender and health (Wyrod 2013).

11. This perspective on sexuality draws much inspiration from Foucault (1978). It also dovetails with other historians of sexuality, especially Laqueur (1990), who describes radical shifts in conceptions of female sexuality over the course of Western civilization. Female sexual desire went from being framed as active and voracious to passive and muted, Laqueur argues, in response to women's growing power and status in society.

12. Other gender research in Africa emphasizes that gender identities have been, and continue to be, articulated with age, wealth, and other forms of hierarchy (Amadiume 1997; Beoku-Betts and Njambi 2005; Mikell 1997; Nnaemeka 2004; Ogundipe-Leslie 1994; Oyewumi 1997, 2000; Steady 1987, 2006; Tamale 2006).

13. My emphasis on these three aspects of masculinity is also influenced by Connell's (1987; 1995, 74) three-part model of the structure of gender: labor (the

sexual division of labor), power (the overall subordination of women and dominance of men), and cathexis (the practices that shape and realize desire, especially sexual desire).

14. This insight is in keeping with sociological perspectives of gender as a complex, multidimensional social structure that encompasses processes on individual, interactional, and institutional levels (Acker 1990; Connell 1987; Glenn 1999; Lorber 1994; Ridgeway and Smith-Lovin 1999; Risman 2004, 2011).

15. This time period also has significance for understanding the changing landscape of AIDS treatment. During my initial fieldwork antiretroviral medications were not widely available, but by 2009 they were more accessible in Kampala. In 2015, they were even more widely available in Kampala and much of Uganda more generally.

16. I use a pseudonym for this organization and for all my informants. The names of places have not been changed (Bwaise, Kawempe, etc.), although I have taken care to avoid including information that could reveal an individual's identity, occasionally altering details to preserve anonymity.

17. I talked with the husband and wife, or wives, together and individually, and found that informative and insightful discrepancies between couple and individual interviews often emerged. For a more detailed discussion of the methods I employed in this part of my fieldwork, see Wyrod 2013.

18. Like other Bantu languages, Luganda nouns are based on a stem that is modified by the addition of a prefix. The stem -ganda, for example, is modified with the prefix *mu-* for person, the prefix *ba-* for people, the prefix *bu-* for place, and the prefix *lu-* for language. Thus a *Muganda* lives in *Buganda* and speaks *Luganda* with other *Baganda*.

2. THE MAKING OF MASCULINITY
IN URBAN UGANDA

1. In contrast to the Victorian mores of British missionaries and colonists, however, Ganda men recognized women's sexual desire and that a husband should be able to satisfy his wife's legitimate sexual needs (Kisseka 1973, 150; Obbo 1980, 78). A woman's sexual relationship with anyone other than her husband, however, was unacceptable (Kyomuhendo and McIntosh 2006, 76).

2. Literally translated as "that which is feared," *ekitiibwa* references notions of honor, glory, prestige, dignity, and respect. In the highly stratified kingdom of Buganda, notions of honor, or ekitiibwa, were well developed by the early nineteenth century and have played a central role in Ganda social life. As the linguist John Murphy (1972, 210) notes, it "is perhaps the greatest ideal and most sought after attribute of the Baganda. It has an importance comparable to that of 'face' in the Orient."

3. These elite women included the *Namasole* (queen mother), *Lubuga* (queen sister), *abambejja* (princesses), *bakembuga* (wives of the kabaka), and wives of chiefs (Richards 1964, 257).

4. Until the late 1500s most kabaka had only one or two official wives. In the 1700s, however, this changed drastically as polygyny became institutionalized. Sunna II, for example, who ruled from 1795 to 1856, had 148 official wives, 2,000 reserve wives, and 18,000 maiden servants (Musisi 1991, 769).

5. Some men did allow their wives to use part of their gardens for cotton or coffee cultivation, and the wives controlled the profits (Mair 1934, 95; Richards 1954a, 22). In addition, as part of the Uganda Agreement of 1900, the colonial administration created private property in Buganda. Large parcels of land were originally given to 3,940 elite Ganda men (Richards 1966, 25). Over time, these plots were divided and given to heirs, who could include daughters, or they could be sold to women. Thus in Buganda a unique process allowed women to own private property and cultivate their own cash crops. This also allowed some women to own property in Kampala, which facilitated the emergence of single, independent female householders (Southall and Gutkind 1957).

6. In the 1890s, approximately 30,000 South Asian laborers were brought by the British from British India to construct the Uganda Railway. After the railway was completed, some South Asians remained in Uganda and worked as merchants and government clerks, primarily in Kampala.

7. Kampala's population in 1959 was approximately 100,000, or only 1.5 percent of the total population of Uganda (Kyomuhendo and McIntosh 2006, 91). In 2011, Kampala accounted for 3.5 percent of Uganda's population.

8. Derek Peterson notes that both Ganda royal elites and *bataka* (clan leaders) publicly endorsed monogamous marriage as central to their notion of moral order and to establish themselves as reputable, upstanding, Christian citizens. However, for many elite men "this political and rhetorical focus on monogamous sexual discipline was a convenient fiction" (Peterson 2012, 97).

9. Since the mid-nineteenth century there has been a Muslim minority population in Uganda. Christianity, however, became the de facto official religion, and the entire educational system was originally based on the work of Christian missions (Mair 1940, 3). To this day Muslims are often treated as a special group; for example, separate Muslim marriage and family legal codes have been created that make allowances for polygamous marriage. As Southall (1961, 51–52) argues, this has often had the effect of strengthening "traditional male values," including men's rights to a "plurality of women."

10. The magendo economy (typically translated as black market trade or smuggling) grew out of the price controls imposed by the Amin government mandating both artificially low prices for produce and high exchange rates. Under these controls, Ugandan farmers received little money for crops sold

domestically, which encouraged the smuggling of goods like coffee to neighboring countries for sale at higher prices.

11. Somewhat paradoxically, Amin was at the forefront of African leaders in terms of appointing women to high-level positions in government. As Decker (2013) argues, these appointments were not a reflection of pro-woman policies but instead were made to legitimize his military rule, surround himself with attractive women, humiliate male colleagues, and portray a commitment to women's rights, especially during the United Nations Decade for Women, which began in 1976.

12. During the 1990s, only 5 to 7 percent of women were involved in wage or salaried work, compared to 21 percent of men (Kyomuhendo and McIntosh 2006, 218).

13. Anne Marie Goetz and Shireen Hassim (2003) have highlighted the limits a state-sponsored gender equity program poses for the women's movement in Uganda.

14. The Domestic Relations Bill has a long history. A version was initially proposed, and rejected, in the 1970s. In 2006, parliament reviewed a revised bill and again rejected it. The bill was then split into the Muslim Personal Bill and the broader Marriage and Divorce Bill. While Museveni voiced support of the Marriage and Divorce Bill, members of his party rejected it in 2013.

15. Of particular note is the NGO I volunteered with during my fieldwork, CEDOVIP, which had integrated AIDS prevention activities into their work on domestic violence (Abramsky et al. 2012; Musuya 2011). I discuss this important work in detail in chapter 6.

16. The paradoxes of gender, sexuality, and AIDS that Kampala women have confronted have been the focus of insightful analysis (Davis 2000; Mickleburgh 1998; Ogden 1996; Wallman 1996). In contrast, paradoxes for men have received limited attention.

17. Doyle (2013, 387) agrees with Epstein and Thornton that concurrent, overlapping relationships have indeed been a critical aspect of the Ugandan (and African) AIDS crisis. However, he stresses that more casual, short-term partnerships have also played an important role in HIV transmission.

18. Such issues came to a head in the 2005 "condom crisis," in which a national shortage of condoms was seen as a possible shift in government AIDS policy away from condoms and toward a focus on abstinence and sex only within marriage.

3. PROVIDING IN POVERTY

1. *Muyaye* is derived from *omuyaga*, someone who smokes marijuana. Obbo (1993) and Mamdani (1983) note the term was already widely used in the 1970s

to describe young men who specialized in the magendo smuggling economy that flourished during Idi Amin's regime. Today, abayaye (pl.) are seen as products of the urban slums. Because "youth" is a very broad term in urban Uganda, and can be associated with any unmarried person under forty, even older men could be labeled muyaye. The association between muyaye and youth adds insult to injury when used to describe unemployed men in their thirties. Similar terms exist in other urban African contexts, most notably *utsotsi*, used to describe violent, streetwise male criminals in urban South Africa (Glaser 1992; Mkhize 2004).

2. Cornwall (2003) and Silberschmidt (2001) make similar observations about contemporary gender tensions surrounding women's work and men's attempt to police it in Nigeria, Kenya, and Tanzania.

3. This area first gained its sordid and dangerous reputation in the 1970s when smugglers stopped here on runs between Kigali in Rwanda and Mombasa on the Kenyan coast, hence the name Kimombasa.

4. As noted above, Julius also used "amaanyi" in his description of men's privilege of having multiple wives or girlfriends. The term is often used to describe strong, powerful, or violent men (*omusajja ow'amaanyi*) and can also euphemistically refer to semen (Snoxall 1967, 196). The violent connotations of "amaanyi" are evident in the verb "to rape," *okuliisa amaanyi*, which is literally translated as "to eat with violence."

5. Rafik's usage was typical of how other men I met described their concerns about reversals of "proper" gender relations in contemporary Uganda. Similar examples appear in chapter 4.

6. Aboim (2009, 201) also highlights how African men can be betwixt and between worlds in her research in urban Mozambique, revealing "how men are reconstructing their identities when caught between tradition and male dominance and the Westernized values of the modern equalitarian family." See also Spronk's (2012) rich analysis of men's similar paradoxes in Nairobi.

4. WOMEN'S RIGHTS IN THE REMAKING OF MASCULINITY

1. Elsewhere (Wyrod 2016), I have referred to these dynamics as the *intimate politics of women rights* to capture both how intimate relationships shape women's rights and how women's rights shape intimate relationships.

2. This understanding of rights reflects a hierarchical model of sociopolitical power in which a sole ruler, in this case a king, is at the apex. Beneath the king is a set of interlocking substructures, the smallest being the home and the largest the clan, each with its own head. This political system mandates allegiance of subordinates to superiors, and while justice and *obwenkanya* (equality) are rel-

evant in Buganda, their meanings are more restricted and imply "a situational equality of subjects before a power-holder and decision-maker rather than an ontological equality of persons" (Karlstrom 1996, 489).

3. This man used the verb *okusinga,* meaning "to exceed, surpass, be higher than, stronger than, or superior to." This usage echoes Karlstrom's (1996) observation that Baganda typically held that only one person should be at the head of a given social group or hierarchy. *Okusinga* was often used by men and women when discussing their views on women's rights.

4. Men's concerns about gender equality were also occasionally voiced in relation to "women now marrying men," as noted in chapter 3. In these cases, men used the word *okuwasa* (to marry), a transitive verb conventionally used to describe a man marrying a woman. *Okufumbirwa* (to be married) is the intransitive verb used to describe a woman being married to a man; it would be used to describe a man being married to a woman only in a disparaging way (Murphy 1972). So the use of *okuwasa* here implies women having a type of power conventionally reserved for men.

5. Because Sophie was very reserved and quiet during my initial interview with her and Samuel, I had a female Ugandan research assistant conduct the interview with Sophie alone.

6. Literally, "to climb on, step on, ascend over the man."

7. As noted previously, this use of the active form of the verb to marry (*okuwasa*) implies women now have a type of power typically associated only with men.

8. Even without this agreement, Phoebe had a strong case for claiming the property because her marriage to Wilfred was informal and not legally recognized. Purchasing the land was therefore a business agreement that gave her sole ownership of the property.

9. One of these women, Pamela, was discussed in the previous chapter. Both she and her cowife were also partially successful in getting their husband to use condoms more consistently.

10. This new health problem did prompt some reassessment of certain masculine norms by both men. They both made it clear that they felt pressure, especially from male peers, to leave their HIV-positive partners. Staying in the relationship was a challenge to this simple solution to their problems. For a more detailed discussion of these relationships, see Wyrod 2013.

11. Other research has also shown that HIV-positive women in discordant relationships struggled and largely failed to enforce safe sex with their negative partners, with discordance also consolidating male power (Stevens and Galvão 2007).

12. For a similar critique of human rights more generally in Malawi, see Englund 2006.

5. THE INTERSECTION OF MASCULINITY, SEXUALITY, AND AIDS

1. It was correct that this grassroots men's union was unique in Kampala, and probably Uganda, in 2004. Since 1993 the AIDS Support Organisation had sponsored the small Positive Men's Union, but it was only active sporadically in 2004.

2. All three of these men said they first tested HIV-positive in the mid- to late 1990s.

3. Henry's views on masculinity and work were discussed in chapter 3.

4. I organized this group discussion with the intention of speaking with average workingmen in Bwaise. These men were in their twenties and thirties, Muslims and Christians, and all earning only a few dollars a day. Most had a primary school education or one to two years of secondary school education, and approximately three quarters were Baganda.

5. These figures correspond well to the Uganda HIV/AIDS Sero-Behavioural Survey: 2004–05 (UHSBS 2004–05), a nationally representative survey conducted during my initial year of fieldwork. This survey found that nationally 70 percent of sexually active men and 96 percent of women claimed to have only one partner in the previous year. Figures for Kampala were 65 percent of men and 93 percent of women. The survey also reported that 18 percent of currently married men and 3 percent of married women said they had sex with a "non-marital, non-cohabiting partner" in the previous year (Uganda Ministry of Health et al. 2006).

6. Peter was also briefly discussed in the opening vignette of chapter 1.

7. I conducted nineteen interviews with women in Bwaise in 2004. In this convenience sample, the majority of women were Baganda, ranged in age from 17 to 59, had varied educational backgrounds (from none to secondary school), and were both Muslim and Christian. See the appendix for further information.

8. These ten women were all Baganda, ranged in age from 20 to 45, were both Muslims and Christians, and had education levels from only primary school to some tertiary.

9. According to the UHSBS 2004–05, only 4 percent of sexually active women nationally and 7 percent of women in Kampala reported two or more partners in the previous year (Uganda Ministry of Health et al. 2006).

10. Dense sexual networks that facilitate HIV transmission require a percentage of women, not just men, to have concurrent sexual relationships (Halperin and Epstein 2004; Epstein 2007). Globally, surveys of sexual behavior often fail to capture these relationship dynamics (Wellings et al. 2006, 1708). However, as I stress throughout this book, it is a mistake to conflate the frequency, causes, and consequences of women's and men's concurrent sexual relationships. Women with multiple sexual partners face great social risk to their reputation and bodily

risk of abuse and HIV infection. Men with concurrent partners often gain social status, face little or no threat of domestic violence, and have greater control over safe sex practices.

11. The UHSBS 2004–05 found that nationally Ugandan men reported only seven *lifetime* sexual partners and women two lifetime partners. Figures for Kampala were similar (Uganda Ministry of Health et al. 2006). In addition, Wellings et al. (2006, 1714) note in their comprehensive analysis of sexual behavior globally that some studies indicate that men in some sub-Saharan African countries report *fewer* lifetime sexual partners compared to their peers in industrialized countries.

12. Interestingly, the phrase "zero grazing" was only explicitly mentioned by one person in the 116 interviews I conducted. This man was university educated and one of the only men I considered close to middle class. However, he mistakenly conflated zero grazing with his decision to abstain from all sexual relationships.

6. beyond bwaise

1. Two-thirds of both married and unmarried bodabodamen said they had at least one additional more casual sexual partner in addition to their regular partner (Nyanzi et al. 2004, 245).

2. Parikh (2007, 1205) does discuss one unusual exception to this trend. Men of the Uganda Taxi Owners and Drivers' Association of Iganga created a peer-based program that discouraged extramarital affairs and promoted alternative notions of masculinity "that centered on being responsible not only for the economic well-being of the household but also for the affective well-being of the marital bond."

3. See Setel 1996, 1999 for an early example of AIDS as a paradox of manhood for young men in northern Tanzania forced to migrate to urban areas for work in the early 1990s.

4. Like Spronk (2012), Hunter is careful to emphasize the ambiguities of this modern ideology of male sexuality. He notes that "the meaning of *isoka* is deeply contested among men" (2002, 109), with older men attempting to reinforce the importance of formal marriage, some younger men ambivalent about whether or not to "show off" their girlfriends, and poorer men resentful of rich men's ability to easily attract girlfriends. Like Smith (2014), Hunter also draws out the complexities of how men "do intimacy" in their multiple sexual partnerships. He stresses that these relationships are best understood as a modern version of "provider love" in which men derive pleasure and satisfaction not simply from sex but also from providing gifts and money to their lovers and the intimate bonds this creates.

5. SASA! has been implemented in eight communities in Kampala (not including Bwaise or Kawempe Division). The programs involve community residents, local religious and political leaders, and professionals such as healthcare providers and police officers.

6. The results for physical and sexual violence were not statistically significant, but this was likely due to the small number of communities included in the study (4 control and 4 intervention communities), a common problem of statistical power for community-level trials.

7. The fact that women did not report equally significant changes raises questions about the validity of men's self-reported behavior. However, as the study team notes, "given the study context, in which patriarchy is a dominant aspect, the shifts among men in intervention communities provide encouraging evidence to suggest that SASA! may be making men more cognizant of what they should or could be doing in order to foster more equitable relationships" (Kyegombe et al. 2014a, 10).

8. Smith (2009a, 258) makes a similar point, arguing that "men's extramarital sex happens *because* of a whole range of socially organized opportunity structures, to the extent that women have extramarital sex, it happens *despite* all the social impediments designed to prevent it" (original emphasis).

References

Aboim, Sofia. 2009. "Men between Worlds: Changing Masculinities in Urban Maputo." *Men and Masculinities* 12 (2): 201–24.

———. 2010. *Plural Masculinities: The Remaking of the Self in Private Life.* Aldershot: Ashgate.

Abramsky, Tanya, Karen Devries, Ligia Kiss, Leilani Francisco, Janet Nakuti, Tina Musuya, Nambusi Kyegombe, Elizabeth Starmann, Dan Kaye, and Lori Michau. 2012. "A Community Mobilisation Intervention to Prevent Violence against Women and Reduce HIV/AIDS Risk in Kampala, Uganda (the SASA! Study): Study Protocol for a Cluster Randomised Controlled Trial." *Trials* 13 (1): 96–96.

Abramsky, Tanya, Karen Devries, Ligia Kiss, Janet Nakuti, Nambusi Kyegombe, Elizabeth Starmann, Bonnie Cundill, et al. 2014. "Findings from the SASA! Study: A Cluster Randomized Controlled Trial to Assess the Impact of a Community Mobilization Intervention to Prevent Violence against Women and Reduce HIV Risk in Kampala, Uganda." *BMC Medicine* 12 (122): 1–17.

Acker, Joan. 1990. "Hierarchies, Jobs, Bodies: A Theory of Gendered Organizations." *Gender & Society* 4 (2): 139–58.

Adam, Barry. 2011. "Epistemic Fault Lines in Biomedical and Social Approaches to HIV Prevention." *Journal of the International AIDS Society* 14 (Suppl. 2): S2.

Agadjanian, Victor. 2002. "Men Doing 'Women's Work': Masculinity and Gender Relations among Street Vendors in Maputo, Mozambique." *Journal of Men's Studies* 10 (3): 329–42.

Ahearn, Laura. 2001. *Invitations to Love: Literacy, Love Letters, and Social Change in Nepal.* Ann Arbor: University of Michigan Press.

Ahikire, Josephine. 2003. "Gender Equity and Local Democracy in Contemporary Uganda: Addressing the Challenge of Women's Political Effectiveness in Local Government." In *No Shortcuts to Power: African Women in Politics and Policy Making,* edited by Anne Marie Goetz and Shireen Hassim, 213–39. New York: Zed Books.

Ahlberg, Beth. 1994. "Is There a Distinct African Sexuality? A Critical Response to Caldwell et al." *Africa* 64 (2): 220–42.

aids2031 Consortium. 2010. *AIDS: Taking a Long-Term View.* Upper Saddle River, NJ: FT Press.

Akumu, Patience. 2015. "Women's Rights Violations Don't Need to Kill or Maim to Still Be Violations." *African Arguments,* September 22. http://africanarguments.org/2015/09/22/womens-rights-violations-don't-need-to-kill-or-maim-to-still-be-violations/.

Amadiume, Ifi. 1987. *Male Daughters, Female Husbands: Gender and Sex in an African Society.* London: Zed Books.

———. 1997. *Re-Inventing Africa: Matriarchy, Religion, and Culture.* London: Zed Books.

Amnesty International. 1978. "Human Rights in Uganda." June. Available at www.amnesty.org/en/documents/afr59/007/1978/en/.

Andersson, Neil, Anne Cockcroft, and Bev Shea. 2008. "Gender-Based Violence and HIV: Relevance for HIV Prevention in Hyperendemic Countries of Southern Africa." *AIDS* 22 (Suppl. 4): S73–S86.

Anglemyer, Andrew, George Rutherford, Rachel Baggaley, Matthias Egger, and Nandi Siegfried. 2011. "Antiretroviral Therapy for Prevention of HIV Transmission in HIV-Discordant Couples." *Cochrane Database of Systematic Reviews,* no. 8: CD009153.

Ankrah, E. Maxine. 1991. "AIDS and the Social Side of Health." *Social Science & Medicine* 32 (9): 967–80.

Ashforth, Adam. 1999. "Weighing Manhood in Soweto." *CODESRIA Bulletin,* no. 2: 51–58.

Baeten, Jared, Deborah Donnell, Patrick Ndase, Nelly Mugo, James Campbell, Jonathan Wangisi, Jordan Tappero, et al. 2012. "Antiretroviral Prophylaxis for HIV Prevention in Heterosexual Men and Women." *New England Journal of Medicine* 367 (5): 399–410.

Barker, Gary, and Christine Ricardo. 2005. "Young Men and the Construction of Masculinity in Sub-Saharan Africa: Implications for HIV/AIDS, Conflict, and Violence." Social Development Papers 26. World Bank, Washington, DC.

Barnett, Tony, and Alan Whiteside. 2002. *AIDS in the Twenty-First Century: Disease and Globalization.* New York: Palgrave Macmillan.

Bassett, Mary, and Karen Brudney. 2014. "Treating Our Way out of AIDS?" *American Journal of Public Health* 104 (2): 200–203.

Baylies, Carolyn, and Janet Bujra. 2000. *AIDS, Sexuality and Gender in Africa: Collective Strategies and Struggles in Tanzania and Zambia.* London: Routledge.

Beasley, Christine. 2008. "Rethinking Hegemonic Masculinity in a Globalizing World." *Men and Masculinities* 11 (1): 86–103.

Beoku-Betts, Josephine, and Wairimu Ngaruiya Njambi. 2005. "African Feminist Scholars in Women's Studies: Negotiating Spaces of Dislocation and Transformation in the Study of Women." *Meridians: Feminism, Race, Transnationalism* 6 (1): 113–32.

Bibeau, Gilles, and Duncan Pedersen. 2002. "A Return to Scientific Racism in Medical Social Sciences: The Case of Sexuality and the AIDS Epidemic in Africa." In *New Horizons in Medical Anthropology: Essays in Honour of Charles Leslie,* edited by Charles M. Leslie, Mark Lock, and Margaret M. Nichter, 141–71. London: Routledge.

Bond, George, and Joan Vincent. 1997. "AIDS in Uganda: The First Decade." In *AIDS in Africa and the Caribbean,* edited by George Bond, John Kreniske, Ida Susser, and Joan Vincent, 85–98. Boulder, CO: Westview Press.

Bourgois, Philippe. 2009. *Righteous Dopefiend.* Berkeley: University of California Press.

Brandt, Allan M. 1987. *No Magic Bullet: A Social History of Venereal Disease in the United States since 1880.* New York: Oxford University Press.

Bridges, Tristan. 2014. "A Very 'Gay' Straight? Hybrid Masculinities, Sexual Aesthetics, and the Changing Relationship between Masculinity and Homophobia." *Gender & Society* 28 (1): 58–82.

Bridges, Tristan, and C.J. Pascoe. 2014. "Hybrid Masculinities: New Directions in the Sociology of Men and Masculinities." *Sociology Compass* 8 (3): 246–58.

Brier, Jennifer. 2009. *Infectious Ideas: U.S. Political Responses to the AIDS Crisis.* Chapel Hill: University of North Carolina Press.

Brod, Harry. 1995. "Pornography and the Alienation of Male Sexuality." In *Men's Lives,* edited by Michael S. Kimmel and Michael Messner, 393–404. Boston: Allyn & Bacon.

Bujra, Janet. 2000. "Targeting Men for a Change: AIDS Discourse and Activism in Africa." *Agenda* 44: 6–23.

Bunnell, R., J. Nassozi, E. Marum, J. Mubangizi, S. Malamba, B. Dillon, J. Kalule, J. Bahizi, N. Musoke, and J. Mermin. 2005. "Living with Discordance: Knowledge, Challenges, and Prevention Strategies of HIV-Discordant Couples in Uganda." *AIDS Care* 17 (8): 999–1012.

Burton, Jennifer, Lynae Darbes, and Don Operario. 2010. "Couples-Focused Behavioral Interventions for Prevention of HIV: Systematic Review of the State of Evidence." *AIDS and Behavior* 14 (1): 1–10.

Butler, Judith. 1990. *Gender Trouble: Feminism and the Subversion of Identity.* New York: Routledge.

Caldwell, John, and Pat Caldwell. 1987. "The Cultural Context of High Fertility in Sub-Saharan Africa." *Population and Development Review* 13 (3): 409–37.

Caldwell, John, Pat Caldwell, and P. Quiggin. 1989. "The Social Context of AIDS in Sub-Saharan Africa." *Population and Development Review* 15 (2): 185–234.

Campbell, Catherine. 1997. "Migrancy, Masculine Identities and AIDS: The Psychosocial Context of HIV Transmission on the South African Gold Mines." *Social Science & Medicine* 45 (2): 273–82.

Campbell, Catherine, Yugi Nair, and Sbongile Maimane. 2006. "AIDS Stigma, Sexual Moralities and the Policing of Women and Youth in South Africa." *Feminist Review* 83 (1): 132–38.

Carovano, Kathryn. 1995. *HIV and the Challenges Facing Men.* New York: UNDP HIV and Development Programme.

Carrigan, Tim, R. W. Connell, and John Lee. 1985. "Toward a New Sociology of Masculinity." *Theory and Society* 14: 551–604.

Castells, Manuel. 1997. *The Power of Identity.* Malden, MA: Blackwell.

Cates, Willard. 2011. "HPTN 052 and the Future of HIV Treatment and Prevention." *Lancet* 378 (9787): 224–25.

Chen, Anthony. 1999. "Lives at the Center of the Periphery, Lives at the Periphery of the Center: Chinese American Masculinities and Bargaining with Hegemony." *Gender & Society* 13 (5): 584–607.

Cohen, Jon. 2011. "HIV Treatment as Prevention." *Science* 334 (6063): 1628.

Cohen, Myron, Ying Chen, Marybeth McCauley, Theresa Gamble, Mina Hosseinipour, Nagalingeswaran Kumarasamy, James Hakim, et al. 2011. "Prevention of HIV-1 Infection with Early Antiretroviral Therapy." *New England Journal of Medicine* 365 (6): 493–505.

Collier, Jane. 1997. *From Duty to Desire: Remaking Families in a Spanish Village.* Princeton, NJ: Princeton University Press.

Colvin, Christopher, and Steven Robins. 2009. "Positive Men in Hard, Neoliberal Times: Engendering Health Citizenship in South Africa." In *Gender and HIV/AIDS: Critical Perspectives from the Developing World,* edited by Jelke Boesten and Nana Poku, 177–90. Aldershot: Ashgate.

Colvin, Christopher, Steven Robins, and Joan Leavens. 2010. "Grounding 'Responsibilisation Talk': Masculinities, Citizenship and HIV in Cape Town, South Africa." *Journal of Development Studies* 46 (7): 1179–95.

Comaroff, Jean. 1993. "The Diseased Heart of Africa: Medicine, Colonialism, and the Black Body." In *Knowledge, Power, and Practice: The Anthropology of Medicine and Everyday Life,* edited by Shirley Lindenbaum and Margaret Lock, 305–29. Berkeley: University of California Press.

Connell, Catherine. 2010. "Doing, Undoing, or Redoing Gender? Learning from the Workplace Experiences of Transpeople." *Gender & Society* 24 (1): 31–55.

Connell, R. W. 1987. *Gender and Power: Society, the Person, and Sexual Politics.* Stanford, CA: Stanford University Press.

———. 1991. "Live Fast and Die Young: The Construction of Masculinity among Young Working-Class Men on the Margin of the Labour Market." *Journal of Sociology* 27 (2): 141–71.

———. 1995. *Masculinities.* Berkeley: University of California Press.

———. 2000. *The Men and the Boys.* Berkeley: University of California Press.

Connell, R. W., and James Messerschmidt. 2005. "Hegemonic Masculinity: Rethinking the Concept." *Gender & Society* 19 (6): 829–59.

Cornwall, Andrea. 2002. "Spending Power: Love, Money, and the Reconfiguration of Gender Relations in Ado-Odo, Southwestern Nigeria." *American Ethnologist* 29 (4): 963–80.

———. 2003. "To Be a Man Is More than a Day's Work: Shifting Ideals of Masculinity in Ado-Obo, Southwestern Nigeria." In *Men and Masculinities in Modern Africa,* edited by Lisa Lindsay and Stephan Miescher, 230–48. Portsmouth, NH: Heinemann.

———. 2005. "Introduction: Perspectives on Gender in Africa." In *Readings in Gender in Africa,* edited by Andrea Cornwall, 1–19. Bloomington: Indiana University Press.

Cornwall, Andrea, and Nancy Lindisfarne. 1994. Introduction to *Dislocating Masculinity: Comparative Ethnographies,* edited by Andrea Cornwall and Nancy Lindisfarne, 1–10. New York: Routledge.

Craddock, Susan. 2004. "Beyond Epidemiology: Locating AIDS in Africa." In *HIV and AIDS in Africa: Beyond Epidemiology,* edited by Ezekiel Kalipeni, Susan Craddock, Joseph Oppong, and Jayati Ghosh, 1–10. Malden, MA: Blackwell.

Creighton, Genevieve, and John Oliffe. 2010. "Theorising Masculinities and Men's Health: A Brief History with a View to Practice." *Health Sociology Review* 19 (4): 409–18.

Davis, Mark, and Paul Flowers. 2011. "Love and HIV Serodiscordance in Gay Men's Accounts of Life with Their Regular Partners." *Culture, Health & Sexuality* 13 (7): 737–49.

Davis, Paula. 2000. "On the Sexuality of 'Town Women' in Kampala." *Africa Today* 47 (3): 29–60.

Decker, Alicia. 2010. "Idi Amin's Dirty War: Subversion, Sabotage, and the Battle to Keep Uganda Clean, 1971–1979." *International Journal of African Historical Studies* 43 (3): 489–513.

———. 2013. "On the Promotion of 'Certain' Ugandan Women: Was Idi Amin Feminist or Foe?" In *Women, Gender, and Sexualities in Africa,* edited by Toyin Falola and Nana Akua Amponsah, 225–36. Carolina Academic Press African World Series. Durham, NC: Carolina Academic Press.

Decoteau, Claire. 2013a. "The Crisis of Liberation: Masculinity, Neoliberalism, and HIV/AIDS in Postapartheid South Africa." *Men and Masculinities* 16 (2): 139–59.

———. 2013b. "Exclusionary Inclusion and the Normalization of Biomedical Culture." *American Journal of Cultural Sociology* 1 (3): 403–30.

Demetriou, Demetrakis. 2001. "Connell's Concept of Hegemonic Masculinity: A Critique." *Theory and Society* 30 (3): 337–61.

Deutsch, Francine. 2007. "Undoing Gender." *Gender & Society* 21 (1): 106–27.

Donnell, Deborah, Jared Baeten, James Kiarie, Katherine Thomas, Wendy Stevens, Craig Cohen, James McIntyre, Jairam Lingappa, and Connie Celum. 2010. "Heterosexual HIV-1 Transmission after Initiation of Antiretroviral Therapy: A Prospective Cohort Analysis." *Lancet* 375 (9731): 2092–98.

Dowsett, Gary. 2013. "Prevention as Hyperbole; Culture as Concupiscence." *HIV Australia* 11 (1): 43–45.

Doyle, Shane. 2013. *Before HIV: Sexuality, Fertility, and Mortality in East Africa, 1900–1980*. Oxford: Oxford University Press.

Dunkle, Kristin, Rachel Jewkes, Heather Brown, Glenda Gray, James McIntryre, and Sioban Harlow. 2004. "Gender-Based Violence, Relationship Power, and Risk of HIV Infection in Women Attending Antenatal Clinics in South Africa." *Lancet* 363 (9419): 1415–21.

Dworkin, Shari. 2015. *Men at Risk: Masculinity, Heterosexuality, and HIV Prevention*. New York: New York University Press.

Dworkin, Shari, Christopher Colvin, Abbey Hatcher, and Dean Peacock. 2012. "Men's Perceptions of Women's Rights and Changing Gender Relations in South Africa Lessons for Working with Men and Boys in HIV and Antiviolence Programs." *Gender & Society* 26 (1): 97–120.

Dworkin, Shari, Megan Dunbar, Suneeta Krishnan, Abigail Hatcher, and Sharif Sawires. 2011. "Uncovering Tensions and Capitalizing on Synergies in HIV/AIDS and Antiviolence Programs." *American Journal of Public Health* 101 (6): 995–1003.

Dworkin, Shari, and Anke Ehrhardt. 2007. "Going beyond 'ABC' to Include 'GEM': Critical Reflections on Progress in the HIV/AIDS Epidemic." *American Journal of Public Health* 97 (1): 13–18.

Dworkin, Shari, Abigail Hatcher, Chris Colvin, and Dean Peacock. 2013. "Impact of a Gender-Transformative HIV and Antiviolence Program on Gender Ideologies and Masculinities in Two Rural, South African Communities." *Men and Masculinities* 16 (2): 181–202.

Dworkin, Shari, and Lucia O'Sullivan. 2005. "Actual versus Desired Initiation Patterns among a Sample of College Men: Tapping Disjunctures within Traditional Male Sexual Scripts." *Journal of Sex Research* 42 (2): 150–58.

Dworkin, Shari, Sarah Treves-Kagan, and Sheri Lippman. 2013. "Gender-Transformative Interventions to Reduce HIV Risks and Violence with

Heterosexually Active Men: A Review of the Global Evidence." *AIDS and Behavior* 17 (9): 2845–63.

Emslie, Carol, Damien Ridge, Sue Ziebland, and Kate Hunt. 2006. "Men's Accounts of Depression: Reconstructing or Resisting Hegemonic Masculinity?" *Social Science & Medicine* 62 (9): 2246–57.

England, Paula, Emily Shafer, and Alison Fogarty. 2008. "Hooking up and Forming Romantic Relationships on Today's College Campuses." In *The Gendered Society Reader,* edited by Michael Kimmel and Amy Aronson, 531–47. New York: Oxford University Press.

Englund, Harri. 2006. *Prisoners of Freedom: Human Rights and the African Poor.* Berkeley: University of California Press.

Epstein, Helen. 2005. "God and the Fight against AIDS." *New York Review of Books* 52 (7): 47–50.

———. 2007. *The Invisible Cure: Africa, the West, and the Fight against AIDS.* New York: Farrar, Straus & Giroux.

Epstein, Helen, and Julia Kim. 2007. "AIDS and the Power of Women." *New York Review of Books* 54 (2): 39–41.

Epstein, Helen, and Martina Morris. 2011a. "Concurrent Partnerships and HIV: An Inconvenient Truth." *Journal of the International AIDS Society* 14 (13): 1–11.

———. 2011b. "HPTN 052 and the Future of HIV Treatment and Prevention." *Lancet* 378 (9787): 225.

Epstein, Steven. 1996a. "A Queer Encounter: Sociology and the Study of Sexuality." In *Queer Theory/Sociology,* edited by Steven Seidman, 145–67. Cambridge, MA: Wiley-Blackwell.

———. 1996b. *Impure Science: AIDS, Activism, and the Politics of Knowledge.* Berkeley: University of California Press.

Esacove, Anne. 2010. "Love Matches: Heteronormativity, Modernity, and AIDS Prevention in Malawi." *Gender & Society* 24 (1): 83–109.

———. 2013. "Good Sex/Bad Sex: The Individualised Focus of US HIV Prevention Policy in Sub-Saharan Africa, 1995–2005." *Sociology of Health & Illness* 35 (1): 33–48.

European AIDS Treatment Group. 2014. "Community Consensus Statement on the Use of Antiretroviral Therapy in Preventing HIV Transmission." European AIDS Treatment Group, Brussels.

Fallers, Lloyd. 1964. "Social Mobility, Traditional and Modern." In *The King's Men: Leadership and Status in Buganda on the Eve on Independence,* edited by Lloyd Fallers, 158–210. London: Oxford University Press.

Fallers, Margaret. 1960. *The Eastern Lacustrine Bantu (Ganda and Soga).* London: International African Institute.

Faludi, Susan. 1999. *Stiffed: The Betrayal of the American Man.* New York: W. Morrow.

Farmer, Paul. 1999. *Infections and Inequalities: The Modern Plagues.* Berkeley: University of California Press.

———. 2005. *Pathologies of Power: Health, Human Rights, and the New War on the Poor.* Berkeley: University of California Press.

Fenstermaker, Sarah, Candace West, and Don Zimmerman. 1991. "Gender Inequality: New Conceptual Terrain." In *Gender, Family, and Economy: The Triple Overlap,* edited by Rae Blumberg, 289–307. Newbury Park, CA: Sage.

Ferguson, James. 2006. *Global Shadows: Africa in the Neoliberal World Order.* Durham, NC: Duke University Press.

Foreman, Martin. 1999. *AIDS and Men: Taking Risks or Taking Responsibility.* London: Panos.

Foucault, Michel. 1978. *The History of Sexuality, Volume 1: An Introduction.* New York: Random House.

Fritz, Katherine, Willi McFarland, Robert Wyrod, Charles Chasakara, Knox Makumbe, Admire Chirowodza, Chamunorwa Mashoko, Timothy Kellogg, and Godfrey Woelk. 2011. "Evaluation of a Peer Network–Based Sexual Risk Reduction Intervention for Men in Beer Halls in Zimbabwe: Results from a Randomized Controlled Trial." *AIDS and Behavior* 15 (8): 1732–44.

Gagnon, John. 1990. "The Explicit and Implicit Use of the Scripting Perspective in Sex Research." *Annual Review of Sex Research* 1 (1): 1–43.

Galvão, Jane. 2005. "Brazil and Access to HIV/AIDS Drugs: A Question of Human Rights and Public Health." *American Journal of Public Health* 95 (7): 1110–16.

Gamson, Joshua, and Dawne Moon. 2004. "The Sociology of Sexualities: Queer and Beyond." *Annual Review of Sociology* 30 (1): 47–64.

Gibbs, James. 1965. *Peoples of Africa.* New York: Holt, Rinehart and Winston.

Gibson, Diana, and Anita Hardon, eds. 2005. *Rethinking Masculinities, Violence, and AIDS.* New Brunswick, NJ: Transaction Publishers.

Glaser, Clive. 1992. "The Mark of Zorro: Sexuality and Gender Relations in the Tsotsi Subculture on the Witwatersrand." *African Studies* 51 (1): 47–68.

Glenn, Evelyn. 1999. "The Social Construction and Institutionalization of Gender and Race: An Integrative Framework." In *Revisioning Gender,* edited by Myra Marx Ferree, Judith Lorber, and Beth Hess, 3–43. Thousand Oaks, CA: Sage.

Goetz, Anne. 2003. "The Problem with Patronage: Constraints on Women's Political Effectiveness in Uganda." In *No Shortcuts to Power: African Women in Politics and Policy Making,* edited by Anne Goetz and Shireen Hassim, 110–39. London: Zed Books.

Goetz, Anne, and Shireen Hassim, eds. 2003. *No Shortcuts to Power: African Women in Politics and Policy Making.* London: Zed Books.

Goitom, Hanibal. 2013. "Uganda: Women Judges Voice Concern over Domestic Violence." *Global Legal Monitor,* July 8.

Greig, Alan, Dean Peacock, Rachel Jewkes, and Sisonke Msimang. 2008. "Gender and AIDS: Time to Act." *AIDS* 22 (Suppl. 2): S35–S43.

Groes-Green, Christian. 2012. "Philogynous Masculinities: Contextualizing Alternative Manhood in Mozambique." *Men and Masculinities* 15 (2): 91–111.

Gupta, Geeta. 2000. "Gender, Sexuality, and HIV/AIDS: The What, the Why, and the How." *Canadian HIV/AIDS Policy & Law Review* 5 (4): 86–93.

———. 2002. "How Men's Power over Women Fuels the HIV Epidemic." *British Medical Journal* 324 (7331): 183–84.

Gupta, Geeta, Justin Parkhurst, Jessica Ogden, Peter Aggleton, and Ajay Mahal. 2008. "Structural Approaches to HIV Prevention." *Lancet* 372: 764–75.

Hallett, T., J. Aberle-Grasse, G. Bello, L. Boulos, M. Cayemittes, B. Cheluget, J. Chipeta, et al. 2006. "Declines in HIV Prevalence Can Be Associated with Changing Sexual Behaviour in Uganda, Urban Kenya, Zimbabwe, and Urban Haiti." *Sexually Transmitted Infections* 82 (Suppl. 1): i1–i8.

Halpenny, Philip. 1975. "Three Styles of Ethnic Migration in Kisenyi, Kampala." In *Town and Country in Central and Eastern Africa,* edited by David Parkin, 276–87. London: Oxford University Press.

Halperin, Daniel, and Helen Epstein. 2004. "Concurrent Sexual Partnerships Help Explain Africa's High HIV Prevalence: Implications for Prevention." *Lancet* 364 (9428): 4–6.

Hansen, Holger. 2013. "Uganda in the 1970s: A Decade of Paradoxes and Ambiguities." *Journal of Eastern African Studies* 7 (1): 83–103.

Haram, Liv, and C. Bawa Yamba. 2009. *Dealing with Uncertainty in Contemporary African Lives.* Uppsala, Sweden: Nordiska Afrikainstitutet.

Hattersley, C. W. 1908. *The Baganda at Home.* London: Religious Tract Society.

Heald, Suzette. 1995. "The Power of Sex: Some Reflections on the Caldwells' 'African Sexuality' Thesis." *Africa* 65 (4): 489–506.

Hearn, Jeff. 2004. "From Hegemonic Masculinity to the Hegemony of Men." *Feminist Theory* 5 (1): 49–72.

Heimer, Carol. 2007. "Old Inequalities, New Disease: HIV/AIDS in Sub-Saharan Africa." *Annual Review of Sociology* 33 (1): 551–77.

Hickel, Jason. 2012. "Neoliberal Plague: The Political Economy of HIV Transmission in Swaziland." *Journal of Southern African Studies* 38 (3): 513–29.

Higgins, Jenny, Susie Hoffman, and Shari Dworkin. 2010. "Rethinking Gender, Heterosexual Men, and Women's Vulnerability to HIV/AIDS." *American Journal of Public Health* 100 (3): 435–45.

Hirsch, Jennifer. 2003. *A Courtship after Marriage: Sexuality and Love in Mexican Transnational Families.* Berkeley: University of California Press.

Hirsch, Jennifer, and Holly Wardlow, eds. 2006. *Modern Loves: The Anthropology of Romantic Courtship and Companionate Marriage.* Ann Arbor: University of Michigan Press.

Hirsch, Jennifer, Holly Wardlow, Daniel Jordan Smith, Harriet Phinney, Shanti Parikh, and Constance Nathanson. 2009a. Introduction to *The Secret: Love, Marriage, and HIV,* edited by Jennifer Hirsch, Holly Wardlow, Daniel Jordan Smith, Harriet Phinney, Shanti Parikh, and Constance Nathanson, 1–22. Nashville, TN: Vanderbilt University Press.

———, eds. 2009b. *The Secret: Love, Marriage, and HIV.* Nashville, TN: Vanderbilt University Press.

Hollway, Wendy. 1984. "Women's Power in Heterosexual Sex." *Women's Studies International Forum* 7 (1): 63–68. Special Issue, "Men and Sex: A Case Study in 'Sexual Sexual Politics.'"

Hunter, Mark. 2002. "The Materiality of Everyday Sex: Thinking beyond 'Prostitution.'" *African Studies* 61 (1): 99–120.

———. 2004. "Masculinities, Multiple-Sexual-Partners, and AIDS: The Making and Unmaking of Isoka in KwaZulu-Natal." *Transformation: Critical Perspectives on Southern Africa* 54 (1): 123–53.

———. 2005. "Cultural Politics and Masculinities: Multiple Partners in Historical Perspective in KwaZulu-Natal." *Culture, Health & Sexuality* 7 (4): 389–403.

———. 2010. *Love in the Time of AIDS: Inequality, Gender, and Rights in South Africa.* Bloomington: Indiana University Press.

Iliffe, John. 2005. *Honour in African History.* Cambridge: Cambridge University Press.

Illouz, Eva. 1997. *Consuming the Romantic Utopia: Love and the Cultural Contradictions of Capitalism.* Berkeley: University of California Press.

Ingraham, Chrys. 1994. "The Heterosexual Imaginary: Feminist Sociology and Theories of Gender." *Sociological Theory* 12 (2): 203–19.

———. 2002. "Heterosexuality: It's Just Not Natural!" In *Handbook of Lesbian and Gay Studies,* edited by Diane Richardson and Steven Seidman, 73–82. London: Sage.

Jackson, Stevi. 1996. "Heterosexuality and Feminist Theory." In *Theorising Heterosexuality,* edited by Diane Richardson, 21–38. Buckingham: Open University Press.

———. 1999. *Heterosexuality in Question.* Thousand Oaks, CA: Sage.

———. 2005. "Sexuality, Heterosexuality and Gender Hierarchy: Getting Our Priorities Straight." In *Thinking Straight: The Power, Promise, and Paradox of Heterosexuality,* edited by Chrys Ingraham, 15–38. New York: Routledge.

Jemmott, John, Loretta Jemmott, Ann O'Leary, Zolani Ngwane, Larry Icard, Anita Heeren, Xoliswa Mtose, and Craig Carty. 2014. "Cluster-Randomized Controlled Trial of an HIV/Sexually Transmitted Infection Risk-Reduction Intervention for South African Men." *American Journal of Public Health* 104 (3): 467–73.

Jenness, Valerie, and Sarah Fenstermaker. 2014. "Agnes Goes to Prison: Gender Authenticity, Transgender Inmates in Prisons for Men, and Pursuit of 'the Real Deal.'" *Gender & Society* 28 (1): 5–31.

Jewkes, Rachel, M. Nduna, J. Levin, N. Jama, K. Dunkle, A. Puren, and N. Duvvury. 2008. "Impact of Stepping Stones on Incidence of HIV and HSV-2 and Sexual Behaviour in Rural South Africa: Cluster Randomised Controlled Trial." *British Medical Journal* 337: a506.

Johnson-Hanks, Jennifer. 2006. *Uncertain Honor: Modern Motherhood in an African Crisis*. Chicago: University of Chicago Press.

Kajubi, Phoebe, Edward Green, Esther Hudes, Moses Kamya, Alison Ruark, and Norman Hearst. 2011. "Multiple Sexual Partnerships among Poor Urban Dwellers in Kampala, Uganda." *JAIDS Journal of Acquired Immune Deficiency Syndromes* 57 (2): 153–56.

Kaler, Amy. 2003a. "'My Girlfriends Could Fill a Yanu-Yanu Bus': Rural Malawian Men's Claims about Their Own Serostatus." *Demographic Research*, Special Collection 1 (11): 349–72.

———. 2003b. *Running after Pills: Politics, Gender, and Contraception in Colonial Zimbabwe*. Portsmouth, NH: Heinemann.

———. 2010. "Gender-as-Knowledge and AIDS in Africa: A Cautionary Tale." *Qualitative Sociology* 33 (1): 23–36.

Kalichman, Seth, Leickness Simbayi, Allanise Cloete, Mario Clayford, Warda Arnolds, Mpumi Mxoli, Gino Smith, et al. 2009. "Integrated Gender-Based Violence and HIV Risk Reduction Intervention for South African Men: Results of a Quasi-Experimental Field Trial." *Prevention Science* 10 (3): 260–69.

Kalipeni, Ezekiel, Susan Craddock, Joseph Oppong, and Jayati Ghosh, eds. 2004. *HIV and AIDS in Africa: Beyond Epidemiology*. Malden, MA: Blackwell.

Kampala Capital City Authority. 2012. "Updating Kampala Structure Plan and Upgrading the Kampala GIS Unit." Kampala.

Kandiyoti, Deniz. 1988. "Bargaining with Patriarchy." *Gender & Society* 2 (3): 274–90.

Karim, Quarraisha, Salim Karim, Janet Frohlich, Anneke Grobler, Cheryl Baxter, Leila Mansoor, Ayesha Kharsany, et al. 2010. "Effectiveness and Safety of Tenofovir Gel, an Antiretroviral Microbicide, for the Prevention of HIV Infection in Women." *Science* 329 (5996): 1168–74.

Karlstrom, Mikael. 1996. "Imagining Democracy: Political Culture and Democratisation in Buganda." *Africa* 66 (4): 485–505.

Kim, Julia, Charlotte Watts, James Hargreaves, Luceth Ndhlovu, Godfrey Phetla, Linda Morison, Joanna Busza, John Porter, and Paul Pronyk. 2007. "Understanding the Impact of a Microfinance-Based Intervention on Women's Empowerment and the Reduction of Intimate Partner Violence in South Africa." *American Journal of Public Health* 97 (10): 1794–1802.

Kimmel, Michael. 1996. *Manhood in America: A Cultural History.* New York: Free Press.

———. 2005. *The Gender of Desire: Essays on Male Sexuality.* Albany: State University of New York Press.

Kinsman, John. 2010. *AIDS Policy in Uganda: Evidence, Ideology, and the Making of an African Success Story.* New York: Palgrave Macmillan.

Kipnis, Laura. 2003. *Against Love: A Polemic.* New York: Pantheon Books.

Kippax, Susan. 2012. "Effective HIV Prevention: The Indispensable Role of Social Science." *Journal of the International AIDS Society* 15 (2): 17357.

Kippax, Susan, and Niamh Stephenson. 2012. "Beyond the Distinction between Biomedical and Social Dimensions of HIV: Prevention through the Lens of a Social Public Health." *American Journal of Public Health* 102 (5): 789–799.

Kippax, Susan, Niamh Stephenson, Richard Parker, and Peter Aggleton. 2013. "Between Individual Agency and Structure in HIV Prevention: Understanding the Middle Ground of Social Practice." *American Journal of Public Health* 103 (8): 1367–75.

Kisekka, Mere. 1973. "The Baganda of Central Uganda." In *Cultural Source Materials for Population Planning in East Africa: Beliefs and Practices,* edited by Angela Molnos, 3: 148–62. Nairobi: University of Nairobi.

Kouyoumdjian, Fiona, Liviana Calzavara, Susan Bondy, Patricia O'Campo, David Serwadda, Fred Nalugoda, Joseph Kagaayi, Godfrey Kigozi, Maria Wawer, and Ronald Gray. 2013. "Risk Factors for Intimate Partner Violence in Women in the Rakai Community Cohort Study, Uganda, from 2000 to 2009." *BMC Public Health* 13 (566): 1–9.

Kron, Josh. 2011. "Charges against Ugandan Opposition Leader Are Dropped." *New York Times,* August 9.

Kyegombe, Nambusi, Tanya Abramsky, Karen Devries, Elizabeth Starmann, Lori Michau, Janet Nakuti, Tina Musuya, Lori Heise, and Charlotte Watts. 2014. "The Impact of SASA!, a Community Mobilization Intervention, on Reported HIV-Related Risk Behaviours and Relationship Dynamics in Kampala, Uganda." *Journal of the International AIDS Society* 17 (1): 1–16.

Kyegombe, Nambusi, Elizabeth Starmann, Karen Devries, Lori Michau, Janet Nakuti, Tina Musuya, Charlotte Watts, and Lori Heise. 2014. "'SASA! Is the Medicine That Treats Violence': Qualitative Findings on How a Community Mobilisation Intervention to Prevent Violence against Women Created Change in Kampala, Uganda." *Global Health Action* 7 (25082): 1–10.

Kyemba, Henry. 1977. *A State of Blood: The Inside Story of Idi Amin.* New York: Grosset & Dunlap.

Kyomuhendo, Grace, and Marjorie McIntosh. 2006. *Women, Work & Domestic Virtue in Uganda, 1900–2003.* Kampala: Fountain Publishers.

Lancet Editorial. 2011. "HIV Treatment as Prevention—It Works." *Lancet* 377 (9779): 1719.

Laqueur, Thomas. 1990. *Making Sex: Body and Gender from the Greeks to Freud*. Cambridge, MA: Harvard University Press.

Lindegger, Graham, and Michael Quayle. 2009. "Masculinity and HIV/AIDS." In *HIV/AIDS in South Africa 25 Years On*, edited by Poul Rohleder, Leslie Swartz, Seth Kalichman, and Leickness Simbayi, 41–54. New York: Springer.

Lindsay, Lisa, and Stephan Miescher. 2003a. "Introduction: Men and Masculinities in Modern African History." In *Men and Masculinities in Modern Africa*, edited by Lisa Lindsay and Stephan Miescher, 1–30. Portsmouth, NH: Heinemann.

———, eds. 2003b. *Men and Masculinities in Modern Africa*. Portsmouth, NH: Heinemann.

Lorber, Judith. 1994. *Paradoxes of Gender*. New Haven, CT: Yale University Press.

Low-Beer, Daniel, and Rand Stoneburner. 2003. "Behaviour and Communication Change in Reducing HIV: Is Uganda Unique?" *African Journal of AIDS Research* 2 (1): 9–21.

———. 2004. "Uganda and the Challenge of HIV/AIDS." In *The Political Economy of AIDS in Africa*, edited by Nana Poku and Alan Whiteside, 165–90. Burlington, VT: Ashgate.

Luke, Nancy. 2003. "Age and Economic Asymmetries in the Sexual Relationships of Adolescent Girls in Sub-Saharan Africa." *Studies in Family Planning* 34 (2): 67–86.

Lupton, Deborah. 1999. *Risk*. London: Routledge.

Lurie, Peter, Percy Hintzen, and Robert Lowe. 2004. "Socioeconomic Obstacles to HIV Prevention and Treatment in Developing Countries: The Roles of the International Monetary Fund and the World Bank." In *HIV and AIDS in Africa: Beyond Epidemiology*, edited by Ezekiel Kalipeni, Susan Craddock, Joseph Oppong, and Jayati Ghosh, 204–12. Malden, MA: Blackwell.

Lusher, Dean, and Garry Robins. 2009. "Hegemonic and Other Masculinities in Local Social Contexts." *Men and Masculinities* 11 (4): 387–423.

Lynch, Ingrid, Pierre Brouard, and Maretha Visser. 2010. "Constructions of Masculinity among a Group of South African Men Living with HIV/AIDS: Reflections on Resistance and Change." *Culture, Health & Sexuality* 12 (1): 15–27.

Lyons, Maryinez. 1999. "Medicine and Morality: A Review of Responses to Sexually Transmitted Diseases in Uganda in the Twentieth Century." In *Histories of Sexually Transmitted Diseases and HIV/AIDS in Sub-Saharan Africa*, edited by Philip Setel, Milton James Lewis, and Maryinez Lyons, 97–118. Westport, CT: Greenwood Press.

Magadi, Monica. 2013. "The Disproportionate High Risk of HIV Infection among the Urban Poor in Sub-Saharan Africa." *AIDS and Behavior* 17 (5): 1645–54.

Mair, Lucy. 1934. *An African People in the Twentieth Century.* London: Routledge.

———. 1940. *Native Marriage in Buganda.* London: Oxford University Press.

Mamdani, Mahmood. 1976. *Politics and Class Formation in Uganda.* Kampala: Fountain Publishers.

———. 1983. *Imperialism and Fascism in Uganda.* Nairobi: Heinemann Educational Books.

———. 1996. *Citizen and Subject: Contemporary Africa and the Legacy of Late Colonialism.* Princeton, NJ: Princeton University Press.

Messer, Ellen. 1993. "Anthropology and Human Rights." *Annual Review of Anthropology* 22: 221–49.

Messner, Michael. 1997. *Politics of Masculinities: Men in Movements.* Thousand Oaks, CA: Sage.

Michau, Lori. 2007. "Approaching Old Problems in New Ways: Community Mobilisation as a Primary Prevention Strategy to Combat Violence against Women." *Gender & Development* 15 (1): 95–109.

Mickleburgh, Andrew. 1998. "The Relevance of Marriage for Ganda Women in Bwaise, Kampala, Uganda." PhD dissertation, University of Cambridge.

Miescher, Stephan. 2005. *Making Men in Ghana.* Bloomington: Indiana University Press.

Mikell, Gwendolyn, ed. 1997. *African Feminism: The Politics of Survival in Sub-Saharan Africa.* Philadelphia: University of Pennsylvania Press.

Mills, David, and Richard Ssewakiryanga. 2002. "'That Beijing Thing': Challenging Transnational Feminisms in Kampala." *Gender, Place, and Culture* 9 (4): 385–98.

———. 2005. "'No Romance without Finance': Commodities, Masculinities, and Relationships among Kampalan Students." In *Readings in Gender in Africa,* edited by Andrea Cornwall, 90–95. Bloomington: Indiana University Press.

Mkhize, Nhlanhla. 2004. "Being a Man in South Africa: Who Is a Father?" *ChildrenFIRST* 8 (56): 3–8.

Mojola, Sanyu. 2014. *Love, Money, and HIV: Becoming a Modern African Woman in the Age of AIDS.* Oakland: University of California Press.

Morrell, Robert. 1998. "Of Boys and Men: Masculinity and Gender in Southern African Studies." *Journal of Southern African Studies* 24 (4): 605–30.

———. 1999. "Boys, Men, and Questions of Masculinity in South Africa." In *Questions of Intimacy: Rethinking Population Education,* edited by Linda King, 31–59. Hamburg: UNESCO Institute for Education.

———, ed. 2001a. *Changing Men in Southern Africa.* London: Zed Books.

———. 2001b. "The Times of Change: Men and Masculinity in South Africa." In *Changing Men in Southern Africa,* edited by Robert Morrell, 3–40. London: Zed Books.

Morrell, Robert, Rachel Jewkes, and Graham Lindegger. 2012. "Hegemonic Masculinity / Masculinities in South Africa Culture, Power, and Gender Politics." *Men and Masculinities* 15 (1): 11–30.

Morrell, Robert, and Sandra Swart. 2005. "Men in the Third World: Postcolonial Perspectives on Masculinity." In *Handbook of Studies on Men and Masculinities,* edited by Michael Kimmel, Jeff Hearn, and Robert W. Connell, 90–113. Thousand Oaks, CA: Sage.

Murphy, John. 1972. *Luganda-English Dictionary.* Washington, DC: Catholic University of America Press.

Musisi, Nakanyike. 1991. "Women, 'Elite Polygyny,' and Buganda State Formation." *Signs* 16 (4): 757–86.

———. 1995. "Baganda Women's Night Market Activities." In *African Market Women and Economic Power: The Role of Women in African Economic Development,* edited by B. House-Midamba and F. Ekechi, 121–40. Westport, CT: Greenwood Press.

Musuya, Tina. 2011. "Mobilizing Communities to Prevent Violence against Women and HIV in Kampala, Uganda." In *Women's Health and the World's Cities,* edited by Afaf Meleis, Eugenie Birch, and Susan Wachter, 240–57. Philadelphia: University of Pennsylvania Press.

Nnaemeka, Obioma. 2004. "Nego-feminism: Theorizing, Practicing, and Pruning Africa's Way." *Signs* 29 (2): 357–85.

Nyanzi, Stella, Barbara Nyanzi, Besse Kalina, and Robert Pool. 2004. "Mobility, Sexual Networks, and Exchange among Bodabodamen in Southwest Uganda." *Culture, Health & Sexuality* 6 (3): 239–54.

Nyanzi, Stella, Barbara Nyanzi, and Bessie Kalina. 2005. "Contemporary Myths, Sexuality Misconceptions, Information Sources, and Risk Perceptions of Bodabodamen in Southwest Uganda." *Sex Roles* 52 (1–2): 111–19.

Nyanzi, Stella, Barbara Nyanzi-Wakholi, and Bessie Kalina. 2009. "Male Promiscuity: The Negotiation of Masculinities by Motorbike Taxi-Riders in Masaka, Uganda." *Men and Masculinities* 12 (1): 73–89.

Obbo, Christine. 1980. *African Women: Their Struggle for Economic Independence.* London: Zed Press.

———. 1993. "HIV Transmission: Men Are the Solution." *Population and Environment* 14 (3): 211–43.

O'Brien, Rosaleen, Kate Hunt, and Graham Hart. 2005. "'It's Caveman Stuff, but That Is to a Certain Extent How Guys Still Operate': Men's Accounts of Masculinity and Help Seeking." *Social Science & Medicine* 61 (3): 503–16.

Ogden, Jessica. 1996. "'Producing' Respect: The 'Proper Woman' in Postcolonial Kampala." In *Postcolonial Identities in Africa,* edited by Richard Werbner and Terence Ranger, 165–92. London: Zed Books.

Ogundipe-Leslie, Molara. 1994. *Re-Creating Ourselves: African Women and Critical Transformations.* Trenton, NJ: Africa World Press.

Ojambo, Fred. 2011. "Uganda Inflation Rate Climbs in August to Highest Since 1993." *Bloomberg Business Week*, August 31.

O'Manique, Colleen. 2004. *Neoliberalism and the AIDS Crisis in Sub-Saharan Africa: Globalization's Pandemic*. New York: Palgrave Macmillan.

Orengo-Aguayo, R., and D. Perez-Jimenez. 2009. "Impact of Relationship Dynamics and Gender Roles in the Protection of HIV Discordant Heterosexual Couples: An Exploratory Study in the Puerto Rican Context." *Puerto Rico Health Sciences Journal* 28 (1): 30–39.

Ouzgane, Lahoucine, and Robert Morrell. 2005. *African Masculinities: Men in Africa from the Late Nineteenth Century to the Present*. New York: Palgrave Macmillan.

Oyewumi, Oyeronke. 1997. *The Invention of Women: Making an African Sense of Western Gender Discourses*. Minneapolis: University of Minnesota Press.

———. 2000. "Family Bonds / Conceptual Binds: African Notes on Feminist Epistemologies." *Signs* 25 (4): 1093–99.

Padilla, Mark. 2007. *Caribbean Pleasure Industry: Tourism, Sexuality, and AIDS in the Dominican Republic*. Chicago: University of Chicago Press.

Padilla, Mark, Jennifer Hirsch, Miguel Munoz-Laboy, Robert Sember, and Richard Parker, eds. 2007. *Love and Globalization: Transformations of Intimacy in the Contemporary World*. Nashville, TN: Vanderbilt University Press.

Parikh, Shanti. 2007. "The Political Economy of Marriage and HIV: The ABC Approach, 'Safe' Infidelity, and Managing Moral Risk in Uganda." *American Journal of Public Health* 97 (7): 1198–1208.

———. 2009. "Modern Wives, Men's Infidelity, and Marriage in East-Central Uganda." In *The Secret: Love, Marriage, and HIV*, edited by Jennifer Hirsch, Holly Wardlow, Daniel Jordan Smith, Harriet Phinney, Shanti Parikh, and Constance Nathanson, 168–96. Nashville, TN: Vanderbilt University Press.

Parker, Richard, and Peter Aggleton. 2003. "HIV and AIDS-Related Stigma and Discrimination: A Conceptual Framework and Implications for Action." *Social Science & Medicine* 57 (1): 13–24.

Parkin, David. 1969. *Neighbors and Nationals in an African City Ward*. London: Routledge & Kegan Paul.

Pascoe, C. J. 2003. "Multiple Masculinities? Teenage Boys Talk about Jocks and Gender." *American Behavioral Scientist* 46 (10): 1423–38.

———. 2007. *Dude, You're a Fag: Masculinity and Sexuality in High School*. Berkeley: University of California Press.

Patterson, Amy. 2006. *The Politics of AIDS in Africa*. Challenge and Change in African Politics. Boulder, CO: Lynne Rienner.

Patton, Cindy. 1990. "Inventing 'African AIDS.'" In *Inventing AIDS*, 77–98. New York: Routledge.

Pepin, Jacques. 2011. *The Origins of AIDS*. Cambridge: Cambridge University Press.

Persson, Asha, and Wendy Richards. 2008. "Vulnerability, Gender and 'Proxy Negativity': Women in Relationships with HIV-Positive Men in Australia." *Social Science & Medicine* 67 (5): 799–807.

Peterson, Derek. 2012. *Ethnic Patriotism and the East African Revival: A History of Dissent, c. 1935–1972*. New York: Cambridge University Press.

Pierotti, Rachael. 2013. "Increasing Rejection of Intimate Partner Violence: Evidence of Global Cultural Diffusion." *American Sociological Review* 78 (2): 240–65.

Pigg, Stacy, and Vincanne Adams. 2005. "Introduction: The Moral Object of Sex." In *Sex in Development: Science, Sexuality, and Morality in Global Perspective*, edited by Stacy Pigg and Vincanne Adams, 1–38. Durham, NC: Duke University Press.

Poulin, Michelle. 2007. "Sex, Money, and Premarital Partnerships in Southern Malawi." *Social Science & Medicine* 65 (11): 2383–93.

Povinelli, Elizabeth. 2002. "Notes on Gridlock: Genealogy, Intimacy, Sexuality." *Public Culture* 14 (1): 215–38.

———. 2006. *The Empire of Love: Toward a Theory of Intimacy, Genealogy, and Carnality*. Durham, NC: Duke University Press.

Power, Samantha. 2003. "The AIDS Rebel." *New Yorker*, May 19, 54–67.

Pronyk, Paul, James Hargreaves, Julia Kim, Linda Morison, Godfrey Phetla, Charlotte Watts, Joanna Busza, and John Porter. 2006. "Effect of a Structural Intervention for the Prevention of Intimate-Partner Violence and HIV in Rural South Africa: A Cluster Randomised Trial." *Lancet* 368 (9551): 1973–83.

Ratele, Kopano, Elron Fouten, Tamara Shefer, Anna Strebel, Nokuthla Shabalala, and Rosemarie Buikema. 2007. "'Moffies, Jocks and Cool Guys': Boys' Accounts of Masculinity and Their Resistance in Context." In *From Boys to Men: Social Constructions of Masculinity in Contemporary Society*, edited by Tamara Shefer, Kopano Ratele, Anna Strebel, Nokuthla Shabalala, and Rosemarie Buikema, 112–27. Lansdowne: UCT Press.

Republic of Uganda. 1995. *Constitution of the Republic of Uganda*. Entebbe: Uganda Print and Publishing Corporation.

Richards, Audrey. 1954a. *Economic Development and Tribal Change: A Study of Immigrant Labour in Buganda*. Nairobi: Oxford University Press.

———. 1954b. "Report on Fertility Surveys in Buganda and Buhaya, 1952." In *Culture and Human Fertility: A Study of the Relation of Cultural Conditions to Fertility in Non-Industrial and Transitional Societies*, edited by Frank Lorimer, 351–98. Paris: UNESCO.

———. 1964. "Authority Patterns in Traditional Buganda." In *The King's Men: Leadership and Status in Buganda on the Eve on Independence*, edited by Lloyd Fallers, 256–93. London: Oxford University Press.

———. 1966. *The Changing Structure of a Ganda Village: Kisozi, 1892–1952.* Nairobi: East African Publishing House.

Richey, Lisa. 2011. "Antiviral but Pronatal? ARVS and Reproductive Health: The View from a South African Township." In *Reproduction, Globalization, and the State: New Theoretical and Ethnographic Perspectives,* edited by Carole Browner and Carolyn Sargent, 68–82. Durham, NC: Duke University Press.

———. 2012. "Treating AIDS in Uganda and South Africa: Semi-Authoritarian Technologies in Gendered Contexts of Insecurity." In *Gendered Insecurities, Health, and Development in Africa,* edited by Howard Stein and Amal Fadlalla, 50–71. London: Routledge.

Richter, Linda, and Robert Morrell, eds. 2006. *Baba: Men and Fatherhood in South Africa.* Cape Town: HSRC Press.

Ridgeway, Cecilia. 2009. "Framed before We Know It: How Gender Shapes Social Relations." *Gender & Society* 23 (2): 145–60.

———. 2011. *Framed by Gender: How Gender Inequality Persists in the Modern World.* New York: Oxford University Press.

Ridgeway, Cecilia, and Shelley Correll. 2004. "Unpacking the Gender System: A Theoretical Perspective on Gender Beliefs and Social Relations." *Gender & Society* 18 (4): 510–31.

Ridgeway, Cecilia, and Lynn Smith-Lovin. 1999. "The Gender System and Interaction." *Annual Review of Sociology* 25 (1): 191–216.

Risman, Barbara. 2004. "Gender as a Social Structure Theory Wrestling with Activism." *Gender & Society* 18 (4): 429–50.

———. 2011. "Gender as Structure or Trump Card?" *Journal of Family Theory & Review* 3 (1): 18–22.

Rivers, Kim, and Peter Aggleton. 1999. *Men and the HIV Epidemic.* New York: UNDP HIV and Development Programme.

Robins, Steven. 2008. "'Brothers Are Doing It for Themselves': Remaking Masculinities in South Africa." In *The Politics of AIDS: Globalization, the State and Civil Society,* edited by Maj-Lis Follér and Håkan Thörn, 156–76. New York: Palgrave Macmillan.

Roscoe, John. 1911. *The Baganda: An Account of Their Native Customs and Beliefs.* London: Macmillan.

Rutakumwa, Rwamahe, Martin Mbonye, Thadeus Kiwanuka, Daniel Bagiire, and Janet Seeley. 2015. "Why Do Men Often Not Use Condoms in Their Relationships with Casual Sexual Partners in Uganda?" *Culture, Health & Sexuality* 17 (10): 1237–50.

Rutter, Virginia, and Pepper Schwartz. 2011. *The Gender of Sexuality: Exploring Sexual Possibilities.* Lanham, MD: Rowman & Littlefield.

Rweyemamu, Chrysostom. 1999. "Sexual Behavior in Tanzania." In *AIDS and Men: Taking Risks or Taking Responsibility,* edited by Martin Foreman, 65–78. London: Panos.

Sacks, Karen. 1979. *Sisters and Wives: The Past and Future of Sexual Equality.* Westport, CT: Greenwood Press.

Schilt, Kristen. 2010. *Just One of the Guys? Transgender Men and the Persistence of Gender Inequality.* Chicago: University of Chicago Press.

Schoepf, Brooke. 2004. "AIDS, History, and Struggles over Meaning." In *HIV and AIDS in Africa: Beyond Epidemiology,* edited by Ezekiel Kalipeni, Susan Craddock, Joseph Oppong, and Jayati Ghosh, 15–28. Malden, MA: Blackwell.

Schoepf, Brooke, Claude Schoepf, and Joyce Millen. 2000. "Theoretical Therapies, Remote Remedies: SAPs and the Political Economy of Poverty and Health in Africa." In *Dying for Growth: Global Inequality and the Health of the Poor,* edited by Jim Yong Kim, 91–126. Monroe, ME: Common Courage Press.

Schrock, Douglas, and Michael Schwalbe. 2009. "Men, Masculinity, and Manhood Acts." *Annual Review of Sociology* 35 (1): 277–95.

Schwalbe, Michael. 2014. *Manhood Acts: Gender and the Practices of Domination.* Boulder, CO: Paradigm Publishers.

Schwartz, Pepper. 2007. "The Social Construction of Heterosexuality." In *The Sexual Self: The Construction of Sexual Scripts,* edited by Michael Kimmel, 80–92. Nashville, TN: Vanderbilt University Press.

Seal, David, and Anke Ehrhardt. 2003. "Masculinity and Urban Men: Perceived Scripts for Courtship, Romantic, and Sexual Interactions with Women." *Culture, Health & Sexuality* 5 (4): 295–319.

Seale, Andy, Jeffrey Lazarus, Ian Grubb, Ade Fakoya, and Rifat Atun. 2011. "HPTN 052 and the Future of HIV Treatment and Prevention." *Lancet* 378 (9787): 226.

Segal, Lynne. 1994. *Straight Sex: Rethinking the Politics of Pleasure.* Berkeley: University of California Press.

Setel, Philip. 1996. "AIDS as a Paradox of Manhood and Development in Kilimanjaro, Tanzania." *Social Science & Medicine* 43 (8): 1169–78.

———. 1999. *A Plague of Paradoxes: AIDS, Culture, and Demography in Northern Tanzania.* Chicago: University of Chicago Press.

Sharlet, Jeff. 2010. "Straight Man's Burden: The American Roots of Uganda's Anti-Gay Persecutions." *Harper's Magazine,* September, 36–48.

Siedner, Mark, Nicholas Musinguzi, Alexander Tsai, Conrad Muzoora, Annet Kembabazi, Sheri Weiser, John Bennett, et al. 2014. "Treatment as Long-Term Prevention: Sustained Reduction in HIV Sexual Transmission Risk with Use of Antiretroviral Therapy in Rural Uganda." *AIDS* 28 (2): 267–71.

Silberschmidt, Margrethe. 2001. "Disempowerment of Men in Rural and Urban East Africa: Implications for Male Identity and Sexual Behavior." *World Development* 29 (4): 657–71.

———. 2004. "Men, Male Sexuality, and HIV/AIDS: Reflections from Studies in Rural and Urban East Africa." *Transformation: Critical Perspectives on Southern Africa* 54 (1): 42–58.

———. 2005. "Poverty, Male Disempowerment, and Male Sexuality: Rethinking Men and Masculinities in Rural and Urban East Africa." In *African Masculinities: Men in Africa from the Late Nineteenth Century to the Present,* edited by Lahoucine Ouzgane and Robert Morrell, 189–204. New York: Palgrave; Scottsville, South Africa: University of KwaZulu-Natal Press.

Simpson, Anthony. 2009. *Boys to Men in the Shadow of AIDS: Masculinities and HIV Risk in Zambia.* New York: Palgrave Macmillan.

Smith, Daniel Jordan. 2006. "Love and the Risk of HIV: Courtship, Marriage, and Infidelity in Southeastern Nigeria." In *Modern Loves: The Anthropology of Romantic Courtship and Companionate Marriage,* edited by Jennifer Hirsch and Holly Wardlow, 135–56. Ann Arbor: University of Michigan Press.

———. 2007. "Modern Marriage, Men's Extramarital Sex, and HIV Risk in Southeastern Nigeria." *American Journal of Public Health* 97 (6): 997–1005.

———. 2008. "Intimacy, Infidelity, and Masculinity in Southeastern Nigeria." In *Intimacies: Love and Sex across Cultures,* edited by Willikam Jankowiak, 224–44. New York: Columbia University Press.

———. 2009a. "Gender Inequality, Infidelity, and the Social Risks of Modern Marriage in Nigeria." In *The Secret: Love, Marriage, and HIV,* edited by Jennifer Hirsch, Holly Wardlow, Daniel Jordan Smith, Harriet Phinney, Shanti Parikh, and Constance Nathanson, 84–107. Nashville, TN: Vanderbilt University Press.

———. 2009b. "Managing Men, Marriage, and Modern Love: Women's Perspectives on Intimacy and Male Infidelity in Southeastern Nigeria." In *Love in Africa,* edited by Jennifer Cole and Lynn Thomas, 157–80. Chicago: University of Chicago Press.

———. 2014. *AIDS Doesn't Show Its Face: Inequality, Morality, and Social Change in Nigeria.* Chicago: University of Chicago Press.

Snoxall, R.A. 1967. *Luganda–English Dictionary.* Oxford: Clarendon Press.

Southall, Aidan. 1960. "On Chastity in Africa." *Uganda Journal* 24 (2): 207–16.

———. 1961. "The Position of Women and the Stability of Marriage." In *Social Change in Modern Africa,* edited by Aidan Southall, 46–66. London: Oxford University Press.

———. 1980. "Social Disorganization in Uganda: Before, during and after Amin." *Journal of Modern African Studies* 18 (4): 627–56.

Southall, Aidan, and Peter Gutkind. 1957. *Townsmen in the Making: Kampala and Its Suburbs.* Kampala: East African Institute of Social Research.

Southwold, Martin. 1959. "Community and State in Buganda." PhD dissertation, Cambridge University.

———. 1965. "The Ganda of Uganda." In *Peoples of Africa,* edited by James Gibbs, 83–118. New York: Holt, Rinehart and Winston.

———. 1973. "The Baganda of Central Uganda." In *Cultural Source Materials for Population Planning in East Africa: Beliefs and Practices,* edited by Angela Molnos, 3:163–73. Nairobi: University of Nairobi.

Spronk, Rachel. 2012. *Ambiguous Pleasures: Sexuality and Middle-Class Self-Perceptions in Nairobi.* New York: Berghahn Books.

———. 2014. "The Idea of African Men: Dealing with the Cultural Contradictions of Sex in Academia and in Kenya." *Culture, Health & Sexuality* 16 (5): 504–17.

Steady, Filomina. 1987. "African Feminism: A Worldwide Perspective." In *Women in Africa and the African Diaspora,* edited by Rosalyn Terbong-Penn, Sharon Harley, and Andrea Rushing, 2–24. Washington, DC: Howard University Press.

———. 2006. *Women and Collective Action in Africa: Development, Democratization, and Empowerment.* New York: Palgrave Macmillan.

Stevens, Patricia, and Loren Galvao. 2007. "'He Won't Use Condoms': HIV-Infected Women's Struggles in Primary Relationships with Serodiscordant Partners." *American Journal of Public Health* 97 (6): 1015–22.

Stillwaggon, Eileen. 2003. "Racial Metaphors: Interpreting Sex and AIDS in Africa." *Development and Change* 34 (5): 809–32.

———. 2006. "Racial Metaphors: Interpreting Sex, and AIDS in Africa." In *AIDS and the Ecology of Poverty,* 133–57. New York: Oxford University Press.

Stoneburner, Rand, and Daniel Low-Beer. 2004. "Population-Level HIV Declines and Behavioral Risk Avoidance in Uganda." *Science* 304 (5671): 714–18.

Sumerau, J. Edward. 2012. "'That's What a Man Is Supposed to Do': Compensatory Manhood Acts in an LGBT Christian Church." *Gender & Society* 26 (3): 461–87.

Summers, Carol. 1991. "Intimate Colonialism: The Imperial Production of Reproduction in Uganda, 1907–1925." *Signs* 16 (4): 787–807.

Susser, Ida. 2009. *AIDS, Sex, and Culture: Global Politics and Survival in Southern Africa.* Malden, MA: Wiley-Blackwell.

Swidler, Ann, and Susan Watkins. 2007. "Ties of Dependence: AIDS and Transactional Sex in Rural Malawi." *Studies in Family Planning* 38 (3): 147–62.

Tamale, Sylvia. 1999. *When Hens Begin to Crow: Gender and Parliamentary Politics in Uganda.* Boulder, CO: Westview Press.

———. 2003a. "The Implementation of Quotas: African Experiences." Paper presented at the Southern African Development Community Parliamentary Forum Conference, Pretoria, South Africa, November 11.

———. 2003b. "Out of the Closet: Unveiling Sexuality Discourses in Uganda." *Feminist Africa* 2: 1–6.

———. 2006. "African Feminism: How Should We Change?" *Development* 49 (1): 38–41.

Thomas, Lynn. 2003. *Politics of the Womb: Women, Reproduction, and the State in Kenya.* Berkeley: University of California Press.

Thomas, Lynn, and Jennifer Cole. 2009. "Thinking through Love in Africa." In *Love in Africa,* edited by Jennifer Cole and Lynn Thomas, 1–30. Chicago: University of Chicago Press.

Thornton, Robert. 2008. *Unimagined Community: Sex, Networks, and AIDS in Uganda and South Africa.* Berkeley: University of California Press.

Treichler, Paula. 1999. *How to Have Theory in an Epidemic: Cultural Chronicles of AIDS.* Durham, NC: Duke University Press.

Tripp, Aili. 2000. *Women and Politics in Uganda.* Madison: University of Wisconsin Press.

———. 2010. *Museveni's Uganda: Paradoxes of Power in a Hybrid Regime.* Boulder, CO: Lynne Rienner.

Tripp, Aili, and Joy Kwesiga. 2002. *The Women's Movement in Uganda: History, Challenges, and Prospects.* Kampala: Fountain Publishers.

Uganda AIDS Commission. 2012. "Global AIDS Response Progress Report: Country Progress Report Uganda." Kampala, Republic of Uganda. www.unaids.org/sites/default/files/en/dataanalysis/knowyourresponse/countryprogressreports/2012countries/ce_UG_Narrative_Report[1].pdf.

Uganda Bureau of Statistics. 2002. "The 2002 Uganda Population and Housing Census, Provisional Results." Kampala, Republic of Uganda.

———. 2006. "The 2002 Uganda Population and Housing Census, Main Report." Kampala, Republic of Uganda. www.ubos.org/onlinefiles/uploads/ubos/pdf%20documents/2002%20Census%20Final%20Reportdoc.pdf.

Uganda Ministry of Health, ORC Macro, MEASURE/DHS+, and Centers for Disease Control and Prevention. 2006. *Uganda HIV/AIDS Sero-Behavioural Survey 2004–05.* Calverton, MD: Uganda Ministry of Health and ORC Macro. http://dhsprogram.com/pubs/pdf/ais2/ais2.pdf.

Ullman, Richard. 1978. "Human Rights and Economic Power: The United States versus Idi Amin." *Foreign Affairs* 56 (3): 529–43.

UNAIDS. 2000. "AIDS Epidemic Update." Geneva. http://data.unaids.org/publications/irc-pub05/aidsepidemicreport2000_en.pdf.

———. 2012. "Region Fact Sheet 2012: Sub-Saharan Africa." Geneva. http://www.unaids.org/sites/default/files/en/media/unaids/contentassets/documents/epidemiology/2012/gr2012/2012_FS_regional_ssa_en.pdf.

Vaughan, Megan. 1991. *Curing Their Ills: Colonial Power and African Illness.* Cambridge: Polity Press.

Vitellone, Nicole. 2000. "Condoms and the Making of 'Testosterone Man': A Cultural Analysis of the Male Sex Drive in AIDS Research on Safer Heterosex." *Men and Masculinities* 3 (2): 152–67.

Wagman, Jennifer, Ronald Gray, Jacquelyn Campbell, Marie Thoma, Anthony Ndyanabo, Joseph Ssekasanvu, Fred Nalugoda, et al. 2015. "Effectiveness of an Integrated Intimate Partner Violence and HIV Prevention Intervention in Rakai, Uganda: Analysis of an Intervention in an Existing Cluster Randomised Cohort." *Lancet Global Health* 3 (1): e23–e33.

Wagner-Raphael, Lynne, David Seal, and Anke Ehrhardt. 2001. "Close Emotional Relationships with Women versus Men: A Qualitative Study of 56 Heterosexual Men Living in an Inner-City Neighborhood." *Journal of Men's Studies* 9 (2): 243–56.

Walker, Gregory. 2006. "Disciplining Protest Masculinity." *Men and Masculinities* 9 (1): 5–22.

Wallman, Sandra, ed. 1996. *Kampala Women Getting By: Well-being in the Time of AIDS*. Kampala: Fountain Press; Athens: Ohio University Press.

Wardlow, Holly, and Jennifer Hirsch. 2006. Introduction to *Modern Loves: The Anthropology of Romantic Courtship and Companionate Marriage*, edited by Jennifer Hirsch and Holly Wardlow, 1–34. Ann Arbor: University of Michigan Press.

Warner, Michael. 2000. *The Trouble with Normal: Sex, Politics, and the Ethics of Queer Life*. Cambridge, MA: Harvard University Press.

Watkins-Hayes, Celeste. 2014. "Intersectionality and the Sociology of HIV/AIDS: Past, Present, and Future Research Directions." *Annual Review of Sociology* 40 (1): 431–57.

Wellings, K., M. Collumbien, E. Slaymaker, S. Singh, Z. Hodges, D. Patel, and N. Bajos. 2006. "Sexual Behaviour in Context: A Global Perspective." *Lancet* 368 (9548): 1706–28.

West, Candace, and Sarah Fenstermaker. 1993. "Power, Inequality and the Accomplishment of Gender: An Ethnomethodological View." In *Theory on Gender/Feminism on Theory*, edited by Paula England, 151–74. New York: A. de Gruyter.

West, Candace, and Don Zimmerman. 1987. "Doing Gender." *Gender & Society* 1 (2): 125–51.

———. 2009. "Accounting for Doing Gender." *Gender & Society* 23 (1): 112–22.

Westbrook, Laurel, and Kristen Schilt. 2014. "Doing Gender, Determining Gender: Transgender People, Gender Panics, and the Maintenance of the Sex/Gender/Sexuality System." *Gender & Society* 28 (1): 32–57.

White, Luise. 1990. *The Comforts of Home: Prostitution in Colonial Nairobi*. Chicago: University of Chicago Press.

Wilkins, Amy. 2009. "Masculinity Dilemmas: Sexuality and Intimacy Talk among Christians and Goths." *Signs* 34 (2): 343–68.

Wyrod, Robert. 2007. "Bwaise Town: Masculinity in Urban Uganda in the Age of AIDS." PhD dissertation, University of Chicago.

———. 2008. "Between Women's Rights and Men's Authority: Masculinity and Shifting Discourses of Gender Difference in Urban Uganda." *Gender & Society* 22 (6): 799–823.

———. 2011. "Masculinity and the Persistence of AIDS Stigma." *Culture, Health & Sexuality* 13 (4): 443–56.

———. 2013. "Dialectics of Gender and Health: The Case of HIV Serodiscordance." *Sociology of Health & Illness* 35 (8): 1260–74.

———. 2016. "When Rights Come Home: The Intimate Politics of Women's Rights in Urban Uganda." *Humanity* 7 (1): 47–70.

Wyrod, Robert, Katherine Fritz, Godfrey Woelk, Sheila Jain, Timothy Kellogg, Admire Chirowodza, Knox Makumbe, and Willi McFarland. 2011. "Beyond Sugar Daddies: Intergenerational Sex and AIDS in Urban Zimbabwe." *AIDS and Behavior* 15 (6): 1275–82.

Yeung, King-to, Mindy Stombler, and Renee Wharton. 2006. "Making Men in Gay Fraternities: Resisting and Reproducing Multiple Dimensions of Hegemonic Masculinity." *Gender & Society* 20 (1): 5–31.

Zelizer, Viviana. 2005. *The Purchase of Intimacy*. Princeton, NJ: Princeton University Press.

Index

Note: Page numbers in *italics* indicate figures.

abakazi be tawuni (town women), 55–56, 68
abayaye (thugs) and *muyaye* (thug), 5, 87,
   88, 101, 115, 253–54n1
ABC (abstain, be faithful, use condoms)
   approach: individual behavior emphasized, 206–7; masculine sexual privilege
   persistence and reaffirmation in, 212–13,
   217; moral narrative in, 202; secrecy
   about sexual affairs prompted by, 202,
   210. *See also* abstinence; "be faithful";
   condom use
Aboim, Sofia, 254n6
Abramsky, Tanya, 228
abstinence: condom crisis and, 253n18;
   emphasis on, 20, 202, 212–13, 217; monetary savings linked to, 109; religious
   argument for, 78–79
"abstinence pride" march, 78
ACT-UP (AIDS Coalition to Unleash Power),
   21
Adam, Barry, 227
adultery, punishment for, 51. *See also*
   monogamy
Africa: challenges to male privilege in, 12;
   colonial depiction of Africans as the other,
   16; future of HIV prevention in, 224–32;

smuggling network in, 65; social significance of AIDS in, 19–23, 206, 208–20.
   See also global AIDS pandemic; masculinity in Africa; sub-Saharan Africa; *and
   specific ethnic groups and countries*
age, HIV prevalence and, *14*, 212, 249n4
Aggleton, Peter, 21–22
agriculture: cash crop farming for cotton and
   coffee exports, 53–54, 64, 252n5; effects
   of price controls in, 252–53n10; neoliberal policies' impact on, 70; subsistence
   crops raised by women, 46–47
AIDS: as bewitchment, 199–200; considered
   in decisions about relationships, 109–10,
   194–95; epicenter of Uganda's epidemic,
   175; fatalism about, 102, 103; fluency in
   details and discourse of, 39–40, 113,
   120–21, 169, 181, 184–85; as indigenous
   disease, 22; local script on, 39–40; long-
   term effects of epidemic considered, 8–12;
   masculine sexual privilege persistence
   despite, 120, 125–26, 127–28, 160, 162–
   63, 168–70, 177–79, 184–85, 189–201,
   215–20, 223–25, 240; masculinity
   remade in African context of, 208–24;
   masculinity remade in Bwaise context of,

AIDS (continued)
    8–9, 24–31, 85, 119–22, 177–79; men's
    denial of, 163–70; origins of, 43–44;
    political-economic analysis of, 84–85;
    social problems linked to spread of,
    12–19; social significance of, 19–23, 206,
    208–20; Uganda's successful response to,
    6–12, 22–23, 76–77, 160, 206; women's
    accommodations to and critiques of men
    and, 186–93, 201; women's vulnerability
    to, 16–17, 73, 84–85, 110, 113, 117, 121–22,
    142–43, 150, 155–56, 210, 225–26, 231.
    See also AIDS relief funding; biomedical
    approaches; community engagement; glo-
    bal AIDS pandemic; masculinity, sexual-
    ity, AIDS, and social change intersection;
    and entries beginning with HIV
AIDS Coalition to Unleash Power (ACT-UP),
    21
AIDS counselors: claims about, 113; home
    visits and responsibilities of, 4–5, 161–62;
    for men coming to terms with HIV status,
    168; on men's denials, 162–63; response
    to suicidal thoughts, 164. See also peer
    educators
AIDS Doesn't Show Its Face (Smith), 215–16
AIDS drugs. See antiretroviral drugs
AIDS Information Center, 161
AIDS prevention. See HIV prevention
AIDS relief funding: effects of biomedical-
    focused, 23, 226–27; main sources of, 15;
    for men's groups, 164, 256n1. See also
    biomedical approaches; NGOs
AIDS Support Organisation (TASO), 161, 164,
    168, 256n1
Ali (pseud.), 86–87
amaanyi (strength, sexual strength):
    bewitchment of, 198–99; in carpentry
    work, 106–8; male superiority evidenced
    in, 125; multiple sexual relationships to
    prove, 173; persistent importance of, 51,
    91; violent connotations of, 254n4. See
    also masculine sexual privilege
Ambiguous Pleasures (Spronk), 213–14
Amin, Idi: coup by, 64–65; effects of price
    controls under, 252–53n10; Keep Uganda
    Clean campaigns of, 67; social change
    under, 69; tyrannical excesses of, 65, 66;
    women appointees of, 253n11
Anglicans (Church of Uganda), 91, 109, 112,
    116
Anti-Homosexuality Act (2014), 11–12, 74
Anti-Pornography Act (2014), 11, 74

antiretroviral drugs: global emphasis on, 23,
    226–27, 229; as human right, 21; limits
    of, 219; mentioned, 3; pre-exposure
    prophylaxis (PrEP), 79, 226–27; side
    effects of, 169; timing of availability,
    251n15. See also biomedical approaches
anti-STD campaigns, 58–60
Ashforth, Adam, 84
authority over women, children, and home.
    See male authority over women, children,
    and home; work and male provider ideal

Baganda (ethnic group): focus on, 44; hierar-
    chy and notions of power in, 46–48, 130,
    254–55n2; as intermediaries in colonial
    period, 52–63; as majority in Bwaise, 38;
    marriage traditions of, 3; openness to
    addressing AIDS, 77; in precolonial era
    (19th c.), 44–52. See also Buganda, king-
    dom of; Luganda
bakirerese (restless people), 52, 68
banakyeombekedde (women who live alone),
    51–52, 58, 68, 252n5
Bantu (ethnic group), 44
Barnett, Tony, 65, 66
Basoga (ethnic group), 210–11
"be faithful": emphasis on, 10, 20, 78, 116,
    179–80, 202, 210; men not expected to, 51,
    168, 212; as problematic, 17, 214–15, 229;
    in self-image, 40, 112, 136, 153, 181–82;
    suspicions about, 93–94, 117, 176, 190, 197,
    223; women expected to, 47, 191
Besigye, Kizza, 70
Betty (pseud.). See Edward and Betty
biomedical approaches
—AIDS: emphasis on, 23, 79, 226–27, 229,
    236; moralizing narrative linked to,
    19–20, 60, 77–78, 250n9. See also antiret-
    roviral drugs
—STDs, 59–60
bodabodamen (motorcyle taxi men), 81, 209–
    10, 257nn1–2
Botswana, HIV prevalence in, 13
Boys to Men in the Shadow of AIDS (Simp-
    son), 216–17
Brazil, AIDS drugs as right in, 21
brewing: beer, 55, 56; gin, 141
bridewealth (omutwalo): increases in, 55, 60;
    marriage ritual of payment, 46, 146; mon-
    etization of, 53; payments for multiple
    wives, 50–51; repayment banned in
    divorce, 73–74; repayment required in
    divorce, 50, 60

British colonial system: anti-STD campaigns in, 58–60; anxieties about independent urban women, 55–56; changes in men's roles in, 54–55; characteristics of, 53–54, 251n1; destabilizing trends in marriage under, 60–63; gender relations ideology in, 56–58, 59, 249–50n5, 251n1; indirect rule of, 44, 52–53; land privatized in, 53, 252n5; public health regime of, 15–16, 43; South Asian workers imported, 54, 252n6. *See also* Christianity

Buganda, kingdom of: culture of, 24–25, 29–30, 203–4, 251n2; hierarchical structure of, 46–50, 254–55n2; independent women in, 51–52, 55–56, 230; Kampala as center of, 38, 44, *45*; notions of *eddembe* (rights) in precolonial, 129–30; polygyny in, 50–51; postindependence violence in, 65–66; precolonial capital (*kibuga*) of, 44, 46; women's work in, 46–47, 49. *See also* Baganda; Luganda

Bush, George W., 78

Bwaise: author situated in, 38–40; current changes in, 234–36; described, 1–5, 31, 33–35, 80–82; everyday survival and gender tensions in, 85–90; flooding and open sewers in, 2, 4, 13, 31, 82, 99, 138, 170, 174, *175*, 181, 234, 235, 240; future of, 239–40; housing examples, 2, 33, *33*, *129*, *133*, 133–34; interconnections evidenced in, 205–6; main intersection in, 170–71, *171*, 234, *235*; map, *32*; postindependence flight to, 65–66; reputation of, 82–83; secondary school in, 24–25; ubiquity of AIDS in, 5–6; unregulated urban development in, 63; women of, *187*. *See also* Bwaise businesses; everyday life; Kimombasa section

Bwaise businesses: auto parts store, 91; bicycle and motorcycle taxis, 80–81, 209–10, 257nn1–2; brothels (lodges, guest houses), 99–101, *100*, 102, 235; cell phone repair, 114; commercial strip of, *9*, 33–34, *34*, 81, 83; cooking and selling *maandazi*, 3, 4, 138, 139, 141, 142; current situation of, 235–36; electronics shop, 237–38; furniture store, 89, 194–95; hardware shop, 86, 171–73; hotel, 235; housewares store, 90, 91–92; laundry, 195–96; official and informal eateries, 81–82; pharmacy, 146, 235; restaurant, 190–91. *See also* Kibira carpentry workshop; markets

Bwaise Health Clinic (pseud.): activities at, 36, 37; closure and demolition of, 236,

239; essentialist views about male sexuality and patriarchy in, 162–63; first impressions of, 160–61; PMCTC Health Fair and, 165–66; services of, 161–62

Bwaise Positive Men's Union (AIDS support group): conceptions of masculinity in, 167–70; denial and stigma in living with AIDS, 166–67; founding, 36; growth of, 164–65; loss of space for meetings, 236; meetings and goals, 163–64, 225; reluctance to test discussed, 165

Caldwell, John, 250n6
Caldwell, Pat, 250n6
Cameroon, AIDS origins in, 43
carpentry: author's apprenticeship in (*see* Kibira carpentry workshop); as men's work, 35–36; as semiskilled occupation, 103–4, 108; switching jobs in, 114; typical workshop for, *104*

Catholics: mentioned, 123, 134, 136, 138, 139, 174, 190, 195; polygyny practiced by, 176, 191; sexual identity males at boarding school, 216–17; wedding of, 3

Center for Domestic Violence Prevention (CEDOVIP): AIDS prevention integrated with domestic violence prevention in, 253n15; founding and goals, 36, 37; gender equality advocacy of, 132; SASA! programs implemented by, 228–29, 258nn5–7

character (*empisa*), of women, 49, 62, 148, 149

children: born HIV-positive, 168; devotion to, 123–26, 127; end of marriage and concerns for, 142–43; as official wife's duty, 178; personal and cultural expectations to produce, 182, 185

China National Aero Technology, 236

Christianity: born-again and evangelical believers, 11–12, 78, 116–18, 186, 210); Church of Uganda (Anglican) noted, 91, 109, 112, 116; cost of church weddings, 60; marital fidelity encouraged, 116–17; marriage laws and sexuality concerns in, 57–60, 73; multiple sexual relationships despite, 176, 180; patriarchy and monogamy linked in, 186; political fictions in, 57, 252n8; respectability idea in, 55; rise of Pentecostalism, 78; secrecy about sexual affairs prompted by, 202, 210; syphilis campaigns of, 59–60, 78; women's demands influenced by, 53. *See also* Catholics

Christine (pseud.), 1–6, 39, 239
Church of Uganda (Anglican), 91, 109, 112, 116
civil service employment: men in, 64; neoliberal policies' impact on, 70; women's participation in, 130–31, 253n11
civil wars (Uganda, 1970s and 1980s), 16
cohabiting couples/partners, 129, 133; high infection rates among long-term, 192; HIV interventions for, 226. See also Couples Research; HIV-discordant couples; intimate sexual relationships; men's multiple sexual relationships; and specific couples
Cole, Jennifer, 15
colonial period. See British colonial system
Colvin, Christopher, 250n9
Comaroff, Jean, 15–16
community engagement: AIDS discussed, 22–23; home visits to those with AIDS, 161–62; importance of, 161–62; indigenous HIV prevention programs, 228–31, 258nn5–7; organizational efforts at, 36; Straight Talk clubs as, 24–25. See also AIDS counselors; Bwaise Health Clinic; Bwaise Positive Men's Union; peer educators; public awareness and discourse
companionate marriage: Christian ideology of, 59; growing salience of ideology of, 17; maintaining appearance of, 122; masculine sexual privilege and, 213–15, 250n8
compensatory sexuality: hegemonic masculinity emphasized in, 27–28; precarious work linked to, 96–103, 119–20, 211–12; in response to women's rights discourse, 210–11. See also men's multiple sexual relationships
condom use: accepted but limited, 174, 179; efficacy in stopping HIV, 22; encouraged at Straight Talk club, 24; of HIV-positive couple, 168–70; hopes for children vs., 183; inconsistent use, 196, 197, 199, 200; men's refusal, 136, 150, 153, 190, 192, 219; SASA! program and, 229; shortage crisis and, 253n18; as symbol of impersonal sex, 215; wives' insistence on, 5, 94, 95, 255n9; young Catholic men socialized against using, 216–17
Connell, R. W., 250–51n13
Cornwall, Andrea, 84, 254n2
Couples Research: demographics of participants, 247; research methodology, 37, 251n17; summary of findings, 155–59;

Ugandan women's rights as context of, 128–32. See also interviewees; and specific couples

David (pseud.), 174–77
Decker, Alicia, 66, 253n11
Decoteau, Claire, 250n9
Demographic and Health surveys, 231
demographics: Bwaise residents, 33; of Couples Research participants, 247; of HIV prevalence, 14; of interviewees, 246; Kampala's growth, 63; Kampala vs. Uganda, 252n7; national census of virgins proposed, 78; percentage by gender in wage work, 253n12; rural vs. urban in colonial period, 53
Dennis (pseud.): on amaanyi and work, 106–8; background, 105; on intimate relationships, money, and AIDS, 109–12, 120–21. See also Kibira carpentry workshop
division of labor: male authority in public sphere, 75–76; in precolonial Buganda, 46–50; refigured in agriculture, 50, 53–54, 252n5. See also double standard; male authority over women, children, and home; patriarchal attitudes
divorce and/or separation: bridewealth repayment banned in, 73–74; bridewealth repayment required in, 50, 60; example of, 193; history of, 143–44; independent women after, 52, 67, 187–88; legislative efforts on, 11, 72, 253n14; women's right to, 50, 52, 62, 125, 150. See also marriage
Domestic Relations Bill (proposed), 72, 253n14
domestic violence: changing views on, 140; gender inequality evidenced in, 73; rejection of, 142; in response to quarrels, 146; rights-based approach to prevention, 36; women's views on, 62, 187. See also rape
Domestic Violence Act (2010), 10, 73, 74, 158–59
domestic violence prevention: HIV prevention linked to, 226, 228–29, 258nn5–7; sexual violence and marital rape discussed in, 73, 152, 159. See also Center for Domestic Violence Prevention
"domestic virtue model," 56–57, 75, 76
double standard: evidenced in blame for AIDS, 97–98, 189–90; failure of women's rights discourse to confront, 210–11; men's extramarital affairs buttressed by, 170, 215–16; in precolonial Buganda, 51.

See also division of labor; masculine sexual privilege; men's multiple sexual relationships
Doyle, Shane, 69, 77, 230, 253n17
Dworkin, Shari, 158

economic conditions: HIV transmission linked to, 16; neoliberal policies and, 70, 75, 231–32; postindependence growth and volatility in, 64; recent economic growth, 75, 233–36. See also *magendo* economy; political economy; poverty; un- and underemployment; work
economic inequality: AIDS entangled with, 84–85, 230–32; increased, 234–35, 240; persistence and widening of inequalities, 29–30, 70, 208, 223; similarities across sub-Sahara, 220. *See also* gender inequality; poverty; un- and underemployment
eddembe (rights, freedom, liberty, peace): income as reinforcing, 149–51; meanings of, 129–30. *See also* rights; women's rights
education: after-school club focused on sex ed, 24–25; expectations of income due to, 184; women's access increased, 90, 131. *See also* AIDS counselors; peer educators
Edward and Betty (pseud.): commitment to each other, 181–82; Edward's current situation, 238; Edward's multiple relationships and secrecy, 183–84, 202, 224; Edward's work and financial struggles, 180–82; failure of relationship, 184–85; modern egalitarian relationships juxtaposed to Edward's masculinity, 213
Edwina (pseud.). *See* Isaac and Edwina
ekitiibwa (honor, respect): meanings of, 47, 251n2; protected as married women, 149–50; rechanneled into Christian, Westernized respectability, 55; role of, 47–49. *See also* male status
elites: colonial grooming of men, 54; decline of women's status, 56–57; HIV/AIDS less a concern for (Kenya professionals), 213–14; independence and sexual freedom of female, 49, 51; land given to male, 252n5; marriage and sexuality concerns of, 57–58, 252n8; types of female, 252n3
emirembe (peace), 144
empisa (character), of women, 49, 62, 148, 149
employment. *See* un- and underemployment; work
Epstein, Helen, 22, 25, 230, 250n6, 253n17

Esther (pseud.), 190–93
ethnic groups: divisions of, 64; in Uganda, 44, *45*
—SPECIFIC GROUPS: Bantu, 44; Basoga, 210–11; Gisu, 24–25; Haya, 77; Igbo, 214; Lango, 64; Luo, 212–13; Muhindi, 98; Nilo-Hamitic, 44; Nilotic, 44; Nkole, 77; Zulu, 217–18, 219, 257n4. *See also* Baganda
ethnography. *See* Bwaise; interviewees; methodology
everyday life: AIDS fluency in, 39–40, 113, 120–21, 169, 181, 184–85; AIDS role in shaping, 3–6, 8, 198–201; *bakirerese* as leaders in fashion, 68; gender tensions in, 85–90; lived masculinities in, 28–29, 31–35, 221–24; nightlife scene in, 5, 63, 82–83, 98–100, 112, 113, 116; official ideology vs. conduct in, 57, 252n8; participant observation of, 35–37; rhetoric of women's rights integrated in, 154–59; stigmatization of AIDS in, 166–67. *See also* Bwaise; gender relations; HIV-discordant couples; intimate sexual relationships
extramarital sexual relationships. *See* intimate sexual relationships; men's multiple sexual relationships

family planning: contraceptive injections, 136, 151–53; tubal ligation, 169. *See also* condom use
Family Planning of Uganda, 181
Farmer, Paul, 16
female circumcision, outlawed, 73
female sexuality: blamed for spread of disease and immorality, 66–67, 172, 176–77, 189–90, 216; complexities of, 230; male anxieties about in colonial period, 58–60; normative notions of, 26, 57; shifting conceptions of, 250n11; social construction of, 147. *See also* family planning; gender inequality; gender relations; intimate sexual relationships; women
femininity: adapting women's rights to notions of, 147–54; irrational quality of, 28; normative notions and "proper," 62, 69, 144, 149, 230
Ferguson, James, 220
FIDA (Uganda Association of Women Lawyers), 142, 143
Foucault, Michel, 250n11
funding. *See* AIDS relief funding; NGOs

gambling, 143
Ganda men. *See* men
Ganda women. *See* women
GDP (gross domestic product) rates, 70
gender: biological sex distinguished from,
    139–40; as complex, multidimensional,
    and dynamic, 29–30, 251n14; HIV preva-
    lence by, *14*; interactionist view of, 28–29;
    structure of, 250–51n13
gender and health dialectics: AIDS epidemic's
    altering of, 21–23; AIDS fluency in,
    39–40, 113, 120–21, 169, 181, 184–85; ter-
    minology of, 250n10. *See also* Bwaise
    Health Clinic; public awareness and
    discourse
gender differences: *amaanyi* and carpentry
    in relation to, 106–8; in dealing with
    AIDS, 164–66; in HIV testing and sup-
    port group attendance, 162–63; in rela-
    tionships among men vs. women, 167. *See
    also* gender inequality
gender equality: male authority retained in
    accommodation to, 138–41; men's rejec-
    tion of, 131–32, 133–38; negotiating male
    authority and, 146–54; public discourse
    on, 71–73. *See also* women's rights
gender equity: Ganda power structure and,
    130, 131; limits of, 71, 73, 130, 230,
    253n13; monogamy linked to, 186; resist-
    ance to, 134–41; women's rights framed
    as, 155, 157–58
gender inequality: male sexuality and persist-
    ence of, 220–24, 240; men's extramarital
    affairs buttressed by, 215–16; SASA!
    program focused on, 228–29, 258nn5–7;
    sexual dynamics as reinforcing, 157–58;
    women's vulnerability to HIV due to, 16–17,
    84–85, 225–26, 231. *See also* economic ine-
    quality; hegemonic masculinity; poverty
gender relations: AIDS as constraint on
    women's agency in, 156–59; altered nor-
    mative discourses of, 8; anxieties about,
    11–12; changes in, 29–30, 71–73, 197;
    Christian ideology of, 59; constructed in
    everyday life, 28–29; "domestic virtue
    model" of, 56–57, 75, 76; economic condi-
    tions linked to, 218–19; everyday tensions
    in, 85–90; in HIV-discordant relation-
    ships, 93–95, 120, 124–26, 127–28,
    156–57, 255nn10–11; HIV-positive men's
    modest remaking of, 166–67; long-term
    tensions in, 10–11; male accommodation
    to changes in, 138–41; political economy

intertwined with, 16–17; in postindepend-
    ence turmoil, 66–69; role in AIDS epi-
    demic, 5–6; women's income as altering,
    149–51. *See also* intimate politics of wom-
    en's rights; male authority over women,
    children, and home; masculine sexual
    privilege; women's rights; work and male
    provider ideal
gift giving, 47, 54–55. *See also* bridewealth
Gisu (ethnic group), 24–25
global AIDS pandemic: biomedical and mor-
    alizing narrative of AIDS in, 19–20, 60,
    77–78, 227, 250n9; gender dynamics in,
    224–32; origins of, 43–44; response to
    African crisis of, 15; Uganda's place in,
    6–12, 23, 43, 76–77, 160, 206. *See also*
    ABC (abstain, be faithful, use condoms)
    approach; AIDS relief funding; biomedi-
    cal approaches; NGOs
Global Fund to Fight AIDS, Tuberculosis, and
    Malaria, 15
Goetz, Anne Marie, 253n13
government: blamed for women's rights,
    211–12; surveillance of women, 11, 59–60,
    66–67, 74. *See also* civil service employ-
    ment; *and specific presidents*
Great Britain: patriarchal mores of, 56–57,
    59, 251n1; public health regime of, 15–16,
    43; Uganda protectorate of (*see* British
    colonial system)
gross domestic product (GDP) rates, 70
Gutkind, Peter, 60–62, 67, 69, 72

Hassim, Shireen, 253n13
Hattersley, C. W., 53
Haya (ethnic group), 77
hegemonic masculinity: AIDS intertwined
    with, 219, 224–32; complex issues in,
    229–30; concept, 26–29; interdepend-
    ence of ideals in, 222–24; protection of,
    despite changes, 29–30; women's accom-
    modations to and critiques of, 186–93;
    young Catholic men socialized into, 216–
    17. *See also* male authority over women,
    children, and home; masculine sexual
    privilege; work and male provider ideal
Henry (pseud.), 86, 171–73, 177
HIV-discordant couples: curiosity and ques-
    tions about, 183; failure to enforce safe
    sex in, 255n11; masculine sexual privilege
    renegotiated in, 93–95, 120, 124–26,
    127–28.156–157, 207, 225; pressure to
    leave HIV-positive partner, 255n10

HIV-positive status: as bewitchment, 199–200; children born as, 168; of couples living together, 168–70; fear of, 110, 113, 121; laws on, 11, 249n3; personal crisis for men with, 127, 164–65; secrecy about, 93, 124, 164, 165; younger vs. older men, 212. *See also* Bwaise Positive Men's Union; HIV-discordant couples; Post-Test Club

HIV prevalence: decrease in, 6, 13, 15, 76; increase in, 249n2; in long-term relationships, 192; peak of, 249n1; in South Africa, 217; in sub-Sahara, 13, *14*, 15; in Uganda, *14*, 22, 240

HIV prevention: anti-STD campaign compared with, 59–60; "collective efficacy" in, 22; domestic violence prevention linked to, 226, 228–29, 258nn5–7; essentialist views about male sexuality and patriarchal culture in, 162–63; faith-based approaches, 78–79, 116–17; future in African context, 224–32; individual responsibility as, 19–20, 250n9; masculine sexual privilege persistence and reaffirmation in, 112, 116, 121, 201–4, 206–7, 212–14, 217; open talk about AIDS and sexual behavior, 6–7, 76–77, 157; peer educators' efforts in, 12–13, 180–82; PMCTC (preventing mother-to-child transmission) Health Fair, 165–66; pre-exposure prophylaxis (PrEP), 79, 226–27; social changes as, 21–23; sociologically sophisticated approaches, 227–29, 258nn5–7; teen programs for, 24–25, 161; "treatment-as-prevention" approach, 23, 79, 226–27; women's rights discourse in, 158–59. *See also* ABC (abstain, be faithful, use condoms) approach; abstinence; AIDS counselors; antiretroviral drugs; "be faithful"; Bwaise Health Clinic; condom use; HIV testing; zero grazing approach

HIV Prevention and Control Act (2014), 11, 249n3

HIV spread: dense sexual networks as key factor in, 6–7, 18, 23, 77, 185–86, 193–94, 200–201, 213, 230, 256n10; fewer sexual relationships to limit, 173–74; likely first arrival, 63; men's multiple sexual relationships as factor in, 63, 119, 172–73, 176–79; opportunities for, 12, 66, 69; recent increase in, 10, 249n2; studies of, 8; in sub-Sahara, 13, *14*, 15; women's vulnerability to, 16–17, 73, 84–85, 110, 113, 117,

121–22, 142–43, 150, 155–56, 210, 225–26, 231

HIV testing: claims about, 183; facility for, 160–61; fear of results in, 137, 197; men encouraging men in, 166; men's refusal of, 150, 154, 165; routinely done, 150, 177; sexual satisfaction and need for, 178, 194

Hollway, Wendy, 25

homesteads (*maka*), 46–47, 48, 54. *See also* land and property

homosexuality, 11–12, 21, 74

Hope (pseud.), 161–63

households. *See* male authority over women, children, and home

Hunter, Mark: on AIDS and multiple sexual relationships, 85, 121; ambiguities and complexities considered, 257n4; on gender vs. earnings arenas, 120, 158; on *isoka* ideal (Zulu man with multiple sexual partners), 217–18, 219, 257n4; on women's rights and AIDS, 218–19

Iganga town: masculine sexual privilege in, 210–11; taxi owners' association in, 257n2

Igbo (ethnic group), 214

Iliffe, John, 47, 48, 55, 57

indigenous approaches to AIDS. *See* Bwaise Health Clinic; Bwaise Positive Men's Union; community engagement

individualism: biomedical and moralizing narrative of, 19–20, 60, 77–78, 227, 250n9; in precolonial Buganda, 48

individual responsibility: behavior change in, 77–78; *bodabodamen* and, 209–10, 257n2; generic AIDS prevention strategies focused on, 78, 202, 206–7; HIV-positive men on, 167; neoliberal focus on, 231–32, 250n9; pragmatic decisions about, 109–12, 121; proper notion of, 20. *See also* ABC (abstain, be faithful, use condoms) approach

inequalities: AIDS epidemic's highlighting of, 21–22; changing contexts while preserving, 27–28. *See also* economic inequality; gender inequality

international development agencies, 71–72, 131–32, 139. *See also* NGOs

International Monetary Fund (IMF), 70

interviewees: approach to, 37–38; current situations of, 236–39; demographic characteristics of, 246, 256nn7–8; differences in couple vs. individual interviews, 251n17; men's group, 177–79, 256n4 (*see also*

interviewees *(continued)*
    Bwaise Positive Men's Union); pseudo-
    nyms for, 251n16. *See also* Couples
    Research; methodology
intimate politics of women's rights: concept,
    128, 254n1; male authority enforced
    despite verbal rhetoric on rights, 133–38;
    male authority retained in accommoda-
    tions to rights, 138–41; negotiating HIV-
    discordant relationship in, 93–95, 120,
    124–26, 127–28, 156–57, 255nn10–11;
    negotiating women's rights and male
    authority in polygyny, 145–54; remaking
    masculinity and, 154–59; Ugandan con-
    text of, 128–32; woman's property rights
    and resources deployed in, 140, 141–42,
    143–44, 255n8
intimate sexual relationships: AIDS as con-
    straint on women's agency in, 156–59;
    colonial period changes in, 60–63; com-
    plex moral landscape of, 73–74; dense
    networks of, 6–7, 18, 23, 77, 185–86,
    193–94, 200–201, 213, 230, 256n10;
    fraught with tensions and conflicts,
    177–79, 183–86, 187, 193–94; gendered
    nature of AIDS and, 224–32; HIV-posi-
    tive couple in, 168–70; HIV-positive
    women in, 156, 255nn10–11; number of
    lifetime partners, 257n11; "proper" behav-
    ior in, 37, 73; risks for women vs. men,
    256–57n10; tracing webs of, 193–201,
    229–32; women blamed for problems in,
    126, 144, 146, 173, 196; women's distrust
    and fear in, 182–83, 186–89; women's
    multiple, 192, 193, 198, 200, 256–57nn9–
    10; women's rights in context of, 128; as
    women's security in postindependence
    turmoil, 66. *See also* cohabiting couples/
    partners; Couples Research; HIV-dis-
    cordant couples; men's multiple sexual
    relationships
Isaac and Edwina (pseud.): Edwina on wom-
    en's rights, 125–26; as HIV-discordant
    couple, 124–26, 127–28, 156; home and
    family of, 123–24; male sexual privilege
    maintained by Isaac, 127–28
isoka (Zulu man with multiple sexual part-
    ners), 217–18, 219, 257n4
Issa (pseud.): on AIDS, 100–102; characteris-
    tics of, 96–97; compensatory sexuality of,
    120; current situation of, 237; Dennis
    compared with, 111, 112; escapism of,
    98–99, 101, 102–3; male sexual privilege

of, 119–20, 121; work frustrations of,
    97–98, 101, 119

jaboya system (fishermen and female fish
    sellers), 213
Jacqueline (pseud.), 91–95
James (pseud.), 195–201
Jesus Life Church, 116–17
Joseph (pseud.), 163–64, 167–70
Julius (pseud.): Dennis compared with, 112;
    economic success and multiple wives of,
    90–92; HIV-positive status of, 93–95;
    Issa compared with, 103; male sexual
    privilege of, 119–20

kabaka (king), 46, 47–48, 252n4
Kaler, Amy, 18–19
Kalif (pseud.), 173–74, 177
Kampala: as center of Buganda, 38, 44, *45*;
    central business district of, *7*; Chinese
    presence increased in, 236; city divisions
    in, 34–35; described, 31; development and
    growth, 54, 63, 233–34; economic stratifi-
    cation increased in, 208; as epicenter of
    AIDS pandemic, 43; Keep Uganda Clean
    campaigns in, 67; map, *32*; midcentury
    changes in gender and sexual relations in,
    60–63; nightlife and prostitution areas in,
    82–83; official consolidation of, 63; postin-
    dependence social and moral terrain in,
    67–69; "walk to work" protests in, 70. *See
    also* Bwaise; Kawempe Division
Karlstrom, Mikael, 130, 255n3
Kawempe Division: map, *32*; poverty in, 31
Kawempe General Hospital (Bwaise), 236
Keep Uganda Clean campaigns, 67
Kenya: agriculture in, 53; AIDS among Luo
    in, 212–13; AIDS as paradox for men in,
    211; "disempowered" men in, 85; gender
    tensions and working women in, 254n2;
    normative masculinities and modern rela-
    tionships in, 213–14, 254n6
Kibira carpentry workshop: *amaanyi* and
    masculinity ideal encapsulated in, 106–8;
    author's apprenticeship in, 35–36, 37, 40,
    105, *106*; decline of business, 110–11;
    demise of, 235–36; described, 104–5;
    opening of, 109; as typical carpentry shop,
    103, *104*; workflow in, 105–6. *See also*
    Dennis; Rafik
Kimmel, Michael, 83–84
Kimombasa section: in daytime, *96*; nightlife
    of, 98–100, 112, 113; reputation of, 96,

254n3; work frustrations in, 97–98, 101.
See also Issa
king (*kabaka*), 46, 47–48, 252n4
kingdom of Buganda. *See* Buganda, kingdom
of
Kippax, Susan, 227
Kisekka, Mere, 51
KwaZulu-Natal (South Africa), *isoka* (Zulu
man with multiple sexual partners) in,
217–18, 219, 257n4
Kyegombe, Nambusi, 229, 258n7
Kyomuhendo, Grace, 47, 56, 67, 72, 75

Land Act (1998), 72
land and property: precolonial Ganda men's
need for, 46; privatization under colonialism, 53, 252n5; "real" men defined by,
176; women's rights to inherit and own,
140, 141–42, 143–44, 252n5, 255n8. See
also *maka*
Lango (ethnic group), 64
Laqueur, Thomas, 250n11
laws and decrees: anti-homosexuality, 11–12,
74; anti-pornography, 11, 74; customary
marriage, 57; domestic violence, 10, 73,
74, 158–59; female genital mutilation
banned, 73; HIV testing and status, 11,
249n3; land, 72; marriage, 57, 58; venereal diseases, 67; women as minors until
age thirty, 56
Leavens, Joan, 250n9
Lesotho, HIV prevalence in, 13
Lindsay, Lisa, 27
Lion's Club (Bwaise), 98–99, 113, 116
Love, Money, and HIV (Mojola), 212–13
Love in the Time of AIDS (Hunter), 217–19
Luganda (language): "human rights" in,
129–30; in interviews, 38; noun forms in,
251n18; terms for active vs. passive marriage in, 115, 140, 255nn4, 7; "to rape" in,
254n4. *See also* Baganda; Buganda, king-
dom of
Luo (ethnic group), 212–13
Luwero Triangle, 65–66

Madina (pseud.). *See* Musa, Madina, and
Rashmi
magendo economy (black market trade or
smuggling): beginnings of, 65, 252–
53n10; disease spread via, 16, 65; men's
participation in, 66; *muyaye* term and,
253–54n1; routes of, 254n3
Mair, Lucy, 49, 54–55, 58, 60

maka (homesteads), 46–47, 48, 54. *See also*
land and property
Malawi, media, men, and HIV transmission
in, 18
male authority over women, children, and
home: accommodation to women's rights
while retaining, 138–41; approach to
studying, 28–31, 29; enforced despite
rhetoric on women's rights, 133–38; ideal
of (male authority), 30, 49, 52, 130–32;
interdependence of sexuality and work
with, 222–24; male anxieties about loss
of, 58–59, 61–62, 89–90; monetary earnings linked to, 75–76; monogamy and,
186; negotiating women's rights while
maintaining, 146–54; in precolonial
Buganda, 46, 47–50; threats to, 71–73,
207–8, 210–11; women's limited power in
negotiating changes, 91–95; women's
resources and rights used in challenging,
141–42, 143–45; women's tactics to
assuage men in, 68–69. *See also* marriage;
masculine sexual privilege; work and
male provider ideal
male honor. See *ekitiibwa*; male status
male provider ideal. *See* un- and underemployment; work; work and male provider
ideal
male sexuality: AIDS role in shaping, 8–9;
costs and benefits of normative notions of,
177–79, 217; political economy of, 83–85;
pragmatic approach to, 109–12, 121; racial
stereotypes of, 15–16, 18–19, 27, 185–86,
220, 231, 249–50n5; as reservoir of privilege, 112–19; sex drive depicted as spontaneous, insatiable, innate force, 25–26, 97,
163, 172, 178, 185–86, 212; social construction of heterosexuality, 24–27; work
as performance of, 90–96; young men's
escapism in, 98–99, 101, 102–3. *See also*
compensatory sexuality; masculine sexual
privilege; masculinity, sexuality, AIDS,
and social change intersection; work and
male provider ideal; zero grazing
approach
male status: caught between AIDS and masculine sexual privilege, 112, 116, 121, 201–
4, 206–7, 212–14, 217; competition in,
113–14; of *isoka* ideal (Zulu man with
multiple sexual partners), 217–18, 219,
257n4; "manhood acts" and, 27–28, 222–
23; money as symbol of, 171, 174, 176;
money linked to, 41–42, 48–49, 54–55,

male status *(continued)*
76, 86–87, 89, 171, 174, 176, 209–10; multiple sexual relationships as proof of, 51,
127–28, 172–73, 176, 177, 178–79, 184–85,
191–92, 208–11, 256–57n10; of *omwami*
(husband) vs. *omusajja* (man), 182;
polygyny as marker of, 50–51, 52; providing for family as emblem of, 30, 53–55,
56, 90–96, 177; social mobility linked to,
47–49; struggle to maintain in poverty,
202–3; urban life and, 109, 175–76. *See
also* masculine sexual privilege; men's
multiple sexual relationships; money;
work and male provider ideal
Mamdani, Mahmood, 253–54n1
Mandeni (KwaZulu-Natal, South Africa),
isoka (Zulu man with multiple sexual
partners) in, 217–18, 219, 257n4
Margaret (pseud.), 112–15, 117, 118
marital fidelity. *See* "be faithful"
markets: men's cash crop farming and participation in, 53–54; opportunities for
men and women in, 58, 81–82, 173, 175;
women discouraged from participation in,
56; women's dominance in, 70–71. *See
also* Bwaise businesses; *magendo*
economy
marriage: arranged, 134, 147; balancing
equity with duties in, 219; changes in
colonial period, 60–63; changes in serodiscordant couple's relations, 124–26,
127–28, 156; colonial categories and codes
on, 57, 58; costs of, 46–47, 52, 58, 60, 111;
critique of, 250n8; customary, 57 (*see also*
polygyny); "free," 61; high HIV risk for
women in, 215; ideal of, 146; *okuwasa* vs.
okufumbirwa, 115, 140, 255nn4, 7; in precolonial Buganda, 46, 47–50; "proper," 50,
58, 78; women on success in, 68–69;
women's rights in informal type of, 139,
255n8. *See also* bridewealth; companionate marriage; divorce; intimate sexual
relationships; male authority over
women, children, and home; polygyny
Marriage and Divorce Bill (proposed), 11,
253n14
Marriage Ordinance (colonial), 57, 58
Mary (pseud.), 4, 5–6
masculine sexual privilege: approach to studying, 28–31, *29*; companionate marriage
and, 213–15, 250n8; concept of, 8–10,
209; dense sexual networks created in,
6–7, 18, 23, 77, 185–86, 193–94, 200–201,

213, 230, 256n10; family planning as
problem in, 151–53; HIV transmission
linked to, 17–19; ideal of, 30, 51, 172–73;
interdependence of authority and work
with, 222–24; among Luo in Kenya, 212–
13; "manhood acts" and, 27–28, 222–23;
men's recognition of threats to women in,
89–90; perceived threats against, 11–12;
persistence and reaffirmation in HIV prevention programs, 112, 116, 121, 201–4,
206–7, 212–14, 217; persistence despite
AIDS, 120, 125–26, 127–28, 160, 162–63,
168–70, 177–79, 184–85, 189–201, 215–20,
223–25, 240; poverty entangled with,
179–86, 193–94; reaffirmed and accepted
as status quo, 190–92, 201; reaffirmed in
ABC approach, 212–13, 217; safe sex practices and, 168, 203; social construction of,
25–26, 221–24; synergistic dynamics of
economic success and, 90–96; tracing
implications of, 193–201, 229–32; urbanization and, 60–63, 109; valorization of,
24–25; women's accommodations to and
critiques of, 186–93, 201; women's rights
rhetoric and persistence of, 150–59; work
and male sexuality as reservoir of, 112–19;
young men's escapism in, 97, 98–101,
102–3. See also *amaanyi*; male authority
over women, children, and home; male
status; men's multiple sexual
relationships
masculinities: Amin's model of, 66–67,
253n11; being HIV-positive as counter to
key components of, 164–67; carpentry as
encapsulating, 106–8; changing normative notions of, 69, 203–4; in daily life,
28–29, 31–35, 221–24; economic acquisitiveness and work as marker of, 54–55,
83–84; expansion of AIDS linked to,
17–18; modern egalitarian relationships
juxtaposed to, 213–14; multiple types and
identities possible in, 27–28; political
economy of, 83–85; procreation essential
to, 46; remaking in context of AIDS and
Bwaise, 8–9, 24–31, 85, 119–22, 177–79;
remaking in context of social significance
of AIDS, 19–23, 206, 208–20; remaking
in context of women's rights, 154–59;
social process and themes of, 28–31, *29*,
206–9; wife as marker of maturity, 139.
See also hegemonic masculinity; male
authority over women, children, and
home; masculine sexual privilege; mascu-

linity, sexuality, AIDS, and social change intersection; masculinity in Africa; work and male provider ideal

masculinity, sexuality, AIDS, and social change intersection: approach to studying, 160–63; costs and benefits of normative notions of male sexuality in, 177–79, 217; Joseph as exemplar of, 167–70; men's denial in context of, 163–67; paradoxes of precarious work in, 172–74; persistence of masculine sexual privilege in, 120, 125–26, 127–28, 160, 162–63, 168–70, 177–79, 184–85, 189–201, 215–20, 223–25, 240; poverty's interplay with, 179–86; pragmatic navigation of dangers, 174–77; reason for persistence of masculine sexual privilege in, 112, 116, 121, 201–4, 206–7, 212–14, 217; social problems and spread of AIDS in, 12–19; social significance of AIDS in, 19–23, 206, 208–20; tracing implications of, 193–201, 229–32; women's accommodations to and critiques of, 186–93, 201. *See also* Bwaise Health Clinic; Bwaise Positive Men's Union; masculinities

masculinity in Africa: interconnected themes in, 206–9; sexuality, gender inequality, and remaking of, 208–24

Matthew (pseud.), 24–25

McIntosh, Marjorie, 47, 56, 67, 72, 75

Medi (pseud.), 105, 108

medical narrative. *See* biomedical approaches

men: ambivalence and anxieties about women's rights and independence, 49, 55–56, 68, 72–73, 89–90, 125, 134–35, 196, 222; attitudes toward provider role, 86–88; blamed for HIV spread, 3, 6, 137, 143, 186–89, 192, 200; in colonial period, 53–55, 58; definition of "real man," 99; diversity of lived experiences, 28–29, 221–24; essentialist notions of, 26–27; HIV prevalence by age, *14*, 249n4; male-only peer groups of, 214–15; in precolonial era, 46–50, 251n2; pressured to leave HIV-positive partners, 255n10; "proper," 27, 47, 50, 75, 106–7, 119–20, 215, 218, 222–24; racial stereotypes of, 15–16, 18–19, 27, 185–86, 220, 249–50n5; sexual control and agency of, 9; urban male breadwinner identity possible, 64; vulnerability to HIV infection, 18, 84, 127, 179; women's accommodations to and critiques of AIDS and, 186–93, 201. *See also* Bwaise Positive

Men's Union; male authority over women, children, and home; male status; masculine sexual privilege; men's multiple sexual relationships; work and male provider ideal

"Men Make a Difference" (UNAIDS World AIDS Campaign, 2000), 18

men's multiple sexual relationships (including extramarital): of Amin, 66; changes in, 60–63, 168; dense sexual networks created in, 6–7, 18, 23, 77, 185–86, 193–94, 200–201, 213, 230, 256n10; escapism, comfort, and stress relief in, 85, 196–97; as factor in AIDS, 63, 119, 172–73, 176–79, 253n17; as hegemonic aspect of masculinity, 186–93, 201; informal marriage ended due to, 142–43; male status proven by, 51, 127–28, 172–73, 176, 177, 178–79, 184–85, 191–92, 208–11, 256–57n10; men's ambivalence about, 215–16; motivations in, 118–19, 214–15; official ideology vs. conduct of, 57, 252n8; pragmatic decisions about, 109–12, 121; "provider love" in, 257n4; remade in KwaZulu-Natal, 217–18, 257n4; secrecy about, 17, 60, 114–15, 122, 179–85, 191, 195, 202, 210, 214–15, 224; secrecy about HIV-positive status in, 93, 124, 164, 165; struggles to support (*see* work and male provider ideal); women's toleration to a point, 113–18; young Catholic men socialized into, 216–17; young men's banter about, 97, 98–101, 102–3. *See also* cohabiting couples/partners; HIV-discordant couples; intimate sexual relationships; masculine sexual privilege; masculinities; polygyny

methodology: focus and motivation, 8–12, 30–32; immersive nature of, 38–40; research methods, 35–38. *See also* interviewees

Mickleburgh, Andrew, 209

Miescher, Stephan, 27

migration: emergence of new types, 53; to urban areas, 54–56, 63, 64, 65–66

military and police forces: Amin's model of masculinity in, 66–67, 253n11; autocratic use of, 64; role in *magendo* economy, 65; violence against "walk to work" protesters, 70. *See also* National Resistance Army

Mohamed (pseud.): accused of witchcraft, 198–201; two wives of, 194–95; on unemployed men, 89

Mojola, Sanyu, 212–13

money: difficulties of earning, 18, 97–98, 101, 119, 139, 142–45, 196–97, 207–8, 211, 217–18; interviewees' current situations in relation to, 236–39; intimate relationships and AIDS in relation to, 109–12, 120–21; as key to masculine ideal, 41–42, 48–49, 54–55, 76, 86–87, 89, 171, 174, 176, 209–10; lack of, as motivation for avoiding relationships, 184; as motive for women's multiple partners, 192; as prerequisite for multiple sexual relationships, 173–74, 212; to start businesses, 134, 136, 149, 151; women's income as altering gender relations, 149–51. *See also* bridewealth; poverty; un- and underemployment; work; work and male provider ideal; working women

monogamy: AIDS as motivation for, 125; ambiguity about, 57–58; Christian ideology of, 59, 73; endorsed but not upheld, 57, 252n8; history of, 121, 223; men's claims of, 109, 111–12, 179–82, 194; pragmatic vs. ideal approach to, 186; in precolonial era, 50–51; promotion of, 10, 77–78, 117–18; secrecy of affairs in, 202, 206–7, 210, 229; women's claims of, 5–6, 187–92. *See also* zero grazing approach

motorcyle taxi men (*bodabodamen*), 81, 209–10, 257nn1–2

Mozambique, male dominance vs. equalitarian family paradox in, 254n6

Muhindi (ethnic group), 98

Mukasa (pseud.), 164

multiple sexual relationships. *See* intimate sexual relationships; men's multiple sexual relationships

Munyankole (ethnic group), 167

Murphy, John, 251n2

Musa, Madina, and Rashmi (pseud.): home, marriages, and children, 145–46; negotiating women's rights and male authority in, 146–54; as typical example, 155–56

Museveni, Janet, 78

Museveni, Yoweri: autocratic tendencies emerging, 75, 231–32, 234; challenges facing, 69–70; Chinese alliances of, 236; gender and sexual relations tensions under, 73–74, 75–76, 131; Marriage and Divorce Bill supported by, 253n14; neoliberal reforms of, 70, 75; power gained by, 66; proactive response to AIDS, 76; sexuality-related laws signed by, 10–11; women's situation under, 70–73, 130–31, 159

Musisi, Nakanyike, 50, 51, 88

Muslim Personal Bill, 253n14

Muslims: legal treatment of, 252n9, 253n14; mentioned, 134, 173, 180; polygyny of, 73, 94, 146, 194–95

Musoga (ethnic group), 98

muyaye (thug) and *abayaye* (thugs), 5, 87, 88, 101, 115, 253–54n1

National Resistance Army, 66, 130

neoliberal citizenship. *See* individual responsibility

neoliberal economic restructuring, 70, 75, 231–32

NGOs (nongovernmental organizations): AIDS-related, 161; gender equality ideas disseminated by, 131–32; legal aid from, 142, 143; locals' work for, 13, 139, 180–81, 238; masculinity considered by, 226; SASA! programs of, 228–29, 258nn5–7; women's rights supported by, 71–72

Nigeria: AIDS and moralizing discourses in, 12; gender tensions and working women in, 254n2; men often viewed as useless in, 84; social significance of AIDS in, 214–16; women's rights and duties in, 158; women's vulnerability to AIDS in, 122

Nilo-Hamitic (ethnic group), 44

Nilotic (ethnic group), 44

Nkole (ethnic group), 77

Nyanzi, Stella, 209–10

Obama, Barack, 79

Obbo, Christine, 67–69, 89, 253–54n1

Obote, Milton, 64–66

obuyniza (authority, power), meanings of, 49–50, 92, 124

okubaliga (extramarital love affairs). *See* intimate sexual relationships; men's multiple sexual relationships

okusinga (to exceed, surpass, be higher than, superior to), 255n3

O'Manique, Colleen, 20

omutwalo. See bridewealth

omwenzi (womanizer), 93–94, 110, 177

One Man Can program, 226

Pamela (pseud.), 91–95, 255n9

paradoxes: AIDS as, 12, 257n3; dynamics of multiple factors in, 112, 118, 186, 210–12, 216, 223, 253n16; hegemonic masculinity as, 28, 227–28, 254n6; precarious work as,

172; urban life as, 62–63. *See also* men; women

Parikh, Shanti, 121–22, 158, 202, 210–11, 214, 215, 257n2

Parker, Richard, 21–22

patriarchal attitudes: Amin's model, 66; British model, 56–57, 59, 251n1; Christian model, 78–79, 186; modest reformulation of, 219, 258n7; traditional legitimation of, 26–27; typology of, 83–84. *See also* gender relations; hegemonic masculinity; male status

Patrick (pseud.), 12–13

Paul (pseud.), 2–3, 4–5, 6

peace (*emirembe*), 144

peer educators, 12–13, 180–82. *See also* AIDS counselors

Pentecostalism, 78

PEPFAR (President's Emergency Plan for AIDS Relief, U.S.), 15, 20, 78–79

Peter (pseud.): on cousin's sexual behavior, 181–85, 224; family of, 4, 6; girlfriend of, 238–39

Peterson, Derek, 252n8

Phoebe (pseud.). *See* Wilfred and Phoebe

Plan International (NGO), 139, 181

PMCTC (preventing mother-to-child transmission) Health Fair, 165–66

political economy: everyday survival and tensions over gender relations in, 85–90; HIV transmission linked to, 16–19; of masculinity and sexuality, 83–85; pragmatic decisions in context of, 109–12, 121; synergistic dynamics of economic success and masculine sexual privilege in, 90–96

politics: of Anti-Homosexuality Act, 11; women's expanded roles in, 71, 130–31. *See also* political economy

polygyny: AIDS concerns in, 150, 153, 194–95; allowed for Muslim minority, 252n9; of Amin, 66; Christian disapproval of, 57–58, 59; financial pressures of, 146, 151; HIV-discordant relationships in, 93–95, 120; as marker of male status, 50–51, 52; negotiations in, 91–92; viewed as man's decision, 176; women's accommodation to, 191–92; women's objections to, 62; women's rights negotiated in, 145–54. *See also* men's multiple sexual relationships

population. *See* demographics

Post-Test Club, 162, 236

poverty: attitudes toward responsibility for, 86–88; factors in spread of AIDS rooted in, 4–5, 6, 16, 84–85, 230–32; interven-

tions hampered by, 219; male attitudes toward working women and, 89–90; masculine sexual privilege in context of, 179–86, 193–94, 202–3; support for multiple wives, 195; women's rights and, 159; of women who forgo new relationships, 187–88. *See also* economic inequality; money; un- and underemployment; work and male provider ideal

pre-exposure prophylaxis (PrEP), 79, 226–27

President's Emergency Plan for AIDS Relief (PEPFAR, U.S.), 15, 20, 78–79

Prohibition of Female Genital Mutilation Act (2010), 73

property. *See* land and property

prostitution. *See* sex workers

public awareness and discourse: AIDS and sexuality in, 5–7, 13, 22–23, 76–77, 157; gender equality, 71–72, 131–32; HIV-positive status, 162; homosexuality, 74; moralizing and anxieties in, 11–12

public health initiatives: anti-STD campaigns, 58–60; medicalized notion of sexuality in, 20. *See also* biomedical approaches; Bwaise Health Clinic; Bwaise Positive Men's Union; community engagement; HIV prevention; NGOs

public morality campaigns, 19–20, 60, 77–78, 250n9

Rafik (pseud.): carpentry work of, 105, 108; conversion of, 116; current situation of, 237–38; intimate relationships of, 112–16, 117–19; male sexual privilege of, 120, 202, 213

Raising Voices (NGO), 36, 228

Rakai district, as epicenter of AIDS epidemic, 175

rape: Luganda term for, 254n4; marital, 73, 152, 154, 159, 207; in postindependence upheaval, 66–67, 69

Rashmi (pseud.). *See* Musa, Madina, and Rashmi

religiosity, in AIDS prevention campaigns, 78–79. *See also* Christianity; Muslims

restless people (*bakirerese*), 52, 68

Richard (pseud.), 165

Richards, Audrey, 47, 49, 53, 60

Ridgeway, Cecilia, 203

rights: to AIDS drugs, 21; of humanity, 129–30; legal reforms attempted, 10–11; precolonial notions of, 129–30. *See also* women's rights

Robins, Steven, 250n9
romantic love. *See* companionate marriage; intimate sexual relationships
Roscoe, John, 50
Rose (pseud.), 115–16, 117–18, 238

safe sex practices: in HIV-discordant couples, 255n11; openness to, 77; some men's aversion to, 25; understanding need for, 168; wives' leverage in, 94, 95, 219. *See also* condom use; HIV testing
same-sex relations, 11–12, 21, 74
Samuel and Sophie (pseud.): as atypical example, 155; HIV testing and, 137; homeownership of, 133–34; male authority enforced despite women's rights rhetoric, 133–38; Musa and family compared with, 147, 151–52; separate interview of Sophie, 255n5; Sophie's death, 137; Wilfred and Phoebe compared with, 144
Sarah (pseud.), 168–69
SASA!, 228–29, 258nn5–7
school visits, 24–25. *See also* education; young people
Schrock, Douglas, 27–28, 222–23
Schwalbe, Michael, 27–28, 222–23
secrecy: about contraceptive injections, 136; about enacting masculine sexual privilege, 179–85; about woman's business, 149; "be faithful" dictate as prompting, 214–15, 229; of extramarital affairs, 17, 60, 114–15, 122, 179–85, 195, 202, 210, 214–15, 224; of HIV-positive status, 93, 124, 164, 165; of *magendo* economy, 65
separation. *See* divorce and/or separation
serodiscordant couples. *See* HIV-discordant couples
Setel, Philip, 257n3
sexuality: altered normative discourses of, 8; anxieties about, 11–12; colonial attempt to control, 15–16, 59, 249–50n5; open talk about AIDS and, 6–7, 76–77; permissive culture of, 63; persistence of gender inequalities and, 220–24; in postindependence turmoil, 66–69; social construction of, 24–27, 147. *See also* biomedical approaches; female sexuality; homosexuality; intimate sexual relationships; male sexuality; men's multiple sexual relationships; public awareness and discourse
sexually transmitted diseases (STDs): Amin's decree on, 67; colonial campaigns against, 58–60; prevention programs, 238;

response to AIDS and, 77–78. *See also* AIDS; HIV prevalence
sex workers: brothels (lodges, guest houses) in Bwaise, 99–101, *100*, 102, 235; comment on, 125; counselor focused on helping, 181–82, 238; as entrepreneurs, 57–58; increased number of, 63; independent town women as, 55, 56
SHARE program, 229
Silberschmidt, Margrethe, 85, 120, 211–12, 254n2
Simpson, Anthony, 216–17
slum communities: growth in Kampala, 61; as milieu conducive to experimentation, 67–68; number of, 34–35; use of term, 33. *See also* Bwaise; Kimombasa section
Smith, Daniel Jordan: on AIDS in Nigeria, 12, 122; on extramarital sex occurrence, 258n8; on normative masculinities vs. modern relationships, 214–16; referenced, 257n4; on women's rights and duties, 158
Sniper (pseud.), 97
social change: AIDS as prompting, 24–31; masculine sexual privilege largely untouched in, 203–4; working women as vanguard in, 68–69. *See also* masculinity, sexuality, AIDS, and social change intersection
social processes: AIDS as force in, 21–23, 24–31; Christianity and, 57–58; in liberal sexual culture and nightlife scene, 63; masculinity as, *29*; monetization of, 17, 250n7; questions about, 29. *See also* AIDS; gender relations; marriage; masculinities; men's multiple sexual relationships; women's rights
Sonke Gender Justice Network, 226
Sophie (pseud.). *See* Samuel and Sophie
South Africa: colonial legacy in, 15–16; HIV prevention linked to domestic violence prevention in, 226; *isoka* (Zulu man with multiple sexual partners) in, 217–18, 219, 257n4; male street criminals in, 253–54n1; multiple sexual relationships scrutinized in, 121; Treatment Action Campaign of, 21; women's desire to earn money in, 120, 158
Southall, Aidan, 60–62, 65, 67, 69, 72, 252n9
South Asian migrants, 54, 65, 252n6. *See also* Muhindi
Southwold, Martin, 48
Soweto, men often viewed as useless in, 84
Speke, John Hanning, 52

Spronk, Rachel, 213–14, 215, 257n4
Ssempa, Martin, 78
STDs. *See* sexually transmitted diseases
Stillwaggon, Eileen, 16, 250n6
Straight Talk clubs, 24–25
strength. See *amaanyi*
sub-Saharan Africa: colonial legacy in, 15–16; demographics of AIDS in, 13, *14*, 15; gender inequality and HIV spread in, 225; number of lifetime partners reported by men in, 257n11. *See also specific countries*
Summers, Carol, 59
Sunna II (*kabaka*), 252n4
Swaziland, HIV prevalence in, 13
Swidler, Ann, 215
synergistic dynamics of AIDS and women's rights. *See* intimate politics of women's rights
syphilis campaigns, 59–60, 78

Tamale, Sylvia, 11–12
Tanzania: AIDS as paradox for men in, 211; "disempowered" men in, 85; gender tensions and working women in, 254n2; migration in, 16, 257n3
TASO (AIDS Support Organisation), 161, 164, 168, 256n1
taxes and taxation, 53, 56
terror campaigns, 64, 65
Thomas, Lynn, 15
Thornton, Robert, 22, 253n17
thugs (*abayaye*) and thug (*muyaye*), 5, 87, 88, 101, 115, 253–54n1
Townsmen in the Making (Southall and Gutkind), 60–62
town women (*abakazi be tawuni*), 55–56, 68
transactional sex concept, 17, 250n7
Treatment Action Campaign (South Africa), 21
Tripp, Aili, 75

Uganda: Chinese presence increased in, 236; Christianity as de facto official religion of, 252n9; civil wars in (1970s and 1980s), 16; as epicenter of AIDS pandemic, 43; hip-hop culture of, 2; HIV prevalence in, *14*, 22; homophobia in, 11–12; independence gained (1962), 63; parliamentary seats reserved for women in, 71; postindependence turmoil in, 64–69; success in response to AIDS, 6–12, 22–23, 76–77, 160, 206; as women's rights leader in Africa, 7, 36, 71. *See also* British colonial system; Buganda,

kingdom of; demographics; ethnic groups; laws and decrees; Luganda
Uganda Agreement (1900), 252n5
Uganda Association of Women Lawyers (FIDA), 142, 143
Uganda Constitution, 71, 74, 131
Uganda Constitutional Court, 11, 74
Uganda Council of Women, 71
Uganda HIV/AIDS Sero-Behavioural Survey, 256nn5, 9, 257n11
Ugandan Women's Network, 74
Uganda Railway, 252n6
Uganda Supreme Court, 73–74
Uganda Taxi Owners and Drivers' Association of Iganga, 257n2
Uganda Youth Development Link, 181
UNAIDS World AIDS Campaign (2000), 18
un- and underemployment: AIDS-related health issues impacting, 165; crisis of masculinity in, 84–85; daily insecurity of, 13, 30, 85–90, 97–98, 101, 230–31; persistence of, 240; as personal failing, 49; role in HIV transmission, 16, 18; urban migration and, 54–56, 63, 64, 65–66. *See also* work and male provider ideal
United Nations Decade for Women, 253n11
United States: evangelical missionaries from, 11–12; hip-hop culture and clothing in, 5; PEPFAR plan of, 15, 20, 78–79; response to African AIDS crisis, 15
urban areas: changes in gender and sexual relations in, 60–63; current changes in, 233–36; effects of neoliberal policies in, 70, 75, 231–32; experimentation and social change in, 67–69; male status symbols in, 55, 109; migration to, 54–56, 63, 64, 65–66; women's economic roles in, 70–71, 88–90; women's rights and remaking masculinity in context of, 154–59

Vaughan, Megan, 59
Venereal Diseases Decree (1977), 67
Vincent (pseud.), 165
violence: *amaanyi* linked to, 254n4; postindependence, 65–66; structural, 16; against "walk to work" protesters, 70; women vulnerable to sexual, 66–67, 69. *See also* domestic violence; military and police forces; rape
Vitellone, Nicole, 25

"walk to work" protests, 70
Watkins, Susan, 215

Wellings, K., 257n11
Whiteside, Alan, 65, 66
Wilfred and Phoebe (pseud.): income and home of, 138–39; Phoebe's property rights and resources, 140, 141–42, 143–44, 157, 255n8; tensions over social changes and, 144–45; Wilfred's accommodation to women's rights while retaining authority, 138–41
witchcraft, accusations of, 198–201
womanizer (omwenzi), 93–94, 110, 177
women: access to education, 90, 131; accommodations to and critiques of male sexual behavior, 186–93, 201; activism of, 71–73, 131–32; attitudes toward men as providers, 87–88; blamed for HIV spread, 66–67, 93–94, 124, 150, 170, 176–77, 189–90, 197, 216; in colonial period, 53–56, 58–62, 252n5; complicit in men's secrecy, 202; desire for well-being and peace, 144; differences in navigating masculinity, 221; empisa (character) of, 49, 62, 148, 149; exchange of sex for gifts from men, 17, 250n7; HIV prevalence among, 13, 14, 249n4; independent, modern, urban types of, 55–56, 211–12, 230; men's ambivalence and anxieties about rights and independence of, 49, 55–56, 68, 72–73, 89–90, 125, 134–35, 196, 222; multiple sexual relationships of, 192, 193, 198, 200, 256–57nn9–10; paradoxes faced by, 12, 62–63, 253n16; postindependence rhetoric on, 64; in precolonial era, 44, 46–47, 49–52, 55–56, 230, 251n1; "proper," 49, 56–57, 62, 67, 144, 149, 153, 158, 172, 192; relationships with men rejected by, 187–88; respected as married women, 149–50; sexual needs recognized, 251n1; as soldiers, 130; surveillance of, 11, 59–60, 66–67, 74; vulnerability to HIV infection, 16–17, 18, 73, 84–85, 95, 110, 113, 117, 121–22, 142–43, 150, 153, 155–56, 179, 210, 225–26, 231; who live alone (banakyeombekedde), 51–52, 58, 68, 252n5. See also women's rights; working women
women's movement, 71–73, 131–32
women's rights: backlashes against and criticism of, 72–73, 131–32, 197, 224; economic-intimacy dialectic inflected by, 218–19; gender inequality and marital rape in context of, 73, 152, 154, 159, 207; institutionalization of, 10–11, 71, 126–27,

128–32, 219; limits of, 155, 157–58, 203, 207, 210–11, 240; mobilized for safe sex practices, 168, 203; mobilized in informal marriage, 138–45, 255n8; negotiated in polygyny, 145–54; okusinga in relation to, 255n3; rebuffed in marriage, 133–38; remaking of masculinity in context of, 154–59; role in protection from HIV infection, 125–26, 127, 156; Uganda as leader in, 7, 36, 71; using resources but downplaying discourse of, 144–45. See also intimate politics of women's rights
—SPECIFIC RIGHTS: to divorce, 50, 52, 62, 125, 150; to inherit and own property, 140, 141–42, 143–44, 252n5, 255n8; to refuse sex, 228; to work, 148–51, 153–54, 155, 219
work: increased opportunities postindependence, 64; limited cash-earning opportunities in, 54–55, 61–62, 72–73; as marker of male respectability, 55; as master narrative, 83–85; precarious nature of, 96–103, 119–22, 172–74, 218. See also Bwaise businesses; carpentry; un- and underemployment; work and male provider ideal; working women
work and male provider ideal: approach to studying, 28–31, 29; carpentry as path to, 104–8; compensatory sexuality and, 96–103, 119–20, 211–12; context of, 80–83; difficulties of embodying, 18, 97–98, 101, 119, 139, 142–45, 196–97, 207–8, 211, 217–19; everyday survival and gender tensions over, 85–90; ideal of (male provider), 30, 53–55, 56, 70, 119, 177; increased opportunities postindependence, 64; interdependence of authority and work with, 222–24; masculine sexual privilege linked to success in, 90–96, 171–73, 208; paid employment as new key to, 54–55, 75–76; pragmatic decisions about, 109–12, 121; setbacks in postindependence turmoil, 66; traditional medicine and limited income in, 145–46; in urbanizing Kampala, 48–49; working women as threat to, 72–73; young men's failure in, 97–98, 101, 102–3. See also male authority over women, children, and home; money; un- and underemployment; working women
working women: capital and support to start businesses, 134, 136, 149, 151; desire to earn money, 120, 158; economic inde-

pendence struggles of, 68–69; income-earning strategies of, 3, 4, 30, 56, 57, 58, 88–89, 151, 153, 180, 182, 190–91; job opportunities for, 70–71, 81–82, 141; male anxieties about, 49, 72–73, 89–90, 134–35, 196, 222; male authority in home and, 139–40; negotiating male authority and income of, 147–54; in nursing, 112–14; percentage of, compared to men, 253n12; precolonial precedent absent, 47; as "proper" wives, 67. *See also* agriculture; *banakyeombekedde*; Bwaise businesses; markets; sex workers
World Bank, 70

young men: attitudes toward AIDS, 100–102, 103; author viewed as model for, 40; community-based organization of, 181–82; contradictions articulated by, 223–24; cultural backgrounds of, 24–25; current situations of, 237–38; frustrations and escapism of, 98–101, 102–3; as peer counselors, 12–13; socialized into hegemonic version of masculinity, 216–17. *See also* peer educators; *and specific interviewees*

young people: HIV prevalence by age, *14*, 212, 249n4; HIV prevention programs for, 161; nightlife of, *5*, 63, 82–83, 98–100, 112, 113, 116. *See also* public awareness and discourse

Zambia, masculinities and HIV/AIDS in, 216–17

zero grazing approach: as dependent on women's sexual relations with partners, 172–73; goal of, 22–23, 77; masculine sexual privilege reaffirmed in, 112, 116, 121, 201–4, 206–7; as men's primary prevention strategy, 174, 177; pragmatics of, 111–12; use of term, 257n12

Zulu (ethnic group), 217–18, 219, 257n4

CPSIA information can be obtained
at www.ICGtesting.com
Printed in the USA
LVHW032158280423
745597LV00001B/57